AMERICAN BONDS

Princeton Studies in American Politics
Historical, International, and Comparative Perspectives
Ira Katznelson, Eric Schickler, Martin Shefter,
and Theda Skocpol, Series Editors

A list of titles in this series appears at the back of the book

American Bonds

How Credit Markets Shaped a Nation

Sarah L. Quinn

PRINCETON UNIVERSITY PRESS

PRINCETON AND OXFORD

Copyright © 2019 by Princeton University Press

Published by Princeton University Press
41 William Street, Princeton, New Jersey 08540
6 Oxford Street, Woodstock, Oxfordshire OX20 1TR

press.princeton.edu

All Rights Reserved

Library of Congress Control Number: 2019930955
ISBN 978-0-691-15675-0

British Library Cataloging-in-Publication Data is available

Editorial: Meagan Levinson and Jacqueline Delaney
Production Editorial: Mark Bellis
Jacket Design: Amanda Weiss
Jacket Credit: "Settlement on the Prairie," early American engraving, 1884 / iStock
Production: Jacqueline Poirier
Publicity: Nathalie Levine and Julia Hall
Copyeditor: Sarah Vogelsong

This book has been composed in Adobe Text Pro and Gotham

Printed on acid-free paper. ∞

Printed in the United States of America

10 9 8 7 6 5 4 3 2 1

CONTENTS

List of Illustrations   vii

Acknowledgments   ix

Abbreviations   xiii

1   The Problem and Promise of Credit in American Life   1

2   The Credit Frontier   22

3   Three Failures   48

4   Credit as a Tool of Statecraft   69

5   From a Nation of Farmers to a Nation of Homeowners   88

6   Mortgage Bonds for the Small Investor   107

7   The Rise of Federal Credit Programs   124

8   Off-Budget and Decentralized   150

9   A Return to Securitization   174

10   What We Owe One Another   199

Notes   213

Index   277

ILLUSTRATIONS

Tables

1.1	The Policy Work-Arounds	9
2.1	Selected Early Land Laws	26
2.2	Public Domain Land Sales and Collections, 1813–1819	27
5.1	Holders of Residential Mortgage Debt, 1896–1930	93
6.1	Selected Regulatory Responses: New York State and Federal Government	119
8.1	Mortgage Debt by Type of Holder, Selected Years, 1940–1970 (in Billions)	160
8.2	Mortgages for Existing Homes by Maturity and Loan-to-Value Ratio, Selected Years	171

Figures

1.1	The Policy Work-Arounds	9
2.1	Land Grant Map, 1893	34
2.2	Advertisement for Land Bought on Credit from Railway, 1872	35
3.1	Number of U.S. Banks by Region, 1870	57
3.2	Banks in Five Southern States, 1880	58
3.3	Louisiana Corn Merchants' Cash and Corn Prices, with Implied Interest Rates, 1886–1896	59
5.1	Proportion of Americans Living in Urban Areas	89
6.1	Real Estate Bonds as a Portion of Outstanding Nonfarm (Residential and Commercial) Mortgage Debt, 1896–1952	109
8.1	Mortgage Debt by Type of Holder, 1940–1970	161
8.2	Government Outstanding Direct vs. Guaranteed Loans, 1932–1950 (in Billions)	172

8.3 Growth of Outstanding Direct and Guaranteed Loans, 1952–1970 (in Billions)   172

9.1 Effective Limit Adjustments in the 1960s   187

ACKNOWLEDGMENTS

This project began as an attempt to understand why government officials played such a large role in the creation of the modern mortgage securitization market. Given that most people think of cutting-edge financial development as something done by private entrepreneurs, I wanted to know why policymakers had been so central in the early days of the industry. Some digging in the archives revealed a bitter political fight over a government plan to use an early form of securitization to manipulate the federal budget. Through a series of twists and turns that I will discuss in chapter 9, these contentious budget politics eventually triggered both the spin-off of Fannie Mae and federal support for a revitalized system of private securitization.

In the process of solving one problem, I had stumbled onto an even bigger one: Why was the federal government experimenting with securitization in the 1950s and 1960s? And how could it be that in the late 1960s the federal government held over $30 billion in loans and guaranteed another $70 billion, which formed the pool of assets that it was selling off? Nothing about those facts fit with my existing understanding of a staid, boring postwar federal government. It was becoming clear to me that the forces behind the government's use of securitization were older, more political, and more expansive than I initially understood. To fully grasp what happened meant reaching back even further. What began as an investigation of securitization in the 1960s now became a deeper dive into the co-evolution of securitization and federal allocative credit programs since the founding of the nation. This deeper dive was a much larger project and took a much longer time to complete. In the years that followed, I accrued a great many debts.

The research was funded by the Institute for New Economic Thinking, the Kauffman Foundation, the University of Washington, and the Michigan Society of Fellows. Parts of chapters 8 and 9 were published in the *American Journal of Sociology*. I thank Sherman Maisel for sharing his papers, and John Padgett for sharing his personal collection of postwar housing materials. At the Lyndon B. Johnson Presidential Library, archivist Allen Fisher was a generous and expert guide to the files. I am also grateful to Eric Schwartz for shepherding the project through publication at Princeton University Press, Eric Crahan for guiding it through the review process, and Meagan Levinson for bringing it home.

A team of research assistants helped make the analyses that follow possible. Reed Klein helped tremendously in the preparation of the manuscript. Mark Igra researched the bond houses of the 1920s and the changing debt limits of the 1960s. Among other things, Emily Ruppel assisted with research of the school loan programs. Other students took turns tracking down articles, digitizing documents, and checking and compiling federal budget reports on the credit programs, work that is still ongoing: Pragya Kc, Nicole Hathaway, Jake Lemberg, Amy McCormick, Brooke Lee Wieser, Sripriya Navalpakam, Cindy Gudino, Kalyah Bojang, James Maltman, Xinguang Fan, Alexis Yezbick, Alyssa Ahmad, Ellen Kortesoja, Patrick Choi, Alexis Chouery, and Lynette Shaw, who oversaw these efforts for some of this time. Julia Hon, Ayanna Meyers, Kari Hensley, and Elana Messer all provided much-needed assistance with the manuscript at different stages. The book is clearer and crisper thanks to Sarah Vogelsong's copyedits of the pages that follow.

I am grateful to those people who took the time to listen and share comments at the following events at conferences, workshops, and colloquia: the SCOPES workshop at the University of Washington; the SCANCOR and Economic Sociology Workshop at Stanford; and talks and colloquia at the University of Michigan Society of Fellows, Northwestern University's Sociology Department, the University of Washington's Department of Geography, the Center for Comparative Research at Yale University, Harvard Business School's Organizational Behavior Group, the University of Washington at Bothell's School of Business, and the University of Pennsylvania's Department of Sociology. Parts of this work were also presented at the Relational Work Conference at UC Davis; the Social Studies of Finance Seminar; the All-University of California Group in Economic History Conference; the Progressive Politics of Financial Regulation Conference at the Allard School of Law; the University of Michigan's Economic Sociology Workshop and Interdisciplinary Committee on Organizational Studies; the Financial Innovation, Diffusion and Institutionalization: The Case of Securitization conference; and sessions at the American Sociological Association and Social Science History Association. I thank particpants at each for their questions and comments.

Work on this project began at the University of California Berkeley under the guidance of Neil Fligstein and Heather Haveman in the Sociology Department. Their reputations speak for themselves. From the start this work also benefited from the insights of Dwight Jaffee, who helped track down key players and uncover old rumors; he was crucial to the development of this book. Marion Fourcade also provided invaluable guidance and inspiration to the end. For sharing their insights on drafts and in conversations, I thank Fred Block, Bruce Carruthers, Gerald Davis, John Hall, Greta Krippner, Richard Lachmann, John Padgett, Monica Prasad, Mark Rose, Herman Schwartz, Michael Schwartz, Aaron Shaw, and Kiyoteru Tsutsui. A special thanks to members of writers' groups who made sure the chapters of this book ended up better than they started: Nick Wilson, Damon Mayrl, Laura Mangels, Kristen Jafflin, Siri Colom, Brian Lande, Greggor Mattson, Alice Goffman, and Cristobal Young. Lynne Gerber and Ariel Gilbert Knight deserve special recognition for the sheer volume of pages they read over the years.

Colleagues at the University of Washington provided invaluable feedback and support. I thank Steve Pfaff, Edgar Kiser, Alexes Harris, Kate Stovel, Jerry Herting, Nathalie Williams, Aimee Dechter, and Megan Finn. At the Michigan Society of Fellows, I was helped greatly by Don Lopez and Linda Turner. Many other fellow travelers through Berkeley, Michigan, and Washington provided much-needed advice and encouragement: Rachel Best, Sophie Van Ronsele, Holice Kil, Brian Lande, Jennifer Randles, Stephanie Mudge, Bryan Sykes, Hana Brown, Lily Cox-Richards, Clare Croft, Roger Grant, and Sara McClelland.

Steve and Cindy Kapusta opened their home so that I would have a place to write when I desperately needed it. Marcy and Evan Sagerman gave us shelter when we were flooded out of our home. I doubt I would be a sociologist if not for the inspiration of Marc Steinberg and Pat Miller at Smith College. I doubt I would have had the nerve to write a book if not for the early encouragement of Terry Culleton at George School.

My deepest thanks go to my family. Thank you to Marsha Lehman and Dana Groner, who have given me more gifts than can be listed here. Thank you to my siblings for support and friendship: T. J. Quinn and Colleen Diskin, Katherine Quinn and Kenny Thring. In the years I worked on this book, their children—Liam, Ally, Eleanor, Maddy, and Mikey—have all grown into people I like and admire. Thank you to the Kapustas for welcoming me into a family with such warmth: Jean and Nikki, Jason and Bridget, Steve and Cindy and Helga. I remain thankful for the love and support of people no longer here: Sylvia and Alvin Lehman, Joe and Al Kapusta, and especially my father Tom Quinn, who pushed his children to appreciate the value of good questions. I think he would have gotten a kick out of my writing a book.

Above all, I thank Brian Kapusta for his understanding, intelligence, and generosity of spirit. Brian, this book is for you. I marvel at my great luck, to get to travel through this world with you and Scout.

ABBREVIATIONS

CCC   Commodity Credit Corporation

FDIC   Federal Deposit Insurance Corporation

FEMA   Federal Emergency Management Agency

FFLA   Federal Farm Loan Act

FHA   Federal Housing Administration

FHLB   Federal Home Loan Bank

FHLBB   Federal Home Loan Bank Board

FLA   Farm Loan Association

FMHA   Farmers Home Administration

FNMA   Fannie Mae/Federal National Mortgage Association

FSLIC   Federal Savings and Loan Insurance Corporation

GDP   gross domestic product

GNP   gross national product

HOLC   Home Owners' Loan Corporation

HUD   Housing and Urban Development

MBA   Mortgage Bankers Association

NAACP   National Association for the Advancement of Colored People

NHA   National Housing Act

NRA   National Recovery Administration

PC   participation certificate

RFC   Reconstruction Finance Corporation

S&L   Savings and Loan

SBA   Small Business Administration

SBICS   Small Business Investment Corporations

SCC   Southern Commercial Congress

SEC   Securities and Exchange Commission

SPV   special purpose vehicle

TARP   Troubled Asset Relief Program

USAID   United States Agency for International Development

USBLL   United States Building and Loan League

USDA   United States Department of Agriculture

VA   Veterans Administration

AMERICAN BONDS

1

The Problem and Promise of Credit in American Life

Finance is always social. It is social not just because it distributes profits and risks among people, but also because those profits and risks are distributed on the basis of understandings, usually unspoken, of what people can imagine owing to and sharing with one another.

This insight is so foundational as to perhaps seem trivial, but it often gets lost when people talk in the technical language of finance: of liquidity, risk profiles, and asset classes. That technical language, useful for understanding the dynamics of capital flows, frequently obscures the social character of finance and keeps us from considering another vital set of questions we might ask: Why do people consider a given system reasonable in the first place? How do groups decide what they owe to one another as members of a community or nation?

In the broadest sense, this book is a sociological excavation of finance. It seeks to unearth the logics buried under jargon and taken-for-granted assumptions. To do this, *American Bonds* traces the historical evolution of two powerful, behind-the-scenes forces in U.S. credit markets, securitization and federal credit programs, from the founding era through the 1960s. The book's core contribution is to show how early American land and housing policy gave rise to a wide-reaching politics of credit allocation in the twentieth century. It makes the case that U.S. government officials have long used landownership, housing markets, and easy credit as policy tools, and that they have done so in an elusive search for not only ways to avoid the redistribution of wealth while still ensuring widespread economic opportunity, but also ways to effectively govern within a remarkably complex and fragmented political system. It is a history with implications for how we think of America's underappreciated developmental state, its market-heavy social policies, and its volatile financial systems.

The Background and the Cases

The backdrop for this story is the sheer historical magnitude of America's real estate markets. Already by 1890 nearly half of U.S. households were owner-occupied, and a staggering four-fifths of farming households headed by people over the age of 60 were owner-occupied.[1] Such high levels of homeownership required a massive amount of credit to circulate, and in the right way: not just among businesses, but among families; not just in cities, but in rural areas; not just among the well-off, but among ordinary people; not just in the short term, but long enough for families to pay off the sizable debt.[2] This was no easy feat, as other scholars have noted. Mortgages are risky and costly transactions, ones that many banks avoided, either partially or completely, for long periods of time.[3] Especially in the nineteenth century, moving the nation's capital reserves from eastern centers across a vast frontier into the hands of small borrowers was a challenge. In earlier eras, as now, lenders could glut a market with credit amid a speculative fever. America's mortgage markets—centered on the most economically and emotionally significant debt held by ordinary families—were also endemically unstable and inefficient.

American mortgage markets are therefore old, expansive, morally super-charged, and highly consequential. All of this is ideal for a study of the social life of finance. Mortgage markets' long and troubled history also provides a context in which to understand the two cases at the heart of this book: securitization and federal credit. Both evolved as ways to manage the risks and costs associated with lending and, in so doing, improve the flow of credit across the nation. Mortgage markets are therefore at the center of the analysis that follows.

To say that mortgage markets are at the center of this story is not to say that this book is exclusively concerned with mortgages. Credit circulates, and so do lending techniques. Following developments in securitization and federal credit back through U.S. history means periodically addressing domains like farming, commercial real estate, and railroads. Furthermore, a key lesson of this book is that credit is a multipurpose political tool. Every chapter describes how people use credit to solve their problems, decisions that are shaped by the challenges of governance within an institutionally fragmented political system. *American Bonds* therefore covers a great deal of ground even as it returns to the matter of mortgage markets and to the question of how securitization and federal credit moved money into them.

WHAT IS SECURITIZATION?

Securitization is a financial technology that repackages loans for resale.[4] Just as undesirable cuts of meat can become more appetizing when combined into a sausage, loans can be made more desirable to investors by being combined in a pool that diversifies those loans' risks. Bonds can then be issued that give investors a share of the pool. Alternatively, a large loan or asset, like the mortgage for a skyscraper, can be divided up and sold in smaller pieces, as certificates or bonds. To extend the culinary metaphor, the key issue becomes who gets the prime cuts (the rights to the first repayments, or senior debt) and who gets the offal (that is, subordinated debt that only pays out after other classes of bondholders are paid).

In today's securitization markets, sellers pool assets within special purpose entities (that is, trust or shell companies) in order to remove those assets from their balance sheets. Complex financial formulas then determine how the expected income from those assets will back bonds that bear different levels of risk. When those pools are made up of mortgages, the bonds are called mortgage-backed securities. The financial engineers who design these pools typically arrange for some kind of credit support that ensures certain bondholders will get paid even if the assets in the pools, like mortgages, default. Examples of credit support are insurance policies purchased from another company or guarantees from a governmental agency.

In short, securitization is a way of reselling existing loans. As such, it is part of a secondary market. The primary market is where the loans are first issued. Robust secondary markets boost primary markets because they attract new customers and provide existing customers with more ways to raise funds. Anyone who has purchased a car expecting to one day resell it or trade it in has experienced this process at work.

Securitization is a revolutionary technology, best known for the role it played in the turn-of-the-millennium housing bubble. Bolstered by a friendly regulatory environment, computing power, and new information technologies, the mortgage securitization market went through explosive growth in the 1980s. Soon every kind of debt—school loans, auto loans, credit card obligations—was securitized. Financiers boasted that this represented a breakthrough in risk management. It was to be a new era of credit access for poorer borrowers, constituting nothing less than the democratization of credit. As investors came running from around the world, the banking industry reshaped itself around securitization. Economists Greenwood and Scharfenstein estimate that as the boom was reaching its peak between 2000 and 2006, "all of the incremental growth in household credit as a share of GDP [gross domestic product] was securitized."[5] Sales slowed but did not stop after the market crashed. In 2016, an average of $210 billion worth of securitization issuances were traded *daily*.[6]

Why study historical iterations of the securitization market? Long before our current market emerged in the 1960s, the United States had major mortgage bond markets in the 1830s, 1870s, and 1920s. This book uses these earlier markets to analyze the different social logics of securitization; it is, to my knowledge, the first book to do so. This book also uses securitization's political history to better elucidate the relationship between states and markets. Most people associate revolutionary financial technologies with private entrepreneurship. As historian Louis Hyman writes, however, this world-changing version of securitization "began with the federal government."[7] Quasi-governmental mortgage dealers Fannie Mae and Freddie Mac built the market in the 1970s and 1980s, and remain powerful forces in it today. Even before then, in the 1960s, government offices used securitization to sell off government-held loans as a way to raise off-budget funds. Those sales point to an even larger story. It was not just any part of the government that incubated securitization: it was the federal credit programs.

WHAT ARE FEDERAL CREDIT PROGRAMS?

Federal credit programs direct and promote the flow of credit in the economy. Today the U.S. federal government reports that it owns $1.3 trillion in loans and guarantees another $2.5 trillion through a web of credit programs embedded within a range of governmental agencies.[8] That combined total of $3.8 trillion, accumulated over decades, is nearly as large as the entire $4 trillion reported federal budgetary expenditure for 2017. The total for federal credit jumps to $8.5 trillion if you include in the calculations other obligations like the guarantees offered by Fannie Mae and Freddie Mac (which remain under government conservatorship but are excluded from the budget because they are officially privately owned entities) or the Federal Reserve's holdings of mortgage-backed securities acquired after the 2008 meltdown.[9] As economists Mariana Mazzucato and Randall Wray note, around a third of all privately held debt in the United States is backed in some way by the federal government.[10] And even that impressive amount is not a full account of government support for credit markets. Add tax expenditures that encourage lending, and the extent of government credit support gets even larger. Between 2005 and 2009, the period that covers the apex of the millennial housing boom, the mortgage interest deduction amounted to a $434 billion incentive for borrowing.[11] None of this even touches on efforts of state and local governments. Federal credit programs are not, therefore, the entirety of government credit support in the United States, but rather an institutional center for such efforts. As such, they have something to teach us about the role of credit in the American political economy.

The actual federal credit programs take many forms: some issue loans, some provide guarantees and insurance, and some buy and sell existing loans. They are also old: nineteenth-century credit support helped build roads, railways, canals, western irrigation systems, and more. Credit programs operate across policy domains: the Commodity Credit Corporation (CCC) uses loans to subsidize farmers; the U.S. Agency for International Development

(USAID) gives loans to other countries as a form of foreign aid; the Federal Emergency Management Association (FEMA) and the Small Business Association (SBA) provide loans as a mode of domestic disaster relief.[12] Through its credit programs, the federal government has bolstered nearly every sector of the economy, with extensive backing harnessed for core industries: first agriculture, then housing, and most recently education. Credit programs are not just financial conduits. They are also institution builders. The Federal Farm Loan Act (FFLA) promoted the use of the long-term amortizing mortgage. The SBA underwrote the early venture capital industry. The Export-Import Bank pioneered certain kinds of overseas lending.

Despite their importance, large gaps remain in our knowledge of how these programs developed. Existing research glosses over the nineteenth century or looks narrowly at specific sectors rather than how the programs operate as a group.[13] In some cases, scholars analyze credit programs as instances of something else, like industrial policy, governmental partnerships, or Progressive Era politics.[14] While I owe a great debt to this research, much of which I draw on throughout this book, major questions about the history and implications of federal credit, as a mode of policy in its own right, remain unanswered. We know little, for example, about the rise of credit as a tool of statecraft in the United States or the ramifications of this for developmental or social policy. Scholars like Susanne Mettler, Christopher Howard, and David Freund have called for a more in-depth examination of federal credit allocation.[15] This book takes up that call.

WHY STUDY SECURITIZATION AND FEDERAL CREDIT TOGETHER?

Securitization and federal credit programs have repeatedly influenced one another's development. The chapters that follow will show that early government credit support for rail and roads pulled settlers across the continent and helped turn the United States into an agricultural powerhouse. Western settlement drummed up demand for credit on the frontier, where brokers used securitization to facilitate farm lending. As these efforts failed, populist farmers concluded that a stronger central government was their best chance for securing regular access to cheaper credit, a shift in political opinion that enabled the total overhaul of the farm credit system in the Progressive Era, a policy that in turn set precedents for the New Deal. In the postwar era, the credit programs incubated the modern securitization market. When lawmakers used securitization to boost the nation's struggling mortgage markets, they set the course for a revolution in American mortgage markets.

This back-and-forth between federal credit programs and securitization can teach us something. It is indicative of how private and public actors work together and over long periods of time to build markets, even within the supposedly laissez-faire-friendly context of the United States. As an examination of the role of states in markets, *American Bonds* extends a long line of research into how governments make modern capitalist markets possible.[16] This body of scholarship has already shown that modern states and markets grew up together. Healthy markets generate a tax base that funds governments, and governments in turn help markets thrive by providing stable property rights, developmental policies, official currency, regulations, risk protections, and emergency protections.[17]

Financial markets are a core part of this history of state–market relations, because financial markets are special public goods. Finance is the seat of money and credit, of national savings, capital, profits, and reinvestment. If financial markets are inefficient, money trickles when it should flow. If financial markets are unfair, capital gathers in one part of the system at the expense of the rest. If financial markets are rapacious—too fraudulent, corrupt, or speculative—bad debts accumulate like an infection in a bloodstream. Because finance circulates through various other markets, government efforts to ensure its proper functioning can have far-reaching ramifications. Greta Krippner has shown that government efforts to manage the flow of money and credit sparked America's transition to a new era of financial capitalism in the 1970s and 1980s.[18] She is one of many scholars whose work reveals that U.S. federal involvement in markets is far more expansive, and generative, than typically appreciated.[19] *American Bonds* contributes to this effort by showing how America's complex political system influenced the way that the U.S. federal government historically engaged with credit allocation.

The paired cases of securitization and federal credit also provide a multidimensional look at the morality of financial markets. At no point did securitization represent a pristinely rational approach to risk management. Loan pools are essentially little moral worlds: they require decisions about who belongs and who is excluded, who gets profits and who bears losses, who is allowed to exit the deal and under what conditions. Their design reflects how people conceive of their financial relations and obligations to one another. While securitization is useful for understanding these little moral worlds, the federal credit programs illuminate the big moral world of political economy. A mortgage pool of loans from the Veterans Administration (VA) issued with government guarantees is not just a contract between a borrower and a lender, but a bond between a borrower, a lender, and a larger community that now bears the risks associated with its soldiers' loans. The process for reallocating or issuing credit involves decisions about which groups or businesses are too important to go without access to capital and which ways of lending are preferable.

Here the analysis follows the lead of sociologists like Viviana Zelizer, Bruce Carruthers, and Marion Fourcade, who analyze exchanges as part of the process through which people understand, define, and negotiate their social connections.[20] Financial markets are part of how we delimit the role of the government in credit markets and that of credit markets in society. They help determine the extent to which Americans must use market exchange to meet fundamental needs like housing, education, and healthcare; they also help determine the degree of social support available within the realm of market exchange. Those decisions are never just about potential economic returns; they are also about national priorities and values.

In all, the paired histories of securitization and federal credit provide complementary perspectives on how credit allocation operates at the center of the U.S. political economy. By showing how specific practices entail judgments about who should get what, the book illuminates some of the social logics behind who gets profits and who gets risks in American credit markets. And by showing how lawmakers turn to land and credit to solve a host of political problems, this book situates housing and credit within a larger pattern of political fragmentation and conflict that goes back to the earliest days of the nation. It is to that larger context the chapter now turns.

A Fractured Nation

A key contention of this book is that U.S. housing and credit policies operate within a larger context of governmental complexity. That context has been detailed by scholars of American political development, a field that explains how the nation's core political institutions have developed over time.

The U.S. government is sprawling and fragmented by design, a result of the founders' decision to balance the authority of the central government with that of individual states. This dispersion of political power has led to the development of a government with nearly 90,000 units spread out over the nation's states, counties, cities, towns, special districts, and school districts, as William Novak notes.[21] At the center of this sprawl is a political core made up of the three branches of the federal government, whose powers are balanced against one another's. The complexity is reproduced within each branch. The two chambers of Congress work through a welter of committees, 20 in the House and another 21 in the Senate. The judicial branch is divided into three levels and 94 federal districts, all of which are "naturally passive" because their power is only activated externally.[22] The Department of Justice alone includes 40 offices that share law enforcement authority with other entities like state troopers, county sheriffs, military police, and immigration and customs enforcement officers. This structure has resulted in competing seats of authority and a veritable gauntlet of veto points that any policy must run.[23]

All nations have groups with varied interests that clash, but the United States, because of its sheer size and complexity, creates more opportunities for

conflict than most. The most brutal of the divisions that give rise to such conflict are America's racial divides, institutionalized through slavery, Jim Crow,
and mass incarceration, which compromised American democracy in the past
and continue to fester today. In the nineteenth century American racism inter-
sected with hardening regional divides that increasingly separated the industrial North, the Cotton South, the wheat- and cattle-filled Great Plains, and the
timber- and produce-rich West Coast.[24] These cleavages were the foundation
for distinct economies, lifestyles, and worldviews that became an existential
threat to the nation in the lead-up to the Civil War. Today, a mix of geography,
economy, culture, and race mark an increasingly hostile gap between "blue"
coastal elites and the "red" heartland. Other divides cut across space: the separation of the haves and have-nots, of gender and ideology.

This combination—fragmented political institutions that overlay complex
social divides—defines American political life. When polarization is especially
high and interest groups are strong, the structure can result in gridlock, or
even devolve into what Francis Fukuyama has called a "vetocracy," in which
groups use veto points to grind government to a halt.[25] Scholars like Michael
Sandel and Gary Gerstle have similarly observed that this highly fragmented
system can only work given some basic agreement about shared goals and
rules for political discourse.[26] Without that basic agreement, paralysis results.
Political scientist Eric Shickler points out that even at its best, the American
political structure forces the kinds of compromise that do not bring consensus
so much as they produce lingering dissatisfaction, since, by definition, none
of the negotiating parties get exactly what they want. To make matters worse,
since those advantaged by a previous agreement have an interest in protecting
their gains, new rules tend not to replace previous arrangements so much as
overlap with or modify them. Shickler concludes that the American style of
pluralism is particularly "disjointed."[27]

Political and social fractures did not stop the federal government from
growing, but they did change how it grew. Government officials devised ingenious ways to avoid veto points, link various seats of power, and generally
compensate for the system's shortcomings. While they are almost always used
in some kind of combination, for analytical clarity it can help to group these
diverse policies into three types: partnerships, inducements and incentives,
and market forms. These work-arounds, which are summarized in figure 1.1
and table 1.1, are regularly incorporated into government entitlements, regulations, and subsidies.

Partnerships are collaborations with local governments and private entities,
either to design or to implement policy. With Damon Mayrl, I have written
about the various forms these collaborations take, from simple contracts (as
when the federal government hired a subsidiary of Halliburton to build holding

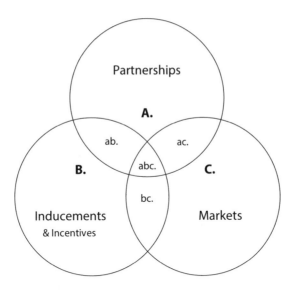

FIGURE 1.1. The Policy Work-Arounds

TABLE 1.1. The Policy Work-Arounds

	Work-Around	Example
A	Partnerships	U.S. federal government charters the nonprofit Red Cross to provide rehabilitation to veterans after the First World War.
ab	Partnerships with incentives/ inducements	AmeriCorps is a public–private partnership. Its Segal Education Award program offers forgiveness for direct government loans for AmeriCorps members who later work full-time for eligible nonprofits and government agencies and make payments for 10 years.
B	Incentives and inducements	Tax deductions for charitable giving
bc	Market-based inducements and incentives	The UNICOR Federal Bonding Program provides theft insurance for businesses that employ former inmates.
C	Market forms	FEMA uses cost-benefit analyses to evaluate hazard-mitigation projects.
ac	Market-based partnerships	U.S. federal government charters the for-profit Federal National Mortgage Association to promote the nation's secondary mortgage market.
abc	Incentives built in to market-based partnerships	Small business set-asides give preferred access to government purchases and contracts to businesses owned by women, people from disadvantaged backgrounds, and service-disabled veterans.

cells in Guantanamo Bay) to complex hybrid organizations that share control and costs (like port authorities).[28]

Inducements and incentives direct private individuals and companies toward desired actions. Tax breaks encourage people to buy homes, have children, save for retirement, or donate to charity.[29] Inducements like high-occupancy vehicle lanes encourage carpooling. Increasingly, inducements are taking the form of subtle "nudges."[30] For example, by switching a government program to one that people must opt out of (rather than opt in to), the government can increase rates of participation in programs; this strategy has been used to provide more retirement benefits to veterans and more school lunches to low-income children.[31] Often the ability to partner or trade with the government is the incentive, such as when priority for a government contract goes to companies with a good safety compliance record.

Market forms entail the application of market tools in political spaces. They include strategies with origins in market spaces and market techniques that privilege efficiency over core political logics (like rights), such as the use of cost-benefit analyses to evaluate government programs. To some extent, the use of market forms derives from the government's long and frequent use of partnerships. Sometimes partnerships are with nonprofits, but frequently they involve alliances and contracts with for-profit businesses and firms.[32] Researchers have observed a global rise in market forms under neoliberalism, but this book will focus on earlier historical iterations.[33]

These work-arounds have multiple political advantages. Partnerships circumvent veto points and avoid jurisdictional battles by shifting authority and expenses into private hands. Inducements and incentives minimize expenses. Tax expenditures are overseen by revenue committees, which makes them easier to implement than programs routed through the veto-ridden appropriations process.[34] Nudges use the power of modern behavioral science to manipulate people into voluntarily making choices the government wants them to make. Richard Thaler and Cass Sunstein defend the approach as "a relatively weak, soft, and non-intrusive type of paternalism" that people tend to prefer to regulations that are openly restrictive, involve punishments or fines, or cost more money to enforce.[35] By directing markets, government officials can appease constituents without openly redistributing resources through taxation and spending.

Partnerships, incentives, and market forms all recruit citizens into the work of governance. Some scholars see them as a kind of colonizing power that constitutes an underappreciated strength of the U.S. federal government.[36] State power can be measured not just in terms of centralized control, but in generalized influence. Viewed this way, the federal government's capacity to branch out—to incorporate private groups in the rule of law and to seed desired action rather than just take it—is not a sign of the administrative weakness of the central government, but a measure of the state's considerable breadth of reach.

The political advantages of policy work-arounds come at a cost, however, because they aggravate the underlying issue of government complexity. Suzanne Mettler warns that inducements and market forms "obscure the role of government and exaggerate that of the market."[37] Steven Teles calls the resulting morass of policies a "kludgocracy" in which "an army of consultants and contractors" with an interest in creating ever more complex programs further gums up the political works.[38] Elisabeth Clemens has compared the American state to a Rube Goldberg machine, "an immensely complex tangle of indirect incentives, cross-cutting regulations, overlapping jurisdictions, delegated responsibility, and diffuse accountability."[39] Within this tangle, complex policies wrap around core institutions like vines covering a trellis.

Land, housing, and credit have always been part of this complex web of American statecraft. The distribution of land is a relatively straightforward aspect of this entanglement: the public domain was a resource that the national government could distribute in lieu of taxing and spending.[40] Even when the land was cheap or free, its distribution had ramifications for national credit markets because people still needed to borrow to build and farm. Credit did not just support land policy, however. Because credit fuels growth, it has long been a favored market form in its own right. A closer look at the politics of credit can clarify why.

The Political Lightness of Credit

Credit can generate growth. It gives borrowers access to funds and goods today based on a promise to repay the debt, with interest, in the future. Borrowers can use these funds to buy things, which raises demand, or build and sell things, which increases supply. Economic historian William Goetzmann has called credit a "time machine," arguing that this ability to turn expected future values into current resources did nothing less than make modern civilization possible.[41] The political usefulness of credit as such a time machine has not been lost on lawmakers. Across generations and party affiliation, officials have realized that carefully orchestrated engagements with finance can please constituents, save tax dollars, and avoid political gridlock. I use the metaphor of lightness to convey the many levels of political flexibility credit entails and how this has mattered in American political life.

Credit programs are *fiscally light*. They can yield big results for low costs. Guarantees of loans do not require expenditures when issued; as contingent liabilities, guarantees only result in a charge if a borrower defaults. Direct loan programs are more expensive at the moment when money is lent but nevertheless offset expenditures by generating income through fees or repayments or by selling off government-held loans.[42] Furthermore, credit programs can be easily set up as partnerships, with shared financing costs and reduced overhead, which makes them administratively light. Entities like the Commodity Credit Corporation or Fannie Mae straddle governmental boundaries: they can be just private enough to stay off the federal accounts (since they issue their own debt and so are not funded through the Treasury) but public enough to follow government mandates and receive special support.[43]

Credit programs also have a kind of budgetary lightness. Budgets determine the rules of the game for government spending, which makes them powerful disciplinary institutions to which officials continually orient themselves.[44] Inconsistent and improper accounting among the federal credit programs has obscured their costs in official accounts, allowing the government to raise and spend off-budget funds; accounting in these programs was not modernized until the 1990s, and watchdogs warn that official numbers still understate the programs' activities.[45] Subsidies within the programs, like below-market interest rates, cost the government money but, like tax expenditures, do so in the form of money-not-collected.

The abstract nature of credit facilitates this lightness. For all that credit is tied to some of the most concrete parts of life—actual dollars used to buy real objects—the debt is itself simply an agreement. Credit is a promise that money exchanged will be repaid, an obligation extended over time.[46] As a promise, it has no preexisting organic or material state. Rather, people create systems to organize, record, track, and enforce borrowers' obligations and lenders' rights. That characteristic of credit—its role as a space of classification, a thing defined in the last instance through processes of accounting and categorization, trust and commitment—can be powerfully harnessed in political contexts. Credit markets, because they deal in promises over time, are highly sensitive to questions of legitimacy, trust, and reliability. Governments, when they are stable and not in crisis, are specialists in legitimacy, trust, and reliability.

New theories of state power allow for deeper understanding of this elective affinity between politics and credit markets. At the center of modern governments, writes sociologist Pierre Bourdieu, is "the production and canonization of social classifications," a special capacity that he calls "symbolic power."[47] As the word "canonization" indicates, a government does not create these understandings of state classifications out of whole cloth, but rather puts an *official stamp* on existing notions. Official stamps matter because the authority and power behind them can be transformative. Government support for currency, for instance, is what allows money to be readily and widely exchanged.[48]

When it comes to credit markets, governments have many options for using their symbolic power to induce desired outcomes. Some of these options are classic forms of regulation. Adjustments to banking rules (like requirements for holding reserves) or to the Federal Reserve's open market window are among the best known of such strategies and generally work in broad strokes, influencing the overall level of credit and money in the economy. The credit programs, in contrast, more readily work like precision instruments and direct credit exactly where the government wants it to flow.

A theory of symbolic power also clarifies how credit programs came to have a kind of *ideological lightness*. Credit programs give government officials a great deal of rhetorical leeway because they combine market forms with partnerships and inducements and are used for many purposes.[49] Historian David Freund found that designers of the New Deal housing credit programs talked about them as "essentially non-interventionist" efforts that "unleashed" private capacities.[50] A 2016 special budgetary report on credit and insurance introduces the programs as both a response to market failures and a means of combating inequality.[51] This polysemy is useful for lawmakers, who must answer to multiple audiences with conflicting agendas. With Damon Mayrl, I have argued that government officials' ability to manage such understandings is an important part of policymaking.[52]

One lesson from this book is that credit's ideological lightness was not inevitable. While existing research tends to take for granted that Americans like markets and so like credit programs, that assumption neglects how frequently people are offended by any sort of boundary transgression. Indeed, the boundaries between states and markets are especially fraught.[53] Many nineteenth-century Americans rejected national government involvement in credit markets as a corrupt and paternalistic form of overreach, an understandable stance given the rampant patronage politics of the day. Progressive reformers did not just build a modern civil service; they also reframed federal government credit support as a form of self-help and set a path for the more expansive use of credit as a tool of statecraft that developed during the New Deal.

There are political costs to credit's political gains. Notably, guarantee programs save on immediate expenditures but can be costly in cases of default. Credit programs also miss out on revenue: they socialize risks of loans while letting private firms keep the profits from repayments. There are also organizational trade-offs associated with credit programs. These programs frequently compromise administrative transparency, coordination, and control. Moreover, the act of pumping out loans and guarantees is inflationary, which was not an immediate problem in the New Deal, when economic growth was so desperately needed, but became a major concern in the 1960s. Then, with inflation high and money tight, economic advisors lamented that credit programs undermined their attempts to cool the economy.

Despite these political and organizational trade-offs, the overall advantages of federal credit for lawmakers and bureaucrats are considerable. Under the right conditions, credit distribution promises growth without costs, without appearing to redistribute wealth, and without the polarizing specter of government overreach. Credit allocation can seem like a mild kind of policy even as it boosts entire industries. Viewed this way, it is not surprising that lawmakers have so often used credit allocation to manage tough distributional issues and veto points—or that, as a result, credit programs emerged as a key part of America's complex style of statecraft.

Credit and America's Peculiar Developmental State

I have argued that government officials use credit to navigate the rocky terrain of American politics. But what does this mean for how we think about the U.S. economy? Today's massive securitization industry speaks to how credit policies can impact global markets. It is only one example of many. The chapters that follow will also show that credit programs are not intermittent, marginal, or even limited to addressing flaws in credit markets. Credit programs have historically supported everything from railroads and farming to housing and energy. Credit has been used for disaster relief, foreign policy, and military efforts. It has been integral to the promotion of amortized mortgages, overseas lending, venture capital, and more.

In making this point, *American Bonds* brings credit allocation to the fore of our understanding of U.S. government officials as creative and consequential market participants.[54] In the field of sociology, Fred Block and colleagues have argued for the existence of a U.S. "developmental network state" that works through brokerage and research funding. The support by the Defense Advanced Research Projects Agency (DARPA) of the early Internet is a quintessential example of the world-changing capacity of government brokerage and research support.[55] Economist Mariana Mazzucato builds on this insight to argue that the American government should be thought of as a visionary entrepreneur that specializes in long-term investments for innovations with low early returns and high risks—the kind of big gambles that scare away private investors but open up new markets.[56] Most of the significant technologies used in the iPhone, she notes, trace back to some government effort to fund or facilitate the innovation. Legal scholars Robert Hockett and Saule Omarova refer to the mass of government economic subsidies and investments as the "developmental financial state."[57]

The United States never had a developmental state akin to that of a nation like France or Japan, where the growth of specific markets was subject to extensive centralized planning. But it is also true that American markets grew with considerable help from the state. The extent of U.S. government support for the economy is larger than most people realize. This is nowhere more consequential than in the housing sector. The website of the Federal Housing Administration (FHA) boasts that the agency is the world's largest mortgage insurer, having backed 47.5 million properties as of 2017.[58] Half of U.S. residential mortgages outstanding today were connected in some way to Fannie, Freddie, or the Federal Home Loan Banks.[59] In times of crisis, when the normal government programs are combined with bailout efforts, the level of government support of markets can reach jaw-dropping proportions. In 2009, the special inspector general for the Troubled Asset Relief Program testified to Congress that the total potential liability of the U.S. federal government through its various guarantees and bailouts in a worst-case scenario amounted to $23.7 trillion—the equivalent of 150 percent of that year's GDP.[60]

Block's theory of a developmental network state argues that U.S. developmental policy is generative rather than controlling, reliant on bottom-up change instead of top-down direction. A look at credit allocation bears this out. Political economist John Zysman studied European industrial policies and found that activist industrial governments used financial systems as "the muscle and the apparatus" to move an economy.[61] In France and Germany, governments used their influence over a centralized banking system to ration credit. Zysman concludes that "the single discretion necessary to all state-led industrial strategies" is credit *allocation.* [62] He further notes that such a strategy necessarily failed in nations like the United States where robust capital markets allowed companies to circumvent government attempts at credit rationing through banks.

Zysman is right about the importance of credit for economic development, but he misses the potential effectiveness of decentralized credit policies. Historically, the U.S. government continually induced change in domestic markets, but its credit distribution was diffuse, like a sprinkler, rather than streaming from a main source, like a spigot. Continual recalibrations to U.S. markets were made through the decentralized network of the credit programs. The modern securitization market stands as an example of how that approach can work. Credit is a valuable policy tool everywhere, but the use of that tool is shaped by particular political and economic contexts. In nations where political life is more centralized, so too is governmental credit allocation.

To be clear, I am not arguing that government officials are exclusively responsible for the growth of U.S. credit markets, or even the rise of the modern securitzation market. On the contrary, the book is full of examples of nongovernment actors making important breakthroughs, not the least of which are private companies' efforts to develop securitization deals in the postwar era, discussed in chapter 9. My point is rather to contribute to scholarship that moves creative government activities in markets from the margins to the center of the story. To clarify how government officials have mattered is not to say that private firms have therefore been inconsequential, but to paint a more detailed picture of how markets are made. A focus on government actors at key junctures yields a more detailed account of how government officials work with and alongside nongovernment actors to build an economic world.

Land, Homes, and Credit as Social Policy

Land and housing programs have long served as America's functional equivalent of a European welfare state. Political scientist Laura Jensen argues that nineteenth-century land distribution was effectively a welfare program used to placate and provide for the population. Land distribution was an early *entitlement*, especially for white male veterans.[63] Housing scholars like Schwartz, Kemeny, and Castles have posited a trade-off between homeownership and welfare programs, making the case that the U.S. government directed family savings over the life course through credit and tax policies that promoted homeownership.[64]

America's market-friendly social policy is not just a story of land and housing, but also one of easy money and credit access. Gunnar Trumbull has observed that in the early twentieth century, American labor saw consumer credit as a safety net for striking workers and so forged a pro-credit political coalition with a hypercompetitive banking industry eager to branch into consumer markets.[65] In a sweeping historical analysis, Monica Prasad argues that nineteenth-century farmers inadvertently set the United States on this path when they promoted a progressive tax system that ultimately failed to fund a more expansive welfare state. An underfunded welfare state combined with a pro-consumption bias (farmers wanted policies that encouraged people to buy their produce, after all) to create political support for cheap credit. The key insight here is that robust consumer credit markets and weak welfare states can be reinforcing systems: in the absence of a stronger welfare state, American families latched on to credit as a lifeline, which created pressure for government officials to ensure its supply.[66]

If credit can substitute for social policy, it is because credit programs can do many of the things that welfare programs do: smooth consumption and cushion families during emergencies, compensate for low wages, and secure cardinal resources like housing, healthcare, and education.[67] While credit provides economic support through lending, it does not follow that all of its benefits are repaid with interest. If the government issues a loan at a below-market interest rate, this is a subsidy. So too if the government forgives a loan or allows someone to refinance on easier terms, that is money in the bank for recipients.

When it comes to its use as a mode of social policy, credit's ideological lightness means that recipients of federal credit are protected from the dishonor sometimes associated with welfare programs.[68] That is because credit is a market form and so comes without the stigma associated with charity. But while a program like Social Security is not stigmatizing because someone has *already paid* into it, that arrangement is flipped with credit programs: borrowers get the payment first and repay it later. Instead of accumulating dishonor, the borrower builds a credit history and has a chance to become an owner of a home or business. In this way, credit programs provide status and enhance financial citizenship.[69] The open obligation of the credit form—the fact that there is repayment—helps people overlook the various opportunities and subsidies also transferred through this process. Subsidies and state assistance then appear to be forms of self-help.

Credit and Racial Inequality

The government's extension of its symbolic power through credit has frequently been politicized along racial lines and used in racially exclusionary ways. Examples of credit's role in upholding white supremacy run throughout this book. Before the Civil War, southern congressmen sought to protect the national balance of power that ensured the entrenchment of slavery by denying credit support for western infrastructure development, and southern states guaranteed mortgage bonds that included slaves as human collateral. After the Civil War, southern states used strict lending laws to lock in a system of labor controls and debt peonage that hit black farmers first and hardest. After the New Deal, credit programs thrived while efforts at European-style centralized planning failed, in part because southern congressmen did not see credit programs as a threat to white supremacy.

Racist credit politics were never just a southern issue, of course. Perhaps the most famous example of the national scale of these practices is the Federal Housing Administration's insurance program that helped many families who had no credit record secure their first mortgages. This was a crucial boost, because it gave families a chance to build wealth that could be tapped in emergencies or old age, or be passed along to later generations. In the postwar era, these government-insured mortgages overwhelmingly went to white families. As political scientist Chloe Thurston has argued, people of color excluded by the housing credit programs fought for inclusion in them from the creation of those programs.[70] There is a large body of research that shows how the exclusion of families of color from the housing credit programs created lasting differences in wealth, as well as differences in access to the best public schools and job opportunities.[71]

When families of color were excluded from the largesse of the housing programs, they lost out on multiple fronts: the chance to build what became the main form of wealth for American families, access to higher-quality schools in tax-rich suburban neighborhoods, the chance to build a credit record on forgiving terms, and a chance to get all of this support in a way that was entirely divorced from the stigma associated with receiving welfare. Historian David Freund has investigated the legacy of New Deal housing credit programs and concluded that these programs' racial policies had lasting implications for the nature of northern white racism. With the contributions of the credit programs downplayed as mere market corrections, white families saw their resulting sprint up the social ladder not as an achievement made easier through credit hoarding, but as deriving exclusively from their hard work and so signifying their virtue and deservingness.[72]

If credit is a time machine, it is not only dollars that flow through it: credit continually carries forward the prejudices and inequalities of the past. There has been no time period or region in which credit distribution has not been distorted by racism. Here, then, is another way we can think of the lightness of credit policy: as historically serving the interests of white Americans.

Distribution in America

It is by looking at economic and social policy together that we can grasp the overall implications of the use of land and credit as a mode of distribution in the U.S. political economy. The real payoff of these strategies is the promise that accompanies them of not needing much social policy at all: the acceptance of the idea that market growth should alleviate poverty and, with it, the need for redistribution. Lizabeth Cohen has studied the postwar era and concluded that suburban consumerism became a civil religion because "it promised the socially progressive end of economic equality without requiring politically progressive means of redistributing existing wealth."[73] Greta Krippner has investigated the financial turn of the 1970s and 1980s and found that lawmakers used financial deregulation to avoid openly rationing resources (lawmakers preferred that "the market" take responsibility for hardship).[74] Scholars like Wolfgang Streeck, Colin Crouch, and Raghuram Rajan have all observed lawmakers around the world using easy credit to compensate citizens for low wages and frayed social safety nets in the era of neoliberalism.[75]

By tracing the history of securitization and federal credit programs over a long time, this book connects these insights and clarifies the overarching pattern of their development as it played out in the context of American history. Federal credit is an important tool of statecraft, one reaching back to the earliest days of the nation. It has always been implicated in distributional politics. The meaningful change from the nineteenth to the twentieth century was the extent to which lawmakers approached credit allocation as a backstop or primary lever. Viewed this way, the government's involvement in the securitization market is not surprising, but typical, and typical not just of housing policy, but of an array of credit policies—credit policies that are in turn typical of the use of markets as one facet of the generally complex style of American statecraft.

The contribution of this book is not just to make sense of credit's role in the U.S. political economy, but also to illuminate how the social logics of distribution operate *within* credit markets. We see this operation in the distinct historical approaches to the design of mortgage bonds. Populists built co-operative protections for borrowers into their loan pools. A century later, government-guaranteed mortgage bonds reflected the social logic of the credit state, in which state-promoted financial development and risk redistribution served as an alternative to wealth redistribution.

The point here is an extension of an old insight within economic sociology: financial tools are designed by human beings who grapple with concrete problems imbued with political pressures, historical contingencies, and shared understandings.[76] Culture and politics are always the material out of which people come to understand their interests and desires, and develop strategies for pursuing them. Social life is not like soft flesh covering an underlying, bone-hard economic truth. It is the marrow. It is the stuff from which economic life is built.

Researching Credit Politics in Time

This is a work of historical sociology that draws on existing research to theorize social processes. The method follows what Theda Skocpol has called the "targeted primary" approach, which draws from secondary materials and supplements them with original research to fill in details as needed. In this case, reports from the Progressive Era informed my analysis of the emergence of the Federal Farm Loan Act, and original archival research clarified early government use of securitization for asset sales.[77] As the title indicates, *American Bonds* is exclusively a study of the United States, so it does not include systematic comparisons with other nations. That said, I hope this study generates knowledge that will be useful to other scholars who make such comparisons, and chapter 10 will consider why we might expect some of these relationships to matter elsewhere.

Paul Pierson has noted that analyses that cover long time spans are ideal for identifying relationships between systems of institutions, which may unfold slowly or unevenly over many years.[78] An approach that necessarily trades depth for historical breadth, the long view is well suited for a study of the relationship between American political institutions and credit markets, one of this book's primary goals. Methodologically, this book also borrows from Jeffrey Haydu's insight that institutions are instances of iterative problem solving, which means scholars can approach them as both elements to connect and cases to compare.[79] This study applies the same logic to financial techniques: I analyze how new financial tools create resources and problems that influence later groups, and I treat financial tools as objects to compare in order to better understand social logics of exchange that are hard to see in isolation.

The analysis starts with a watershed land policy in the founding era. It ends with a 1968 regulatory change that reorganized the housing credit program Fannie Mae and authorized it to trade in government-guaranteed mortgage-backed securities. The year 1968 is a reasonable end point because it marked a key policy transformation: the nation was leaving behind an older New Deal system and turning toward a new one organized around securitization, the system still in place today.

While I will briefly examine the effects of these shifts on later events in chapter 10, the book does not cover in detail the millennium-era housing boom that so famously implicated securitization and Fannie Mae in the economic collapse of the first decade of the twenty-first century. Instead, it analyzes the older, less well-studied roots of that market. *American Bonds* is not a history of the recent housing and credit crisis, then, but a prehistory of that crisis. To the extent that those deep structures persist, it is perhaps a prehistory of crises still to come.

Looking Ahead

The chapters that follow compare different modes of mortgage finance over time, paying special attention to the interaction of political institutions and mortgage markets. Because the book links financial technologies to their broader social contexts, some chapters emphasize large-scale historical transformations, while others look more closely at specific markets.

The first half focuses on the volatile world of nineteenth-century mortgage finance. Chapter 2 traces the development of the nation's patchwork mortgage market and early crisis-prone credit programs. The latter include land-sales-on-credit schemes intended to raise funds to pay down Revolutionary War debt, as well as the controversial, crisis-prone railway programs. Chapter 3 begins at the end of the nineteenth century, as the problem of credit provision reached a boiling point, and compares three approaches to pooling loans from this period to show how they articulated competing visions for a rapidly changing political economy. Failures at this time set the stage for future credit programs. Chapter 4 shows how Progressives returned to the issue of farm credit distribution in the early 1900s and drew on European precedents to reframe credit allocation as a way for the central government to help people help themselves. Chapter 4 also shows how political conflict shaped the development of the federal farm loan system, a breakthrough in allocative credit that set precedents for policies to come.

The second half of the book focuses on the explosive rise of both residential mortgage markets and federal credit in the twentieth century. Chapter 5 shows how, as the United States transitioned from an agricultural to an industrial nation, mortgage lenders promoted homeownership as the new measure of independence, success, and virtue. This chapter also discusses how a growing federal government in World War I took new steps into housing policy. Chapter 6 takes a close look at the postwar boom in mortgage bonds, this time made up of smaller slices of large mortgages for commercial buildings like skyscrapers. The market heated up at the close of the 1920s as lenders marketed mortgage bonds to families. The collapse of this market in the early 1930s wiped out the private market for mortgage bonds completely and led to regulatory prohibitions against small-investor purchases of mortgage bonds.

The New Deal brought the creation of Fannie Mae and other housing credit programs, and also heralded a much broader expansion of credit as a tool of statecraft. This is the focus of chapter 7. Here we see how government officials used the ideological and fiscal lightness of credit allocation to find a more palatable, but still effective, alternative to European-style economic planning. Chapter 8 reviews the evolution of federal credit programs in the postwar era into a sprawling, decentralized system with housing at its center. Chapter 9 shows how that system incubated securitization, and how that in turn helped set the terms for the reorganization of housing finance in 1968. The analysis shows how budget politics can shape the type of credit policies that are crafted. The concluding chapter discusses how the events recounted throughout the book help us understand the housing bubble of the early 2000s. It also draws lessons for sociological theories of states and markets.

Considered together, these chapters show how political institutions shape government participation in markets. They reveal how competing moral visions of the American political economy are written into specific ways of pooling and dividing loans. And they detail how Americans have repeatedly turned to land, housing, and credit in an elusive search for widespread economic opportunity that comes without the attendant costs of political conflict, financial risk, or large-scale redistribution. The chapters present, in other words, the enduring problem and promise of credit in American life.

2

The Credit Frontier

The United States has always been in the real estate business, and so it has always had to grapple with the distribution of mortgage credit.[1] This chapter introduces the problem of farm credit distribution in the nineteenth century and discusses some early examples of how federal credit and securitization were mobilized in response to it.

The first half of the chapter looks at the federal government's use of credit as a policy tool, focusing on two instances: the sale of land on credit to raise funds to pay down Revolutionary War debt and the use of land and credit as supports for the transcontinental railroads. The United States expanded by 3.7 million square miles between 1783 and 1867 as European settlers spread over the continent.[2] For a small nineteenth-century national government that lacked political power and administrative capacity, the acquisition and distribution of the public domain loomed large. Land was an essential political resource. Sold to raise revenues, it was a fiscal tool. Given away to soldiers, it was an instrument of social and military policy. Granted to the railways, it was a form of economic development. Nineteenth-century selective credit programs usually served as ad hoc and temporary ways to support or supplement the use of land as a policy tool.

The second half of the chapter looks at the demand for farm mortgage credit in the West and South as the nation spread over the continent. Land is a massive absorber of capital, and even when farmers received land for free, settlers and farmers used mortgages to raise funds to improve and work the land. As settlers pushed inland in the nineteenth century, they did so in a series of surges that followed a typical pattern. A rise in the price of a commodity (like cotton or wheat) or the opening up of a territory by a new railroad would draw settlers with hopes of getting rich. This would cause a spike in land prices, and the promise of returns would eventually overwhelm the risks and transaction costs that would otherwise slow mortgage investment. Capital would flow into the region from New York, Philadelphia, or London. Excitement would encourage fraud, speculation, and overproduction. The boom would eventually culminate in panic, bust, and finally recovery. Some farmers who lost their property would sink into tenancy, while others would move farther west to try again. Each major boom and bust cycle was followed by recrimination for the land policy that supported it, sometimes resulting in the creation of a new approach to land or credit distribution or bank regulation.

A mix of banks, insurance companies, intermediaries, and individuals, moved credit from the capital-rich cities to more sparsely populated regions spread out over the continent. In the South, this process included early experiments with mortgage-backed bonds in the 1830s. Since slaves were mortgaged in the Cotton South, these bonds were secured not just with land, but with, as historian Bonnie Martin has put it, "human collateral."[3] These bonds were also guaranteed by state governments, putting the support of states like Louisiana and Mississippi behind the trade.

In all, this chapter shows that land and credit have always been part of how Americans have sought to resolve disputes over who should get what and part of how government officials have sought to avoid more direct modes of taxing and spending. Securitization and federal credit have long been part of American distribution politics as well.

Public Lands, Sold on Credit

Before the emergent national U.S. government had the right to tax, it had the right to distribute public lands.[4] The way that Congress distributed those lands was indelibly shaped by another governmental obligation: responsibility for paying the nation's debts.

The U.S. federal government entered the 1790s deep in the red, with $80 million in obligations, representing roughly 40 percent of the gross national product (GNP). Over $12 million of that was owed to foreign creditors, mainly France and Holland.[5] The total debt included the wartime debts accrued by the states, which Hamilton had pushed for control over in a bid to strengthen the central government and bind the states together. In addition to paying down the debt, the national government needed to finance its ongoing land acquisitions (the Louisiana Purchase alone cost $15 million) and its military campaigns against Native Americans. Raising funds to cover those expenses was no small problem in a nation short on specie and famously resistant to taxation.[6]

Land had two important fiscal functions: it could be distributed in lieu of other payments, and it could be sold. During the war, cash-strapped revolutionaries pledged land to soldiers and English deserters as compensation for their service. Laura Jensen explains that land distribution operated alongside pensions as an early entitlement program, and that the government provided land access to entire classes of citizens, starting with soldiers and veterans.[7] After the war, land distribution to soldiers and armed settlers doubled as military policy. Paul Frymer argues that the national government purposefully used the land offices to overwhelm American Indian and Mexican populations with white settlers.[8] In their analyses, Jensen and Frymer each observe that land distribution had its own kinds of fiscal and ideological benefits. It was a cheap way to appease populations. It blurred welfare with warfare.

Land could also be sold off. Thomas Jefferson in 1776 had objected to "selling lands at all," a policy that was consistent with his commitment to a republican vision of a nation of independent yeoman farmers. In this view, the small farmers had a right to those lands, so it was unfair to generate revenue at their expense.[9] Nevertheless, by the mid-1780s the national debt had become a pressing concern, and this shaped land policy. When the United States defaulted on payments to France, the founders looked to land sales to pay down the national debt. Poor credit was not only an embarrassment, but also a threat to national defense: it made it hard to raise funds quickly to mobilize an army in an emergency. Despite his earlier reservations, Jefferson proceeded with the task of drafting the first of the Land Ordinances in 1784 (although it was the Ordinance of 1785 that Congress passed and implemented as policy). Later, as president, Jefferson signed an act that authorized the military to expel squatters on public lands.[10] On August 4, 1790, Congress pledged that the proceeds from land sales would be "applied solely" to the repayment of the war debt.[11]

Every aspect of land sales was politically fraught. The founders rejected the idea of direct sales to foreign investors, which Pelatiah Webster compared to "killing the goose that laid an egg every day in order to tear out all at once all that was in her belly."[12] Instead, they argued, domestic sales could raise funds without sacrificing national autonomy. Even then, matters of lot size and price and location of sales were controversial. The potential to collect revenue had to be balanced against the dangers of speculation, settlers' demands for cheap land, and eastern landholders' worries about lowered property values and heightened labor shortages. In the end, sales proceeded through a modified version of the New England township system, with a floor placed on prices to keep their value from dropping too low. First set at $1 per acre at auction, the price of land was raised by Congress to $2 per acre in 1796. In a break from the New England model, and in line with the more scattershot southern system of settlement, there was no requirement for purchasers to develop or settle the land.[13]

This commitment to sales came with its own political challenges. To protect its landed interests, the federal government now had to drive off squatters, which meant potentially using the military against citizens. Land surveys were slow, and the public land states had to adjudicate a massive number of cases concerning competing and conflicting titles. Selling the land also required administrators. From the outset, wealthy speculators formed land companies that acted as middlemen, purchasing large tracts directly from the government with the intention of distributing them later to settlers. For the government, the land companies promised a swift influx of money with relatively little inconvenience. The Ohio Land Company won the right to purchase 1.5 million acres at a low price, for example, but it failed as a result of its own trouble raising funds. Large amounts of land company tracts eventually reverted back to the public domain. Historian Paul Gates notes that if such early companies had been more successful, they may well have displaced the federal government as the organizational center of land disbursement on the frontier.[14]

The first government land sales were not particularly successful either. Receipts for transactions conducted between 1785 and 1795 show that sales amounted to less than 1 percent of the national debt, and buyers purchased fewer than 50,000 acres from 1797 to 1800.[15] One problem was that competitors undercut the auction prices. Both the states and land companies sold land at lower prices than the federal government, as did many soldiers who chose to unload their military bounties rather than actually settle on rough lands. Another problem was that buyers were allowed to use depreciated government bonds for the purchase of land.[16] Many settlers could not afford even the depreciated payments, and they found little recourse in America's early banks, which catered to elites and merchants.[17]

Congress took various steps to increase revenues. In 1787 land sales were authorized to be made "on time," with a third of the amount put down and the remainder due in three months.[18] Even these credit terms were a stretch for many settlers, however.[19] Provisions for federal credit were relaxed over a period of years: loan tenure moved from three months (1787) to one year (1796), then four years (1800), and eventually five or six years (1804). In addition to allowing sales on credit, Congress removed fees, allowed settlers to defer interest payments, and offered discounted prices to people who paid in cash. It also reduced the size of lots, from 640 to 360 acres in 1800 and to 160 acres in 1804 (this continued over time, with lot size dropping to 80 acres in 1820 and 40 acres in 1832). Land sales north of the Ohio went from "practically nothing" in 1800 to over half a million in 1805.[20] In 1812 the Land Offices were created as a bureau within the Treasury to oversee the distribution of the public lands.[21] Major changes to the federal land distribution laws are summarized in table 2.1.

Government credit and easier terms did not entirely eliminate the need for private lenders. Settlers who could not raise the 20 percent down payment

TABLE 2.1. Selected Early Land Laws

Law	Description
Land Ordinance of 1785	Provided for the sale of lands, broken into 640-acre lots, at a minimum price of $1 per acre.
Land Act of 1797	Allowed for the sale of land "on time" with a third of the amount due at purchase and the remainder due in 3 months.
Land Act of 1796	Allowed for the sale of land with a 20 percent down payment plus an additional 30 percent in 30 days, with full payment in a year, at 6 percent interest. Raised the price of land to $2 per acre.
Land Act of 1800	Extended credit for up to five years.
Land Act of 1820	Ended the sale of land on credit; replaced it with cash sales at $1.25 per acre.
Species Circular, 1836	Executive order from Andrew Jackson requiring payment in specie to the Land Offices.
Preemption Act of 1841	Granted squatters first rights to bid on land they had developed if they had lived there more than two years.
Graduation Act of 1854	Lowered prices for certain public lands.
Homestead Act of 1862	Granted land to settlers with a fee of $50.
Pacific Railway Act of 1862	The first of a series of acts between 1862 and 1871 that authorized direct federal land grants and loans for transcontinental railways.
Banking Acts of 1863 and 1864	Created a national banking system with a pyramid reserve structure and restrictions on issuing new mortgages or holding mortgages for longer than five years.

within the 40-day window turned to the lenders who regularly attended government land auctions. Others turned to land jobbers and "land sharks," speculators who typically purchased tracts at government auctions and immediately resold them at higher prices and on credit.

An early tax expenditure policy also supported the sales. Congress sought to improve sales by getting new states to agree not to tax land purchased on credit that was still being paid off. This was justified by the notion that a title did not pass to the borrower until the loan was paid off, which meant that the states would be taxing land officially owned by the federal government. To help make up for states' lost revenues, the national government granted 3 to 5 percent of the sale back to state coffers, with the funds earmarked for internal developments.[22] This plan was inaugurated by Ohio and was subsequently copied by other states. While best understood as a government transportation and economic development policy, it was also motivated by the tax and revenue implications of credit sales.[23]

TABLE 2.2. Public Domain Land Sales and Collections, 1813–1819

Year	Acres	Amount Sold	Amount Collected	Unpaid Balance
1813	270,240	$621,225	$726,507	$2,114,135
1814	865,136	$1,784,560	$1,174,697	$2,723,947
1815	1,120,233	$2,340,188	$1,368,517	$3,695,668
1816	1,622,829	$3,567,272	$1,658,197	$5,604,745
1817	2,032,042	$4,768,771	$2,344,211	$8,029,304
1818	2,529,174	$7,463,705	$3,243,308	$12,461,477
1819	5,675,646	$17,681,793	$5,954,450	$24,220,528

Source: Paul Wallace Gates, *History of Public Land Law Development*, ed. U.S. Public Land Law Review Commission, Management of Public Lands in the United States (New York: Arno Press, 1979), 136. Totals include lands west of the Mississippi for 1819 only. Lands north of the Ohio River, Mississippi, and Alabama are included for 1813–1819.

There were early signs that collections would be a problem. Treasury Secretary Albert Gallatin noted that land sales on credit would create a class of debtors hostile to the government.[24] Others warned that sales of land on government credit encouraged speculation. In 1812, a House committee on public lands urged an end to the credit system. "Men are seduced by the temptation," it warned, "which the credit held out to them, to extend their purchase beyond their means of making payment."[25] Western advocates for government credit responded that opponents were thwarting growth for selfish sectional reasons.[26] Despite concerns, land sales on credit remained a popular policy that brought in $1 million to $2 million in the middle of the decade (table 2.2). When settlers ran into trouble with payments, Congress passed relief acts to grant them more time. The first such act, passed in 1806, allowed 309 settlers an extension on repayments. Congress then passed a dozen more relief acts *before* the market bottomed out in the Crash of 1819.[27]

BOOM YEARS

One way to understand the role of credit in a crisis is through the work of Charles Kindleberger. "The pattern," says Kindleberger, building on the insights of Hyman Minsky, "is biological in its regularity."[28] A financial crisis starts with an outside shock to the system that creates a new economic opportunity. The end of a war, changes in money supply, deregulation, and new financial instruments are all common "shocks." The shock creates an incentive for people to borrow in hopes of cashing in on the new opportunity; this demand for credit is met with an increase in supply. Existing banks lend more, new banks form, and unregulated lenders multiply. New kinds of assets or money may emerge as people seek to circumvent existing constraints on the money supply. Not all expansions of credit cause a bubble, but all bubbles depend on credit expansion.

The next stage of a financial crisis is a period of euphoria or mania. As new people with access to (sometimes new forms of) money enter the market and compete for goods, prices rise even higher. Expansion then transforms into a bubble, and the resulting frenzy can spread into new markets (there is usually more than one object of speculation) and other nations. Manias are fertile ground for fraud, which can take the form of blatantly illegal practices or just questionable ones. But as long as confidence is high most people will ignore signs that the system itself has gone awry. The good times last as long as more people are buying than selling. At some point, however, a sense of unease creeps in, confidence collapses, and the bubble deflates. This correction is often, but not always, accompanied by a panic.[29] Lenders, worried that they are overextended, start to retrench. Interest rates rise, currencies can depreciate, and funds can flow out of a nation. Economist Irving Fisher talks about this as the "debt disease," noting that leverage is the mechanism that transforms speculation into a true economic catastrophe.[30] Banks call in their loans, which forces debtors to undertake fire sales of commodities that further drive down prices. Low prices can drive businesses into bankruptcy. A race commences to cash out before the prices hit bottom. The debt that fueled the market's growth now speeds its decline. This results in lowered output, unemployment, and hoarding.

In the early nineteenth century, the end of the War of 1812 was the shock that set the nation on a course for a land boom. Peacetime brought an end to the naval blockade and sparked the resumption of maritime trade. Reopened trade led to a massive influx of cheap European goods and a renewed outflow of American commodities. Farmers now shipped goods to Europe, where years of war and poor harvests had decimated crops. Prices rose for sugar, tobacco, wheat, and cotton.[31] The rush to capitalize on these rising commodity prices drove up prices on farmland. As prices mounted, banks mobilized. The number of U.S. banks rose from 88 to 392 between 1811 and 1818, and the total circulation of bank notes rose from $45 million to $100 million between 1812 and 1817.[32] When the Second Bank of the United States was chartered in 1816, its western branches, such as those in Pittsburgh and Lexington, followed the state banks in aggressively issuing notes that went to fund trade and land purchases.[33]

As the market for land heated up, the federal government increased sales, and the high cotton prices drew more settlers to the South. In 1816 the federal government sold 209,000 acres in Alabama. Three years later, sales in that state had jumped to 1.3 million acres.[34] The general market expansion stretched the boundaries of the nation. By 1819 Indiana, Mississippi, Illinois, and Alabama had all become states.[35] Bidding wars drove up prices to new heights, reaching highs of $32 an acre in Missouri and $69 an acre in Huntsville, Alabama, in 1816, as sales of public lands mounted.[36]

CRISIS AND CORRECTION

Unease crept in during the summer of 1818. As the required $4 million in payments for the Louisiana Purchase debt came due, the Second Bank of the United States, chastened by scandals and worried about its dwindling specie reserves, took steps to rebuild its holdings of gold and silver coins by restricting its own lending and specie redemptions.[37] The retraction caused the state banks to call in their loans, setting off a series of bank failures.[38] At a time when the period of most mercantile loans was fewer than 90 days, the contraction ripped through the economy.[39] Debtors sold property to repay loans, and prices dropped. Between 1817 and 1819 cotton prices fell by a half.[40] In an extra blow to farmers, a respite from war and bad harvests allowed European crops to recover, which further depressed demand for American produce.

On the frontier, low prices and scarce money caused some places to revert to barter or use grain and whiskey as a stand-in for money.[41] The eastern regions were also hit hard. In Philadelphia 1,808 people were sent to debtors' prisons in 1819. That same year, the average farm worker's wage plummeted from $1.50 to 50 cents in Massachusetts, and the count of public paupers jumped from 8,000 to 13,000 in New York City.[42]

The bottom fell out of the public land market. Prices tumbled back to the $2 per acre floor, and sales dropped from $13.6 million in 1818 to $1.7 million in 1820.[43] By the end of 1820, borrowers owed $24 million to the government, and Congress worried about how much of that it would ever see.[44] It responded by passing 11 more relief acts by 1832.[45] Most allowed for longer repayment times. Some allowed settlers to give up part of their land and apply funds toward the rest, while others forgave interest on the debt or reduced prices in exchange for prompt repayment. These acts were often purposefully designed to benefit settlers but exclude absentee speculators. As the crisis played out, millions of acres were forfeited back to the government.

As with any financial crisis, the people who lived through it struggled to make sense of what had just happened. Some blamed the national government's practice of paying soldiers in land bounties. Others railed against the banks, including the Second Bank of the United States and the aggressive lending in which its western branches engaged. As one critic at the time railed, "Capitalists, both real and fictitious, have engaged extensively in this business [of land speculation]. The banks have conspired with the government to promote it; the former by lending money to the speculator, the latter by its wretched system of selling land on credit."[46] Senator Thomas Hart Benton raged against the Second Bank's vast accumulation of debts amid the crisis:

"All the flourishing cities of the West are mortgaged to this money power. They may be devoured by it at any moment. They are in the jaws of the monster! A lump of butter in the mouth of a dog! One gulp, one swallow, and all is gone."[47] The years that followed were fertile ground for the antigovernment, antibank vitriol of Andrew Jackson's populist Democrats.[48]

In response to the crisis, Congress overhauled the land distribution system.[49] The federal government stopped selling land on credit in 1820. As a kind of consolation prize, it lowered the price of land to $1.25 an acre and began selling it in smaller, 80-acre lots.[50] Over the objections of some western congressmen who still supported the credit system, the cash bill passed by a resounding 133 to 23 majority.[51] After 1823 the Second Bank of the United States refrained from mortgage lending as well.[52]

In retrospect, the land sales on credit were never a terribly effective source of revenue. The management of squatters and land distribution had been a significant expense, and repeated relief acts chipped away at profits. As table 2.2 shows, actual collections of revenue from land sales lagged far behind the total balance of the sales, so that by 1819, according to land historian Paul Gates, the unpaid balance of debts to the government amounted to four times the amount collected. The best years of exports coincided with a glut of cheap European imports. It was those tariffs that made the biggest contribution to paying down the national debt: the $1.7 million of revenue collected from land sales in the boom year of 1816 was dwarfed by customs collections of $36.6 million (see table 2.2).[53] The federal government now exited the business of securing or providing credit for farmers until the Progressive Era. It did continue to oversee the distribution of public lands, doggedly seeking revenue through cash sales throughout the 1830s.

Land and Loans for Development

There was another major way that the government used land and credit as political tools in the nineteenth century: to support the early infrastructure development efforts known at the time as internal improvements. The economic and social development of the nation required the movement of people into habitable land. This meant building canals and harbors and lighthouses, roads and railways. It also meant draining swamps and irrigating drylands. All this was accomplished through a mix of public and private efforts.

The dynamics of these internal improvement politics illustrate the complexity of American government discussed in the introduction. The role of the federal government in distributing and developing land was one of the most controversial issues of the early and mid-nineteenth century. Jacksonian Democrats, who were especially active in the West and South, strongly objected to the national government's involvement in banking, a systemic national program of internal improvements, and land sales—all of which were understood as a diversion of public resources for private gain.[54] On one hand, the ferocity with which the Jacksonians attacked government involvement in banking and internal improvements stands as a reminder that government use of credit is not inherently uncontroversial or depoliticized. On the other hand, the ferocity of these fights means we must also take care not to overstate the consistency or uniformity of antistatist sentiment in American history.[55] Jackson himself used the national government to build harbors and promote trade, and the largest congressional appropriations for internal improvements before the Civil War occurred during his presidency.[56] (The nation's largest federal improvement before that, the construction of the National Road, began under Jefferson.) Moreover, even for the Jacksonian Democrats, the laissez-faire rejection of government involvement was exclusively a federal issue: public and private alliances were generally accepted on the state and local levels. State- and local-level internal improvements programs were robust and played a major role in the creation of infrastructure like roads, canals, dams, and the first railroads.

Moreover, there were always lawmakers who, in the Hamiltonian tradition, fought for a more energetic role for the national government in the economy. Republican nationalists like John Quincy Adams and Henry Clay concluded from the Crash of 1819 that the federal government should use centralized planning to achieve independence from European markets through orderly economic growth.[57] Clay's "American System" proposed to use land sales and tariffs (and a national bank) to fund internal improvements and to support business. One scholar summarizes the history of internal improvements as "the prolonged failure of the majority to establish its favored policy."[58] A more energetic national role in internal improvements was not uniformly unpopular so much as it was terrifically divisive over long periods of time, much like the issue of national healthcare is today.

These ideological divides combined with sectional interests and institutional fragmentation to hamper federal internal improvements. Twenty-one out of 53 presidential vetoes that occurred before the Civil War were related to internal improvements.[59] Specific projects were relatively easy to derail on a national stage, since a given road or canal was likely to be opposed by anyone who saw it as offering an unfair advantage to a competitor. The more visionary the plan for systematic development, the more groups would align against it.[60]

As fights over slavery in the run-up to the Civil War intensified, they came to subsume debates about land sales and internal improvements. As it became clear that western settlers rejected the extension of slavery, the southern states increasingly resisted any plan that could promote the West and so upset the nation's balance of power. For the same reason, lawmakers in the Northeast came to see economic development as a bulwark against the expansion of slavery and a chance to tilt the balance of power in their favor.[61] This standoff mostly paralyzed land and internal improvement policy. Steven Minicucci estimates that Congress appropriated $42.6 million for internal improvements between 1790 and 1860—less than a third of what local governments spent and about a seventh of what state governments directly spent on such projects in that time.[62] For most years before the Civil War, direct expenditures for internal improvements stayed well under 5 percent of the federal budget.

For all that national government involvement in internal improvements—and especially more systematic approaches to the challenge—was hampered, scattershot efforts did proceed, even early on. The first national internal improvement was the 1789 construction of a lighthouse at the mouth of the Chesapeake Bay in Cape Henry, Virginia. The first of a series of lighthouses built to illuminate maritime trade routes along the Atlantic coast, it had direct economic benefits.

As political scientist Brian Balough argues, the internal improvements that were made on the federal level are important examples of a national developmental state, one that relied extensively on public–private coalitions and mixed enterprise.[63] While some efforts, like funding for the Army Corps of Engineers or the lighthouses, involved direct expenditures, land grants were also important developmental policy tools. The national government not only granted land to companies working on a project (like a canal or railroad) but also made land grants to states to support specific projects like swamp drainage and famously to support schools and education (the most famous of these grants being the 1962 Morrill Act's provision of land for public universities).[64]

Land grants allowed the national government to give entrepreneurs a re-source to monetize. In his history of canal and railroad promotion, Carter Goodrich writes of the "obvious advantages" of land grants from the point of view of the government: land was a subsidy that appeared "costless" and avoided "the unpleasant necessities of raising taxes or borrowing money or incurring current deficit."[65] Once companies resold government-granted land they could mortgage it to raise funds. One English capitalist commented of the Illinois Central Railroad in 1856 (which received 2.5 million acres through a land grant in 1850): "This is not a railroad company, *it is a land company*."[66] Many other railways benefited from congressional aid routed through state governments as well.[67]

It is hard to overstate the importance of this support of railways for economic development. Few people at the time failed to recognize that towns would soon spring up wherever railroads were built, and across the nation town jobbers hustled to bring railroads to targeted areas to increase the value of the land there. Overland travel would soon be free from the restrictions posed by weather and nature.[68] The draw of migrants westward meant not only that new towns would be built, but also that there would be new markets for goods manufactured back east. In this way railways could spark a virtuous circle of growth. But railways also involved tremendous cost and risks, far beyond what most domestic investors were willing and able to invest. Proponents of government support argued that public action must be taken to encourage the development of the rails, lest private financiers' limits on raising capital impede national growth.

With the Pacific Rail Act of 1862, the national government took a massive step forward in supporting transcontinental railroads through a mix of land grants, loans, and guarantees—a mix designed to build a transnational railway without raising taxes.[69] This was possible because the onset of the Civil War changed the political calculus for internal improvements. The secession of the southern states removed what was then the primary barrier to national-level internal developments. At the same time, the onset of war created a demand for tracks to move military supplies and soldiers, although most of the building would happen after the war.[70]

The land grants gave the railroads land to build on, land to sell to settlers to raise funds, and, most important, land to collateralize as mortgage bonds.[71] By 1871 the federal government had granted railroads rights to up to 175 million acres (the railways eventually used over 131 million); rights to another 50 million acres were granted through the states.[72] Some of these granted lands were still occupied by Native Americans. The acreage was dispersed in alternating blocks along the tracks, forming a checkerboard pattern that had earlier been used to aid the building of the canals (see figure 2.1 for an example of this pattern).[73] The government retained ownership of blocks of land interspersed throughout this grid so as to directly profit from the subsequent rise in land values. Railways also sold land to settlers; figure 2.2 is an 1872 advertisement of land sales by the Burlington & Missouri River Railroad Co., which offered loans at 6 percent on a 10-year basis. While profitable, payments from such land sales trickled in over a period of years, so they did not meet the railways' need for working capital.[74] For that, land had to be monetized immediately, which meant dealing with capital markets.

Credit support was a major part of national railway policy, boosting the effectiveness of the land grants. In 1862 and again in 1864, the federal government provided $50 million in bonds to the transcontinental railroads. It was, in the words of historian Richard White, "taxless finance at its most grandiose."[75] For each mile of road built, the railway could borrow, depending on the terrain, $16,000 to $48,000 in 30-year government bonds with 6 percent interest, with a guarantee of payment of principle and interest from the United States.[76] It was this loan structure that drove the companies' race to lay down track.[77] These bonds were designed to appeal to European investors like large British banks, which used American intermediaries, like Kidder Peabody in Boston, to

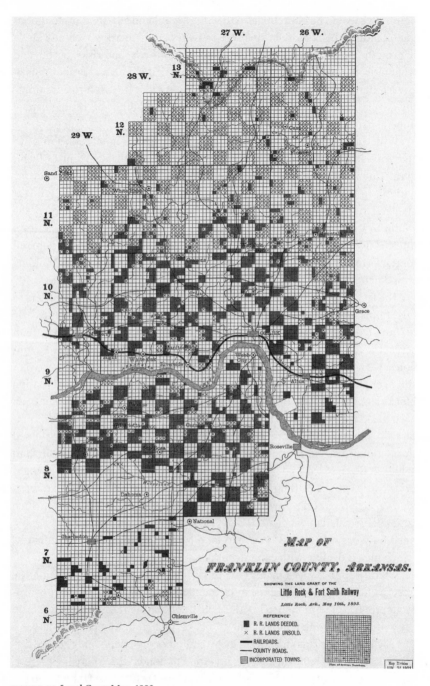

FIGURE 2.1. Land Grant Map, 1893
Source: Little Rock & Fort Smith R.R. Co., "Map of Franklin County, Arkansas; Showing the Land Grant of the Little Rock & Fort Smith Railway," in United States General Land Office, *Railroad Maps, 1828 to 1900* (Washington, D.C.: Library of Congress, 1893).

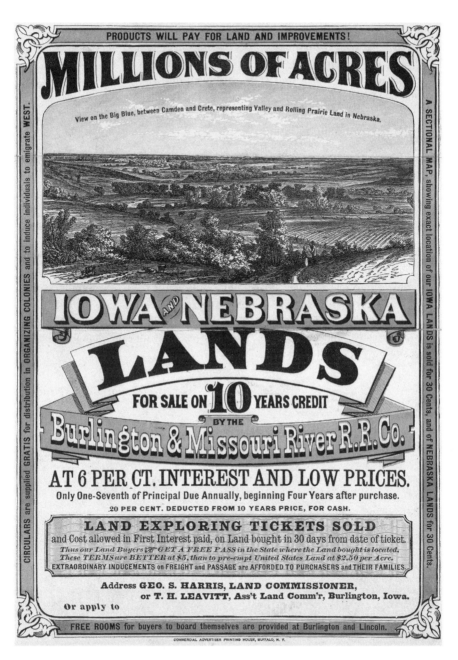

FIGURE 2.2. Advertisement for Land Bought on Credit from Railway, 1872
Source: Burlington & Missouri River Railroad Co., "Millions of Acres. Iowa and Nebraska. Land for Sale on 10 Years Credit by the Burlington & Missouri River R. R. Co. at 6 Per Ct Interest and Low Prices" (1872), in Library of Congress, *An American Time Capsule: Three Centuries of Broadsides and Other Printed Ephemera* (database), https://www.loc.gov/collections/broadsides-and-other-printed-ephemera/about-this-collection/.

invest.[78] A quarter of a million dollars in new railway debt entered the market within four years after the war.[79] British investors had poured an estimated $1.7 billion into U.S. railways by 1898.[80] Between the end of the Civil War and 1873, 35 million miles of track were built, and the number of railways in operation doubled in under a decade.[81]

Then came the Crash of 1873. Within two years, 121 railroads had defaulted on over $500 million in bonds. By 1878, railroad stock prices had dropped 60 percent from their 1973 high.[82] Thirty percent of railway tracks were under receivership in the 1870s.[83] As the nation once again took stock of the economic devastation swept in by the end of the boom-bust cycle, news media unearthed stories of corruption, overbuilding, watered-down stocks, faulty accounting, and fraudulent overcharges. Using its construction company, Credit Mobilier, the Union Pacific had raised over $74 million—$14 million more than it had cost to build the actual railroad. Company men had pocketed the extra funds and bought off congressmen and senators in the process. Not only had government officials failed to protect the people—they had participated in the corruption that ran rampant through the nation at the time. As farmers pushed for more regulation of the railroads, the corporations countered that the real problem was the improper involvement of the government in private business.

Up until this point in American history, people generally understood corporations as public–private hybrids, special government-aided ventures wherein the nation conferred special rights in return for the provision of a public good. If a corporation had a special privilege—say, control over a waterway, the ability to impose a tax in the form of a toll, or limited liability—it was because the effort was seen as contributing to the public welfare and so deserving special dispensation. But in the Gilded Age, a great push from the corporations, aided by pro-business courts, replaced that understanding with a new vision of the corporation as an independent body with natural rights. In this view, the corporation was not an extension of the state, but something to be protected from government encroachment. "The land grant experience not only put an end to the practice of railway grants," writes sociologist Frank Dobbin, "but brought the notion of federal participation in economic development to an early end."[84] Of course, federal participation in the market was not entirely over, as Dobbin himself notes. It would reemerge, but in other forms, and always with a nod to the enduring ideal that the state should act like a "referee," and not a player, whenever possible.[85]

The provision of federal credit and the use of federal lands to secure private credit had initially seemed to offer something for almost nothing. Instead, it ended up producing such a terrific disaster that corporations were able to use the government's role in the scandal to deflect further attempts to regulate them.

Credit in the South

Like the western farmer, the southern planter had to borrow to purchase land, improve it, farm it, and somehow keep the family going until the crop could be harvested and sold. In the slave states, these costs could include the expense of buying and owning another person. "The empire of cotton was at its heart an empire of credit," writes Sven Beckert.[86] And in that empire of credit, planters used land, slaves, and cotton to borrow from the world's most sophisticated financial centers. In Louisiana in 1837, for example, over half of the $39 million of paid-in capital in its banks came from Europe (especially Britain and Holland), while nearly a fifth was raised from U.S. cities (mainly New York, Boston, and Philadelphia).[87] Alongside these institutions, the famous market intermediary of the South, the factor, himself acted like a mobile one-stop shop and bank. The factors brought supplies when they came, took crops like cotton and sugar as they left, and floated credit along the way. In return, they received credit from the banks or other financiers, like British firms.[88]

Slavery meant that people could be mortgaged like land. Thomas Jefferson's Monticello was funded through a mortgage on 150 slaves.[89] Edward Baptist notes that by the 1840s, the 2 million enslaved people in the United States represented a market value of $1 billion, roughly a fifth of the entire nation's wealth.[90] When human beings are traded like objects, they constitute a form of movable or chattel property. Compared to land, slaves could more easily be sold in smaller units and could be transferred across space. Bonnie Martin's survey of southern mortgages found ample evidence of people using slaves as collateral. While most often a mortgage was yet another way to extract value from the body of a slave, Martin also found records of freed people who used mortgages to purchase the freedom of others.[91]

The normal logic of credit and collateral take on a stark horror in the context of slavery. For the enslaved, credit's capacity to act like a "time machine" meant that a person's own capacity to be violently forced into a life of unpaid labor—and to bear children who could also be forced to do the same—was the very thing that financed their enslavement. Or consider the use of pooling to diversify risks: when the collateral for a loan was a human being, groups of slave-backed mortgages were used to lower the risk that the market value of any one person would decline as a result of age or illness. Baptist stresses that when human beings are used as collateral for a loan, it is a human being who is surrendered to pay off a debt. The risk of economic loss to the lender, or of loss of land for the buyer, is transmuted into the risk of family separation and displacement for the slave.[92]

The common practice of using slaves as collateral was part of an early nineteenth-century experiment with mortgage-backed bonds. This experiment

emerged out of a group of southern property banks (sometimes called plantation banks or planters' banks).[93] The first of these was founded in New Orleans,
the port through which capital, goods, and slaves flowed in and out of the
region and one of the nation's great cities in the 1830s.[94] The idea came from
J. B. Moussier, an indebted enslaver who ran a sugar plantation as a side business.[95] In search of new ways to attract capital to the region, and in so doing
solve his own worsening financial problems, Moussier teamed up with planters
to promote a new property bank.

The effort came to fruition with the 1827 charter of the Consolidated Association of Planters of Louisiana, an institution authorized to operate alongside
the state's commercial and public improvement banks. The Consolidated Association was capitalized with $2 million in mortgages on cultivated land paid
in by farmers who received shares in $500 increments. Shares gave farmers
the right to receive dividends and later draw up to one half of the value of their
mortgage, which could include mortgages on slaves. The original plan for the
bank to sell its bonds ran into trouble. Investors were uninterested in investing in the unknown property bank. At that point, two steps were taken that
would help the sales proceed. First, the state of Louisiana agreed to guarantee
the bank's bonds. Second, the mortgages backing the bonds were placed in
collateral trusts.[96] As Edward Bapist stresses, this meant the bonds were more
like today's mortgage-backed securities. The change offered enough risk protection to attract overseas investors, and bonds sold quickly in London and
Amsterdam.

The success was soon copied. Louisiana's Union Bank was chartered in
1832, capitalized with $8 million of bonds backed by $7 million in mortgages
on slaves and improved land. It was followed in the next year by the Citizens
Bank, whose paid-in capital included slave mortgages. By 1840, Louisiana was
the most credit-rich, monetized state in the nation.[97] Other states followed its
course. Arkansas, Florida, and Mississippi chartered banks funded by mortgages on land and people in the 1830s. The territory of Wisconsin even tried to
set up a similar bank, but Congress repealed the effort.[98] Despite their origins
in mortgage banking, most plantation banks involved themselves in business
with merchants; after the initial capitalization, the banks generally preferred
to issue commercial loans.[99] At this time, according to Fritz Redlich, these
plantation banks were among the most important movers of capital in the nation.[100] Given the centrality of slaves to the cotton market, this movement of
money was also a movement of human beings. "In the course of a mere four
years," writes Baptist, "from 1833 to 1836, 150,000 enslaved people were moved
from the old states to the new."[101]

What was the social logic of these mortgage pools? On one hand, they reflected a broader logic of state governance. It was common for state banks, especially in the South and the West, to act like development banks; in this way,

state legislatures regularly supported internal improvements at midcentury, helping to build roads, improve riverways, and expand rail.[102] For states in the Cotton South, the activities of these development banks included, but were not limited to, transportation projects. Overall, the property banks were a kind of developmental approach to agriculture.

On the other hand, the bonds were very much a piece of the moral economy of slavery, which turned black bodies into property. Edward Baptist notes that the structure of the bonds themselves derived profits from, and displaced risks onto, slaves: it was enslaved people who would be sold if the deal failed. These mortgage-backed bonds therefore reflect the political and moral economy of state-level developmental banking in the slave-holding South: financial risks were widely dispersed but were transmuted for slaves into particular risks of loss and displacement, even as these individuals were denied any claim to the profits.

The pioneering Consolidated Association of Planters of Louisiana operated for 14 years and then took 40 more years to liquidate.[103] As a series of such banks failed in the Crash of 1837, the states struggled with the burden of paying off the debt they had guaranteed.[104] The state of Mississippi—where all but 2 of the state's 25 banks closed in 1837—repudiated its debts and was blacklisted by international lenders and unable to borrow through the Civil War period.[105] The nation's experiments with mortgage bonds were far from over, however. As Americans struggled to move credit across the frontier and attract it from Europe, they continued to experiment with different ways of tapping the land and organizing risks. The next chapter will compare three failed experiments with pooling mortgage debt that unfolded at the end of the century.

Credit on the Western Frontier

Farmers in the West faced an entirely different set of issues than those of the Cotton South. Much had changed since the days of eighteenth-century subsistence farming. Now, a prospective farmer from the East had to move a family over the Appalachians, purchase land and livestock, construct buildings and fencing, and buy seed, equipment, and enough food and supplies to survive until the first harvest. In general, nineteenth-century tools were more useful and more expensive, which made them a larger proportion of the overall cost of farming than they had been in the eighteenth century.[106] The settlers' need for credit, therefore, persisted through a series of changes in national land distribution policy: the adoption of cash sales and lower land prices in 1820; the placement of restrictions on land sales that required payment to be made in specie under Jackson in 1835 (a move designed to prevent speculation); the granting of preemption in 1841, under which squatters officially won the right to be the first bidder on the lands they had improved;

the passage of the Graduation Act reducing the price of unsold lands in 1854; and the provisions of the Homestead Acts that gave away the land for "free" (with a $50 fee) in the 1860s.[107] Most of these policies were hard-won battles for the West, defended on grounds that they would discourage speculators. None, however, addressed the demand for credit.

To gain a sense of the expenses that nineteenth-century western farmers faced, consider the recollections of George Ade, the son of a cattle baron:

> The untouched prairie which was not wholly or partly submerged was a crazy quilt of high-stemmed and gorgeously colored flowers from late spring until the killing frosts of autumn. To break through the ribbed soil, bury this wild growth and convert a tangy and fibrous flower garden into a corn field was a whale of a job. Every low spot on the prairie was a slough rank with reeds and cattails, and breeding ferocious gallinippers by the millions. Also a large kind of horse-fly, called the "green head," which was so warlike and blood-hungry that when it attacked a horse in swarm formation, it would either kill him or weaken him so much that he had no value as a work animal. Oxen were used in breaking raw prairie, and even these tough and thick-skinned animals suffered tortures when attacked by armies of green heads.
>
> The first ditches . . . were deep furrows made with a thirty inch plow. As many as thirty yoke of oxen would be used in one ditching outfit. On level ground the big plow could be pulled along, ripping and tearing through the tough roots of the bull grass and needle grass and the ironweeds and all the other knotty growth, by fifteen yoke of oxen. In mushy ground and bad going the whole thirty yoke had to be used, some of them to move a capstan ahead of the gang and also to supply power when the pull had to be made by capstan. . . . You will understand that reclaiming the prairie was no job for a weakling, a lazybones or anyone not prepared to meet a payroll.[108]

This is an account of lands in northwestern Indiana, some of the most difficult to break—so difficult, in fact, that poorer settlers passed them over. Nevertheless, it brings to life the costs of settlement and reminds us that expenses would have increased with farm size.[109] A settler who wanted to establish a homestead in the Midwest in the 1850s and 1860s could have expected to pay $500 for his property at the low end and upwards of $1,000 or $1,500 at the higher end.[110] Costs could be even higher for free blacks, who might be required to post a $500 or $1,000 security bond to settle in many states, including Ohio and Illinios.[111] Preemption allowed settlers a year or two to get established before having to purchase a title, which gave farmers a chance to profit from a harvest before buying the land. But many hopefuls found their capital was still tied up in the farm and the tools needed to operate it when the time came to purchase the land.[112] Farmers looked to credit to move, to improve the land, and to ride out hard times. Consequently, they turned to merchants and manufacturers who sold goods "on time." Farmers also used mortgages to purchase land and borrow against its value, much like people do today with home equity loans.

To understand the difficulties that attended such lending, consider the long-term farm loan secured with a mortgage on the land from the perspective of the lender. Mortgage lending can be tricky under the best of circumstances. It requires some understanding of the quality of the land, any buildings or improvements upon it, and the capacities and character of the investor. Farm credit further depends on the cooperation of nature: rain must fall, and disease must spare crops and livestock. The property rights of lenders depend on local politics: a judge must be counted on to enforce the contract. In case of default, the lender must manage the taxes, upkeep, and sale of the property. Add great physical distance to the mix, and it is not hard to see how risks and information costs mounted as one moved farther west and deeper into the South.[113]

A typical mortgage in the second half of the 1800s ranged from 3 to 10 years in length and required a down payment of 40 to 60 percent of the property value. These loans were not usually amortized (with the principle slowly paid down over the life of the loan). Instead, payments went toward the accrued interest, and the principal was due in one large "balloon" or "bullet" payment at the end. Families often took out smaller second and third mortgages to help cover the cost of the land, and lenders frequently allowed farmers to roll over loans if they could not pay in the initial term.[114] In other words, the shorter terms of mortgages during this period does not mean that most people paid off their loans in that time, but that lenders had regular chances to exit the relationship. One study of Pebble Township, Nebraska, found that 47 percent of the 114 people who claimed government lands under the Homestead Act there mortgaged them at one time or another, with nearly half doing so within a year of securing a title.[115]

Who supplied these mortgages? The major institutional players that would come to dominate twentieth-century U.S. mortgage markets were not in fact terribly influential on the frontier. Cooperative mortgage lenders like savings and loans (S&Ls) and building societies sprang up in the 1830s, but they kept to cities and towns. They tended to operate in population-dense urban areas where it was much easier to monitor borrowers, where workers were likely to have regular income, and where local builders frequently volunteered time in the local nonprofit savings cooperative in order to support their main businesses.[116] The U.S. census did not ask about home and farm mortgages until the 1890s. Without access to national level data, scholars of nineteenth-century economic history draw from studies of specific towns or regions and gather historical records from related industries (like banking and insurance). This work indicates that a complex mix of lenders moved credit across the frontier.

INDIVIDUALS

Informal lending systems stayed active far later in U.S. history than most people realize. The "non-institutional lender" category is a residual classification that economic historians have traditionally used to lump together individuals, small trusts, nonprofits, and other kinds of companies, so this designation was not used to exclusively represent family or individual lenders, though families and individuals seem to have dominated this category in earlier periods.[117] Non-institutional lenders represented about half of mortgage holders in the 1890s and held an estimated 30 percent of U.S. mortgage market holdings into the 1930s. It was only after the Second World War that non-institutional lenders held less than a fifth of the nation's mortgages.[118] Some research that looks not at bank portfolios but at overall mortgage or bankruptcy records has found remarkably high levels of peer-to-peer lending.[119] In a new study, Bonnie Martin sampled over 10,000 mortgages from Virginia, South Carolina, and Louisiana over select years before the Civil War and found that 80 percent of the capital in her sample was generated through what she calls "neighbor-to-neighbor" transactions.[120]

INSURANCE COMPANIES

Insurance companies later became major holders of mortgage debt, and for good reason: insurers invest over long time horizons. But while insurance companies regularly participated in nineteenth-century mortgage markets, insurance as a whole was not an especially large industry before the Civil War. After the 1860s, when the industry expanded, insurers tended to invest in their home states due to a mix of preference and regulatory restrictions.[121] Records show that insurance companies were regular participants in farm mortgage markets and helped move money across regions. That said, overall the mortgage markets may have been more important for the insurance industry than the insurance industry was for the mortgage markets in the nineteenth century.

COMMERCIAL BANKS

Banks were a vital but uneven presence in mortgage markets in the nineteenth century. This is partly because of the prevailing notion that banks should limit their business to short-term business lending. Especially during the first part of the century, commercial banks focused on short-term lending to elites and merchants, and stayed out of the business of lending to small borrowers. This made them an inconsistent source of mortgages.

A complex regulatory landscape also shaped the extent to which banks offered mortgages during this period and to whom. In the first half of the century, banking was widely considered to be a special privilege that was granted to a group in order to promote the general public welfare. As such, banks were chartered through legislation, and that legislation was regularly a point of contention between advocates of banking (in the Hamiltonian tradition) and those who saw banks as sometimes necessary but frequently a threat to the independence and decency of the common man (in the Jeffersonian tradition). Political showdowns over banks meant that the national banking system flickered in and out of existence. At points the national banks promoted mortgage markets, at points they didn't, and sometimes they disappeared entirely (in 1811–1816, and then again from 1836 to the Civil War).

The states ran parallel banking systems. Some states chartered public banks, while others preferred public–private hybrids. Some were generous with private charters, while others were stingy.[122] All of this affected bank capital in a general sense. More specific to mortgage markets, some states required banks to hold a portion of their capital in mortgages, and others prohibited this practice (in accordance with the popular notion that banks should deal only in short-term merchant credit). These variations were not just across space, but over time. As the previous section noted, property banks, mostly operational in the South, were active for a time and then closed. A state might have an easy banking policy in boom years followed by severe constraints after a crash. Iowa, for instance, constitutionally banned the issuance of bank charters from 1846 to 1857. During that time private banks could operate, but they could not issue notes.[123]

As the century progressed, "free banking" regimes released new banks from the burden of securing a charter. Under "free banking," a state automatically granted a charter to anyone who met basic statutory requirements, allowing notes to be issued against government bonds. The practice spread through the states in the 1840s and was the default regime in most by the 1850s. Still, many free banks resembled hedge funds that were capitalized not through deposits but via local elite shareholders, many of whom preferred to lend to merchants, wealthier families, or larger speculators.[124] Based on extensive studies of the antebellum era, banking expert Howard Bodenhorn roughly estimates that up to one-half or two-thirds of the free bank and property bank portfolios at this time consisted of mortgages.[125]

After the Civil War, a new set of national banking laws once again reshaped the national flow of credit. Partly in response to calamitous experiences with bank lending on the frontier, the new rules limited the conditions under which nationally chartered banks could acquire and hold mortgages and restricted intra-state banking by taxing state bank notes.[126] Richard Sylla has argued that once national banks were shut out of the real estate market, the flow of capital across state lines dwindled. Largely unable to invest in mortgages, these banks redirected their investments to manufacturers. This slowed agricultural development but promoted an even more rapid pace of eastern industrialization.[127] State banks continued to operate in the West, where their local knowledge gave them an advantage, and country banks were an important source of mortgage credit for rural farmers in the later years of the century.[128]

In sum, a settler's access to mortgages through banks varied a good deal according to time and place during the nineteenth century. Pennsylvania's four state-chartered banks in 1803 neglected the entire western half of the state.[129] In contrast, state banks in Michigan and Illinois financed entirely new towns in the 1830s.[130] Building on the colonial tradition of property banks and loan offices that used land as collateral to issue notes and loans to "melt down" property, some states created land banks that dealt in mortgages.[131] But even the existence of a property bank did not automatically mean that small borrowers would have access to credit on an ongoing basis, since some of these institutions were capitalized by mortgages but largely focused on commercial loans for most of their existence.[132] This is one reason why individual mortgage lenders and intermediaries were so important.

THE INTERMEDIARIES: BROKERS AND BOOSTERS

A strata of intermediaries operated alongside the nation's networks of banks throughout the nineteenth century, occupying a crucial niche between the institutionalized world of chartered banks and the institutionalized world of peer-to-peer lending. These were the nation's brokers, speculators, town jobbers, factors, land agents, and landsharks. Because they traveled, they were especially important to the movement of money over regions and across state lines. (Chapter 3 will provide a detailed look at mortgage brokers' experiments with mortgage bonds in the 1870s.)

Moneylenders, backed by wealthier families, trusts, banks, or insurance companies, were a fixture at auctions in the middle of the century. Reputable agents might receive a commission of 2.5 to 5 percent off a loan to squatters. Historian Allan Bogue tells of one lending partnership that was careful to cultivate a good reputation with farmers because working with the best, most responsible borrowers made for a better investment.[133] Others took advantage of settlers and used inflated resale prices and other gimmicks to circumvent usury limits. During booms, rates of return for town jobbers approached 40 percent in the 1830s and even 120 percent in the 1850s.[134] Very successful land agents effectively grew into private banks over time; this happened, for example, in Iowa during the prohibition of chartered banks, and with cotton factors before the Civil War.[135]

In many cases, the intermediaries who brought credit to a region led the way in early land settlement, lobbying for surveys, purchasing land from the government, laying out townships, and using aggressive sales tactics to draw out investors or settlers, often with overblown claims about the habitability of isolated and rough lands.[136] Captain Charles Williamson, a land agent for an English syndicate called the Pulteny Association, spent $1.37 million between 1792 and 1799 to develop lands in Bath, New York. He built a road, a hotel, and also a racetrack, and then hosted fairs near the Pulteny offices to attract buyers. In a 1796 letter to the *Wilkesbarre Gazzette*, the father of a young English investor bemoaned that his son, caught up in the scheme on his travels through the United States, had "returned both a speculator and a gentleman, having spent his money, swapped away my horse, caught the fever and ague, and what is infinitely worse, that horrid disorder which some call the 'terraphobia.'"[137]

As the nation expanded, developers would identify an area with some kind of geographical advantage (like a waterway), lobby for a survey or money-making internal development (like a road, canal, or railway), design a town, and then head east to woo families to settle there. Town-building could take other forms as well, of course. Sometimes schools (like Cornell), religious groups (think Salt Lake City), and, in the early twentieth century, companies (like Hershey) took the lead in development.[138] In practice, the lines between speculator, lender, and settler were easily blurred. Land was a popular investment in the nineteenth century. Plenty of farmers and politicians who openly derided speculation often participated in the practice themselves; George Washington, Benjamin Franklin, and Aaron Burr, for example, all dabbled in it. Well-established settlers might borrow to purchase extra acres in the upswing of a boom, when the possibility of riches could tempt even the holiest of community members:

> Everyone was imbued with a reckless spirit of speculation. The mania, for such it undoubtedly was, did not confine itself to one particular class, but extended to all. Even the reverend clergy doffed their saceredotals, and eagerly entered into competition with mammon's votaries, for the acquisition of this world's goods, and tested their sagacity against the shrewdness and more practiced skill of the professed sharper.[139]

In the great tradition of human capriciousness, the historical record is dotted with people who saw their own ventures as reasonable but hated to see others do the same. Some farmers and squatters who passionately defended open access to land and the value of homesteading when it served their own interests abandoned those principles entirely when a new batch of homesteaders wanted to settle nearby.[140]

An Enduring Problem

As the young federal government pursued the Jeffersonian vision of a land populated by independent farmers, property ownership was crystallized as a core component of the U.S. political economy. But land does not generate wealth on its own. It is capital that turns plots of land into productive farms or residences. Credit distribution, which entails the movement of capital across time and geographic and social space, poses challenges under the best of circumstances. Frontier lands, with their long travel times, sparse populations, and underdeveloped institutions, are particularly hard on credit markets. In the nineteenth century, the sheer expanse of land that loomed as a source of wealth also impeded the flow of credit needed for that wealth to be realized.[141]

As Miles Colean has pointed out, America's liberal policy of land distribution was not matched by a federal policy of credit distribution to develop that land.[142] State governments were the locus of power and regulation, but the overarching problem of credit distribution required national-level coordination. In a fractured national political context, where both institutional design and popular sentiment suppressed extensive taxation, the land proved a powerful draw to politicians. Land promised to generate wealth for the people and revenues for the state—if not in sales, then in an expanded tax base—but only as long as it could be purchased and developed. From this perspective, we can read the history of public railway finance as a variation on a theme that had played out much earlier with the Land Offices: an attempt by politicians to unlock the value of the land that ended in failure, scandal, and retreat. Entering the field of credit meant being politically responsible for it. This posed no small hurdle in a nation riven by conspiracy thinking, patronage politics, and sectional divides.

By 1890, about a third of American farm owners carried a mortgage that covered 30 to 40 percent of the value of their land. This varied by location, of course: in Kansas, about 60 percent of farmers had a mortgage, while in the southern states, the rate was much lower, at about 40 percent (however, higher rates of tenancy in the South indicate that many southern families had not graduated to mortgage free–ownership but rather remained tenant farmers).[143] In the highly mortgaged western states, a typical farm mortgage matured over somewhere between two and four years but carried an interest rate closer to 8 or 9 percent. On the West Coast, mortgages that matured in two years had interest rates topping 10 percent, an amount nearly twice the average rate in the Northeast.[144] In contrast, a typical eastern mortgage matured in six or seven years and had around a 5.5 percent interest rate. Nineteenth-century credit markets were connected, but not seamlessly.[145] Borrowers on the periphery were well aware that they paid more for credit and got it on worse terms.[146]

The issue was not that credit never moved westward, or even that it was never cheap. The real problem was the instability of the market. The 1830s saw a rush into Michigan, Mississippi, Illinois, and Indiana that crashed in 1837. Next was a surge into Iowa, Illinois, Wisconsin, and Missouri that crested in 1857. (In the next chapter I detail another boom cycle in the 1870s and

1880s that involved early forms of mortgage securitization.) In each case, a region with a popular commodity or development—cotton, wheat, meat, a railway—captured imaginations around the world. Land sales spiked: 20 million acres were sold in 1836, and 50 million acres in the 1850s.[147] Money from East Coast and European investors poured into the West in a surge of credit. Like a tidal pool suddenly submerged by the ocean, the frontier region regularly found itself awash in credit—only for that tide to recede with the inevitable market downturn.[148]

How could the United States have a nationally integrated credit market robust enough to support a nation of small property owners splayed out across vast geographic and social distance but also stable enough to avoid the lure of devastating bubbles? This was the problem that New Deal housing policies sought to address and that the Johnson administration was grappling with when it decided to promote the use of mortgage securitization at the close of the 1960s. As the next chapters will show, the Gilded Age and Progressive Era were times of great creative solutions to this challenge as well.

3

Three Failures

Consider the following three failed credit experiments, which together are the focus of this chapter.

First, in the 1870s, brokers and financiers started using mortgage-backed bonds to sell western farm mortgages. By combining mortgages into pools and adding guarantees, sellers of mortgage bonds helped draw credit to the frontier. This contributed to a western land bubble that burst with the Crash of 1893, leading to the collapse of the early mortgage bond market.

Second, in 1887, members of the Southern Farmers' Alliance in Texas embarked on a plan to use cooperative credit to break a system of crop loans that trapped farmers in a perpetual and degrading cycle of debt. Farmers joined together to pool their borrowing and guarantee each other's debts. This was called the *joint-note plan*. After a promising start, the first and largest of the resulting exchanges closed within two years.

Third, in 1892, the People's Party platform included a proposal for a nation-wide system of warehouses, called the *subtreasury*, which would form the basis of a new system of currency and credit. Polarizing and controversial, the plan was never put into action. But it marked farmers' new pursuit of centralized political control as part of their search for economic relief.

Each of these episodes was an attempt to move credit into the periphery (farther west and south, away from the capital centers of the Northeast and Mid-Atlantic) in a way that was quicker, cheaper, easier, more stable, and more reliable than it had been before. To some extent, each involved corporate methods of organizing property and risk. Despite those similarities, however, there were also differences among the three experiments that reveal fundamental divides in how Americans made sense of a rapidly changing economic landscape. Credit always constitutes a bond between borrower and lender. As a result, credit is always subject to moral judgments about what kinds of exchanges are reasonable, desirable, and just.[1] This is true not just in the intimate sense of whether a specific borrower pays his or her debts on time or whether a given lender acts in a fair or predatory manner. Because credit flows through networks and institutions that span continents and even nations, its distribution invokes much larger questions of how governments and markets should be organized.

As Americans experimented with systems of credit distribution at the close of the nineteenth century, they fought over how competing interests should be reflected in a rapidly transforming political economy. Their clashing assumptions and values were built into these lending structures. For example, the laissez-faire vision of the mortgage bond was articulated in the way it combined mortgages, its guarantees, and its lack of oversight. The Texas Alliance exchange's cooperative model of market development generated a system of lending built on shared risks and democratic representation. The People's Party merged that populism with a vision of an active central government that broadly distributed risks and placed significant financial control in farmers' hands.

Americans' opinions of how credit should operate were forged through these lending structures as much as they were reflected in them. With each experiment, communities learned new ways of organizing and making sense of credit and gained new insights about states and markets. Each of these experiences resulted in hard-won insights about the challenges that plague credit markets. These failures set the stage for a federal overhaul of farm credit in the early twentieth century. At stake in these efforts was not just the speed at which money might flow through credit markets, but also the principles that should guide those flows.

Vulnerability and Agitation: Farmers in a Time of Change

The rise of railways, the ascendance of modern corporations, and the emergence of a new federal bureaucracy after the Civil War—each of these events alone was a significant transformation. Together they propelled the nation into a new era. As industrialization transformed the nation's cities, agriculture experienced its own revolution in production. By the late nineteenth century, the staggering output of American farmers was upending world markets.[2] "The most consequential event of the late nineteenth and early twentieth centuries in the Western world was the unprecedented growth of the United States," writes Prasad. "It was a growth of a kind no one had seen before and that no one really knew how to handle."[3] Between 1870 and 1900, the number of

American farms grew by 114 percent to 5.7 million, and the acreage of U.S. farms doubled to over 838 million.[4] American produce like wheat and cotton glutted markets and inaugurated a period of global economic volatility. Instead of bringing unmitigated happiness, unmatched productivity heralded insecurity and confusion.

Farmers in the Great Plains and the South were especially vulnerable to market swings: they were more likely to rely on a single crop like cotton or wheat, more likely to be devastated by drought, more likely to export their goods to Europe, and more likely to depend on unstable world prices.[5] They were also, as we have seen, more likely than other borrowers to pay higher interest rates. Prices that had spiked during the Civil War generally declined for the rest of the century, interrupted only by periodic booms. As a result, farmers with mortgages felt squeezed between high interest rates and low prices.[6] In this context, foreclosure loomed as a terrible degradation.[7] In the South, the low value of land and high demand for cotton meant that crop liens, mortgages on crops, were a more common form of debt than mortgages on the land itself. Many small southern property owners fell into tenancy, while tenants sunk deeper into debt.

Increasingly radicalized farmers saw the threat of foreclosure as part of a more general problem.[8] The commodity chain itself seemed a conspiracy of faraway financiers and opportunistic middlemen.[9] Owners of grain elevators, who sorted and stored farm goods, seemed to give high-quality products unfairly low valuations in order to justify purchasing famers' produce at lower prices. It seemed obscene that railways charged more for short hauls (like the kind a prairie farmer would need to ship goods to Chicago) than for those over long distances (like the kind a middleman would use to ship goods east).[10] In the South, farmers objected to merchants and lenders inflating prices on farm supplies while setting artificially low prices for farm produce. Everywhere it appeared that the prices for farmers' goods were driven down while the prices for the services and supplies farmers depended on were driven up.

In this context, farmers closely watched policies that could change the circulation and value of money. Adjustments that promoted a strong dollar held little appeal for borrowers who did not want to repay debts in currency that was worth more than when they had borrowed it. At the same time, the further prices dropped, the harder it was for farmers to repay their debts.[11] Prasad has estimated that if price deflation is taken into account, between 1869 and 1885 real interest rates on mortgages were so volatile that they sometimes doubled the level of nominal rates.[12] For example, while the nominal interest rate on a five-year mortgage due in 1874 was 8 percent, declining prices meant that the real rate was closer to 16 percent. Any policy that tightened the money supply was especially devastating in the South, where currency shortages effectively forced small farmers into buying supplies with credit instead of cash, which left them vulnerable to a host of exploitative lending terms. In 1865, there was $30.35 circulating per capita in the region, but by 1880 that amount had dropped to $19.36.[13]

Not surprisingly, farmers decried a series of policies that benefited creditors or further contracted the money supply: the repayment of Civil War bonds in gold rather than in less valuable greenbacks, which disproportionately benefited bankers; the return to the gold standard; and the demonetization of silver, which seemed such an egregious decision to cash-hungry farmers that it would go down in history as the "Crime of 1873." Farmers understood these policies in explicitly social terms. When gold was chosen over greenbacks and silver, farmers saw the government as promoting lenders' interests.[14]

These concerns culminated in the emergence of a complex and changing populist movement. This movement tended to follow a pattern: a wave of farmers would organize around an issue or set of issues, that wave would crest and fall, and then some of those farmers would join the next gathering surge in turn. Greenbackism and the Grange thus gave way to the Agricultural Wheel and the Farmers' Alliance, which gave way to the Farmers Union and the labor-friendly People's Party.[15] These organizations used a mix of strategies, sometimes targeting education and self-help as the solution to farmers' problems, sometimes creating cooperatives to promote business interests, and sometimes organizing for political change. The aspects of farmers' movements perhaps best remembered today are those that had a lasting impact on the regulation of industry and currency: Greenbackers' and Free Silverites' forward-looking focus on the currency, Granger laws that established the right of the government to regulate markets (starting with railways and grain elevators), and antimonopolist agitation that eventually resulted in the Sherman Antitrust Act and an empowered Department of Justice.

When the populists demanded that the government block powerful trusts from collusion and price gouging, they were not just targeting specific unjust practices. Populists questioned the very existence and legitimacy of the modern corporation itself, asking whether the state's provision of special privileges was responsible for such large and powerful private corporations and trusts in the first place.[16] At the end of the nineteenth century, the old notion that corporations were special extensions of state powers was being rejected by the courts, which increasingly recognized corporations as independent entities with their own natural property rights worthy of protection from the state. Populists, however, refuted the notion that corporations were the natural and inevitable result of progress and sought to deny corporations any privileged status that might threaten the security of the small farmer in the new economic order. Here farmers occupied a complex position. As property owners, product sellers, and speculators, farmers generally identified as profit-seeking businessmen. Yet in their indebtedness, farmers could also identify with laborers as fellow producers similarly subordinate to a more powerful class.[17]

Organizational scholars have honed in on this period as one of the most creative and generative in U.S. history, in part because such dramatic social changes and complex identifications resulted in a proliferation of new organizational forms.[18] When sociologist Elisabeth Clemens studied this period, she concluded that organizations played a central role in determining people's strategies of action, and that they did so partly by shaping people's sense of what was possible, moral, and acceptable: it was through their experiences in these multifaceted populist organizations that farmers came to believe not only that the government should reign over the trusts but that the state should actively support farmers' business interests.[19] Elizabeth Sanders argues that populist farmers emerged from these efforts as the primary driving force behind the construction of the modern American federal government. Academics have been so focused on industry, cities, and unions, however, that they have largely ignored farmers' significant contributions to American political development.[20]

Unions, cooperatives, exchanges, clubs, pools, trusts, corporations, commissions, congressional committees—these are all ways of arranging people's activities and responsibilities relative to others. So too are mortgage bonds, cooperative borrowing, and plans for a state-centered model of credit distribution. In the late nineteenth century, the western mortgage bond market reflected what historians have discussed as an American liberal tradition, one that emphasizes unfettered individualism and ambition in the pursuit of commerce. In contrast, the joint-note program and subtreasury plans reflect a countervailing republican tradition, one that pairs the pursuit of commerce with an emphasis on the public good and freedom from domination.[21] So while each of these experiments provided an answer to the problem of the nation's patchwork mortgage market, they did so with diverging implications for how mortgages would circulate in a changing political economy.

Laissez-Faire Credit: The Western Mortgage Bond Bubble

The United States has never been as economically liberal and laissez-faire as modern-day conservatives sometimes imagine. Even at its height of popularity in the nineteenth century, laissez-faire thinking faced formidable critiques from Americans who believed that a strong state was needed to provide for the general welfare.[22] That said, the promotion of laissez-faire ideals was particularly popular in the Gilded Age. Of the three experiments with credit distribution discussed in this chapter, the sale of mortgage bonds is the one that most closely approximates a laissez-faire solution to the problem of moving credit across the nation's patchwork mortgage market.

Existing accounts suggest that land agents, who had long served as middle-men for mortgages on the frontier, began pooling mortgages in the 1870s. Working on behalf of eastern lenders—mostly wealthy families, but also some railroads, trusts, and insurance companies—these land agents discovered that issuing bonds against pools of mortgages saved time and expense, reducing what economists call transaction costs.[23] Historian Allan Bogue, for example, offers a look into the business of J. B. Watkins, a broker who found that pooling mortgages relieved him of the time-consuming hassle of assigning each mortgage to a single investor. Pooling had the advantage of diversifying risks, so that "each debenture bond is, in a sense, insured by all the rest of the series."[24] Moreover, by using a pool, agents could more easily sell mortgages with unusual terms (such as the "vendor's lien note," a contract popular in Texas) that East Coast investors tended to otherwise refuse to buy.[25]

Sellers of western mortgages in the 1870s found that eastern and European investors were eager to buy.[26] One reason was that the series of railroad failures and scandals unfolding by 1873 caused investors to retract from that market. This freed up funds that investors then funneled into the mortgage business. At the same time, yields on U.S. government bonds were shrinking. These government bonds had been popular among investors because they were generally considered a safe investment with a decent return, and because banks and other intermediaries were required by statute to hold those bonds as part of their capital requirements. But by the 1870s, the Treasury was using a budgetary surplus to buy back its bonds, thus decreasing supply. As a result, yields dropped. Global investors were looking for a new safe investment with decent returns. Western mortgages filled that gap.

Existing land agents were soon joined by a new generation of mortgage companies founded in eastern cities and in Europe. Bolstered by capital reserves, these companies started to guarantee their mortgage-backed bonds. Such guarantees relieved investors of the significant credit risks involved in lending out west. If a borrower defaulted, that meant that the lender would still get the expected return, and would do so without the considerable hassle of having to foreclose on and resell a faraway tract of land.[27] While guarantees promised to manage risks for investors, on the other side of the exchange, insurance companies promised to manage farmers' risks. Historian Jonathan Levy has shown that in the 1870s, life insurance agents began targeting farmers with the promise of protecting the family from foreclosure should the man of the family die before the debt was repaid.[28]

The western farm mortgage business grew quickly. By 1893 over 160 mortgage companies existed, most of which had opened within the previous 20 years.[29] Many of these companies had one set of offices in the West to oversee or work with lending agents and another set of offices in eastern or European cities that were responsible for marketing and selling the mortgages and bonds.

The bonds were typically backed by a pool of mortgages held in a trust and matured in 5 to 10 years, though terms ranged from as short as 1 year to as long as 20 years. Using data from regulators in New York and Massachusetts, Snowden has estimated that bonds amounted to one-tenth of the western mortgage market—hardly a dominant presence, but still significant.[30]

Companies that exploited the considerable gap in interest rates between the eastern cities and farm communities reported windfall profits. These high returns attracted well-intentioned imitators as well as scam artists who, in the excitement of a boom, found it easy to borrow money on fake mortgages or simply disappear after collecting funds from investors.[31] As the "farm mortgage craze" mounted, mortgage companies found that they could sell mortgage bonds faster than they could find homeowners in need of loans. Soon the mortgage companies found that the best borrowers already had mortgages.[32]

As with other credit bubbles, lending standards declined as more money flowed into the market. The records of the Mercantile Trust show that the company was selling bonds in Europe faster than its agents could find safe mortgages in the West. In response, the company loosened its loan approval process in an attempt to keep up. Across the market, the quality of mortgages dipped. Agents who were paid on commission found that they could earn bigger fees if they cooperated with appraisers who overvalued the land. Even the more responsible and reputable agents had a tendency to save the best mortgages for the brokerage business and to shunt their most unusual mortgages into pools that investors tended not to examine closely.[33] After the 1873 crash, state examiners reviewed the pools and found that many were undercollateralized. Around 1887, agents at J. B. Watkins in Colorado reported that competition from lenders was creating pressure to ease credit terms: "The great trouble is the competition all over the state, not only in rates, but in the amounts which other companies are willing to lend and also the various privileges that they give or profess to give."[34] By 1888, Watkins had written off the entire state of Kansas. After it concluded that Kansas "is about played out," the company moved on to Texas and Louisiana. Some regulators in eastern states seem to have kept an eye on the market, but it is unclear if or how their efforts affected its trajectory.[35] When drought and depression hit in the 1890s, the highly leveraged and overextended farm mortgage business collapsed.

Many of these events will strike a familiar chord with readers. Intermediaries saw a chance to make large profits by accelerating the flow of mortgage credit and using pooling and guarantees to appeal to investors. Initially successful, these strategies yielded great profits for many. Investors from around the world, disappointed by the staid returns of other investments in the United States, took notice and flocked to U.S. mortgages. It was the nineteenth century's giant pool of money.[36] Fraudsters joined well-intentioned imitators. Brokers conspired with corrupt appraisers to further inflate land values that were already on the rise. Companies became increasingly leveraged as they provided guarantees to investors at home and abroad that their reserves could not actually cover. Without attentive and emboldened regulators to slow the market by other means, the situation escalated until a crash resulted in a painful recovery.

THE POLITICAL ECONOMY OF THE MORTGAGE BOND

In its principles and organizational structure, the mortgage bond market articulated a laissez-faire and corporate model of economic life. Brokers connected East Coast and European investors with borrowers. For investors, risks were mediated by pooling techniques and guarantees offered by brokers seeking to maximize their own profits. For farmers, risk management took the form of insurance sold by for-profit life insurance companies—sometimes the same companies that were selling and bundling the mortgages. The whole market, then, which was largely free from government oversight and regulation, relied on profit-maximizing individuals to devise solutions to the risks and costs of the nation's patchwork mortgage market.

According to historian Jonathan Levy, the mortgage bond specifically reflected the corporate way of understanding risk. Before the 1840s, risk was the technical domain of insurance experts.[37] By the 1880s, he writes, "'risk' became a commonly used extension of the liberal ideal of self-ownership."[38] In this liberal ideal, the proper role of a man was to independently take on risks in search of fortune. The proper role of the government was to stay out of his way. Tinged with Social Darwinism, the liberal ideal posited that a good government should enforce contracts and little else. By this logic, positive government was a form of corrosive paternalism that thwarted competition and undermined the liberal man's ability to help himself.[39]

This is not to say that America's supposedly laissez-faire markets were ever really politically independent. Considerable government resources went into the building of the railroads and other internal improvements. Civil War banking and fiscal policies had bolstered the rise of New York financiers and directed capital toward industry (in part by curtailing the extent of national bank investment in mortgages).[40] Moreover, the entire corporate project depended on the government's willingness to recognize the corporation as a viable, independent form of property. Sociologist William Roy defines corporations as agreements, legitimated and enforced by the government, to selectively collectivize property.[41] "The inescapable fact," political scientist David Ciepley writes, "is that corporations rely on government to override the normal market rules of property and liability and reordain which assets bond which creditors."[42] While proponents of laissez-faire ideals insisted that the corporate form was a natural extension of property rights, many nineteenth-century Americans vehemently disagreed. Antimonopolists insisted that corporations were an extension of state powers and did not represent the natural development of property rights so much as the accretion of special benefits by greedy elites.

The disputed nature of the corporation was adjudicated in the courts, where businessmen found ready allies. Conservative by education and class, many judges enthusiastically supported laissez-faire tenets.[43] Moreover, in asserting the rights of the corporation, judges simultaneously asserted their own authority over that of other branches of government. Through a series of rulings, the courts established the corporation as an entity with its own rights, separate from the state.[44] This was not a privilege universally granted: during this period, courts also ruled that unions constituted a violation of the right to free and unencumbered contract.[45] Nor was the brand of laissez-faire promoted by nineteenth-century businessmen particularly consistent or ideologically pure. Sydney Fine points out that businesses used laissez-faire as rhetoric to deflect regulation and redistribution but readily accepted government efforts to support their own growth or bail them out.[46] The modern corporation was not just a triumph of efficiency, oversight, and coordination, as Alfred Chandler contends: it was also a triumph of political reclassification and a revolution in property rights.[47]

In one of the founding works of organizational theory, Adolf Berle and Gardiner Means wrote that the modern corporation split the atom of property rights by separating ownership and control. The corporation did this when it established that a group of managers could administer and direct the use of property that was owned by others. This was, according to Berle and Means, the final triumph of a new capitalist order over feudalism, since "this dissolution of the atom of property destroys the very foundation on which the economic order of the past three centuries has rested."[48]

If the modern corporation split the atom of property rights, we might think of securitization as a splitting of the nucleus of that atom: it decomposed the concept of beneficial ownership by separating profits from risk. Viewed in this way, securitization is a portable technology for rearranging property rights. It destroys one set of property relations, like a mortgage owned by a single person who both carries the risks of the arrangement and is entitled to its profits, and produces a new arrangement wherein the risks are contractually sheared off from the profits. It was in this willingness to reshuffle property rights on the part of lenders—note that the borrower's mortgage stays uniquely his own—that the mortgage bond market best reflected the laissez-faire ideals and corporate forms of business elites.

Like the corporation, the mortgage bond was a means of selectively socializing capital. Beyond the creation of the pooling mechanism, however, little group identification or advocacy occurred. The use of brokers and contracts thus meant that the market was easily reconciled with the budding liberal ideal of the risk-taking self-made man. Accordingly, the role of the state was limited to protecting and adjudicating property rights. Thus, when the farm mortgage craze crashed in 1893, taking the mortgage bond market with it, there was no bailout akin to the federal debt relief extended to debtors of the Land Office in the 1820s. As self-reliant risk-takers who owed money to private entities, these western farmers were on their own.

Cooperative Credit: The Local Populism of the Alliance Exchanges

In the 1870s, as mortgage bonds accelerated the farm mortgage craze in the West, the particularly brutal system of credit politics in the South was giving rise to a more radical alternative. The Civil War had devastated the southern economy. "The basic difficulty with the South after the war was poverty," writes W.E.B Du Bois of the Reconstruction, "a depth of grinding poverty not easily conceivable even in these days of depression."[49] Grinding poverty combined with a decimated banking system to create a context where credit served as a powerful means of social control.[50] The decimated southern banking system posed additional problems. One study has found that 75 percent of 220 southern banks listed in a national directory closed in 1863 or 1864.[51] When the end of the war wiped out the southern currency and Confederate securities, it took a large swath of southern banks along with them. After the war, this situation combined with new banking regulations and taxes to leave entire regions unbanked.[52] Figure 3.1 shows that in 1870, the Northeast had

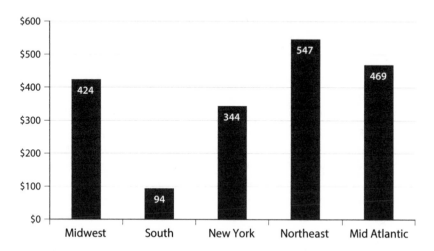

FIGURE 3.1. Number of U.S. Banks by Region, 1870
Source: Table 5 in Matthew Jaremski, "State Banks and the National Banking Acts: Measuring the Response to Increased Financial Regulation, 1860–1870," *Journal of Money, Credit and Banking* 45, nos. 2–3 (2013).

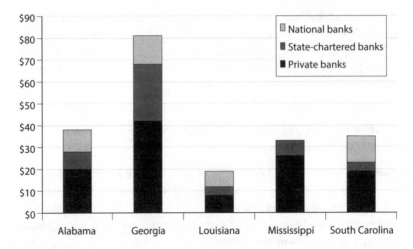

FIGURE 3.2. Banks in Five Southern States, 1880
Source: Table G17 in Roger L. Ransom and Richard Sutch, *One Kind of Freedom: The Economic Consequences of Emancipation*, 2nd ed (New York: Cambridge University Press, 2001).

nearly six times the number of national banks as the South. Figure 3.2 shows that some states, like Louisiana, were in particularly bad shape: New Orleans, for example, had the only state- and nationally chartered banks in Louisiana until 1886.[53] The few banks that remained in the region loaned exclusively to large landholders, who were able to use their access to credit to construct a new system based on tenancy and debt peonage.[54] The federal government, reined in by discontented financiers and worried that redistributing lands would rile northern labor, failed to stop this process.[55] Emancipation also put an end to the longstanding southern practice of using slaves as collateral for loans. Before the war, plantation owners had counted slaves as their main source of wealth and so used them as human collateral.[56]

Because southern land was relatively cheap, valuable crops like cotton emerged as the new preferred source of collateral following the end of slavery. This practice began to be formalized in southern states in the mid-1800s. At the time, there were a great many ways of organizing land rental and labor agreements. The poorest farmers were sharecroppers. As hired laborers who did not own any of the means of farm production, sharecroppers were generally paid out of what they harvested. Their home, supplies, and planting choices were all fully controlled by the landowners. Unlike croppers, tenants used their own supplies and paid a fee for the use of the land. This was more of a land rental agreement than a labor contract, yet given the restrictions on farm credit and supply distribution, the line between these groups remained blurred.

Over time, southern crop lien laws did for tenants what sharecropping had done for laborers: they leveraged economic insecurity, debt, and legal sanctions to concentrate control in the hands of landowners and merchants. Eventually the crop lien laws eroded most of the rights of tenants. In this way, W.E.B. DuBois writes, "the crop lein mortgage was adroitly turned into a labour contract."[57] On the southern "tenant plantations" (which were studied by the federal government in the 1910 U.S. Census), lines between tenant and worker became so blurred that, in the words of historian Harold Woodman, "on such plantations a tenant was simply a cropper with a mule."[58] Crop liens ensured that tenants effectively mortgaged their independence with their crops.

In some places, laws granted lenders extensive rights over the economic lives of debtors: the lender held a mortgage not just on the current crop but on all future crops until the debt was repaid, a provision that scared off other potential creditors. Some lenders had the right to determine what the farmer would cultivate. Because of global prices, the lender usually demanded that cotton be produced, denying farmers even the relief of subsistence farming. The merchant-lender set the terms of the sale and could charge a separate, higher "credit price" for items not purchased with cash—a significant advantage at a time of chronic currency shortages (see figure 3.3). Adding these "credit prices" to the already inflated prices for items, interest in the South for short-term credit could run upwards of 40 percent, and some sources report spikes of over 110 percent.[59] On its own, the combination of currency shortages and credit pricing created a debt trap that was hard for farmers to avoid. Because black farmers started off with fewer resources, they were the first group of tenants to fall into this system of debt peonage and the last to escape it.

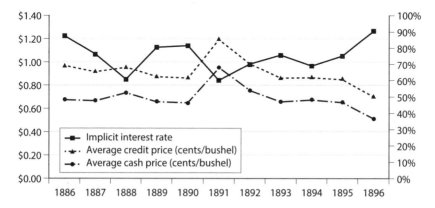

FIGURE 3.3. Louisiana Corn Merchants' Cash and Corn Prices, with Implied Interest Rates, 1886–1896

Source: Table D3 in Ransom and Sutch 2001. For the 1886–1888 period the prices are as of May 1. Thereafter prices are as of June 1.

A host of other provisions also caged in borrowers: indebted farmers could be imprisoned if they moved, some lenders controlled where else the farmer could work, and some places barred northern recruiters from entering the area. Other farmers were forced to sell their crops to landlords and merchants at times when prices were lowest. Once this system was in place, landlords had incredible control, benefiting from not just income from their credit business, but a trapped labor pool. For example, by refusing additional credit or exercising the right to force the farmer to only produce cotton, merchants and landlords could starve their tenants. Michael Schwartz points out that "there was as much centralization of land ownership in 1900 as in 1860, and the largest planters in 1900 controlled as many tenants as their spiritual fathers had controlled slaves."[60] Tenancy and sharecropping, achieved and disciplined through debt, took on properties of slavery.

It was in this context of chronic credit shortages and debt peonage that a cooperative model of credit developed among southern farmers. The Southern Farmers' Alliance, founded in the mid-1870s in Lampasas, Texas, formed as a vigilante group to protect the range and, in the speculative spirit of the nation, also worked to improve local land values.[61] As the Alliance grew, its regular meetings took on many of the functions of the declining Grange, providing a space for community building and agricultural education where members could practice public speaking and publish pamphlets, books, and magazines. It also merged with other organizations, notably the Agricultural Wheel, and eventually became the National Farmers' Alliance and Industrial Union. As the Southern Farmers' Alliance grew in size, the separately organized Northern Farmers' Alliance developed in New York and moved to Chicago. In the Southern Alliance, racism combined with business interests and political ambition drove leaders to segregate the group, going so far as to refuse mergers with other organizations, like the Agricultural Wheel, unless they expelled their existing black members.[62]

Segregated from white movements in the South, black populism developed apace. The Colored Farmers' Alliance, founded in 1886 in Texas, had 1.2 million members by 1891. Southern African Americans had their own populist vision. Unlike its white counterpart, the Colored Alliance had close ties to black churches, focused on literacy and voting rights, and was quicker to see how the entwined political and economically dominant groups were unlikely to cede ground without a strong federal government forcing them to do so.[63]

In cities, laborers' power rested in banding together to stop production. For rural farmers, there was power in standing together to buy and sell goods. In a trenchant and sobering study of the Alliance as a social movement, sociologist Michael Schwartz notes that, depending on local conditions, Alliance farmers boycotted merchants, formed cooperatives to store and sell goods in bulk, and made trade agreements with merchants and store owners in exchange for lower prices.[64] Their efforts regularly met with backlash from local lenders and stores who wanted to preserve the existing system of crop liens and share-cropping. If a local Alliance organized a coop to buy specific farm supplies, for example, local merchants might refuse to conduct any business with known members. There were banks that refused to lend money to Alliance members, warehouses that refused to store Alliance goods, and towns that passed special taxes on Alliance trade.

For farmers organized in the Colored Alliance, anti-Alliance backlash was particularly brutal, as the Leflore County Massacre illustrates.[65] In 1880, a black organizer in Mississippi named Oliver Cromwell established a local chapter of the Colored Alliance and initiated a boycott of local merchants, directing members to shop at an Alliance store in a nearby town. When white merchants threatened retaliation, local black community members rallied in Cromwell's defense. The town erupted in violence. The National Guard, called in to impose order, arrested 40 local black men and turned them over to a local white posse. When the National Guard left, an armed mob terrorized the countryside. The history of the massacre remains shrouded in mystery—it was purposely not recorded in the county news, and a journalist who later went to investigate found locals too terrified to speak of it—but one scholar has estimated the number of dead at 25, and there were reports at the time that the mob killed up to 100 people, including women and children. After the massacre, local white planters issued a notice against the Colored Alliance's plans to "corrupt Negroes to further their intentions and selfish motives" and refused to sell goods to any members of the Colored Alliance.[66] A nearby distributor of an Alliance newsletter was warned not to distribute further materials in the area.

For white Alliance members, who did not face the equivalent terrors of lynch mobs and massacres, the escalating series of backlashes had a radicalizing effect. Schwartz contends that the more local merchants and landlords fought the cooperatives, the more members saw that combating the entire oppressive system of credit, purchases, sales, and distribution was the only way to uplift farmers.[67] Farmers began to think that if the Alliance was to break the system of debt peonage, they needed to create not just cooperative stores, but an entirely new system of credit and distribution to support it.

The Southern Alliance's solution was the concept of the farmers' exchange.[68] Charles W. Macune, a handsome and silver-tongued Wisconsinite who had practiced law and medicine before rising in the ranks of the Alliance, announced the plan in January of 1887. If the Alliance collected $2 from each member, it could build a base of $500,000 to establish an exchange in Texas that could lend that money to farmers to purchase supplies at fair prices. These farmers would later sell their harvest at this exchange, where they would finally get a fair price for their goods. It was a bold plan. Alliance members hailed the Texas Alliance Exchange as a way of "abolishing the awful credit system" and a means of "financial salvation."[69] Excitement mounted, and cities in Texas competed to house it. A deal with the city of Dallas ultimately yielded the Texas Exchange a corner lot with deferred rentals for the building and $3,500 in cash, with a promise of more in the future.[70] The Exchange opened in September in time to sell the cotton harvest. It was an immediate success. Pooling their cotton allowed Exchange members to undercut their competitors' prices. One transaction alone sent 1,500 bales of Exchange cotton to England, France, and Germany.[71] Texas farmers reported savings of over $6 million resulting from lower prices and supply bills.[72] This early success, paired with an active lecture circuit that spread the news, led to the creation of exchanges in other states.

The Texas Alliance Exchange now had a successful record of bulk sales, but since it had opened after the harvest, it had yet to implement its full vision. Furthermore, few members actually paid in to the Exchange, which was seemingly unable to enforce its fee-based structure. As the plan to raise capital from $2 fees floundered, the business relied on startup funds from the city of Dallas. At the same time, the first round of cotton sales only benefited farmers who did not rely on crop liens for credit, since those who had used liens to borrow supplies were already obliged to sell to their local furnishing merchant or landlord. The system offered scant relief to farmers who still faced the prospect of pledging their next year's crop in order to secure supplies.[73]

That November, Macune introduced the Alliance's communal alternative to the crop lien. Farmers could place orders for supplies through their local Alliance and pledge their future crops as collateral. These pledges were over-collateralized to lessen credit risk: farmers promised three times the value that they expected to borrow. To further provide credit support, Alliance members cosigned each other's debts and agreed to let cosigners harvest the crop if something dire rendered a farmer unable to farm his own land. To ensure the soundness of the loan, the joint notes were reviewed at the county level and again at the state level. All these local orders of supplies and all of the joint pledges of collateral were gathered at the Texas Exchange, which then planned to use the joint notes as collateral for loans from southern banks. Those loans would then be used to pay for the farmers' supplies. Called the "joint-note plan," this was an effort to use cooperative credit to circumvent merchant-lenders. The Alliance dispatched lecturers around the region to explain the plan. Groups of farmers, some as few as 8 and some as many as 40, signed up to collectively mortgage their crops and goods and sent orders to the Texas Exchange for supplies.[74]

With the joint-note plan underway, Macune found that wholesale suppliers, drawn by the Texas Exchange's bulk orders, were willing to work with the Alliance. Banks were not. Having placed orders for supplies, Macune was subsequently refused loans throughout the South. One bank in Houston lent him $6,000 on the basis of $20,000 worth of joint notes as collateral. He was turned away in Dallas, and then by banks in Fort Worth, Galveston, and New Orleans.[75] Without credit, the exchange system was on the brink of collapse. Macune accused the banks of maliciously denying credit in an effort to destroy the exchanges.[76] Enraged Alliance members declared June 9 a day of protest and rallied at courthouses across Texas. They raised enough to pay off the Texas Exchange's debts to suppliers, but the damage was done. The Texas Exchange closed the next year because no merchants would provide it credit. In 1890, there were 13 exchanges in total. All closed within three years.[77]

There had long been tension in the farmers' organizations about how overtly political they should be. Opponents of political mobilization warned that entering the mire of politics could corrupt the movement; it was better to focus on self-help, education, or cooperatives. This issue had been debated in the Alliance too, with some pushing for third-party political organization and others, like Macune, a loyal Democrat, pushing to stay officially apolitical. Nevertheless, some Alliance members were involved in politics as early as 1880. Now more turned their attention to the national political stage.[78]

Disabused of their belief in using cooperative means to appeal to the banks for credit, the Alliance moved to wrest control of money from the banks altogether. At the 1888 Texas Alliance convention, Macune proposed the establishment of a treasury within the Exchange that would create a currency for its farmers. In this plan, county Alliances would raise a capital stock of $10,000, and the Exchange would use that as the basis to issue currency to farmers upon deposit of warehouse receipts.[79] With the Exchange faltering, this plan was never put into action, but it reflected a change in focus from communal credit to currency. To break the bonds of credit seemed to require a different course of action: one that focused on the state and money, as well as on national-level politics. As Goodwyn writes, "The discovered truth was a simple one, but its political import was radical: the Alliance cooperative stood little chance of working unless fundamental changes were made in the monetary system. This understanding was the germ of the Omaha Platform of the People's Party."[80]

THE POLITICAL ECONOMY OF THE TEXAS EXCHANGE

The Texas Exchange was a populist experiment with credit distribution. Charles Postel, in his book *Populist Vision*, offers insight into its logic. Alliance farmers were wary of the corporate forms of the monopolies, trusts, and railroads— but they also relied on some of those structures in their own business efforts.[81] Exchanges were corporate in their focus on business interests and in their willingness to have remote centers of centralized power.[82] But these farmers did not understand business interests as inherently individualistic—for populists, they were collective. In an 1888 speech, Macune emphasized the exchange system's fusion of centralized power and collective well-being:

> This plan is pure and simple cooperation. . . . It is calculated to benefit the whole class, and not simply those who have surplus money to invest in capital stock; it does not aspire, and is not calculated to be a business for profit in itself, but is intended to be strictly auxiliary and supplemental to the farming efforts. Another distinctive feature of the exchange plan is that, instead of encouraging a number of stores scattered over the country, each in turn to fall prey to the opposition . . . this plan provides a strong central State head, and places sufficient capital stock there to make that the field for concentrating the fight of the opposition, and a bulwark of strength and refuge for the local store efforts.[83]

This was a self-consciously social vision that saw large-scale organization as a way to help members of a community. At a time when businesses were pressing for a redefinition of the corporation as a person to be protected from the state—an ironic projection of individualism onto the very structure that socialized property—the exchange system saw the possibility of a corporate form that was explicit about its social nature.[84]

The exchanges were also envisioned as a democratic system.[85] The Texas Exchange, for example, had 25 shares of $20,000 each when it was incorporated, and the stockholders holding those shares were elected at yearly state meetings.[86] Alliance leaders were also elected, and at the highest level of authority, executive decisions were often sent to lower-level Alliances for approval.[87] The Texas Exchange specifically applied populist principles to credit markets. Access to the credit market was granted to all Alliance members. Pooling and mutual guarantees redistributed risks within the community. This was a cooperative approach to credit distribution on a broad scale, but it is important to note that it was not a universal one. Because the community was defined in racial terms, the benefit was limited to white farmers.

The National Coordination of Credit: The Subtreasury Plan

Mortgage bonds and Alliance exchanges both envisioned a local and nongovernmental solution to the problem of credit distribution. The People's Party subtreasury plan, however, called on the federal government to ensure the fair distribution of farm credit on a national scale.

The People's Party was the locus of populism's next great wave. A third party wrought of the alliance between farmers and labor, it sought to use scientific principles of government to protect the nation's producers from the predations of big business and finance. The 1892 Omaha Platform reflected a populist-inflected brand of capitalism: support for unions, nationalization of railways and the transportation system (since both were natural monopolies), a revamped land policy that cut out speculators and foreign investors, the free coinage of silver, electoral reform, an income tax, and, most important for the purposes of this chapter, a new subtreasury plan presented by Macune himself.[88]

Like the Alliance exchanges, the subtreasury plan was designed to break the entire oppressive southern system of credit and distribution. Unlike the exchanges, it sought to use the federal government's authority over the money supply to do so. Any county that produced over $500,000 in goods would qualify for a warehouse. Farmers storing goods in the warehouse would get certificates of deposit to sell on the market. Macune thought this would put $550 million worth of greenbacks into circulation—no small promise of relief for currency-starved regions.[89] Any farmer who deposited goods in one of the warehouses could borrow up to 80 percent of the value of those goods at a 2 percent interest rate, a revolutionary prospect for farmers whose short-term loans had interest rates that could exceed 40 percent. The initial plan, hatched in the South, focused exclusively on crop deposits. It was later amended to provide mortgages to farmers so as to better appeal to farmers in the West.

The subtreasury fused the exchange system's emphasis on credit with a Greenback focus on money. It put farmers instead of bankers at the center of the nation's money supply and sought to give local markets an advantage over futures markets in big cities. When he first announced the plan, Macune posed it as an alternative to just focusing on education and efficiency (an appealing option from a more conservative, laissez-faire standpoint) or finding respite in cooperative ventures (the focus of earlier populist efforts). Instead, he urged farmers to demand that the government even the financial playing field: "By organization, a united effort can be brought to bear on the authorities that will secure such changes in the regulations that govern the relations between different classes of citizens."[90] Macune's point was that farmers needed to gain control over the government so they might wrest control from the banks.[91] For farmers who proudly identified as followers of Jackson and Jefferson, the pursuit of a large government that would back a national financial system was not an obvious choice, but populist leaders developed a (sometimes tortuous) way of reconciling their agenda with the farmers' self-understanding, arguing that the populists were the true inheritors of Jefferson's and Jackson's commitment to democracy and liberty, while their opponents were Hamiltonian in their commitment to protecting the moneyed elite.[92]

The subtreasury plan was both popular and controversial. In the South, the People's Party used it as a wedge issue to turn struggling farmers against the Bourbon Democrats. "However painfully—and it was quite painful in some states," Lawrence Goodwyn writes, "the politics of the subtreasury, fashioned some twenty-six years after Appomattox, became the sword that

cut the ancestral bonds to the party of the fathers."[93] Bankers and conservatives ridiculed the subtreasury plan as unconstitutional, a dangerously naïve
and inflationary scheme that would fuel speculation. In the face of backlash,
general support for the plan waned, even in the South.

Support for the subtreasury was finally undermined altogether when
Macune was banned from the Alliance following the revelation that he'd been
secretly paid by Democrats to lure votes from the People's Party in the 1892 elections. By 1893, free silver had replaced the subtreasury on the national agenda.
Farmers thereafter primary sought relief through efforts to ease inflation.

THE POLITICAL ECONOMY OF THE SUBTREASURY

The subtreasury reveals how populism's evolving organizational repertoire
moved toward a national solution to credit distribution. The Alliance itself
relied on bureaucratic power that was centralized in remote locations but
nevertheless could be held accountable through democratic means, and the
failure of the Texas Exchange led many to believe that only a strong federal
government could pry loose the bankers' stranglehold on credit. Subsequently the People's Party convinced many farmers that a large-scale financial
program coordinated by a central state could be reconciled with Jeffersonian
and Jacksonian ideals.

Given all of this, small government no longer seemed to many farmers
the best response to political corruption; making the national government
stronger and more independent was preferable.[94] Against the advocates of
laissez-faire liberalism, proponents of the general welfare state believed that
an independent national government could promote well-being and economic
growth. The subtreasury articulated that vision in the realm of capital and
credit. If the state was going to be granting privileges to corporations, why
should bankers and industrialists, and not farmers, be in charge of the financial
system? In its embrace of a strong central state that would help organize risks
on a national scale, this was a plan that incorporated a broader public into the
organization of the nation's credit and currency.

As the Democratic Party subsumed the People's Party and populism declined, agitation for control over farm credit declined with it. Elisabeth Clemens notes that as farmers entered the twentieth century they largely abandoned
the fraternal and cooperative solidarity that had once infused their business interests. As a result, she contends, farmers transformed from populists focused
on self-help and resistance to the political control of others (like trusts) to
economic corporatists seeking administrative control of their own markets.[95]
Drained of their populist animus, farmers' organizations increasingly came to
resemble corporations, trusts, and railways. Here the volatile economic climate
likely played a role. Farm prices started rising in 1896. As prices mounted,

farmers who had managed to avoid sliding into tenancy found their fortunes improved and left their poorer counterparts to their own devices.

For the well-off farmer, a world of catalogs, mechanized farming, automobiles, and telephones awaited.[96] For the rest, tenancy, crop liens, and sharecropping lay ahead. When the issue of rural mortgage credit was next brought to the national stage, it was championed in decidedly different ways by middle-class Progressive reformers.

Reversing the Tides of Power and Credit

Credit circulated widely but unevenly at the close of the nineteenth century. Capital and currency that had made their way west inexorably flowed back eastward, either through trade or through the system of reserve banks. Each of the three experiments discussed in this chapter sought to move eastern capital out to the western and southern peripheries while managing the risks and costs associated with that lending. Notably, each used some kind of pooling mechanism to manage risks, but those mechanisms operated in very different ways. The mortgage bond directed risks to brokers and financiers, who were expected to manage them through sound business practices in exchange for considerable profit. The joint-note plan sought to redistribute risks and protect profits among willing communities of farmers. The subtreasury imagined the use of government-designed nonprofit corporate structures to disperse risks across the nation.

These ways of organizing credit were not just technical devices. They reflected moral visions for a changing political economy. The mortgage bond expressed laissez-faire ideals. It relied on profit-seeking, risk-bearing individuals—unencumbered by the state—to find a solution to a market mired in high transaction costs and pervasive risks. The joint-note plan expressed a populist commitment to using cooperation and democratic principles in the pursuit of local interests. The subtreasury merged that populism with the belief that a strengthened central state could manage and promote well-being through national-level coordination. In this third vision, the nation as a whole would help carry the risks associated with farming. Each system of risk management articulated a deeper set of understandings of what was possible and desirable for American markets and governments.

One of the lasting lessons of this period is the mutual constitution of states and markets. Steven Skowronek famously characterized late nineteenth-century U.S. government as a state of "courts and parties."[97] The Civil War gave rise to a larger federal bureaucracy than had previously existed, but the U.S. government still lacked many of the hallmarks of a modern national government that had already been developed in Europe: an independent civil service, an executive budget, a standing peacetime army. At the same time that

U.S. political power was generally diffused, the nation's capital remained concentrated in the nation's urban centers. Money that did flow to the periphery still tended to reaccumulate in eastern cities through a combination of trade and reserve banks.[98]

For reformers, the rapid growth of the American economy demanded a political response; state governments were not equipped to manage corporations and capital flows that operated on a national scale. From 1877 to 1900, a vanguard of bureaucrats and administrators undertook an effort to extend the power of the executive. As Elizabeth Sanders notes, farmers were a central part of the push for the modern American state as well. Grangers' demands for regulated railways and warehouses, Greenbackers' assertion of the central government's authority over the monetary supply, and the People's Party's plan for the subtreasury were all part of the farmers' vision for a new role of the federal government in the sphere of economic growth. Despite populists' electoral failures, they succeeded in setting an agenda that the Progressives would later bring to fruition.[99]

The late nineteenth century was a time of transition, a period when new forms of statecraft and economic power were coming into existence. This transition proved both lurching and inconsistent: older ways seemed to have been outgrown, but the shape of what was to come was at once blurry, promising, and alarming. Americans fought over what that new order would look like. In the struggle for position, credit was an important battleground. Populists fought to accumulate political power in a central government, in part so that credit could better flow to the periphery. They were fighting to reverse the tides of power and credit in the nation, helping power accumulate in the center so that credit could better radiate outward. The stories of the populist farmers remind us that if credit distribution has been part of the federal government's organizational repertoire since its modern inception, it is in part because farmers' demands for credit helped call the modern federal government into existence.

4

Credit as a Tool of Statecraft

We have seen that troubled credit markets stretch back to the earliest days of the nation. And we have seen that government officials since the Revolution have used land distribution to raise funds and encourage growth, strategies that sometimes led them into the field of credit markets. But in the nineteenth century, countervailing forces—like sectional standoffs and farmers' distrust of the national government—limited how national officials used credit. State governments regulated credit markets, but this often impeded the regional flow of credit. So, while credit distribution across the nation's patchwork market demanded a national-level solution, no clear resolution materialized. In the 1880s and 1890s, private attempts to move credit across the frontier failed, sometimes spectacularly. Populist agrarians in the 1890s succeeded in changing how farmers organized themselves and how they thought about the national government, but by the end of the century, the reform of long-term farm credit distribution systems had receded from farmers' focus.[1]

In 1916, after nearly a century of being out of the business of farm mortgages, the federal government passed the Federal Farm Loan Act, a policy that overhauled the nation's system of farm credit distribution and created a completely new network of lending organizations. Why this policy, at this time? That is, why, after nearly a century of inaction, at a time when farmers were not especially agitated about the issue, did the federal government finally act to address farm credit? And in a nation known for its anti-statist sentiment, how did the federal government come to organize an entirely new network of lending cooperatives?

The answers to these questions lie not just in the general expansion of federal power at this time, but more specifically in how Progressives drew from European precedents to reframe the old problem of rural credit. Worried about banking troubles and the social decline of the countryside, reformers of the early nineteenth century had focused on the perennial problem of credit distribution. As the three failed experiments of the late 1800s revealed in the previous chapter, dealing with farm credit meant grappling with the extent to which farmers, bankers, or government bureaucrats should have authority over credit.[2] In the German system of *Landschaften*—land banks funded by mortgage bonds called *Pfandbriefe*—Progressives found a technical solution for the distribution of credit across a vast and depopulated space. They also found a moral justification for selective credit as a means by which the federal government could help farmers help themselves. American Progressives thus replaced their earlier, more radical farm credit politics with a more moderate vision of government-supported credit as an inexpensive way of supporting self-help. In the nineteenth century, proposed credit policies had been divisive along sectional and class lines. In the twentieth century, credit policies often transcended such bitter divides.

With a few important exceptions, scholarship on American political development has generally neglected the FFLA.[3] Compared with other hallmarks of Progressive Era state building—the creation of the Federal Reserve, the professionalization of the civil service, the modernization of the army, and the expansion of regulatory powers through agencies like the Interstate Commerce Commission and Federal Trade Commission—the FFLA seems relatively unimportant. Nevertheless, it was a turning point in the use of selective credit as a tool of federal statecraft in the United States. The FFLA provided federal credit on a national level that was administered through public–private partnerships and bolstered by tax expenditures. Its structure was the organizational expression of a political vision in which a strong central state helps people help themselves—but without being paternalistic, and avoiding the need for sacrifice or redistribution from other Americans. It was a dream, in other words, of a kind of frictionless involvement of the federal government in everyday life. By tracing the lead-up to this policy, we can see how Progressives forged a new array of cultural and organizational approaches to federal credit that would later proliferate across policy arenas.

Progressives Rediscover the Rural Credit Problem

After a conversational lull in the earliest years of the twentieth century, the problem of "rural credits" in the United States again became a topic of frequent debate between 1907 and 1913. In the national debate on banking reform that arose in the aftermath of the 1907 crash, the National Monetary Commission issued a report that included details about a promising German system that relied on mortgage bonds.[4] In the spring of 1912, the same year the report was released, President Taft commissioned America's ambassadors in Europe to study European systems of farm credit. He did so at the urging of Myron Herrick, a former governor and banker from Cleveland who was then ambassador to France and who had been giving speeches on the marvel of European credit institutions.[5]

Herrick took the lead in writing up a report that encouraged Americans to adopt the German system of rural credit. The report noted that implementing a German system of mortgage bonds could promote farm credit in part by turning mortgages into a "fluid and popular" investment.[6] Taft endorsed the position and invited state governors to a White House meeting to discuss how the states could implement such a system through uniform legislation that might lead to the creation of a nationally chartered bank supported with federally guaranteed bonds. His invitation stressed, however, that this would be a system "of, for, and by the farmers of the United States."[7]

At the same time, bankers turned their attention to farm credit with the creation of the American Bankers Association's Agricultural Commission in 1911. By December of 1913, the commission was producing *The Banker Farmer*, a monthly magazine dedicated to showing how sound banking could help solve the needs of farmers.[8] The Federal Reserve Act of 1913 had provided a degree of agricultural credit relief, as it authorized national banks to issue mortgages to farmers. (The authorization was added by President Wilson, who needed the support of farmers to pass the bill.[9]) Within three years, commercial banks had lent $45.7 million to farmers.[10] Under Federal Reserve restrictions, however, nationally chartered banks could only invest a quarter of their capital and issue mortgages of five years or less.[11] The rural credit problem was far from resolved.

Concerns about the social well-being of rural America drew further attention to the problem of farm credit. The reformers who made up the Country Life movement in the early 1900s worried that urbanization was draining talent from rural areas and thereby undermining the nation's agricultural foundation.[12] Mounting food prices further reminded a burgeoning middle class that the decline of the countryside came at the expense of the entire nation.[13] In 1908, President Theodore Roosevelt convened the Country Life Commission at the urging of Horace Plunkett, a charismatic Irishman who had toured the United States telling of his great success in organizing Irish farming cooperatives.[14] The commission's primary mandate was not credit distribution, but how to bureaucratize and rationalize farms, conserve land, protect the soil, and lower food prices.[15]

Unlike the populists, reformers in the Country Life movement—which included a growing cadre of newly professionalized rural sociologists—did not blame financiers and middlemen for farmers' problems but instead identified "social disorder" as the central issue.[16] It is perhaps unsurprising, then, that the Country Life Commission subsequently concluded that economic hardship was the main cause of that social disorder. Make farm living "good and profitable,"

and "social cohesion" would follow, it declared.[17] Among other recommendations, the report emphasized the usefulness of cooperatives—including credit
cooperatives—as a way to cure isolation and grow the farm economy.

The Country Life Commission's report of 1909 reveals how Progressive
efforts to avoid open class confrontations resulted in a politically moderate
approach to credit policies. Christopher Shaw notes that the commission "repeatedly shied away from actions that risked exposing class conflict," seeking
reforms that allowed them to do so.[18] As a result, the commission avoided
touchy subjects like immigration and tenancy. One might think that in such a
context, credit would have been similarly elided, as it had been a site of divisive
class politics a mere decade earlier. Yet while the commission did not discuss
credit extensively (in the 65-page report, credit received a mere paragraph of
attention), it discussed it matter-of-factly: while making a broader case for cooperatives, the report argued that a cooperative credit organization would end
the destructive crop lien system, provide "loans on the best terms," and prevent
the drain of capital into urban centers.[19] State and national governments should
not run such organizations, the report noted, but should encourage their development. In this way the government could help farmers help themselves.[20]

This Progressive approach to federally organized rural credit distribution
therefore stripped away the radicalism of the populists and in doing so found a
middle ground. Eastern business interests saw rural credit as a way to support
their own enterprise by growing markets.[21] Bankers saw an opportunity for
profit. Democrats and Republicans recognized farmers as an important voting
bloc and saw a chance to woo them through credit reform. The notion that
rural credit needed study and repair now had broad support.[22]

Into these debates stepped David Lubin. A Jewish refugee from Poland,
Lubin had worked his way across the United States and settled in California.
Side by side with his half-brother, Harris Weinstock, Lubin grew a small store
in Sacramento into one of the West Coast's largest department store chains.[23]
A trip to the Holy Land in 1884 convinced Lubin that yeoman farming was the
key to a more enlightened and democratic society. After returning home, he
purchased an orchard and organized farmers, eventually helping to establish
the California Fruit Growers' Union. While Harris Weinstock would go on to
become a noted U.S. labor organizer, Lubin worked to unite farmers around
the world, hailing the values of international coordination, scientific research,
and improved global communication.

In 1908, the king of Italy, at Lubin's behest, sponsored the creation of the
International Institute for Agriculture. Eventually absorbed into the United
Nations, the institute gathered and disseminated global data on crop production and prices. After its establishment, Lubin turned his full attention to the
rural credit movement. Inspired in part by a successful system of farm credit
distribution in Germany, Lubin believed that better access to credit would

allow American farmers to compete with more powerful financial trusts and middlemen.[24] "With a pamphlet mill at his disposal, a mailing list of some fifty thousand farm organizations, an inexhaustible stock of Biblical quotations and moral parables, and the confidence of a self-taught economist," historian Daniel Rodgers writes, "Lubin bombarded his countrymen with what he had found."[25]

In May of 1912, the Southern Commercial Congress (SCC), an influential regional trade association, invited Lubin to give a lecture. Lubin promptly convinced the SCC to send a delegation to tour Europe to explore alternatives for organizing American farm life. Called the American Commission, the delegation would send two men from each state to Europe alongside representatives from Canada.

In that year's presidential campaign, the Democratic, Republican, and Progressive Party platforms all called for a study of European credit systems.[26] Subsequently, President Taft signed a bill authorizing a smaller delegation representing Congress to tour Europe as well. Named the United States Commission, it was to travel with the SCC's larger American Commission. A massive review of European credit systems was now underway.

The American and U.S. Commissions: Europe and the Promise of Self-Help

As the two commissions prepared to depart together for Europe, Clarence Owens, director of the American Commission and simultaneously an appointed member of the U.S. Commission, endorsed a statement from David Lubin:

> By far the most important question before the American commission is that of how the American farmer can obtain the money. The question has largely been settled in some countries by government agency. But no such settlement of the case is possible in the United States. The United States is far removed from sympathy with paternalism. If money is to be obtained there, it must be had without recourse to governmental sources.[27]

In other words, delegates specifically sought a nongovernmental solution to the problem of farm credit. In fact, Lubin, like others, already had his eye on the German system of cooperative banks that used collectively guaranteed mortgage bonds to provide a stable stream of credit to farmers.

Progressives who toured Europe were common at the time, but Rodgers has called the two commissions' tour one of "the most extraordinary" of the era."[28] The commissions headed as far north as Norway and as far south as Egypt. Subcommittees traveled west to Killarney, Ireland, and east to Moscow. Everywhere the delegates immersed themselves in European agriculture.[29] Back in the United States, the *New York Times* reported on their progress.[30] Delegates broadly investigated rural life, examining everything from cooperatives and education to credit and insurance. Italian speakers outlined experiments with small-scale lending to support small-plot tenant farming. Swedish lectures offered detailed exegeses of cow breeds and their different milk outputs. An Egyptian speaker focused on cotton production. French lecturers explained how democratic ideals were reflected in their systems of credit. In Norway, "an error of misunderstanding" sent a confused subcommittee on a tour of a slaughterhouse; delegates reported that while surprised by the experience, they were nevertheless very impressed with the facility's efficiency and cleanliness.[31] In England, delegates were taken aback by the backwardness of the country's system of credit distribution, given England's leadership in developing consumers' cooperatives. In Ireland, Horace Plunkett charmed his visitors by explaining how cooperatives allowed farmers to help themselves. In the Netherlands and Spain, delegates found counterparts who were similarly looking across Europe for ways to better their own systems of rural credit.

The centerpiece of the tour was Germany, the nation that had consistently led the way in developing cooperative borrowing institutions.[32] In German cities, the Schulze-Delitzsch banks facilitated cooperative borrowing, while in rural German villages, cooperative Raiffeisen banks provided short-term small loans. Most importantly, the Germans seemed to have solved the problem of providing a stable supply of mortgage credit to farmers using a system of lending cooperatives that flourished alongside a set of for-profit joint-stock banks. Speakers explained that Germany had risen to agricultural prominence despite mediocre soil as a result of its superior credit institutions.[33] Among those institutions, the delegates were particularly interested in the Landschaften.

The Landschaften are a network of German land banks in which farmers' cooperatives issue bonds, called Pfandbriefe, secured by farm mortgages. A Prussian merchant founded the first Landschaft in 1770, during the rule of Frederick the Great, to solve a problem much like the one faced by the United States in the late nineteenth and early twentieth centuries: the need to move credit across a vast, sparsely populated area.[34] Limited at first to the large estates of Prussian nobles, Landschaften eventually extended across provinces and grew to address the needs of peasants. By 1913, a farmer could borrow up to two-thirds of the value of his land from a local Landschaft through a 45- to 54-year amortizing mortgage. Instead of directly receiving money, the farmer received a Pfandbriefe—a bond guaranteed by the Landschaft—and then sold it on an exchange. The German government gave the Pfandbriefe special status, treating them much like government bonds and allowing them to serve as legal investments for widows' and orphans' funds. Because each Pfandbriefe was tied to a mortgage, the bonds could be considered "mortgages under another name."[35] Over time, some Landschaften created banks to assist the farmers' Pfandbriefe sales, and by the early twentieth century, some had branched into the life insurance business as well. German speakers on the commissions' tour explained that the Landschaften had played a central role in the development of German agriculture and wealth. With this system, the Germans had built an impressive 150-year record of success, one that had inspired the development of similar systems in Austria, Hungary, Switzerland, Russia, Romania, Denmark, Sweden, and France.[36]

The system was set up to minimize risk. Land was conservatively valued: each property was subject to three separate estimates, and the lowest one was used. Committees oversaw the process and could demand additional valuations by Landschaft officials. Landschaft members then made sure that properties did not deteriorate. Each Landschaft was chartered by the king and regulated, and the king also appointed officers to review all of their accounts annually. Half of 1 percent of every loan payment was set aside to create a reserve. Each Pfandbriefe was backed by both a specific mortgage and the Landschaft itself. All members of the Landschaft were liable for the organization's debts up to the full commercial value of their own property. The system created distance in the relationship between borrower and lender, but it tightened the relationship among borrowers, who were now responsible for each other's debts. Because the Pfandbriefe could be redeemed or sold at any point, it was more liquid than a mortgage—"the perfect type of secure investment," according to a Landschaft director from Berlin.[37] During the Napoleonic wars, when the Prussian government defaulted on its interest payments, the Pfandbriefe traded at a value higher than that of government bonds.[38]

Built for stability, the Landschaften never promised windfall gains for investors. The Pfandbriefe bore a decidedly unsexy return of 3 to 4 percent interest. "The Germans prefer to sleep well rather than eat well," explained one lecturer.[39] Another speaker claimed that the system was "free from every tendency to profit making."[40] With the community organizations overseen by the king and government employees at the helm, the Landschaften subordinated individual profits to community well-being.

Despite the success of the German system, a German political economy professor lecturing in Halle warned the Americans that while the Landschaften were the "perfect" solution for mortgage credit, differences in political structures could make the economic arrangement untenable in the United States. "You have what we call a 'spoils system,' but with us all officers . . . are appointed [by the king] for life, and so they are absolutely independent," he observed. The safety of the system was not only in the pooling mechanism but also in the reliability of the safety checks: conservative valuation of the land, regulatory oversight, generous reserves, and clear delineations of liability for guarantees. Speakers carefully reviewed each mechanism. When a delegate asked how the Prussians dealt with defective land titles, the speaker simply dismissed the question: "Well, that is an impossible thing in Prussia. We have no defective titles." The German farm credit distribution system rested on a foundation of independent oversight and bureaucratic reliability.[41]

Upon its return, the U.S. Commission submitted its recommendations in an official report. Overall, the report lauded the scientific techniques, cooperative spirit, and educational systems its members had seen in Europe before turning to focus on rural credit.[42] The commission recommended that the United States implement a version of the German system. As the parties behind the nineteenth-century mortgage bond market, the Farmers' Alliance Exchange, and the subtreasury had realized, the core insight was that pooling mortgages, and thereby diversifying risk, could lower the costs associated with farm lending: "It is the merging of the credit demands and the property resources of many individuals, somewhat similarly situated, into one financial transaction." The most important aspect of this mechanism was the creation of a bond backed by mortgages—"an invention to render liquid the value of real estate"—to supply capital to farmers. The commission assured readers that this was simply a logical extension of the corporate form into the field of agriculture.[43]

But what kind of organization should produce these mortgage bonds? The report noted that reasonable people could disagree on whether a borrowers' collective (which presumably carried the most benefit for farmers) was preferable to a joint-stock bank (the structure that best reflected the interests of financiers), or whether something in between was the best solution. Recognizing that to be a complicated issue, the report nevertheless put forward model legislation that included a borrowers' collective similar to a Landschaft on the logic that a collective would have the added benefit of instilling cooperation among farmers. The government would facilitate the formation of these organizations, keep the bonds "under rigid government supervision," and then ensure the bonds' success by exempting them from taxes and classifying them as viable investments by regulated entities like banks.[44] Restricting loans to landowners should prevent speculation. In this way, the government's job was to help farmers help themselves.

What the report did not directly say, but what is nevertheless revealed by its discussion, was that cooperatives would not only solve the social problems of isolation but also address the quintessentially *political* burdens of administration and cost. Consider the following statement:

> In every instance in Europe where government capital has been granted to establish mortgage credit, the results have been favorable to the agricultural interests of that nation. It is our opinion that such aid should not be extended in the United States. Our farm property is computed to be worth $40,000,000,000 and is rapidly increasing in value. Surely this vast property, whose value is as stable as the foundations of our Government,

is sufficient to attract capital in ample volume to improve and cultivate its area, without subvention from our Government Treasury. The idea of Federal aid is always attractive and commands many able and earnest advocates; but self-help should be the motto of our new agriculture. If given the opportunity, under liberal enactment of law, the savings of our nation will gladly invest in this safe field and relieve the Federal Treasury of any necessity to finance the project. It is wise legislation, rather than liberal appropriations or loans, which rural credit mostly needs at our hands.[45]

Three notable claims are being made here. First, a program run through bond-issuing organizations would have low long-term costs. Given "wise legislation" that made the farm mortgages less risky, private funds would suffice to pay for the program. Second, a few tweaks to the market could unlock the value represented by the nation's land, here estimated at $40 billion. The value of the land could be used to bootstrap its own development, thus relieving the need for federal expenditures. Third, cooperatives, as intermediaries in the credit market, could also serve as political intermediaries insofar as they allowed the federal government to extend its influence without seeming paternalistic by promoting self-help among the farmers. With cooperatives in place, people did not have to choose between government paternalism and self-direction. This is why, in the midst of a proposal to totally overhaul the farm credit system, the report could claim that "the farmer needs no special privilege and wants no special privilege, and none should be extended to him."[46] European precedents provided not just a system of risk management, but also a justification for government action in which partnerships with private actors legitimated government involvement.

Commission members were sincere in their search for an organizational solution that could plausibly be considered a nonpaternalistic form of government action. The delegates' critiques of the French system reveal this. French speakers, much like speakers in Germany and Ireland, used the language of self-help when describing their rural credit program: "Help yourself and the State will help you," explained one lecturer.[47] Another claimed: "The main concern of France has been to see that our agricultural credit should rise from below—that is, from out of the very midst of our rural democracy. . . . The government stimulates independent initiative, but does not replace it."[48] Yet the French system was much more centralized than the German one. In 1910, the French government created a long-term mortgage system inspired by the Landschaften, but with important differences. France's Credit Foncier had a 25-year monopoly on long-term mortgage lending, whereas in Germany, joint-stock banks competed with the Landschaften. Moreover, the heavy hand of the state was seemingly revealed in the financing of the French system through a central bank: the Bank of France supplied loans to regional banks, which supplied loans to local banks, which then lent up to 8,000 francs to small farmers with 15-year amortizing terms and 2 percent interest.

Americans in the commissions, however, saw a fundamental contradiction between French claims to be supporting a system of self-help and the centralized, monopoly-secured French organization of mortgage banks. While the French presented their system as a bottom-up democratic credit system, a later report from delegates Metcalf and Blank boldly concluded that "France ignores the doctrine of self-help."[49] Indeed, they went so far as to cite English banking expert Henry Wolff: "France would not be France if the state had not put its own gilded finger into the pie, lavishing subventions." Metcalf and Blank noted that while they had previously seen Germany as the more paternalistic state, the tour had convinced them that France was the truly paternalistic regime.[50] In their view, while the Prussian government had managed a quasi-governmental, closely regulated system of farm mortgages for 150 years, it was not behaving paternalistically, because the system did not involve large federal expenditures or monopolies.[51] In other words, federal action that worked through a hybrid public–private structure with low fiscal outlays was preferable.

While the American commissions' report proposed a new, federally organized system of lending through farmers' cooperatives, not all of the delegates agreed that cooperative lending institutions were the best solution. A minority report argued that cooperatives would not work in the United States for cultural reasons, since restless, stubbornly independent, and ambitious American farmers would not tolerate the communal obligations and conservative approach a Landschaft-type system demanded. Cooperatives worked in Europe, these dissenters argued, because European farmers were simpler and less ambitious, uneducated and narrow-minded "plodder[s]" content to tend family lands. Because these European farmers stayed in their communities and avoided speculation, their markets were less volatile, and they had strong social similarities and connections to rely upon: "Such organizations [Landschaften] are all of one race, with, naturally, a similarity of ideas, habits, desires, and methods of living."[52] But Americans, according to the report, being prone to move in search of wealth, were less attached to their neighbors and thus less willing to shoulder their burdens absent a close connection. By this logic, it was hubristic to think that a European solution could be so readily adapted to the U.S. context. Better to make smaller adjustments to existing banks and regulations (like state usury laws to lower rates) than to artificially force a cooperative spirit, especially in the field of credit, where booms and busts came at a terrible price for the entire community.

Despite warnings in Germany about the problems that could come from implementing the required regulation in the U.S. context, neither report expressed concerns about whether the federal government had the adequate administrative capacity to oversee such a system. Civil administration reform was by this time already underway, with Progressives fighting to replace patronage appointments with an independent, professionalized civil service.[53] What boded well for the farm credit reformers was that the part of the government best known for its reliability, competence, and independence was the agency closest to the farmers: the United States Department of Agriculture (USDA). Founded during the Civil War and elevated to cabinet status in 1889, the USDA had emerged in the twentieth century as a respected agency with considerable administrative capacity.[54] In his study of American bureaucratic development, Daniel Carpenter has shown that in the 1920s the USDA acted as a legitimate and reliable broker, coordinating among politically active but divided farmers' groups.[55] As the modern federal government took shape, the USDA led the way in its professionalism and scientific expertise. If there was a single office in the federal government best suited to the task of approximating a German system of oversight, the USDA was it.[56]

But delegates on the frontline of adapting the Landschaften to the U.S. context were untroubled by the government's regulatory capacity. The more important question, the one that received far more attention, was whether American culture could sustain the kind of cooperation needed to successfully create mortgage pools.

The Legislative Path to the Federal Farm Loan Act

By 1913 there was broad agreement that the federal government should act to improve the supply of farm credit in a more substantial way than the Federal Reserve Act allowed. Yet even among supporters there was little consensus on what exactly reform should look like. As they jockeyed for control of the legislation, bankers decried the farmers' proposals as paternalist—or worse, socialist. Farmers for their part contended that bankers were once again trying to profit at their expense.

Representatives whose constituents were heavily made up of farmers sought direct government loans early in this process. In January of 1913, Senator Ellsworth Bathrick of Ohio presented a bill that would allow the Treasury to directly lend money to farmers; a year later, he joined with Senator George Norris of Nebraska to propose that the Department of Agriculture issue loans with 4 percent interest directly to farmers.[57] While not all of the nation's farmers supported direct loans, the Grange and the Farmers Union both endorsed Bathrick and Norris's proposal and sent out 60,000 letters supporting their bill.[58]

Bankers, meanwhile, pushed for a system that would place farm mortgages under their control. Claiming that direct loans would undermine the spirit of self-help, Duncan Fletcher—the Florida senator who had led the U.S. and

American Commissions through Europe and authored their official report—introduced a bill for rural credit in August 1913 that would create farmers' lending organizations financed through local banks.[59] This was effectively the proposed legislation he had laid out in the United States Commission report. It was quickly dismissed by farmers as a power grab by the bankers. Fletcher followed up five months later with a bill co-authored by Representative Ralph W. Moss, a Democrat from Indiana. The Moss-Fletcher bill proposed a for-profit banking model financed by tax-exempt mortgage bonds and subject to reliable regulation. While Wilson endorsed it, farmers insisted that banks would not fairly serve farmers' interests, and the legislation stalled.[60]

Never a group to passively watch events unfold, mortgage bankers also organized. In May of 1914, representatives of mortgage houses met in Hotel Astor in New York to form the Farm Mortgage Bankers Association and promote themselves as "a distinct, well recognized profession." After forming special publication and legislation committees, the association immediately set out to provide an alternative to "agitators" who were "concerning themselves chiefly with foreign systems and conditions." Unable to stop farm credit reform from proceeding, the association proposed that the federal government charter and regulate for-profit banks.[61]

In May 1914, as legislation languished and mortgage bankers organized, a joint House and Senate committee, led by Democratic senator Henry Hollis and Democratic representative Robert Bulkley, sought a compromise. The Hollis-Bulkley plan proposed a regional land bank system in which the federal government would initially capitalize 12 banks with $500,000.[62] The plan was popular in Congress but disliked by the American Bankers Association. President Wilson, who sought support from farmers but was loath to appear to have given them special treatment lest he violate a core principle of his New Freedom agenda, objected to the bill, remarking, "It is unwise and unjustifiable to extend the credit of the Government to a single class of the community."[63] With a presidential veto looming, populists from Arkansas and Oklahoma filibustered for two days.[64] The bill managed to pass in the House, but then it lingered unsigned in the White House for two years. It was only when facing the pressures of a presidential election that Wilson, eager to gain the farm vote, revived the legislation. Thus it was the Hollis-Bulkley bill that became the Federal Farm Loan Act, signed into law in July of 1916.

The Credit Compromise: The Farm Loan Act of 1916

The act that passed in 1916 did not find a middle ground between bankers and farmers so much as it simply capitulated to the demands of each: farmers got their lending cooperatives, bankers got their for-profit banks. Each system was granted the right to raise funds by issuing tax-exempt mortgage bonds through banks officially classified as government instrumentalities. The newly created Federal Farm Loan Bureau, headed by the Federal Farm Loan Board, oversaw both systems from Washington, D.C.[65] This was an Americanized version of the German system, offering farm mortgages ranging in value from $100 to $10,000 that would be paid off in 5 to 40 years, with interest capped at 6 percent.[66]

This system of cooperative lending, built to appease farmers, was backed by 12 land banks, each covering a distinct region of the nation. Each land bank lent money to farmers in its region through cooperatives called Farm Loan Associations (FLAs). Every time an FLA secured a loan for one of its farmers, that farmer invested a small amount (5 percent of the loan) in his local association. That association was then required to also invest a small amount (again, 5 percent of the loan) in the land bank. The more the members of a given association borrowed, the larger their investment in that association and, through that, its regional land bank. Unlike the Pfandbriefe, which a Landschaft issued to a farmer, tax-exempt bonds were issued by the land banks directly on capital markets.[67] Since the land banks were not commercial banks and no one could withdraw deposits from them, the issue of short-term and long-term credit mismatch was resolved. Unlike the German system, American farmers would not be asked to take great responsibility for others' debts. Instead, a farmer's liability was limited to double his investment in the FLA. If a farmer owned $10 in FLA shares, his liability was capped at $20. The FFLA authorized the Treasury to capitalize each of the 12 land banks at $750,000, with the capitalization paid down as members of the FLAs purchased shares, a process completed in 1947.

Land banks depended on a vast network of lending cooperatives that did not yet exist. Consequently, the Department of Agriculture and the Federal Farm Loan Board immediately set out to create them. A massive campaign, carried out through the distribution of pamphlets and the placement of testimonials in existing journals and magazines, encouraged farmers to form local FLAs. "This is a very great and important thing," proclaimed a farmer in one of the Farm Loan Board's pamphlets. "It may be the greatest blessing the farming world has ever had bestowed on it since the passage of the homestead act [*sic*]. It gives the farmer control over their own finances if they care to assume it."[68] In addition to these enthusiastic testimonials, pamphlets explained the new system, detailed how to organize a local cooperative, and described how amortization worked.

The FFLA simultaneously authorized charters for private joint-stock banks. Like the land banks, these institutions could raise funds by issuing tax-exempt bonds and were highly regulated: they were permitted to operate in two states only; they were required to issue the same standardized, amortized mortgages with interest capped at 6 percent used by the land banks; and the Farm Loan Bureau had the power to grant or refuse their bond issuances.[69] Although these were investment banks and thus not allowed to take deposits, some were set up by other commercial banks.[70] In the first years following the passage of the FFLA, some surmised that the joint-stock banks—considered more efficient, market-based solutions that did not try to force cooperation among farmers— would ultimately prevail over the land banks.[71]

This extension of federal power, like many other such extensions, was adjudicated by the courts.[72] Despite assurances from the Farm Loan Board that mortgage brokers were welcome to set up joint-stock banks, most saw the system as an unwelcome and unfairly advantaged encroachment on their business.[73] In 1920, a mortgage broker named Charles W. Smith saw a chance to challenge the constitutionality of the new system. When Smith's own trust company, Kansas City Title & Trust, invested in FFLA bonds, Smith sued, arguing that the tax-exempt bonds were unconstitutional, and that therefore the trust company had violated Missouri banking regulations when it purchased them. As a result, the Treasury halted the sale of FFLA bonds, and the growth of the loan system stalled.[74] In 1921, the Supreme Court upheld the legality of the tax exemption on the grounds that the Federal Farm Loan Act had qualified the land banks as federal depositories. Even though they were never used as such, the designation alone was enough to qualify them as a legal agent of the federal government and therefore subject to tax exemptions.[75]

Both the court case and the onset of World War I slowed the development of the land and joint-stock banks. The land banks opened in March of 1917; the tax-exempt mortgage bonds they issued were designed to lure investors struggling to sell in a market that was now flooded with Liberty Bonds.[76] As a result, the FFLA was amended in January 1918 to allow the Treasury to purchase the bonds. By July 1919, the Treasury held nearly $136 million in mortgage bonds—about half of its total issuance at the time.[77] The constitutional challenge was an additional hurdle. In February of 1920, the Farm Loan Board suspended new applications, and for the second half of 1920, the bond sales stopped completely while the Treasury waited for a ruling on the constitutionality of the tax exemption.

By the end of 1920, the land banks had lent out nearly $350 million in mortgages, and the joint-stock land banks had issued $77 million.[78] At the end of 1922, the first full year of lending after the war and the constitutional challenge, the land banks were offering farm mortgages at a national average of 5.7 percent interest, and joint-stock banks at an average of 6 percent, their maximum allowable rate. In contrast, insurance companies offered farm loans at an average of 6.3 percent interest, and commercial banks at 7.3 percent.[79] By 1923, there were 70 joint-stock banks operating throughout the nation, and together they had issued $190 million in loans that year; in the four states where they were most active—Iowa, Ohio, Indiana, and Illinois—they financed a third of the market.[80] By 1927, the land banks held almost a fifth of the nation's farm debt, and by the end of 1929, 4,662 Farm Loan Associations had been formed.[81]

Despite this growth, by the late 1920s both systems were showing signs of distress. The Land Bank of Spokane failed in 1924, followed by two joint-stock banks in 1927. In 1932, when Depression era investors were unwilling to purchase mortgage bonds, the Treasury injected $125 million worth of stock into the land banks, followed by additional relief funds for land and joint-stock banks through the Reconstruction Finance Corporation. In the midst of the New Deal, with federal power more securely established, the Farm Loan Acts of 1933 only saved the land banks. The joint-stock banks were liquidated.[82]

The Political Economy of the Federal Farm Loan Act

The FFLA, with its cooperative credit structure, obviously owed much to the agrarian populism of the late nineteenth century. Nevertheless, the bankers, academics, and middle-class Progressive reformers who helped design it stripped the most radical features of populism from that collective structure. Gone was the direct responsibility for a neighbor's debt that existed in the exchanges and in some European systems. Under the FFLA, farmers formed cooperatives, but each borrower was liable only for double his own share of the land bank, and votes were based not on membership but on shares held. Like the subtreasury, the farm loan system reserved a place for the federal government in credit distribution, but in a very different way than had been envisioned by Macune in the heyday of the subtreasury fight. Farmers wrested some control over their credit supply from the bankers and the government, but not the issuance of currency itself, as populists had once demanded.

Thus the FFLA was emblematic of a typical Progressive Era compromise: the federal government could provide much-needed economic stability as long as it openly deferred to the private market. This logic is reflected in the structure of the FFLA. The inclusion of the joint-stock banks signaled that government was not displacing private enterprise; the government's investment would be repaid, which limited its lasting role to that of a regulator. In form it looked similar to the Federal Reserve Act of 1913, wherein the government supported and mediated disputes among the commercial banks. In the late nineteenth century, writes Frank Dobbin, "the idea that economic life should be organized by subnational governments seeking to promote regional economic development in collaboration with business interests gave way to the idea that the economy should operate as a free market under a state that established the ground rules for competition."[83] The proper role of the government, by this logic, was to serve as a referee that enforced rules but did not otherwise interfere with the market, if possible.[84]

Yet this "hands-off" approach was always more aspirational than accurate. As Dobbin has noted, there have been many instances when Americans have called on the state to curtail the accumulation of concentrated power.[85] Many scholars have shown that the policies of federal and state governments have always been integral to the development of the American economy, from the provision of funds to private enterprise (as we saw with the railroads) to an array of policies and court rulings that have set property rights to advantage large corporations.[86] In the early twentieth century, the national government was expanding to check the power of the industrial giants it had earlier helped to create.

These same contradictions of American statecraft in this more modern American political economy are written into the structure of the FFLA. The government used a complex framework to claim a hands-off approach even as it built a system of credit distribution from scratch. One academic observer at the time noted that "in spirit the Act was revolutionary—its authors were convinced that American methods were not worth saving; and the machinery for which it provided was greatly complicated by the fact that it did not represent the ideas of any single group of reformers."[87] For all that the 12-bank structure mimicked that established by the Federal Reserve Act, the creation of lending cooperatives meant that the FFLA was a far more complicated, experimental, and entrepreneurial design. Thus, at the very moment that the federal government accumulated new powers, it exercised those powers through an ingenious array of policy tools—credit, expenditures, and partnerships—that dispersed authority.

In *The Rise of the Public Authority: State Building and Economic Development in Twentieth Century America*, Gail Radford argues that the FFLA was part of an ongoing process of establishing hybrid, mixed-enterprise organizations as viable political forms in the United States.[88] As such, the FFLA can be seen as an extension of the same trend that placed regulatory responsibility in the hands of public authorities (like port authorities) that acted as quasi-governmental bodies to manage transportation and commissions (like the Interstate Commerce Commission). In doing so, the federal government drew from precedents set by states and municipalities, which struggled in the absence of a reservoir of funds generated by property taxes to develop low-cost techniques of governance. Tax expenditures are popular for similar reasons. Christopher Howard argues that tax write-offs and exclusions are attractive because they allow government officials a great deal of leeway to effect change without having to raise taxes.[89]

What mixed-enterprise partnerships and tax expenditures have in common with credit provision are low costs and classificatory ambiguity that skilled actors can leverage for political gain. The fiscal advantages are perhaps the most obvious draw of these programs. By sharing the costs of capitalization with private companies, the federal government saves funds, effectively borrowing the existing capacity of the private sector. Tax expenditures cost the government a great deal in lost income over time but generally have the benefit of inducing desired behaviors (like home buying) without generating a backlash for raising taxes. Credit programs involve large outlays but generate income over time. And when all of these features are combined, the usefulness of each is magnified. When run through mixed-enterprise corporations, credit programs can raise funds outside of the normal appropriations process, with tax exemptions helping ensure their success. This process did not work perfectly with the FFLA, but it worked well enough to be repeated and fine-tuned.

The political usefulness of these three organizational forms—credit, partnerships, and tax expenditures—resides not just in their low costs, but in their capacity to invite multiple interpretations. A paper written with my colleague Damon Mayrl discusses how this works.[90] People place things into categories as a first step toward analysis, evaluation, and meaning making.[91] There are social rules for classification, and scholars have outlined an array of penalties people face if they violate these rules. For example, stock analysts give lower and less consistent ratings to unfamiliar kinds of businesses, and audiences may dislike films that span multiple genres.[92] Foundational categories like race and gender can give rise to extensive, sometimes violent forms of social control and policing. But a growing sociological literature reveals that in some contexts, spanning or violating categories leads to gains.[93] Russell Funk and Dan Hirschman show that financial entrepreneurs use ambiguity to avoid regulation.[94] Wendy Griswold shows that books that have ambiguous meanings may have more cultural power and attract more attention.[95] John Padgett and Christopher Ansell show that savvy actors like the Medici family used ambiguity to gain political power, calling the hard-to-read strategies the Medicis deployed a form of "robust action" because of the considerable strategic advantage they afforded.[96]

Theories of classification allow us to see that public authorities, tax exemptions, and selective credit programs are useful organizational forms in part because they court ambiguity by troubling typical patterns of classification. Hybrid entities give political actors the ability to draw simultaneously from private capacities and from special government privileges like tax exemptions. Indeed, this was the basis on which the FFLA was challenged: it was improper, opponents argued, to officially classify the land and joint-stock banks as government instrumentalities. By being both public and private in nature, partnerships allow government officials to claim simultaneously that they are addressing a problem and that they are not displacing private efforts. But this classificatory advantage is context-specific. Thirty years earlier, before the subtreasury experience led farmers to abandon the more strident forms of Jacksonian anti-statism, such efforts would have been more likely to have been met with a strong effort to police the boundary between state and market.

We can see here how credit's classificatory properties gave it a useful political lightness in the context of twentieth-century politics. Direct loans bring in revenue, and promises of future obligation do not show up as large expenditures on government accounts. Requiring few personnel, these policies also have low administrative costs. Furthermore, once it was reframed by progressives, credit emerged in the early nineteenth century as ideologically light: it could be framed either as a government action supporting self-help or as a mere market correction. In a nation increasingly aware of the need for national coordination, where a group of people remained dedicated to the tenets of laissez-faire but the political process demanded political compromise, such flexible policy tools would prove remarkably useful and popular.

A New Path for Credit Policy

Before the FFLA, federal lending programs were Band-Aids designed to solve narrow problems on a short-term basis. After the federal attempt to offer credit for the sale of government lands ended disastrously in 1820, the federal government limited its credit support to corporations working on expensive projects that generally benefited the public: capital-intensive entities like road, canal, railway, waterway, irrigation, and steamboat companies. The projects funded by the loans the government issued (like dams and irrigation systems, railroads and canals) might last, but the system of financing that made them possible eventually expired.

The farm loan system was federal credit support of an entirely new scale and scope. With the FFLA, the system of ongoing credit distribution for a specific group was itself the target of the policy. This was precedent-setting. The land bank system was copied as early as 1923 with the Federal Intermediate Credit Banks, a system of 12 regional banks that provided shorter-term (six-month to three-year) loans to farmers.[97] The Federal Home Loan Bank, created in 1932, also followed this model, both in its use of a hybrid banking structure and in its support of longer-term amortized loans. Finally, the model was replicated in New Deal housing finance policies and became one of the most important legacies of the federal credit policies.[98] The use of credit as a political tool then took on new forms as public–private partnerships and tax expenditures expanded as major tools of governance in their own right.

The FFLA was passed before the American farming market fell off a precipice. During the First World War, American farmers would grow rich selling crops to European nations whose own farms had been decimated by the fighting. When European farming recovered after the war, American farmers failed to scale back their production, once again glutting the market.[99] The decline in U.S. agriculture was sudden and devastating. Farm income dropped by half and land values by a fifth in 1920 and 1921.[100] Prices stabilized but did not recover before the Depression and the Dust Bowl caused even greater distress. When these later troubles arose, however, the federal government now had an arsenal of credit tools to deploy in response.

5

From a Nation of Farmers
to a Nation of Homeowners

In 1880 only one-quarter of Americans were city dwellers, but an urban transition was well underway. In the following decade, the western frontier was officially declared settled, and over one-third of Americans lived in or around cities. By 1920, half of the population lived in cities or suburbs, as figure 5.1 shows. (Today, over three-quarters of Americans do.) As industry and manufacturing drew Americans into cities, selling land became more profitable than tilling it for farmers living near growing urban centers.[1] Speculators set to work converting the farms into suburbs. Between 1880 and 1900, housing construction in and around cities exploded: in Denver, for instance, housing stock grew by 413 percent.[2]

When the nation's economy shifted away from agriculture, its housing and financial needs shifted with it. Urban mortgage credit works differently than rural credit. Cities are free from some of the worst commercial risks of farming, such as the dangers of pestilence and drought. Cities also lower information costs for lenders: population density and geographic access make it easier for creditors to know and monitor borrowers. Over the nineteenth century, cooperative savings societies grew and spread in the nation's cities.

The group of cooperative lenders known as thrifts—a category that included the building and loans, savings and loans, and mutuals—sold not only mortgages, but also a vision of a better life achieved through savings and homeownership. For these lenders, homeownership was a means to cultivate a nation of disciplined, honorable, civic-minded men. This vision was built into the deep logic of their lending structures, which brought into being a

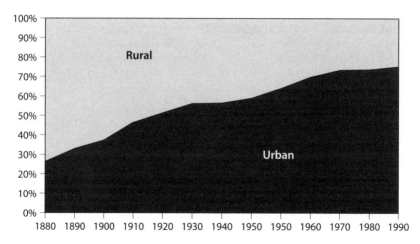

FIGURE 5.1. Proportion of Americans Living in Urban Areas
Source: "Table Aa716–775: Population, by Race, Sex, and Urban-Rural Residence: 1880–1990," *Historical Statistics of the United States.*

small local community of equals working together to lift themselves up. Lending cooperatives developed in the nation's towns and cities over much of the nineteenth century. When a group of "national thrifts" started selling mortgages for profit across state lines in the 1880s and 1890s, the more local and community-minded organizations rejected the challengers as violating the true cooperative spirit of the thrift movement and organized the United States Building and Loan League (USBLL) in response to the threat. The USBLL's first actions were to denounce the nationals and call for state-level regulation to protect their local markets.

On the national level, direct federal government support for urban mortgage credit was delayed until the First World War, when a set of housing crises led to national experiments in the building and financing of urban homes. These programs were temporary, but they helped change how many Americans thought about housing policy, introducing the idea that such policy was an integral part of economic growth and a potentially appropriate site of federal involvement, especially when organized through partnerships and credit support.

Political scientist Paul Pierson has noted that institutions persist in part because complementary institutions reinforce them.[3] As with a rope, the intertwined nature of the various strands of political and economic life of a nation make the sum of those parts stronger. Over the twentieth century, residential housing finance became an important strand of the U.S. political economy, not just by moving credit, but also by helping to link homeownership with people's deepest sense of what it meant to be a successful American.

What Makes a Man Independent?

Over the nineteenth century, homeownership replaced yeoman farming in the American imagination as a kind of idealized experience that many aspired to have. To understand what an accomplishment homeownership was perceived to be, it is necessary to consider the nineteenth-century worldview.

Early Americans valued property ownership for specific political reasons. "Dependence begets subservience and venality, suffocates the germ of virtue and prepares fit tools for the designs of ambition," Thomas Jefferson wrote.[4] In the longstanding American republican ideal, with its roots in the Jeffersonian tradition, working for someone else made a man reliant on another person for his well-being. This dependency was thought to compromise freedom of action and thought, and even the autonomy of a man's actual vote.[5] In contrast, a man who owned property—as a farmer, craftsman, or small businessman—governed himself. This freed him to contemplate and follow his ideals.

In this republican worldview, the very act of acquiring and maintaining property was thought to instill in the owner the civic virtues of reliability, integrity, self-restraint, and strong character.[6] Self-governance was the bedrock of the nation, and property ownership made self-governance possible. It was only after 1815 that tenants started gaining the right to vote in most states. In South Carolina, men without property were disenfranchised until the Civil War.[7] This social stigmatization and political marginalization of renters persists. Ananya Roy has argued that the United States is still defined by a "paradigm of propertied citizenship," illustrated, for example, by the way that homeless people are denied access to public spaces afforded to others.[8]

The rise of manufacturing presented no small challenge to this way of thinking. Factories and industry produced wage labor as surely as they produced commodities. Self-employment dropped from 67 percent of the population in 1870 to 37 percent of the population by 1920.[9] Viewed through the lens of the republican tradition, with its Lockean belief that property ownership promotes political investment and stability, the transition from agriculture to manufacturing was potentially a dangerous transition into dependency.

Homeownership offered a solution to this looming problem. The ideal of self-governance at work could be reconstituted as that of self-governance at home. After all, could not all the gains associated with independent work also be realized through a kind of domestic dominion?[10] Purchasing a home required frugality, hard work, and reliability. Owning a home, like owning a business, instilled in men a neighborly obligation and sense of pride. All of this created better *citizens*: "A man who has earned, saved, and paid for a home will be a better man, a better artisan or clerk, a better husband and father, and a better citizen of the republic."[11] Civic virtue was thus grafted onto the act of owning a home, with the promise of rescuing masculine independence. The detached home itself stood as a physical representation of this independence, the manicured lawn signaling an appreciation for and mastery over nature.[12]

Homeownership did not just instill civic virtues; it also promised to have a pacifying effect on labor. Since the 1830s, housing reformers had warned that tenements were breeding grounds for disease and leftist politics alike.[13] Reformer Lawrence Veiller argued that moving workers from tenements to single-family homes had pacifying potential.[14] As Americans worried about the destabilizing ramifications of showdowns such as the Pullman strike, some argued that raising wages would mollify workers by enabling them to obtain better housing, although most housing reformers were interested in better living standards for the poor, not homeownership per se.[15] The old saw that property ownership encouraged a more conservative citizenry was not lost on reformers of all stripes: "It is an advantage to a mill-town employer to have property-owning employees," wrote one author. "The labor force is more stable and there is less likelihood of a strike, the employees not wishing to jeopardize their positions after a house has been acquired, lest they have to move."[16] For immigrants, owning a home would promote assimilation, or "Americanization." A working homeowner was thought to be a small capitalist, and so less likely to riot or strike.[17]

Homeownership and suburbanization are distinct trends. Many Americans owned homes outside of the suburbs, and not all suburban families were homeowners. However, the rise of residential homeownership in the United States coincided with the rise of suburbanization, and this timing linked the trends in the American experience and imagination. The nation's earliest suburbs were bastions of economic elites, but by the 1860s suburban homes were being marketed to middle-class families of more modest means. Smaller lots close to rail lines allowed professionals to commute to the city.[18] While early suburbs are commonly imagined as a white space, historians have shown that a diverse group of Americans played a role in suburban development. In western cities like Los Angeles, working-class families settled in the spaces between suburb and city.[19] And in the 1910s and 1920s, one in six African Americans moving north as part of the Great Migration settled in the suburbs. A fifth of the black U.S. population lived in the suburbs before the 1940s.[20]

Unlike the farm, where families labored side by side, Americans increasingly came to see home life as fundamentally distinct from men's work. Large cities and large machines had made the new middle class possible. Suburbs now offered an escape from both.[21] Suburban homes were places where middle-class women and children could be protected from the dangers of the larger economic and social world, a great improvement on apartment life.[22] Advocating federal programs that supported single-family detached homes surrounded by a yard (an English garden–style home popular among reformers), Edith Elmer Wood observed that "in the smaller cities, the only excuse for apartments is for celibates, childless couples, and elderly people whose children have grown up and scattered."[23] Catherine Beecher, one of the first designers and open proponents of the American suburban home, saw better-designed homes as an opportunity to bolster a "model family commonwealth."[24] Similarly, the slogan "As Is the Home So the Community and the Nation"[25] cast the suburban home as a microcosm of the civic virtue of the whole.

The ideal was not simply to live in a detached single-family home with a yard, but to own it. Walt Whitman proclaimed that "a man is not a whole and complete man unless he owns a house and the ground it stands on."[26] From the late nineteenth through the early twentieth century, residential home-ownership in the United States climbed. In 1890 only slightly over one-third of nonfarm households were owner-occupied, as compared to a full two-thirds of farming households.[27] This gap had shrunk considerably by 1930: home-ownership for farmers had dropped to 54 percent, and urban homeownership had risen to 46 percent. Yet even those numbers fail to capture the extent to which Americans, including city dwellers, were able to achieve the goal of being a homeowner. Economic historian Richard Sutch notes that if you set aside younger households still saving up their down payments and focus just on households headed by people over the age of 60, some 83 percent of farm households and 58 percent of nonfarm households were owner-occupied even in 1890.[28] Approximately 28 percent of these farm and nonfarm homes were mortgaged in the 1890s, but these numbers too shift by age group. Sutch esti-mates that 30 to 36 percent of homes owned by people in their 30s and 40s in 1890 were mortgaged, whereas fewer than one in five homes owned by people aged 60 and older were still carrying that debt.[29]

HOW DID THESE NEW METROPOLITAN AMERICANS BUY THEIR HOMES?

In the early twentieth century, buying a home in a city was not cheap. For all that the nation's farmers complained that they paid more for mortgages in the eighteenth century, the land they purchased was far less expensive than city property. By the turn of the twentieth century, the costs of wood and other materials were rising. While consumer prices rose by 20 percent between 1895 and 1914, building costs increased by 50 percent.[30] Housing reformers had succeeded in advocating new construction codes, but this too drove up building costs.[31] City dwellers in the United States had relatively high wages, and in suburbs where land was cheaper (like the greater Los Angeles area in the early twentieth century), some people saved and economized to build their own homes—especially working-class migrants out of the South who carried with them a deep suspicion of debt.[32] Nevertheless, many Americans still needed or chose to borrow to purchase their homes.

TABLE 5.1. Holders of Residential Mortgage Debt, 1896–1930

Year	Total Debt (Millions)	Non-institutional	Commercial Banks	Mutuals	S&Ls	Life Insurance	Other
1896	$2,711	50%	5%	20%	16%	6%	3%
1900	$2,917	51%	5%	22%	13%	6%	3%
1905	$3,520	45%	8%	23%	13%	7%	3%
1910	$4,426	37%	10%	25%	16%	9%	3%
1915	$6,012	37%	9%	24%	18%	9%	3%
1920	$9,120	42%	9%	20%	20%	6%	3%
1925	$17,231	38%	11%	18%	23%	8%	3%
1930	$27,649	38%	10%	16%	22%	10%	3%

Source: Kenneth Snowden, "Table Dc903-928: Debt on Nonfarm Structures, by Type of Debt, Property, and Holder: 1896-1952," *Historical Statistics of the United States*. Numbers refer to nonfarm debt held outside of mortgage bonds.

Where did those mortgages come from? Americans living in cities in the nineteenth and early twentieth centuries still relied extensively on informal lending. As table 5.1 shows, as late as 1930, non-institutional investors held nearly 40 percent of residential mortgages. At a time when stock market investing was mainly the domain of elites and mortgages were shorter-term investments, housing markets attracted the funds of small savers.[33] Table 5.1 also reveals the limited role of bankers in the residential mortgage market: between 1900 and 1930, commercial banks doubled their share of residential mortgage debt, but only from 5 to 10 percent.

Life insurance companies invested in more mortgages as they grew. In the early twentieth century these companies kept highly diversified portfolios and were more likely to invest in railroad and government bonds.[34] When they did invest in mortgages, insurance companies skewed heavily toward larger commercial buildings.[35] The real story of nineteenth-century urban mortgage markets, then, is the rise of lending cooperatives.

COOPERATIVE LENDERS

Mutual savings banks were formed in the United States starting in the early 1800s as a way to support smaller, poorer savers whose regular incomes allowed them to accumulate some savings but who lacked access to banks.[36] The earliest mutuals focused on savings in case of injury and loss and so largely ignored housing in favor of assets such as government bonds.[37] Over time, however, the mutuals became involved in the housing market, and by the end of the nineteenth century, one-third of their holdings were in mortgages. By 1893 the mutuals held approximately one-fifth of the nation's urban mortgage debt.

Their share of this debt started to decline in the 1920s, because they remained concentrated in the North and East while construction shifted westward.[38]

The same conditions that led to the rise of the mutual lending societies also spurred the creation of building and loan societies, precursors of the savings and loans that would dominate midcentury mortgage lending.[39] Homeownership was the core of the building and loans' mission. The first one, founded in 1831 and modeled after the English building societies, was the Oxford Provident Building Association. Its activities started with a loan of $375 to Comly Rich to buy a small two-story home, one that still stands in Philadelphia at 4276 Orchard Street.[40] A second building society was founded in 1836 in Brooklyn. From the 1830s to the 1880s, these societies spread throughout larger cities in the Northeast and Midwest.[41] A survey in 1893 found that there were 5,600 building societies in operation.[42] By 1900, building societies had somewhere between 1.4 and 1.75 million members and held over half a billion dollars in assets.[43]

The mutuals, buildings and loans, and S&Ls together were called the thrifts. By the start of the Great Depression, they represented approximately 40 percent of the American residential mortgage market. While demographic shifts caused the mutuals' market share to decline, the building and loans offset this loss, providing an important financing mechanism for urban and suburban expansion. They often offered better terms than other lending institutions: using amortization allowed the thrifts to issue mortgages with an average term length of 8 years in 1900, a number that had increased to 12 years by 1930.[44] Much of the growth of this industry had occurred outside the purview of any regulation.[45] It was only in the 1880s that states began overseeing the market. By the turn of the century, 40 states had some regulation of residential mortgages on the books, but this mostly consisted of basic reporting rules.[46]

Organized on the community level, thrifts were adapted by America's diverse communities. In his famous study of Philadelphia, W.E.B. Du Bois discusses three building and loans formed in the 1880s that were headed by black teachers, merchants, small business owners, and craftsmen. Two were connected to black churches.[47] Philadelphia was also home to ethnic thrifts like the Amerikanischer Darlehen und Bau-Verein, which did business in their members' native languages and offered immigrants a way to "Americanize" by purchasing homes.[48]

Women were active in the thrift movement. For all the cultural valorization of the male breadwinner, women's role as manager of the household budget—and as the moral center of the home—fit well with the mission of the thrifts.[49] A widow named Maria Catherine Barnes seems to have participated in the nation's first mutual society, although she was subscribed through a male trustee.[50] By 1841, thrifts had started to allow women to join without an intermediary. A government survey in 1893 found that a quarter of thrift members were female, and that nearly all thrifts had some female members.[51] Some women even assumed leadership positions in these organizations; in the 1920s the United States Building and Loan League bragged that building and loans had more female leaders than any other financial industry. In Hawaii, Maria K. Naopala served on the governing board of the islands' oldest building and loan.[52] In New York, Scottish immigrant Ann E. Rae started as a clerk in the Niagara Permanent Savings & Loan Association, became its president in 1917, and went on to lead the New York League and the national U.S. Building and Loan League. When she retired in 1930, the company had $16 million in assets.[53] In Cleveland, Clara and Lillian Westropp formed the Women's Savings & Loan Company, which by 1950 had grown to be the second-largest mortgage lender in Cuyahoga County.[54]

Thrifts were small and local. The average one in 1890 had less than $90,000 in assets and fewer than 200 members.[55] As such, these organizations were able to conduct important checks on risk, including considerations such as character as a point of evaluation in a loan approval process.[56] Managerial roles were filled by local volunteers, many of whom had interests in the housing industry, either through construction or through supporting industries such as building supply. Historian Kenneth Snowden has pointed out that such connections positioned managers as smart evaluators of local market risks and created an incentive for good management, since these individuals had an interest in protecting their local reputations. The flip side of this interest, Snowden notes, is that the thrifts were also limited to the local markets in which their managers operated. This localism would have consequences for the economic development of the nation. Snowden estimates that areas outside of the Northeast and Midwest had higher financing costs due to this market segmentation, with borrowers in the periphery paying anywhere from 12 to 20 percent higher financing costs, depending on how far west they were.[57]

As the thrifts developed, they organized not only as community members but also as an industry. In 1893, the S&Ls created the United States Buildings and Loan League as a trade group to represent their interests, actively pursuing the regulation of thrifts. In 1908 a group of realtors and developers gathered at a Chicago YMCA to form the National Association of Real Estate Boards.[58] These groups were joined by the Mortgage Bankers Association in 1913, the National Federation of Construction Industries in 1918, and the National Association of Mutual Savings Banks in 1920.[59]

MORAL LENDING

Members of thrifts saw themselves not as bankers, but as participants in a social movement that offered an alternative to more powerful and potentially exploitative financial systems. The thrifts used economic relations not simply to manage market risks but to forge stronger social connections and nurture better citizens. In pamphlets and advertisements, speeches and newsletters, the thrifts spread the gospel of better communities through saving. At the first annual convention of the USBLL, the organization formally adopted the slogan "The American Home, the Safeguard of American Liberties."[60] When leaders in the field wrote histories of the industry in the 1930s, they positioned their work as part of a legacy of building societies that stretched back to England and ran through the rise of German cooperatives, the emergence of colonial fire insurance cooperatives, and even the creation of the Knights of Labor and the Farmers' Alliance.[61]

These values were built into the very design of the thrifts, as organizational scholars Haveman and Rao have shown.[62] Early thrifts were savings clubs. Members were shareholders who joined at the moment of founding and pledged regular payments in exchange for the ability to borrow from the group, which dissolved when its goals were met. Early thrifts used terminating plans that closely bound their members. Unlike depositors who could invest and leave at will, members were in the club for its duration, were punished with fees if they wanted to exit, and faced fines or the threat of removal if they were delinquent with their payments. Leadership was democratic and management informal: members elected trustees, and everyday duties were carried out on a volunteer basis. This structure linked neighbors together in a community of economic fate. Everyone borrowed, everyone lent.

The all-in-and-all-out design of the terminating plan had its limitations. New members could technically join after the group was established, but to do so they had to make an investment large enough to cover their share of the value already accrued in the organization. Once in, existing members did not have the option of refusing a loan when their turn came, regardless of how their situation might have changed. Borrowing was compulsory, and the only way to delay doing so was to find another member to take the loan instead.[63] Given these downsides, it is not surprising that people continued to experiment with other organizational structures. Serial plans allowed new members to join with smaller payments on a continuing basis; this unlinked the economic fates of the members but allowed the group to endure after the initial goals were met. The serial plans remained strict, however. Morton Bodfish observes that they resembled a series of linked terminating plans more than a real departure from what had preceded them. In 1893, the serial plans dominated the building and loans industry, making up nearly 60 percent of all such concerns.[64]

As the nation moved through the Progressive Era, the organization of the thrifts again shifted to meet the investment desires of better-off families.[65] The serial plans were joined by an even more flexible set of permanent plans, which introduced passbooks to track individual investments and, in a popular

Dayton plan, used amortization. By the 1930s a version of this Dayton plan, one that issued guaranteed stock, dominated the field. These plans minimized long-term commitments and enforcement: investors could more easily enter and exit the group and save at their preferred rate rather than according to the group's schedule. Formal equality was replaced with new hierarchies. Instead of all members being borrowers and savers, distinctions were introduced between classes of investors: notably, members with guaranteed stock had higher returns, although they could not easily withdraw funds. Control was centralized and formalized as paid managers replaced volunteers.[66]

Reflecting on these changes, Haveman and Rao note that over time the thrifts came to assume a more individualistic and bureaucratic form. Oriented toward profit and efficiency, the Dayton and guaranteed plans were better suited to a more mobile population with unreliable incomes. Yet despite all these changes, these more modern thrifts did not jettison a sense of morality so much as shift it, focusing on core Progressive values of efficiency and scientific management that were layered atop the existing belief in the benefits of thrift and localism.[67] These changes indicate how the thrifts adapted to meet an array of financial needs, from a worker's desire to build savings, to an immigrant's desire to assimilate through homeownership, to the desire of upper-middle-class families to invest their savings.[68]

Through all of these changes, the thrifts maintained a core identity as local, nonprofit, community-minded organizations, an identity that they defended when they believed it was threatened by the emergence of the national thrifts.

THE NATIONALS

The nationals were a group of for-profit building and loans that experimented with nationwide lending, growing quickly in the mid-1800s and failing within two decades. The first of them, the National Building and Loan Protective Union, opened in the mid-1800s in Minnesota.[69] Others soon followed. With head offices in midwestern cities linked to branches and agents fanned out around the nation, the nationals promoted themselves by advertising how their diverse investments and economies of scale resulted in higher returns.[70]

Despite the national thrifts' self-identification, members of local thrifts did not embrace them as part of their community, seeing them as perversions of the cooperative spirit at best and as out-and-out frauds at worst. Vocal critics objected to the very idea that the nationals could even be considered thrifts: they were not local, they were for-profit, and they used brokers. Even worse was their financial structure. Members paid into both a loan fund and a separate expense fund from which managers were paid. Other building and loans dedicated, on average, 1 to 2 percent of their revenue to operating expenses. For the nationals, the amount was 6 to 11 percent.[71] It all was seen as a violation of the spirit of cooperation that had made the thrifts famous. Judge Seymour Dexter, co-founder and first president of the USBLL, railed against them:

> While these associations have assumed the name of the true building and loan association, they are no more entitled to use it as descriptive of their business than a western farm mortgage and trust company or an investment and loan company. The name assumed is a misnomer except the word "national." . . . [T]hey have, as a rule, eliminated from their scheme the modes and principles by which the success of the building and loan association has been secured.[72]

The nationals, in other words, were corporate entities dressed up as cooperatives. They were wolves in sheep's clothing.

In size and market share, the nationals never came close to the success of the local thrifts. Between 1887 and 1897, when building and loans' assets totaled approximately $1 billion, the nationals collected $250 million and loaned $150 million.[73] Even the nationals that were not fraudulent or poorly structured suffered from principal agent problems: field officers had little incentive to protect the interests of the home office. Furthermore, unlike managers of regular thrifts, who had an interest in protecting their own local reputation, managers of the nationals were under no such pressure to ensure the long-term viability of mortgages issued in faraway places.

Many nationals were under strain even before the downturn of 1893. As the market tightened, agents for the nationals scrounged for second-rate mortgages while local lenders beat them to the best local loans.[74] The death knell of the industry came in 1897 with the failure of one of the nation's largest nationals, the Southern Building and Loan Association of Knoxville.[75] More than half of the nationals had failed by 1898, and the half dozen that survived through the turn of the century had collapsed by 1910.[76]

While nationals themselves did not last, the organizational and regulatory response to them did. It was the effort to distance the local thrifts from the nationals that spurred the creation in 1893 of the USBLL, which passed four resolutions against the nationals at its first meeting. This group became a launch pad for larger national mobilization, as locals turned to state regulators in an effort to distinguish their business practices and protect their markets. Ohio, New York, Illinois, and Missouri passed legislation that effectively excluded the nationals from those states. Other states, including Iowa, passed legislation that enacted state supervision of thrifts, requiring reviews of accounts and in some cases laws governing which fees were legal.

In the early twentieth century, the federal government upheld its hands-off stance toward residential mortgage finance, even as it took steps to deal with the more troubled farm credit sector (see chapter 4). A small number of Americans during this time called for a system of government support for housing credit, but such efforts gained little traction.[77] It would take the seismic shift of the First World War to change this status quo.

The Wartime Housing Crisis and Credit Support

War requires equipment—ships and tanks, ammunition and explosives. Equipment requires workers. And workers require shelter and transportation. During World War I, this chain of demands became the grounds for a set of wartime experiments with government home building and residential mortgage lending.

Sociologically, the timing of these early federal housing programs is unsurprising. Governments grow during wartime.[78] Wars build states because wars demand administrative capacity, expertise, and infrastructure. The Civil War resulted in a new banking system, an income tax, and more expansive railroads in the West.[79] Now the First World War established additional domains of state authority. In the arena of credit allocation, this took the form of the creation of the War Finance Corporation in 1918. Capitalized with $500 million and authorized to raise another $3 billion in bond issues, the corporation provided loans and support for essential needs, like the conversion of industries to war-related production. While it would later be used as a justification for the establishment of the much larger Reconstruction Finance Corporation, in and of itself the War Finance Corporation was not particularly large. Some of the most important legacies of wartime credit innovation would occur under the supervision of its counterpart, the Emergency Fleet Corporation, whose officials, facing a labor shortage, were forced to take on a worsening housing shortage.[80]

A housing crisis was at hand even before the United States entered the war. Manufacturing expanded rapidly as Americans moved to supply materiel to the Allies, but towns around production plants and shipyards were unable to meet the demand for housing.[81] In Seattle, a single shipyard existed before 1914. Within three years four new steel yards, a dozen wooden steamship yards, and a new shipbuilding plant had opened.[82] The population of Penns Grove, New Jersey, swelled from 2,000 to over 15,000 as workers arrived to work at the DuPont powder factory.[83] The number of U.S. manufacturing workers, which had stood at 8.2 million in 1915, had increased by 25 percent within three years.[84]

The same expansion of manufacturing that drove up demand for homes also drew funds away from residential construction. New homebuilding shrank by nearly half in 1917 and again the following year when the government implemented wartime limits on household construction.[85] As workers poured into new areas, they crammed into existing housing stock. The result was that workers' actual living conditions worsened even while their housing costs increased. Rent control laws, put in place to prevent profiteering and to protect soldiers' families from eviction, provided only partial relief. As Americans struggled to find suitable homes, industries complained that they could not keep workers that they could not house.[86]

Homebuilders across the nation mobilized to encourage families to continue to buy homes and promoted homeownership as a patriotic act. A successful "Buy a Home" campaign in Rochester, New York, in 1917 was mimicked by Portland broker Paul Murphy in 1918, renamed the "Own-Your-Own-Home" campaign.[87] The effort spread from there, and its influence lasted through the interwar period. When the War Industries Board restricted homebuilding in 1918, it also sought to collaborate with the Own-Your-Own-Home program, and Murphy moved to Washington in 1918 to create a new Own-Your-Own-Home office in the Department of Labor. The office was staffed by industry men and encouraged mortgage lenders to loosen their mortgage standards.[88] In 1919, when the wartime office in the Department of Labor was closed, the office was privatized but reconnected to the government through a very different kind of partnership.

AN ARMY OF LABOR: WORLD WAR I HOUSING POLICY

While the Own-Your-Own-Home campaign cast homeownership as a patriotic act for civilians, another set of government programs moved to more directly secure housing for workers essential to the war effort. Military leaders had sought to address the housing issue even before the United States entered the war in April of 1917. However, they quickly ran into an obstacle: Chicago businessman Edward Nash Hurley, who was the head of the Shipping Board, insisted that the issue of housing was a problem to be solved by manufacturers, not the government. As the housing crisis worsened and labor disputes broke out at shipyards, Hurley conceded the need to request funds from Congress to house the "army of labor,"[89] but he gave a lowball estimate for this request of $35 million. In the Senate Commerce Committee, it was Duncan Fletcher, the Florida Democrat who had helped develop the farm loan system, who raised the amount to $50 million.[90]

The military leaders and congressmen who planned the government response to the housing crisis sought to determine what sort of government action was appropriate in the housing sector, aware that their plans would set precedents that could matter after the war. One issue was whether the government should construct cheaper temporary barracks versus permanent homes. Architects and city planners from the urban reform movement advocated permanent homes, which some saw as a first step toward a more expansive federal housing policy.[91] Shipbuilders and manufacturers also wanted permanent homes in order to attract better workers.[92] Proponents of permanent buildings noted that the English government had chosen to build single-family homes rather than barracks. Architect Clarence S. Stein explained, "Britain had discovered that to get the utmost out of the brawn and brain of her workers she must conserve their health and happiness by giving them proper living conditions."[93] Seeing the potential gain as worth the added cost, and assured by activists that the government's involvement in housing was a temporary wartime incursion, the military concluded that in many cases, permanent buildings were best.[94]

There were three main wartime housing efforts. Least controversial was the Army's Ordnance Department, which planned 16 communities for explosives manufacturers in remote areas.[95] By the end of the war, the branch was housing an estimated 45,000 people. With its construction of temporary homes and U.S. Army oversight, the program raised few questions, even though it built homes for private sector labor.

The second main housing effort was a credit program run by the Emergency Fleet Corporation, which needed to house workers near the nation's shipyards.[96] To meet this need, the Corporation provided mortgages to shipping companies to build on land they already owned.[97] With an allocation of $75 million, it financed the construction of a mix of dorms, hotels, apartments, and homes for 24 shipyards and a turbine plant. It also built roads and trolley systems to transport workers to and from the shipyards.[98] Following the armistice, program head A. Merritt Taylor recommended that projects nearing completion be finished.[99] In the end, 9,158 homes were built.[100] In 1922, when Congress refused appropriations for the Corporation, the office sold some of these mortgages at a discount to help cover its operating expenses.[101] To a large extent, this program fit the mold of earlier forms of national credit support: a temporary solution to solve a targeted problem that was halted as soon as the underlying issue was resolved.

Of the wartime housing programs, the most controversial was the third effort: the United States Housing Corporation, a direct housing program through which the federal government built and owned homes. The Housing Corporation was created as a unit of the Department of Labor. Tasked with providing support for workers in any industry essential to the war effort, it initially planned to provide credit support along the lines of that offered by the Emergency Fleet Corporation, but this proved difficult to coordinate. The shipping programs were concentrated geographically, but the Housing Corporation had to manage a great many industries spread out across vastly different housing markets and concluded that directly building and managing the needed homes was the preferable solution.[102] Early housing organizers and planners had their greatest and most direct involvement in this program. Frederick Law Olmsted, Jr., son of the famed designer of New York's Central Park and San Francisco's Golden Gate Park, headed its town planning division. Lawrence Veiller headed the architectural division and in this role drafted standards that were also adopted by the Emergency Fleet Corporation.[103] The real estate division was staffed by members of the National Association of Real Estate Boards, as Christian Topalov notes.[104]

The Housing Corporation chose to implement an Americanized version of the English garden city. Reformer Edith Elmer Wood noted with dismay that while the British programs determined housing allotments by family size, the U.S. programs allocated houses based on wealth: three-bedroom houses were reserved for higher-paid employees, while two-bedroom homes were assigned to the rest.[105] Communities were segregated, and racial inequalities reinforced. In Norfolk, for example, 70 percent of the space in dorms was earmarked for black workers, but only 45 percent of single-family homes were.[106]

Because the progress of the Housing Corporation's allocation through Congress was slower than that of the Emergency Fleet Corporation, its first authorization of $100 million came through only three and a half months before the armistice was signed.[107] Construction had begun on 44 buildings by December 12, 1918, when Congress ordered the Housing Corporation to stop work on any buildings not already 75 percent completed.

The fact that the federal government owned and managed the Housing Corporation's buildings complicated the program's transition into peacetime. An initial plan to quickly sell the properties came under scrutiny by Americans who feared that a fire sale would benefit well-connected speculators at the expense of average families still feeling the pinch of the national housing shortage. Complaints about the speedy liquidation were lodged by the Progressive National Housing Association, the American Institute of Architects, and the American Federation of Labor. The Army, Navy, and Department of Labor also argued for a system of liquidation that would give priority to families already in the homes and would use a public auction to ensure that a fair value was paid for the buildings.[108]

In the end, the U.S. government transferred 452 units to other government programs. The remaining 5,696 homes were sold for $3,165 each, with 10 percent cash down, 7 percent interest, and priority given to any good tenants already in the homes. By 1930, the Housing Corporation was reporting that it had recovered nearly half of its expenditures.[109] "Various types of comfortable, artistic workingmen's homes have been developed as well as community plans which promise much for the social life of the communities," wrote Emergency Fleet Corporation housing director J. Rogers Flannery, "and if housing developments of the future are planned along the same broad lines as adopted by the Government during the war, this country will have a happier, more contented, and healthier race of people."[110]

The controversy over the Housing Corporation was not solely about its liquidation. Many Americans, especially reformers, held up the Housing Corporation's programs as a successful test case for a more extensive national housing policy.[111] Proponents of a smaller federal government pushed back against such claims by arguing that the Housing Corporation had been pater-nalistic, socialistic, and wasteful.[112] It had allowed reformers, planners, and college professors to personally profit via large salaries as advisors, all at great cost to the nation.[113]

Why did the Shipping Board's credit programs proceed free from criticism while the U.S. Housing Corporation's developments generated such hostility? Wood concludes that "the bugbear of government housing" was to blame.[114] In the fight over whether the federal government should be involved in residen-tial housing, direct action proved far more controversial than credit support.

The legacy of these three wartime housing programs was not in their im-mediate continuation but in their lasting influence. In retrospect, the defenders of laissez-faire had good reasons to be worried. First, as historian Gail Radford argues, the war programs did in fact help change how Americans thought about government and housing.[115] An intellectual and institutional founda-tion for government-supported housing—a growing familiarity with the core issues, a set of actors ready to exert pressure, and model legislation to pass on to Congress—was in the process of formation. After the war, the build-ing and loans (with support from the Department of Labor and the National Federation of Construction Industries) pushed for the passage of the Home Loan Bank Bill. They cited the war programs—and the farm loan programs discussed in the previous chapter—to make their case. This bill was unsuc-cessfully introduced in the summer of 1919 and again in the spring of 1921. The National Association of Real Estate Boards similarly pushed for the right to issue tax-exempt bonds so as to better compete with the farm system. The housing lobby was still relativity weak in these years, and little progress was made on the national level, but a set of political tools was being forged, tools that would be mobilized once the national crisis of the Depression pried open a window of opportunity for change.[116]

A second way in which the war programs exerted a lasting influence was through their effect on the careers of future lawmakers. For instance, during the war Herbert Hoover was already taking an interest in housing from his position in the U.S. Food Administration. Later, as secretary of commerce, he pursued this interest through a set of housing programs. Franklin Delano Roosevelt, as assistant secretary of the Navy during the war, was present at landmark meetings in which the Emergency Fleet Corporation's housing plans were formed.[117] Within two decades, Roosevelt would oversee the creation of a modern residential mortgage support system during the New Deal.

The third way in which the wartime programs mattered was that they re-framed housing policy as an economic issue. Eric Karolak has argued that these programs replaced a longstanding emphasis on social justice with a focus on economic possibilities, what he calls a "production-centered para-digm."[118] Housing was now viewed as a matter of industrial policy, a change in signification that made government action more palatable and even necessary.[119] In the eighteenth century, economic growth had been used to justify government support for internal development. Now residential housing was taking its place as part of the American economic growth machine.

Hoover's Associational State: Housing Policy after the War

The federal government did not build or finance homes in the interwar period, but it did not abandon housing altogether. As head of the Department of Commerce, Herbert Hoover worked to build an associational state that could, as historian Ellis Hawley explains, reconcile a rejection of big government with a Progressive's appreciation for management, planning, and professional expertise.[120] Housing was a core part of that effort.

Hoover's big idea was that private involvement could temper state power. To achieve the latter, he simply needed to harness what was already there: the organizations that had proliferated under populism and progressivism, corporate actors, and the volunteerism that had been newly rejuvenated by the war. An associational state would have efficient and flexible partnerships, not a slow and rigid bureaucracy; it would encourage participation, not force compliance. The associational state was one of private initiative, not patrimonialism. Moreover, by stimulating grassroots activity and fostering "industrial self-government," associational programs would grow their own private replacements. Hoover expected associational programs to recede with the subsequent rise of civic organizations as independent managers, a system that Eldon Eisenach later described as a layer of "parastates" helping to lead and guide the nation.[121]

In Hoover's vision, the Department of Commerce would oversee the entire economy by coordinating the efforts of a variety of agencies, including the Departments of Labor, Interior, and Agriculture. While other offices ultimately thwarted the effort, Hoover was nevertheless able to use the Department of Commerce to advance his vision. His housing programs were typical of this approach. Hoover established the Building and Housing Division, which became a locus of network building, collaborative planning, and information sharing between government officials and private real estate interests.[122] This was an extension of an interest in housing Hoover had developed at the end of the war when, as head of the Food Administration, he observed the struggles of female workers in the food industry to secure decent housing.[123] The Department of Commerce also partnered with the Small House Service Bureau, a group run by architects (who were seeking to enhance their professional status at the time) to distribute free building plans to the public. Another partnership was between Commerce and the Home Modernizing Bureau. Created in 1926 and run by Walter Kohler of the kitchen and bath supply company, the Home Modernizing Bureau encouraged homeowners to update and renovate their homes. It was part of a more general attempt to offset a decline in new homebuilding. A third, larger partnership was with Better Homes of America, which showed model homes around the country and had 16,000 committees nationwide. By 1923, Hoover had been installed as the organization's president.[124]

It was also through the Department of Commerce that the Own-Your-Own-Home campaign renewed its association with the federal government. After the war, the campaign ramped up its promotional efforts, encouraging homeownership through a blitz of radio and film advertisements, pamphlets that detailed how brokers could organize their own local campaigns, and promotional materials in various languages filled with illustrations of white men and women planning to buy homes. One boasted that homeownership "is both the foundation of a sound economic and social system and a guarantee that our society will continue to develop rationally as changing conditions demand."[125] Hoover himself wrote that the "Lack of Homes and Consequent Instability is thriving food for Bolshevism."[126] Here we find the federal government joining in the symbolic construction of homeownership: its association with civic virtue and independence, with political stability and individual success, and with the idealized white suburban family.

When the market crashed and the nation careened into the Great Depression, Hoover's partnerships started to look reckless, greedy, and ineffectual. "Viewed from the altered perspective that took shape after 1929," Ellis Hawley writes, "his emerging private government seemed increasingly undemocratic, oppressive, and unresponsive."[127] By revealing the pitfalls of a less involved form of action, Hoover positioned Franklin Delano Roosevelt to take a different approach.

While the failure of Hoover's vision cleared the way for Roosevelt's more intensive New Deal policies, Roosevelt nevertheless built upon some of Hoover's precedents. Chapter 7 will explore in greater detail how Roosevelt's policies, while a repudiation of the associational vision, nevertheless retained certain aspects of it, especially its willingness to use partnerships. Notably, the Home Modernizing Bureau's collaboration with the Department of Commerce proved a direct precursor to the Better Housing Program's Title I loans to families, a policy that dramatically extended the use of consumer credit in the United States.[128] By 1934, the Roosevelt administration had combined the partnerships with credit support to promote housing and, through that, much of the American economy.

Housing Finance in Institutional Context

The stage was thus set for the wave of federal housing programs that would occur in the 1930s. The federal government was already promoting home-ownership through the Department of Commerce by the 1920s. The war had sensitized government officials to the importance of housing as economic policy and had shown them that credit support was feasible and relatively noncontroversial. The thrifts and mortgage brokers had already formed trade associations and were lobbying for credit support and tax benefits akin to what was available for the farm sector.

When the housing market dipped at the end of the 1920s and crashed in the 1930s, government officials understood these events as a threat to both economic growth and Americans' deepest sense of themselves. When the opportunity presented itself, the nation's mortgage sellers and brokers were well prepared to take their place as a central pillar of the twentieth-century American political economy. They already had proposals in hand.

6

Mortgage Bonds for
the Small Investor

Lewis Mumford once observed that "the skyscraper gave encouragement to all our characteristic American weaknesses: our love of abstract magnitude, our interest in land-gambling, our desire for conspicuous waste."[1] It also gave encouragement to the mortgage bond.

In the 1920s, the recovery of the U.S. housing market after the war years became a housing boom. Goetzmann and Newman found that between 1918 and 1926, there was a 400 percent increase in new housing construction nationwide, a number that may understate even more astronomical increases in certain areas.[2] In Ohio, the Van Swerigen brothers drove land values in Shaker Heights from $240,000 to $88 million in the 1920s. A land rush in Florida carved new towns out of the Everglades. During the Florida boom, the value of building permits in Miami rose from nearly $90,000 to almost $8 million, an 8,881 percent increase. All told, nearly $44 billion was funneled into nonfarm mortgages in the 1920s.[3]

As the nation's overall real estate market boomed, city skylines shot up.[4] Since the nation's first skyscrapers had appeared at the close of the 1870s, they had expanded to accommodate a growing urban population, pushed higher by technological advances like elevators, improved steel frames, and better fire control.[5] If the single-family detached home represented the new American family, the skyscraper signified American enterprise, industry, and commerce.[6] But all that height and technology made skyscrapers expensive, and few institutional investors were in place to fund them. Building and loans were active all over the nation but worked mainly with families. Mutuals extended mortgages for larger buildings and apartments but were concentrated in the Northeast.

The farther west one traveled, the more active banks became, but regulations limited their mortgage lending. Life insurance companies lent everywhere through brokers, but mortgages were only one part of their carefully diversified portfolios.[7]

The mortgage bond market moved into this gap, connecting the savings of American families to this new generation of skyscrapers and commercial buildings. For as little as $100—or $10, if you paid in installments—a person could own a share of the mortgage on the Chrysler Building or the Waldorf Astoria, although the unlucky investors in the latter lost their money when its loan defaulted.[8]

With families now acting as investors in an unregulated financial market, these bond sales reflected the new logic of the *shareholder democracy*. I take this phrase from historian Julia Ott, who observes that the bond drives of the First World War transformed the masses into a nation of bondholders.[9] After the war, Wall Street latched onto the notion that middle-class American families should be investors, an identity previously thought to be appropriate only for a much smaller group of elites. By investing, Wall Street contended, American families could not only build their savings but also gain new ways to participate in the development of the nation. This heightened involvement in the market was one of many changes in the financial lives of American families of the era, who were also purchasing more goods, relying more on credit, and increasingly organizing to protect their purchasing power.

The crux of the shareholder democracy was not just that Wall Street's markets could welcome small investors, but also that those markets *should be unregulated*. As the boom grew into a full-scale bubble, sellers had more reason to exploit the ignorance of small investors, and there was no real government oversight in place to stop them. Emboldened by the wartime bond drives and courted by Wall Street and advertisers, many Americans jumped into the shareholder democracy by investing in mortgage bonds. This was, in retrospect, a recipe for disaster. The crash that followed was severe. By one account, $8 billon of an estimated $10 billion of the nation's mortgage bonds defaulted, a devastating loss for up to 4 million bondholders.[10] As the nation's housing market collapsed, investors used the ignorance of small investors to further bilk them.

The Mortgage Bond Market after the First World War

In the early 1920s, the nation's rapidly recovering real estate market began to spill over into a boom in commercial building. Much of that building was funded by mortgage bonds that took one large mortgage and divided it up into smaller slices.[11] As early as 1893, Peabody Houghteling used such bonds for the Mallard WholeSale Store building in Chicago.[12] In this new approach to

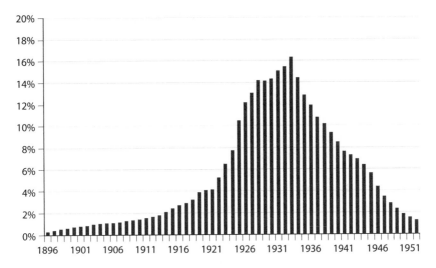

FIGURE 6.1. Real Estate Bonds as a Portion of Outstanding Nonfarm (Residential and Commercial) Mortgage Debt, 1896–1952
Source: Kenneth Snowden, "Table Dc903–928: Debt on Nonfarm Structures, by Type of Debt, Property, and Holder: 1896–1952," in *Historical Statistics of the United States.*

mortgage bonds, entrepreneurs formed a corporation that secured a mortgage for a large commercial property. They would then issue bonds backed by the income generated by the property. A typical bond backed by a first mortgage was sold in denominations of $100, $500, or $1,000. Some were sold as "baby bonds" using a $10 monthly installment plan.[13]

The use of mortgage bonds grew slowly through the First World War and then took off in the 1920s, as figure 6.1 shows. *The Historical Statistics of the United States* estimates that $6 billion in such bonds was outstanding by 1930, representing over 14 percent of all nonfarm mortgage debt that year.[14] Not all mortgage bonds were used to finance commercial buildings; some financed single-family or small multifamily homes.[15] Nor were mortgage bonds the exclusive source of financing for skyscrapers or other large commercial buildings: some mortgage companies issued stocks, for example. But generally, when an investor purchased a mortgage bond, he or she was purchasing a slice of one large mortgage.

The market was remarkably concentrated. One early study found that eight cities dominated the mortgage bond market, with New York and Chicago alone constituting half of all business.[16] A more recent investigation found that between 1911 and 1926, $400 million in mortgage bonds was issued in New York and Chicago, while only about $250 million was issued in the 13 next-largest cities combined, one of which was Brooklyn.[17] Still, bondholders were spread out over the nation, and the bonds they held financed building across the country.[18] The nation's largest real estate bond house, S. W. Straus, had offices in 15 cities by 1922.[19]

The market was concentrated not just in cities but also at the level of the firm. The largest seller by far was S. W. Straus & Co. of Chicago, followed by American Bond and Mortgage Company and G. L. Miller & Co., both of New York.[20] One sample of bonds registered with Moody's rating agency found that Straus alone issued 65 percent of all American mortgage bonds, while American Bond issued 13 percent and Miller issued 6 percent.[21]

At the same time the market for mortgage bonds increased, another market for insuring mortgages grew alongside it. The Title and Guaranteed Company of Rochester, New York, first guaranteed the payment of a mortgage on February 14, 1887.[22] This concern was part of a group of insurance companies that started guaranteeing payment of the principle of and interest on mortgage bonds in New York around the turn of the twentieth century.[23] Bit by bit, the insurance regulation laws in New York bent to accommodate this practice. New York had allowed companies to guarantee real estate titles since 1885. Since 1892, its companies could legally guarantee the payment on some other kinds of debt. Now, starting in 1904, the state specifically made it legal to guarantee mortgage bonds, and in 1911, it authorized insurance companies to buy and sell mortgages.[24] In 1918, the state made it legal for trusts to invest in guaranteed mortgage certificates. The business grew from there. Fifty New York companies dealt in guaranteed mortgages by 1930. The market grew similarly in other large cities.

For all this concentration, there was great variation in how the actual mortgage bonds were created. Some companies took every position in the credit supply chain: they originated mortgages, brokered bonds, guaranteed them, and marketed them. Others specialized in one aspect of the transaction, such as overseeing a trust or insuring bonds. Many firms were independent, while others were affiliated with larger Wall Street banks or, especially in later years, insurance companies. They sold bonds backed by office and apartment buildings, hospitals, churches, homes, theaters, stadiums, warehouses, schools, and even golf courses. Despite all this complexity, however, it is possible to divide the mortgage bond market of the 1920s into three main types of products: mortgage bonds issued by bond houses, guaranteed bonds issued by insurance companies, and participation certificates, also usually issued by insurance companies.

PARTICIPATION CERTIFICATES

About a third of the market for guaranteed mortgage bonds in the 1920s and 1930s was made up of participation certificates. This chapter pauses to discuss them in some detail not only because of their role in the disastrous crash of the market in the 1920s, but also because they went on to play a pivotal role in postwar federal politics, as we will see in chapter 9.

At its base, a participation certificate grants its holder rights to a share of the income generated by a group of mortgages. The use of participation certificates for mortgages in New York started in 1906. By the end of 1932, participation certificates made up $808.5 million of $2.7 billion in outstanding guaranteed bonds. Many of the pools represented by these certificates were large. One held 848 mortgages valued at $10 million, while another held 128 mortgages for a value of $27 million.[25]

In the early twentieth century, participation certificates came to housing markets by way of railroad finance. Scholars have traced their use back to the Schuylkill Company in 1845, but the practice gained more popularity with the expansion of railways in the 1870s.[26] At this time railroad companies placed leases in a trust in order to get around legal restrictions and tax requirements. This structure gave investors rights to flows of payments, but not ownership of the collateral itself. Although this design left investors with a more tenuous legal claim to the collateral, their lack of ownership brought certificate holders tax benefits. Initially, certificates backed by leases were the primary instrument used, but bonds backed by titles held in a trust emerged in later years as well.[27]

All participation certificates were backed by a trust. A government commission that later reviewed the certificates in the 1920s found that "the language of the participation certificates . . . varied widely among the companies, and often within the same company."[28] In the 1920s, some of these real estate trusts held a single large insured mortgage, while others held a pool of mortgages or even other real estate bonds that were themselves backed by mortgages.[29] The certificate guaranteed payment of those mortgages, usually within a 12- or 18-month period following the mortgages' termination date. The trustees of the bond had free rein to substitute mortgages at will without disclosing the swap to certificate holders.[30] Frequently the certificates were referred to as "bonds" and certificate holders were treated like bondholders, but technically these were less straightforward debt instruments than the average bond.[31] Because at least one additional legal layer stood between investors and the underlying assets, the certificates were a kind of subordinated debt.

Contemporary legal experts were confused about what this all meant if the underlying mortgage defaulted. One regulator complained, "The provisions of the certificates are certainly unintelligible to the layman, and the rights created thereby are perplexing to the lawyer."[32] Looking back on the practice, George Alger, chair of New York's Moreland Commission, noted that when guaranteed bonds failed, the holder was left "a fractional owner of a jigsaw puzzle type of security, which, to be of any value, requires the slow and expensive labor of assembly."[33]

While these participation certificates may seem familiar to some readers, and while they carried many of the some hazards of later iterations, it is nevetheless important to note that they were organized according to a somewhat different logic than that governing their more recent counterparts. Today the slicing and dicing of mortgages in pools is justified as a risk management technique for sophisticated investors. Pooling spreads out risks, while divisions within the pools allow investors to select the levels of risk they want. (If an investor wants to be more conservative, he or she pays more for bonds that will be paid out of the pool first. The lower-rated bonds in the pool are paid last but also cost less.) By contrast, in the 1920s and 1930s, risk management was mainly tied to the reputation of the seller or the value of the underlying assets. The pools were primarily a means to transform large mortgages into a form that small investors could consume.[34]

Consider this exchange between an Alger Commission lawyer and Hubert Breitwieser, a vice president at the New York Title and Mortgage Company:

Q. Let us take up the buyers of mortgages that are guaranteed in the order of the conservativism and critical attitude. Whom would you find, in the first place, to be the most difficult to satisfy?

A. *The large insurance companies.*

Q. And you would try to sell to them, and if you could not sell to the large life insurance companies, who were the most critical, who would be the next, whom would you approach next?

A. *The savings banks and the trust companies.*

Q. And then if they failed with the savings banks and the trust companies, then what would they do?

A. *Then the individual and their attorneys.*

Q. And then if they failed with the individual and their attorneys, then we went into the group and tried to sell it to the public through the group mortgage, is that right?

A. Yes, that would be the sequence.[35]

The pools were like a slop bucket that held mortgages rejected by investors who knew better. And it was an expensive slop bucket: sellers piled on all manner of fees—lending fees, title fees, extension fees, servicing fees—in exchange for moving the dregs.[36]

As the above exchange indicates, small-time investors were not the exclusive holders of these certificates. The Bond and Mortgage Company reported that 30 percent of its holdings in 1932 was purchased by trusts. Lawyers Mortgage Company reported that 15 percent of its $435 million in guaranteed mortgages was held by trusts in 1933.[37] Nevertheless, the certificates were overwhelmingly sold to small investors. "In truth," wrote one critic, "[participation certificates] were no better than badly watered stock certificates masquerading in the form of mortgages. They were labeled 'mortgage bonds' simply to increase their appeal to the conservative investment instincts of inexperienced and innocent purchasers."[38]

The exact number of small investors in this market is not known. A congressional committee later estimated that between 4 and 7 million Americans held such bonds. Building on the estimate of 4 million bondholders, it is surmised that 20 million, presumably a number that includes owners' family members, were indirectly affected by the market's collapse.[39]

Real Estate and the Shareholder Democracy

To understand how so many families got caught up in the mortgage bond market, it is necessary to understand how the war sparked a financial transformation for American families. In World War I, over half of the nation's wartime expenses were covered by Liberty Loan, Victory Loan, and War Savings Program bonds, all of which were sold through massive drives that associated bondholding with patriotic duty.[40] In historian Julia Ott's words, investing in a government bond became "a ritual of national belonging," one that was open to workers, women, and immigrants alike. Through this process, "Americans were encouraged to incorporate financial securities ownership into their understanding of national citizenship and national community and to anticipate that widespread ownership of federal debt might transform their society and their state."[41] A third of the nation—34 million Americans—purchased these bonds.[42]

After the war, Wall Street adapted many of the government's techniques for selling bonds, from working with savings clubs to taking out advertisements in women's magazines.[43] The New York Stock Exchange took the lead in extending and solidifying this new sense of a "shareholder democracy." In this worldview, Americans were expected to secure their well-being not through support from the state but by investing in a laissez-faire market. The mortgage bond of the 1920s—with average families as investors and almost no governmental support or oversight—articulated this vision.

It was in this changing world that sellers promoted mortgage bonds as a safe option for the new investor. A 1921 issue of McClure's proclaimed that "bonds and mortgages as a class are more adjusted to the needs of the inexperienced investor than stocks." The article went on to recommend that readers send 25 cents for the ninth edition of the booklet, which was promised to contain a wide range of investment advice.[44]

It was also in this context that some companies specifically marketed mortgage bonds to women. A Securities and Exchange Commission (SEC) report later worried about the exploitation of "teachers, waitresses, domestics and housewives" who had invested in this market. The Straus Company distributed makeup compacts with the company's name printed on them. The Bond and Guarantee Mortgage Company had a specialized woman's department.[45] Halsey Stuart Co. said that a fifth of its customers were women.[46] For female investors, mortgage bonds could symbolize a kind of reasonable step toward feminist independence. A 1922 *Woman's Home Companion* article promoted investment as an integral part of "the economic freedom of women." Offering advice for the novice investor, it went on to state that "carefully selected real-estate mortgages are a high grade and safe investment."[47]

"A PURE INVESTMENT"

Small investors were wooed by advertisements that sold mortgage bonds by touting high returns at low risk. "Freedom from care and worry," announced one advertisement for mortgage bonds; "Changeless Security and a 7% yield," proclaimed another for guaranteed bonds, which went on to refer to its bonds as "a pure investment, with speculative features eliminated."[48] Still another advertisement hailed guaranteed bonds as "the most secure of securities known to man."[49] Editorials sometimes featured investment advice that nudged readers toward advertisers. The Halsey Stuart Company sponsored a weekly nationwide radio show that offered to "increase your knowledge of sound investment."[50]

Because they were linked to solid, lasting buildings, the bonds were framed as a safe choice for good, conservative folk who sought to avoid the wilder speculation of the stock market.[51] Ads might invoke the enduring value of property and the lasting power of great architecture through illustrations of classical architecture, the Parthenon, and Roman aqueducts. A 1923 advertisement from the G. L. Miller bond house featured a picture of the Parthenon over the phrase "A symbol of strength for over 20 centuries."[52] Only three years later G. L. Miller became the first major bond house to collapse.[53]

The reliability and reputation of the bond dealer were other common selling points. Each year the Straus Company updated its record of selling without losses to investors: 39 years, 40 years, 41 years. The company was not legally liable for any payments on the bonds it sold, but it took its reputation seriously. Up until 1931 the company backfilled defaulted payments to bondholders, when it was finally overwhelmed by the onslaught of defaults.

In other cases, advertisements invoked the authority of scientific expertise, sometimes with vague references to scientifically derived safeguards. Marketing materials also trotted out experts. Take this testimonial from a small investor:

I had a savings account with the Schiff Bank, and they sent me several letters by well-educated statisticians, and they showed me how I can live on "easy street." They showed me how to get real-estate bonds, that that is the foundation of America. They also showed me that the real-estate bonds are sounder than American Government bonds. . . . They figured it out for me that by means of buying bonds, that, from the interest, I could be able to pay for rent, gas and electricity, and have quite a bit left over at the end of the year.[54]

The authority of statisticians, allusions to the soundness of real estate, the promise of wealth—sellers used all these techniques. Some issuances were even printed using engravings that resembled Treasury bonds.[55] Every care was taken to communicate the safety and desirability of these bonds.

What about the actual insurance and guarantees that were supposed to safeguard investors? Many bonds without guarantees were marketed as if they had them. One salesman under investigation was later asked if customers had been told that the bonds were not guaranteed despite advertisements of safety. His reply was: "Only when the customer would ask if they were guaranteed."[56] Actually guaranteed bonds were marketed as if they were the safest investments ever devised, although postcollapse autopsies revealed that the actual protections put in place were flimsy; the insurers suffered from high levels of leverage and improper valuation practices, and had failed to anticipate systematic risks. Goetzmann and Newman in recent years sampled the bonds of the time and concluded that "by nearly every measure, real estate securities were as toxic in the 1930s as they are now."[57]

In 1925, the phenomenal growth of the market slowed. In 1926 U.S. housing starts peaked at nearly $4 billion.[58] The real estate bond market stalled out, dipping slightly until it plummeted in 1928. As companies started to fail, the real estate business moved to self-regulate. The American Construction Council, a trade association that had been chaired by Franklin Roosevelt, formed a commission in 1927 to draft a new set of standards for bond sales. Its guidelines for collateralization and valuation were voluntarily adopted by some mortgage bond companies.[59] Years later, however, a congressional report derided the effort as nothing more than smoke and mirrors, because the bond houses "soon abandoned [the reforms] and again began their reckless schemes."[60]

THE CRASH

When the G. L. Miller bond house collapsed in 1926, it was the beginning of the end of the mortgage bond market. One writer estimates that fewer than 20 percent of mortgage companies listed with Moody's at the end of the 1920s were around six years later.[61] In 1927 the New York attorney general issued a warning about the bonds.[62] The industry pressed on: the New York Real Estate Board created the Real Estate Securities Exchange in 1928. By 1930 it was failing, as were a full 80 percent of securities issued in the 1920s.[63] Bonds issued in 1920 retained four-fifths of their value; bonds issued in 1928 recovered less than 40 percent.[64]

By the early 1930s, with more businesses closing and more Americans out of work, the entire real estate market was in turmoil. The value of home prices had dropped by half. Lenders—particularly lenders of the less secure second and third mortgages—responded by refusing to refinance mortgages.[65] By 1933, new building in the United States had ground to a halt. Residential permits for construction dropped from 490,000 in 1928 to under 26,000 a year later. Foreclosures spiked, increasing 71 percent over 1926 levels.[66] Between 1931 and 1935, an average of 250,000 homes foreclosed a year. By the end of that period, 27 states, many of them in the Midwest, had placed moratoriums on foreclosures in an effort to staunch the tide.[67]

As the entire national housing market crumbled, underlying problems in the mortgage market rose to the surface.[68] Mortgage insurers had failed to plan for how a depression would cause all of their mortgages to lose value and become illiquid simultaneously.[69] Reserves were heavily invested in real estate bonds and mortgages, which meant that the value of the reserves plummeted exactly when those reserves were needed.[70] And while mortgage insurers had been required to set aside the equivalent of two-thirds of their capital stock in reserves, there had been no limits on how many guarantees they could issue, which added additional obligations. Other underappreciated risks came to light at this time as well. S&Ls were threatened by the failure of banks that held their deposits. Building and loans were hit particularly hard because of their shared accumulation plans; when members took out a mortgage, they also purchased shares in the organization. The mortgage was paid off when the value of the shares equaled the outstanding value of the mortgage. Now each loss reduced the value of every other person's shares, putting the entire group further behind. Two thousand building and loans were failing by 1933.[71]

As companies closed, the market's underbelly of fraud, corruption, and simple carelessness came to light.[72] The bond houses had made a killing on fees. One issue of $875,000 generated fees of $182,000.[73] Sellers had focused on those high fees and not on the long-term viability of the mortgages, and therefore kept issuing bonds long past the time when good opportunities were gone.[74] Later investigations revealed that the nuts-and-bolts work of assigning mortgages to particular participation certificates was, in many cases, a haphazard affair; one company had "a 22 year old girl who received $16 a week" in charge of making allocations.[75] The field was rife with conflicts of interest and shady dealings. Charles Walgreen, owner of the drugstore business, bought distressed bonds in a building he rented using the names of brokerage employees to hide his identity.[76] Bond houses and insurers hid defaults, sometimes using investors' money to lend out more money in a doomed effort to stay afloat.

Leverage and speculation also proved to be widespread problems.[77] When issuing bonds, mortgage companies often made excessively optimistic assumptions about occupancy and default rates.[78] Appraisers inflated property valuations.[79] Valuations were misrepresented to investors; one appraisal was raised from $14 million to $18 million after a prospectus was already at the printers because the issuer found it had additional debt it wanted to retire.[80] As long as real estate prices were going up, these kinds of problems were seldom noticed, since the property could be sold at a profit.[81] But when prices fell, they proved disastrous. The few market participants who sounded early warnings of overvaluation and fraud were casually dismissed, or worse, attacked for trying to undermine the nation's prosperity.[82]

ADVERTISEMENTS AND PROTECTIVE COMMITTEES

In a kind of one-two punch for smaller investors, many insurance companies and bond houses responded to the crisis by further fleecing their clients. Some companies hired more salespeople as their business declined, hoping to use the income from more sales to pay off the mounting demands from existing clients for payments.[83] George Alger's report to New York state on the failure of the insured mortgage business observed that sellers had "used the depression itself as a sales argument." Salesmen promoted mortgage bonds as a reliable source of income in troubled times or an investment that nervous homeowners could use to stave off foreclosure, as if it would hedge their risks rather than magnify them.[84]

When it came to the participation certificates, trustees used their right to substitute collateral to pay themselves first. Some bond houses "milked" any remaining profits from defaulted buildings by siphoning off remaining income flows.[85] The latter activity was facilitated by the creation of the ironically named "protective committees," which sprang up at the end of 1929 and into the early 1930s.[86] These committees purported to represent the collective interests of scattered bondholders but were actually headed by a small network of lawyers and bankers. Bond houses convened many such groups in an effort to stave off lawsuits and used their lists of clients to organize the holders of the defaulted bonds. Straus alone set up 140 protective committees in Illinois and California and 97 in New York. When it went into receivership, the company held $360 million in bonds from 80,000 investors. Bondholders who joined the protective committees typically signed over power of attorney rights. Once in the committee, bondholders could not leave without paying hefty fees, and in some cases, the committee's permission was needed to leave. Bondholders wooed with frequent updates and detailed correspondence went on to find themselves completely stonewalled by the committee six to nine months later.

What had been marketed as a tool of consumer protection became another source of fraud and self-dealing. The committees collected funds for expenses and charged high management fees that were then distributed to committee members, depositories, and legal counsel.[87] They negotiated for settlements far under market value. One New York building with a valuation of $3.2 million and outstanding bonds of $3.7 million was acquired from bondholders for $750,000.[88] Some committees refinanced the debt to make their own positions superior to that of the bondholders or to skim off the best mortgages, while others delayed bankruptcy resolutions to keep the committee, and therefore their commissions, in business.

In response to the chaos, small investors organized. A protest in Chicago reportedly attracted more than 10,000 people.[89] Angry bondholders sent thousands of letters to government officials calling for action. "I am now past 90 years of age and my earning power is gone, and I expected that this investment would take care of ma and me when we were old, but it is now swept away," said one letter to Congress. Other letter writers demanded action: "I have received $67.50 for my $1,000 bond. Congress should so [sic] something and here's hoping that something is a good investigation."[90] One petition to Congress contained half a million signatures.

STATE REGULATORS: THE CASE OF NEW YORK

In New York, the bond houses could have been investigated under the Martin Act, an antifraud bill that became law in 1921.[91] In 1927, following the collapse of G. L Miller, the New York regulators moved forward under its auspices (this and other regulatory responses are summarized in table 6.1). Led by state attorney general Albert Ottinger, the four-month investigation uncovered various unscrupulous practices of the bond houses, ranging from misleading advertisements to mishandled funds. In response, Ottinger proposed a set of reforms of the houses, which included conflict-of-interest prohibitions; an array of reporting, valuation, and disclosure rules; and the separation of mortgage payments from general operating funds.[92] Many of these rules were not new, just previously unenforced.

Because the guaranteed bonds were insurance products, they were subject to different regulatory authorities. In 1933, the Shackno Act authorized the Insurance Department to take over 18 failing companies, a plan that immediately came under attack as the department struggled to manage the companies. By December, Governor Lehman had instituted an investigation under New York's Moreland Act into the troubled mortgage insurance industry and the state's failed system of regulatory oversight.[93] George W. Alger, a lawyer who had recently come off a successful investigation of the New York parole system, headed it. In a scathing report, Alger singled out participation certificates

TABLE 6.1. Selected Regulatory Responses: New York State and Federal Government

Bond	Seller	Regulatory Response
Real Estate Bonds (Uninsured)	Bond Houses	New York • 1927, New York Martin Act proceedings: four-month investigation headed by Attorney General Albert Ottinger Federal • 1933, Securities Act: Included requirements for companies and securities to be registered • 1934–1936, Sabath Committee: Congressional investigation and hearing concerning the protective committees, headed by Adolf Sabath (D-Ill.) • 1934, SEC Committee: Formed under the 1934 SEC Act to investigate protective committees, headed by William O. Douglas; influenced the Chandler Bill
Guaranteed Mortgages and Participation Certificates	Mortgage Insurers	New York • 1933, Shackno Act: Authorized seizure of 18 insurance companies • 1934, Moreland Commission and Moreland Commission Act: Investigation of failure of insurance regulations, headed by George Alger • 1934–1937, Joint Legislative Committee to Investigate the Guaranteed Mortgage Situation • 1937, New York State Mortgage Commission: Oversaw the management of failed companies' assets Federal • 1933, Securities Act: Included requirements for companies and securities to be registered • 1934, Securities Exchange Act: Included a provision for an investigation of the protective committees

as inherently difficult to regulate. The Moreland Commission proposed the creation of a neutral entity to manage defaulted companies' assets, a proposal that moved forward. Within a year of its creation, the commission set up for this purpose had worked with over 200,000 certificate holders and 15,275 property owners (some of whose holdings were already foreclosed), making it a major mortgage brokerage, servicer, and manager.[94]

Federal Regulation

Much of the main federal response to the mortgage bond crash was subsumed under the more general project of securities regulation, which played out in the wake of the stock market crash.[95] The Securities Act of 1933 did not specifically reference mortgage bonds, but because its broad definition of securities included any "bond, debenture, evidence of indebtedness, certificate of interest or participation," all mortgage bond dealers and their issuances had to be federally registered from that point on.[96] This regulation was followed in 1934 by the Securities Exchange Act, which included a provision initiating an investigation of the protective committees (and entirely bracketed the question of certificates issued by mortgage guarantee companies).[97] SEC chairman Joseph Kennedy chose as its chair William O. Douglas, a former bankruptcy lawyer and Yale Law professor who was later named to the Supreme Court. Douglas brought in another future Supreme Court justice, Abe Fortas, from the Agricultural Adjustment Administration.[98] The SEC commission held a series of hearings, surveyed over 100 protective committees, and produced eight volumes of reports.

At the same time, the Sabath Committee also took on the issue of the protective committees. Headed by Congressman Adolf Sabath (D-Ill.), it was convened to address the concerns of investors who were receiving little, if any, value for defaulted bonds they had contributed to protective committees. The Sabath Committee held hearings in New York, Chicago, Philadelphia, Detroit, and Milwaukee. Its final eight-volume report included 12,000 pages of testimony and a scathing rebuke of the business practice.[99]

RETHINKING LAISSEZ-FAIRE

A damning portrait of laissez-faire emerged from this series of investigations. In April of 1934 the New York Senate and Assembly convened the Joint Legislative Committee to Investigate the Guaranteed Mortgage. The committee concluded that the mortgage guarantee business was fundamentally unsound and should be prohibited.[100] An early U.S. Senate report on the failing market in Washington, D.C., concluded that fraud was the "inevitable result" of the lack of regulation.[101] The message of these reports was that businesses would violate trust and decency unless compelled to do the right thing.

If laissez-faire was flawed, what then constituted a proper government response? If the regulators moved beyond disclosure requirements and started auditing books, was that a form of governmental overreach? Should the management of bankrupt companies be left to courts and bankers, placed under conservatorship of the state, or put in the hands of an independent trustee? There were deep disagreements among government officials. The Sabath Committee wanted a government conservator to run all bankruptcy proceedings, while Douglas's SEC-focused committee wanted the government to oversee but largely sit out of bankruptcy negotiations.[102]

Steps to extend government oversight were met with objections—most prominently, that such a move was a violation of the sanctity of property rights, and that the state was unqualified to manage businesses.[103] Then, as today, not all businessmen fought all regulation. S. W. Straus himself at the time of the Martin proceedings led by Ottinger acknowledged that regulation was a way to rebuild the public's trust in the business:

> We are today standing on the threshold of a new era in the entire invest-ment field, and I believe the day is not far off when the methods of treating and selling every type of investment offered to the American public will be in some manner under strict state or federal government supervision and control. How soon that day will come, I do not know, but it is as certain as tomorrow's sun. . . .
>
> But the tremendous growth of the investment field, especially with the advent of millions of Americans as investors in our Liberty Loan floata-tions, make it necessary that the American public be offered every possible protection.[104]

Hereafter securities regulation would place constraints on the freewheeling creation of publicly marketed securities of all kinds and, as the next chapter will show, would move to put in place new credit supports for housing finance.

New regulation and a strengthened SEC overturned the two core tenets of shareholder democracy when it came to housing finance: the idea that families would invest in mortgage bonds and the idea that the government should take a hands-off stance when it came to mortgage finance. Families could still put their money toward housing, but only as depositors in smaller, local (and now federally insured) S&Ls. While American families continued to invest some of their savings on Wall Street, their days of being mortgage bondholders were over.

The Mortgage Bond Market's Legacy

On October 23' 1935, the director of the SEC's Trading and Exchange Division, David Saperstein, gave a speech to the National Association of Real Estate Boards in Atlantic City, New Jersey. The title of the talk was "Real Estate Bond Issues of the Future."[105] Before taking on this subject, however, Saperstein recounted some sobering facts from the recent past: $8 billion worth of bonds in default, 18 mortgage insurers taken over by the state of New York, and a litany of fraudulent and careless actions that had harmed small-time investors:

> The impact of such a calamity is particularly devastating because of the character of its victims. The individual who buys a real estate security is not ordinarily a speculator or a gambler. He is more likely to be a person of modest means who is induced to invest his savings not so much by any consideration of the merits of the security as by his faith in the concern with which he deals. This was undeniably true in the case of those who

purchased guaranteed mortgages and certificates. Perhaps in no other field of investment did the purchaser so completely assign his judgment to the keeping of others. And seldom has he been more completely betrayed.[106]

Saperstein went on to acknowledge that housing was among the nation's top three industries and its second-largest source of employment. This made it an essential part of the growth of other industries. Sound regulation of housing was therefore needed on multiple grounds: to protect the vulnerable from poor investments, to provide decent homes for the public, and to ensure the stable growth of the economy. He told the group,

> From our present point of vantage we can see with unclouded vision the easy standards which prevailed in a world from which it was commonly believed poverty and hunger had been banished. We now know that those easy standards will not do in today's world or tomorrow's. They must be supplanted by new standards which recognize the simple fact that the investor's interests are of paramount importance not only to himself but to the society which needs him so badly. This point cannot be too strongly emphasized now, at this moment, when the destinies of the building industry and the mortgage business are matters of such grave and universal concern.[107]

In this formulation, the interests of the building industry are so closely aligned with those of the nation as to be virtually identical. Social theorists refer to this kind of conflation as *hegemony*.[108] Here Saperstein was asserting such a link to justify constraints on the industry, but in other contexts, homebuilders and financiers would make claims about national policy on the same grounds. The housing finance industry, however damaged, remained central to the U.S. economy.

At the time this speech was given, the mortgage bond business was still in tatters. Fearing foreclosure, more families chose to rent instead of buy. Investors lacked confidence in real estate securities. The head of the FHA had, the day before, called mortgages "a synonym for nightmare." Some solution was needed, but it was not yet clear what form this would take. To Saperstein, "a new technique of real estate financing must be evolved which will take the curse off the mortgage."[109] However, he could not say what the real estate bond of the future would look like exactly. He posited that new forms of credit support being developed by the FHA would stabilize it and insisted that it had to be safer than the bonds of the past but concluded that the rest was up to the audience members: "The task of winning the investor back to belief in real estate as a medium of investment is, in no small measure, your own."[110]

In retrospect, the most striking aspect of this speech is revealed by its very theme, which Saperstein had been invited to discuss. The room seems to have not yet realized that the private real estate bond market was effectively already dead. Today we know that the crisis had acted like a crucible that burned away all but the most conservative mortgage brokers. The ones who survived reconstituted themselves as brokerage arms of other banks and insurance companies. In 1954, economist Saul Klaman examined the mortgage banking industry and found that fewer than one-fifth of companies registered with the FHA had been founded before the Great Depression.[111] These companies financed themselves through advanced commitments to buy mortgages from banks and insurance companies. This basically made the mortgage dealers brokerage arms of other lending institutions rather than truly independent brokers or bankers.

By 1950, economist Ernest M. Fisher could state that "the mortgage bond issue as an institution has disappeared."[112] Some companies attempted to revitalize it in the 1960s, as chapter 9 will discuss, but without much success. The mortgage bond of the future would now remain dormant until the federal government took up the matter directly.

7

The Rise of Federal Credit Programs

If we imagine markets as distinct systems separate from the rest of social life, it is not hard to see how they could self-correct. A boom, like the housing market in the previous chapter, should lead to overproduction. At some point the overproduction will drive down prices so far that production slows or stops, causing the market to stall. Eventually, when the demand for housing has recovered and reached a level greater than the remaining housing stock, production should pick up again. Disequilibrium thus creates the conditions for a new equilibrium. The theory is beautiful in its simplicity.

The problem with the theory of self-correcting markets is that markets are not distinct systems separate from the rest of social life. People make markets and people lose out when markets self-correct. This was the insight at the heart of Karl Polanyi's masterpiece *The Great Transformation*.[1] Because necessities like land, labor, and money have been commoditized, market corrections are experienced by people as a series of wrenching losses. Families cannot pay rent or afford groceries. Parents lose their sense of worth along with their jobs. For the most vulnerable, market corrections bring the physical violence of cold, hunger, and illness. Market corrections are never as bloodless as the phrase implies.

When people suffer, they demand protection from the state and may make previously unimaginable bargains in search of stability and well-being. This is why the idea of a self-regulating market is a utopian fantasy, Polanyi argues: severe market crises invariably cause political crises. The real choice is not between free markets and managed markets, but rather about where the protection should come from when the market corrects. Do we want the protection to come in the form of a strongman like Mussolini or Hitler, Polanyi asks, or do we want it to intervene in favor of social democracy and market regulation? One way or another, the masses will demand action.

In the face of the Great Depression, Americans fought bitterly over whether attempts to regulate the market necessarily meant sliding into either socialism or dictatorship. Still, the country moved ahead with a wave of policy so extensive that scholars later characterized the New Deal as a "big bang" in American political life.[2] It was followed by another surge in government expansion during the Second World War. Yet while the federal government came out of the 1940s stronger than ever before, it was still riven by deep ideological and sectional divides. Attempts at European-style comprehensive economic planning had failed, as had attempts to provide truly comprehensive welfare protections to all Americans. Despite the considerable expansions of U.S. power at the time, the U.S. government remained decentralized and fragmented, reliant on partnerships, and sensitive to the influence of interest group politics.[3]

While the New Deal is one of the best-studied parts of U.S. history, the fact that this period also saw a "big bang" in the use of credit programs has not been the focus of extensive analysis.[4] This is surprising when we consider that of a list of 31 major New Deal programs identified by one scholar, 15 were credit programs.[5] By the end of the New Deal, selective credit support was no longer limited to farm credit but had spread throughout the American economy, used in more expansive, varied, and systematic ways than ever before. This chapter examines this expansion of credit programs in the New Deal, showing that it was the key moment when credit support came fully into its role as a multipurpose tool of statecraft.

The New Deal credit programs mattered because they helped a fractured political system continue to function. Their appeal rested in how credit programs circumvented the nation's deepest, most intractable fissures. Credit programs allowed government officials to promote specific markets without meeting the various demands of central planning. They could be justified on many grounds and framed as consistent with free-market ideals. Equally important, they could be removed from the budget. The latter characteristic did not please the most stalwart of fiscal conservatives, but it did create more options for maneuvering around them.

This chapter looks at how the Reconstruction Finance Corporation (the financial giant that funded much of the New Deal) and the housing programs served as the institutional centers for the development of U.S. credit policy. Within them, officials expanded the use of credit as a tool of statecraft. At the Reconstruction Finance Corporation, credit emerged as a way to enact targeted, low-cost, off-budget policies throughout the economy. Within the housing sector, Roosevelt used credit to spur homeownership and, through that, construction, employment, and industry.

In both the Reconstruction Finance Corporation (RFC) and the federal housing programs, officials took advantage of the flexibility of the credit programs. In so doing, they built a foundation of credit support for the key pillars of a postwar political economy, all of which relied heavily on consumption and homeownership.

The Problem with the New Deal

The Great Depression posed the problem of not just how to fix broken markets, but how to do so in a way that was consistent with core values of individualism, democracy, and fair play. Ellis Hawley details this dilemma in his book *The New Deal and the Problem of Monopoly*. From the perspective of the early 1930s, it was not at all clear that the government could right the nation's economy without sliding into either socialism or dictatorship. At the root of this confusion was a set of disagreements among New Dealers about the ultimate causes of the Great Depression. As Hawley put it, Americans "have never really decided what to do about [the] industrial order."[6] Antimonopolists argued for decades that big business was incompatible with American values. Despite liberal theorists' contention that corporations were a natural extension of property rights, corporations fit uneasily with the small agrarian ideal of the republican-Jeffersonian tradition. In a world populated by large corporations, laissez-faire did not lead to vibrant competition so much as leave the biggest companies free to squash their competitors.

How did those ideological divisions matter in the context of the New Deal? One group of New Dealers, inspired by Wilson's New Freedom (and Louis Brandeis's antitrust efforts), sought to stop large corporations and decentralize economic power. From their perspective, the government granted too many privileges to big business. Enforced competition could help smaller, more local businesses thrive and, in turn, lessen the need for a larger government to deal with the problem of big business. A second group of New Dealers worked in the tradition of Theodore Roosevelt's New Nationalism and drew from the American love of scientific management. These progressives saw big business as part of the unavoidable march of history and concluded that planning was needed to manage it. Hoover's associational state proffered a third solution: encourage the big corporations and other smaller organizations to become more deliberate and cooperative. If private organizations were more statelike, a large state power would not be needed to check the power of big companies.

The problem was that each group's preferred solution was anathema to the others.[7] If the fundamental issue was that business accrued too many privileges, the answer was to decentralize power and promote competition. But that Wilsonian strategy seemed dangerously naïve to anybody who believed that big business was here to stay, and that bigger government was required to direct it.[8] If the real problem was a failure to properly adjust to this new situation, the answer was to embrace planning and develop a new set of guidelines that could harness and direct the power of the corporations. But the small business–loving Wilsonians wanted to dismantle concentrated power, not facilitate it, and business fought hard against such extensive government activity. The pro-business contingent wanted to encourage the development of Hoover's associational state, in which its members could write and enforce their own standards. But that was a hard sell amid the wreckage of the Great Depression.[9] With such differing opinions and agendas, it was not long after the excitement of Roosevelt's first 100 days that the three groups came to loggerheads.

This clash resulted in "policy deadlock" in Roosevelt's central New Deal economic effort, the National Recovery Administration (NRA). Created in 1933, the NRA was supposed to set standards and even establish prices across many industries. In this it resembled a more European approach to capitalism, a kind of corporatism in which the government brought together business and labor to plan economic development. But with the New Dealers unable to agree on much of anything within the NRA, the agency floundered. When the Supreme Court's *Schechter* decision ruled the NRA unconstitutional in May 1935, it did not strike down a robust program in its prime so much as finally euthanize a slowly dying one. Roosevelt was reportedly relieved that the program was over.[10]

From then on, Hawley explains, economic planning in the United States was of "the exceptional, partial, piecemeal variety."[11] Price fixing and marketing agreements proceeded only in specific arenas: some small businesses, farm prices, the crude oil industry, and the production of the soft black bituminous coal used to generate power and make steel. These industries were so profoundly broken that members set aside internal divisions and lobbied cohesively for planning. In each case, industry participants accepted the regulations and labor standards that came with government planning. And in each case, Hawley explains, they offered up some justification for abandoning the normal rules of competition. Farmers, for example, justified their price supports by asserting that farms were the moral and economic foundation of the nation and so deserved special protections.[12]

With planning relegated to special cases, Keynesian spending offered a more viable path forward for economic development. Keynesian economics focused on consumption, sidestepping the divisive issues of government-managed competition and price setting that had killed the NRA. Moreover, Prasad observes that this consumption-based strategy fit especially well with the existing U.S. political economy because of the incredible productivity and political power of American farmers, who pushed for programs that helped people buy their goods.[13] Keynesianism also had the advantage of not raising the ire of Southern Democrats. As a group, the Southern Democrats helped block economic planning efforts because they saw planning as a potential threat to the dominant southern system of white supremacy. They had no such concerns about the Keynesian approach.

SECTIONALISM AND THE SOUTHERN DEMOCRATS

When it comes to understanding the trajectory of the New Deal, early twentieth-century southern politics are as important to take into account as ideological divides. Ira Katznelson shows the truth of this assertion through his analysis of congressional voting patterns from the early New Deal through the Truman presidency (when, he argues, the nation actually settled on the full scope of New Deal policies). Katznelson observes that while Southern Democrats were major supporters of domestic programs like the Public Works Administration during the first New Deal (the initial burst of programs from 1933 to 1935) and supported a strong military, they blocked any policy that might dismantle southern racial hierarchies. Southern Democrats actually constrained the implementation of a more expansive and cohesive New Deal policy in later years.

Southern Democrats used the array of veto points that the U.S. system offered to block the New Deal programs they disliked.[14] They threatened to vote as a bloc with Republicans. They used the power of seniority in committees, where they held nearly all of the most important chairs, to control legislation. These strategies allowed them to extract considerable compromises from other Democrats. Watered-down labor rights and limited social welfare programs were the outcome. Notably, Southern Democrats were able to exclude domestic and farm workers—two-thirds of all black southern workers—from New Deal labor protections. These New Deal Southern Democrats are why the American welfare state resembles a moth-eaten "crazy quilt" of programs administered at the state level with minimal guidelines and massive holes: they enforced a system in which they would control the flow of national resources locally or else stop the flow entirely. It was Harry Byrd (D-Va.) who led the charge against stronger national standards for Social Security's old age insurance. And when Southern Democrats started to see the labor rights movement as a boon to civil rights, they embarked on a series of attacks on labor protections, culminating in the Taft-Hartley Act of 1947, which eroded many of the rights to organize that labor had secured with the Wagner Act of 1935.[15]

Southern Democrats also helped block the brief resurgence of economic planning during the Second World War. While overall national economic planning had failed with the NRA, a vestige of the planning effort lived on with the National Resources Planning Board, an office created within the Public Works Administration in 1933 to direct its projects. During the Second World War the Board took on a more general economic planning role as part of the war effort, creating an institutional basis for planning that could have persisted after the war. But Southern Democrats saw the office as a potential threat to the existing southern power structure and so used the Appropriations Committee—on which the chair was from Missouri and 14 of 35 Democrats were southern—to block its funding.[16]

Here, then, was another considerable advantage of government spending and Keynesianism: the Southern Democrats as a group saw fiscal policy as no particular threat to their racial order. Of course, some Southern Democrats were strong fiscal conservatives, like Harry Byrd of Virginia. But as a group the Southern Democrats were not dedicated to low government spending per se—they primarily wanted to decentralize power in cases in which such decentralization would allow them to preserve existing racial hierarchies. This set Keynesianism as a political path of least resistance, although it was not without its own challenges.

FISCAL CONSERVATIVES AND THE KEYNESIAN SOLUTION

Keynesian policy itself faced a significant hurdle: the prevalence of fiscal conservativism in both parties. Historian Julian Zelizer reminds us that experts and everyday people alike took for granted the importance of a balanced national budget for a healthy state in the early 1930s. When running for president, Franklin Roosevelt promised to cut expenditures and balance the budget. Once elected, he signaled his commitment to the cause by placing budget hawk Lewis Douglas in charge of the Bureau of the Budget.[17]

Lew Douglas, like other fiscal conservatives of the time, saw government spending as a slippery slope. Spending, once authorized, might never stop. Distrustful of politicians, Douglas believed that government involvement in markets actively interfered with the abilities of markets to heal themselves. For Douglas, the U.S. government should take the role of "umpire," not player.[18] In his dedication to fiscal conservatism, he had a powerful ally in Treasury head Henry Morganthau. Both men believed that deficits eroded the quality of the nation's credit. Both men fought against inflation, arguing that it undermined the value of the middle class's hard-won savings.

Over time, Keynesians like Marriner Eccles at the Federal Reserve gained the upper hand. But in the early years of the New Deal, fiscal conservatism counterbalanced government spending. After all, Roosevelt only really embraced Keynesian principles in 1938, long after he had racked up deficits, seeing no other choice given the dire circumstances of the nation. He planned to return to a policy of budgetary balance as soon as possible, and Morgenthau and Douglas pressured him to do so.[19] As the Depression wore on and Roosevelt continued to spend, Douglas found his arguments ignored and dismissed, and he finally resigned in 1934. (After his resignation, he spoke out against the president's spending.) Morgenthau stuck it out in the administration, but his was a losing battle.

As spending won out over fiscal conservatism in the war years, the structure of the federal administration changed accordingly. Under Harold Smith, the director of the Bureau of the Budget from 1939 to 1946 (when he left to head the International Bank for Reconstruction and Development), the office grew significantly: between 1939 and the end of the war, the Bureau of the Budget's own budget grew from under $400,000 to $3 million, and its staff expanded from 103 people to 512, a growing number of whom were economists (39 by 1947).[20] Meanwhile, the nation's principal remaining outpost of industrial planning, the National Resource Planning Board, was starved of funding and then closed. The fiscally minded Council of Economic Advisers took over its advisory capacities in 1946. In Katznelson's words, the budget now became "an economic policy instrument," heightening its importance as a potential political battleground.[21]

THE BENEFITS OF CREDIT

In the end, the New Deal's "maze of conflicting cross-currents" (in the words of Ellis Hawley) further encouraged a modern federal government that was itself a maze of decentralized power.[22] The federal government was larger and more powerful after the Depression than it had been before, but the states still controlled the distribution of core resources like welfare programs.[23] The era of Hoover's associational state was over, but partnerships remained central to government policy, resulting in a political structure that was highly sensitive to external influence and interest group pressure.[24]

While the story of the New Deal has often been told, scholars of American political development have been less interested in exploring the specific role credit programs played in this fractured system, talking instead in broader terms of Keynesianism and spending. This focus has elided the specific advantages of credit as a tool of statecraft. Under the leadership of Jesse Jones, the RFC offered what historian James Olson has called a "middle way" between the planning efforts of the Left and the fiscal conservativism of the Right.[25] Credit carried marked advantages when it came to each of the three problems outlined earlier: planning, sectionalism, and fiscal conservatism. In contrast to economic planning—which only proceeded for industries that overcame their internal divisions, accepted regulation, and found a special justification for government involvement—credit programs did not require coordination and compromise by industry players. Since pumping up credit was an easier sell than asking for lower prices or production limits, credit could be used to stimulate even the most conflict-ridden industries. Credit programs were financial policy enacted on a piecemeal basis, often through partnerships. This approach was a far cry from the efforts to expand the central administration that so rankled Southern Democrats. Nor did credit programs present themselves as a threat to the existing racial order: on the contrary, academics have singled out the housing credit programs as racist institutions that built wealth for white families at the expense of families of color.[26] As for the fiscal conservatives, credit programs did not appeal to them; however, because credit programs could easily be taken off-budget, they did offer a way around such opponents.

Tracing the history of the Reconstruction Finance Corporation and the housing programs reveals how government officials expanded the use of credit as a mode of spending during the 1930s, both in the spread of credit to new sectors and in the proliferation of techniques of credit allocation. Over time, credit flourished as a policy tool because it could be reconciled with free-market rhetoric, because it could be easily taken off-budget and run through partnerships, and because it could sidestep congressional appropriations and all the veto points that process entailed.

The RFC and the New Credit State

The Reconstruction Finance Corporation started as a relatively small and targeted response to the banking crises of the 1930s. Between 1929 and 1932, lending in the United States dropped by 44 percent.[27] Six hundred banks, holding over a half-billion dollars in deposits, closed in November and December of 1930 alone.[28] Rural banks were strained by depopulation and faced competition from a new generation of credit-proffering retailers; they also suffered for having overlent to farmers in the 1920s.[29] Urban banks were devastated by the collapsed mortgage and stock markets. The Federal Reserve in theory could have stepped in as a lender of last resort, but it was limited in the kind of collateral it could accept, and the Chicago Reserve refused to do much to help failing banks in the midwestern centers of Chicago, Detroit, and Cleveland, which were among the most desperate in the nation.[30]

Still dedicated to the associational ideal, Hoover first encouraged banks to organize among themselves.[31] In the fall of 1931, at a meeting in Andrew Mellon's home, Hoover asked a small group of New York bankers to rescue the failing industry. They reluctantly responded that same October by forming the National Credit Corporation. It was a halfhearted solution plagued by collective action problems: membership was too expensive for the weakest and neediest small country banks, only the most troubled of the next tier of banks wanted to join, and the effort left out much of the financial sector. By the end of November, as banks continued to fail, Hoover moved ahead with a direct government response in the form of the Reconstruction Finance Corporation.

Intended as an emergency measure, the RFC was only authorized to lend for the coming year.[32] Although it had a 10-year charter, Hoover hoped its mere existence would calm the market and so render additional efforts un-necessary. Funded by the Treasury through a $500 million stock purchase, Congress authorized the RFC to issue three times that amount in debt. This was to be the Depression's version of the War Finance Corporation, which had lent money to banks and companies essential for military production during the Great War. It opened with eight divisions and 33 local offices, run by men who had previously staffed the War Finance Corporation.[33]

The RFC's bipartisan board included private bankers and business leaders as well as the heads of the Federal Reserve, Treasury, and Federal Farm Loan Bank. The chairman of the Federal Reserve, Eugene Meyer (who encouraged Hoover to create the RFC and had served on the board of the War Finance Cor-poration), was appointed the first chairman of the new organization's board. Meyer was joined by Secretary of the Treasury Andrew Mellon (who immedi-ately stepped down and was replaced by Ogden Mills) and H. Paul Bestor, the head of the Federal Farm Loan Bank. Charles G. Dawes served as president. Dawes, a brigadier general and former vice president under Coolidge, had served as the first director of the Bureau of the Budget and had already won the Nobel Peace Prize for his plan to lend money to Germany for the payment of war reparations. The other members of the board were representatives of industry, appointed by Hoover and given to Democrats in an effort to make the RFC a bipartisan effort. Harvey Couch was from Arkansas and had experience in banking, railroad, and electric utilities; Wilson McCarthy was from Utah and had experience in agriculture and finance. Rounding out the group was Jesse H. Jones, a Texan with experience in lumber and real estate, whose later 13-year reign over the corporation would substantially expand its growth.[34]

Hoover's limited vision for the RFC was clear in the circumscribed nature of its early loans, which matched the Federal Reserve's conservative terms. Debt was secured with good collateral, issued at 6 or 7 percent interest, and due in six months.[35] Strict terms and high rates were a way to ensure that government support was truly a last resort.[36] The RFC's narrow mission was to assist financial institutions: banks, credit unions, insurance companies, and mortgage companies. Since the banks and insurance companies were heav-ily invested in railroad securities, the early RFC also bailed out the railroads, which at the time faced the added strain of new competition from truck and airline freight delivery.[37]

The early RFC played a crucial role in helping banks whose money was tied up in illiquid mortgages. RFC's doors opened in February of 1932, and its first loan application came from the Bank of America (then called the Bank of America National Trust & Savings Association, with operations limited to California), which used its portfolio of mortgages to secure the loan. The RFC first lent the Bank of America $15 million but later increased this amount to $30 million, eventually lending a total of $65 million. While large banks benefited from large loans, the RFC also made a great many smaller loans to smaller banks: in its first seven months, it issued 90 percent of its bank loans to institutions in small towns (with a population under 50,000). By July, the RFC had made $1.3 billion in loans to 5,520 companies, including 4,964 banks and trusts. This represented a fourth of U.S. banks.[38]

By the summer of 1932, it was clear that the RFC's mere presence would not right the economy.[39] In Congress, liberal Democrats and progressive Republicans pushed for the expansion of the RFC's loans, a change that RFC chair Eugene Meyer resisted. When Congress first sent up a bill that would allow the RFC to lend half a billion dollars to state governments for relief purposes, Hoover vetoed it as a violation of "every sound principle of public finance and government."[40] But for all of Hoover's reticence, he had built a machine for distributing credit, and the nation was about to use it. Even Hoover realized that the worsening market forced his hand. The next bill Congress passed, the Emergency Relief and Construction Act, was signed by Hoover on July 21, 1932.

The Emergency Relief and Construction Act authorized the RFC to lend $300 million to local governments and another $1.5 billion for other public works projects. It also expanded support for farms, including loans abroad for the purchase of U.S. products, agricultural marketing, and stock purchases in the Federal Home Loan Banks. The Treasury paid for this with a purchase of $1.8 billion in RFC stock. The act also reorganized the RFC board, removing the ex officio appointments of the Federal Reserve chair and members of the Farm Loan Commission. At this time, Charles Dawes also resigned as president (in response to a scandal over a failed bank that had received a $90 million RFC loan). The stage was set for the RFC's expansion.[41]

JESSE H. JONES, ADOLF BERLE, AND THE RFC

The same month the Emergency Relief and Construction Act extended the RFC's mission, Jesse H. Jones replaced Dawes as its head. Jones was a Democrat from Dallas who had started off in lumber and had then gotten into the mortgage business to support his lumber sales. This had led to a career in mortgage banking. He had grown into one of the nation's largest real estate developers and had also entered the newspaper business (buying the *Houston Chronicle*) and dabbled in oil (he was an original stockholder in the company that eventually became Exxon).[42] "People learned not to fool with Jesse Jones," Arthur Schlesinger explains in his classic book on the New Deal before describing the man in more detail:

> He was now almost sixty, a great monument of a man, his face square and hard, his lips compressed, his erect seventy-five inches topped by a mass of silver-white hair. He was profane and taciturn in the Texas manner, loved

power, was indifferent to ideology, never read books, had no sentimental illusions about the underdog, and kept his word. He could do business with anybody, even New Dealers, even Wall Street.[43]

Jones was not a modest man. When he later wrote his own account of his time at the RFC, he filled it with praise of his work and character from high-ranking officials. Nor was Jones overly cautious. He would rather ask forgiveness than ask permission. James S. Olson's history of the RFC describes Jones as "blessed with an extraordinary ego and ability to match."[44] Jones viewed the RFC's early lending as timid and short-sighted. With Roosevelt's support, he now set out to remake the organization.[45]

Jones's background provided advantages when it came to dealing with New Deal politics. He was a Democrat appointed by a Republican president. He had banking experience, but as a Texan he was also quick to push back against pressure from New York bankers.[46] He took pride in making sound deals and abided by a strict sense of what the government should and should not do. For instance, Jones thought it was improper for the government to make loans to newspapers or churches—neither of those institutions, he believed, should be in the debt of any government.[47] Similarly, the RFC made no loans to hospitals because Jones felt they should be supported by their local communities.[48] But Jones was willing to expend his own political and social capital in lieu of the RFC's funds for a good cause. When he turned down Archbishop Edward Mooney's request for a loan to save Detroit churches, he directed the archbishop to two banks with Catholic chairmen of the board, who then put together a consortium of Michigan banks that lent the church $21 million.[49]

Jones was eventually granted extraordinary lending powers through the RFC. In June 1940, as France fell to the Nazis, the RFC was authorized to fund military preparations as long as the expenditures were approved by Roosevelt. When a senator observed that this authorized Jones "to lend any amount of money for any length of time at any interest to anyone he chose," the legislation's champion Carter Glass responded: "Yes, but he won't."[50] When the RFC was later folded into other agencies, Jones was given even more authority: he was promoted to the position of federal loan administrator in 1939, and to secretary of commerce in 1940. Moreover, as head of the RFC, Jones was positioned to amass a great deal of political favors. James Olson points out that the 45,000 loans the RFC distributed by 1935 left no congressional district untouched: "To one degree or another, every member of Congress ended up in Jones's debt."[51]

Among Jones's many allies was Adolf Berle, a law professor from Columbia and member of Roosevelt's brain trust. With Gardiner Means, Berle wrote *The Modern Corporation and Private Property*, a landmark work of modern organizational theory that analyzes the corporation as a set of property rights that privileges managers over owners. In 1932, the same year that *The Modern Corporation* was published, Berle was reconceptualizing not only the fundamental nature of property rights, but also the role of the federal government in this new corporate age. He had come to the conclusion that economic recovery rested on federal credit support.[52] In a memo to then-Governor Roosevelt in 1932, Berle argued that troubled money markets were acting as a barrier that prevented the nation's incredible productivity from being directed toward ending poverty. In 1933, Berle wrote that the nation's "greatest single need" was support for institutions that could help refinance the debts of struggling Americans, from "the little farmer in Iowa" to "the big railroad systems."[53] An early fan of Keynes, Berle wanted the federal government to be even more aggressive with credit distribution than Jones, advocating without success for the creation of a new system of regional capital credit banks for business lending.[54]

From the vantage point of early 1933, when the first NRA had not yet failed, men like Berle and Jones saw the RFC as a way to support economic planning.[55] It was not yet clear that credit support would not work in the service of economic planning but instead compensate for its failure. Still, men like Berle and Jones were ready to mobilize the credit of the state on behalf of the struggling nation. The first step in this process was to transform the RFC's original mission: the rescue of the banks.

THE RFC AND THE BANKS

The nation's banking crisis came to a head just as Roosevelt took office. Roosevelt's inauguration was March 4, 1933, just days after the Federal Reserve notified the Treasury that its gold reserves were below the legal limit. On March 5, Roosevelt held a special congressional session to deal with the worsening bank situation. On March 6, he shut down all banks for the next four days. On March 9, Congress passed the Emergency Banking Act. Title III of that bill authorized the Reconstruction Finance Corporation to purchase stock in banks.

Jones had already been a proponent of purchasing stock in banks rather than issuing loans. He believed that the government should be recapitalizing the banks, not putting them deeper into debt. Now, when he was finally authorized to act, the bankers balked at the idea of having the U.S. government as a stockholder. Jones responded to their refusal to sign up for the capitalization program by asking to speak at the convention of the American Bankers Association, held in Chicago during September 1933. There he made a hard sell. "Be smart for once," he said in his speech. "Take the government into partnership with you." Later that evening, after a dinner and a show, he reminded attendees that for all their festivities, half the banks represented in the room were insolvent.[56] In the end, Jones used the Federal Deposit Insurance Corporation (FDIC) to compel the banks' participation. The only way for banks to qualify for the FDIC's deposit insurance program (when it went into effect on January 1, 1934) was for them to qualify as solvent under the FDIC's rules. For the 2,000 banks that were involved in the program, the capitalization deal was their path to FDIC insurance—the only alternative was to publicly pronounce their dire financial straits.

This was how the RFC came to hold over $1 billion in preferred stock in 6,104 banks by 1935. The amount was the equivalent of over a third of U.S. banking capital, held by half of the nation's banks.[57] James Mason, who investigated the RFC's banking policy in 2010, has concluded that the early loans indeed put an additional strain on banks, but that the recapitalization program was successful.[58] Schlesinger credits this program with saving the nation's banking system.[59] The RFC continued to make loans, taking "slow and frozen assets" like mortgages as collateral when other lenders would not.[60] By 1950, the RFC had made $2 billion in loans to 7,343 banks.[61]

MORE CREDIT FOR FARMERS

The Depression slammed into an agricultural sector that was already critically injured, leaving American farmers in a mounting state of desperation. World War I had been a golden age for U.S. farmers, who had thrived by selling produce to war-torn European nations. This boom lasted until Europe's economy recovered. When Americans continued to produce as much as they had before, they flooded the market.[62] Prices fell by 41 percent at the start of the 1920s and plunged another 55 percent during the early 1930s.[63] The still-young farm loan system went into crisis, with half of the Farm Loan Associations insolvent.[64] Small farmers in the Northeast faced foreclosure, while sharecroppers in the South starved. In the big commercial farms of California, dissatisfied workers radicalized and organized.

Hoover had provided some relief with the Agricultural and Marketing Act of 1929, which allowed farmers to extend payments on their loans and injected $500 million into the farm loan system. This act also authorized the government to buy up the nation's excess farm produce.[65] By 1930 the Grain Stabilization Corporation was purchasing grain in the open market and using futures to raise grain prices. But without production limits in place or a plan for what to do with their purchases, the agencies just resold the wheat, which further depressed prices.[66] The Emergency Relief and Construction Act that reorganized the RFC in 1932 also included provisions for farmers, earmarking $36 million to create a network of 12 Regional Agricultural Credit Corporations (called "Regionals") to lend $3 million in each geographical sector for agricultural marketing. When the Regionals were finally set up in August of 1933, farmers complained that their interest rates—set at 7 percent to avoid competition with private lenders—were too high to provide relief. By the end of 1933 the new institutions had only lent out $5 million.

All the while, farmers' anger mounted. By January of 1933, the conservative Farm Bureau warned Washington about simmering unrest. In Iowa, rioting farmers nearly hanged a judge who refused to stop a foreclosure.[67] In response, Roosevelt attacked the problem on multiple fronts outside the direct purview of the RFC. He bailed out the land banks that provided long-term mortgage credit to farmers and signed the Emergency Farm Mortgage Act of 1933, which restructured the debt of land banks and provided extensions for some farmers.[68] Since 1923 the Federal Intermediate Credit Banks had provided short-term credit to cover agricultural supplies. In 1933, the Roosevelt administration combined the management of the Federal Intermediate Credit Banks with that of the land banks under the Farm Credit Administration. Marketing cooperatives like Sunkist, Ocean Spray, and Land O'Lakes got their own credit system in June 1933 with the creation of the Bank for Cooperatives.

The earlier programs had tended to help wealthier businesses rather than the lower rung of tenant farmers and migrant farmworkers. However, starting in 1937, the Farm Security Administration offered loans to the nation's poorest farmers under the Farm Tenancy Act. This program took over the efforts of Rex Tugwell's Resettlement Administration, which had sought to move the nation's poorest farmers and migrant workers (including those hit by the Dust Bowl) onto more arable land, sometimes by providing them with loans to assist the move.[69] By one estimate, the federal government helped with half of the nation's farm loans during the New Deal.[70]

The RFC helped finance many of these New Deal agricultural efforts. By its own report, it helped over a million farmers between February and June of 1932 alone.[71] The RFC loaned $400 million to the effort to rescue the land banks (a loan that was repaid in August 1938). It sent $426 million to Congress to distribute as agricultural aid and $600 million to the Department of Agriculture's rural rehabilitation program (repaid March 1947).[72] It lent $175 million directly to farmers and ranchers and $50 million that went toward the marketing of American produce abroad. All told, the RFC pumped nearly $2 billion into the farm sector.

CREDIT AS PRICE SUPPORTS

During the New Deal, the nation's system of farm price supports was set up as a loan program through the Commodity Credit Corporation. This program serves as a good case for understanding the range of policy agendas officials pursed through the loan form, and it provides insight into how credit programs came to fit within a broader constellation of federal policies.

The CCC, still in operation today, makes loans that are collateralized by the farmer's crops. The key to the CCC's effectiveness as a price support is that the government sets the price of the crops. If the market value of the crop ends up higher than the government's price, then the farmer can sell the crop on the market, repay the loan, and keep the profit. If the market price falls below the government price, then the farmer simply defaults on the loan, and the government keeps the crops. This is a direct subsidy insofar as the government knowingly lets farmers pay back their loans with collateral that does not fully cover the amount borrowed. These instruments are called "non-recourse" loans because the government has agreed, in case of default, to seek no repayment for the loan beyond the crops already pledged as collateral.

According to Jesse Jones, this plan came down personally from Roosevelt, who got the idea from Mississippi cotton planter Oscar Johnson. On October 16, 1933, Executive Order 6340 authorized the RFC to make loans to farmers on the basis of cotton valued at 10 cents a pound, even though cotton was selling for 9 cents a pound at the time. Farmers could get the loans through their local bank or warehouse, which had the option of keeping the loan or passing it along to the RFC.[73] For the trouble of making and servicing the loans, the local bank or warehouse received 2.5 to 4 percent interest on the loan. For the 1934 cotton crop, the RFC made nearly 1.2 million separate loans to farmers against 4.5 million bales of cotton, with the price set at 12 cents a pound.[74]

The next month the CCC made loans to support corn prices. Within a few years, it was also dealing in dairy, tobacco, peanuts, pecans, prunes, and raisins. When teetotaling Henry Wallace, who sat on the CCC board, objected to loans for wine grapes used to make brandy, the RFC made the loan through a partnership with the Bank of America. "It mellowed," wrote Jones, "into exceedingly fine collateral."[75] In 1939 the CCC was transferred to the Department of Agriculture, and in 1948 it was reorganized as a federal corporation.[76]

BEYOND BANKS AND FARMS: CREDIT SUPPORT FOR CITIES, BUSINESSES, AND DISASTER RECOVERY

The RFC's efforts were not limited to banks and farms. Under its auspices, the Rural Electrification Administration used loans and guarantees to bring electricity to the 89 percent of farms that were without it in 1936.[77] The Disaster Loan Corporation, a precursor to later FEMA programs, lent $54 million through 24,900 loans to deal with the aftermath of floods, hurricanes, storms, and blighted crops.[78] As a bank for the New Deal programs, the RFC also supported public works, cities, and counties. The Public Works Administration and the Works Progress Administration received $2 billion from the RFC between 1933 and 1937. The RFC financed some of the nation's largest projects, including the Golden Gate Bridge, a power line linking Los Angeles to the

Boulder Dam, and a 244-mile aqueduct that carried Colorado River water to Southern California.[79] The RFC lent $300 million to cities, which included a $26.3 million loan for the city of Chicago to cover back pay for 19,000 school employees, many of whom were teachers who had gone an entire spring and summer without pay.[80] The RFC also bailed out smaller districts in the West. During the 1920s, districts in drier counties had issued municipal bonds to fund drainage, levee, and irrigation projects. Many of these bonds, which were sold primarily to small investors, were failing by the 1930s. The RFC bought up these bonds at 48 percent of their face value, refinanced them (lowering the interest from 6 to 4 percent), and reissued them with a government guarantee. This put money in the hands of the bondholders and provided relief for farmers from these overextended districts. All told, the RFC put $145 million into drainage, levees, and irrigation districts.[81]

Finally, the RFC started offering business loans in 1934. It paid special attention to manufacturing and medium-sized firms, like southern paper mills and lumber companies in the Northwest. Of the RFC's 9,000 loans—totaling $500 million within four years—half were small loans of $10,000 or less. Larger loans of over $50,000 constituted only 17 percent of the Corporation's allocation in that time.[82] The RFC preferred to partner with private banks when doing these deals and asked banks to share in the loans with private companies or offer to purchase a loan later.[83]

What about the housing market? The RFC was active there as well, as the next section will show.

A New System of Housing Credit

To understand the structure of New Deal housing programs, it helps to recall the state of U.S. mortgage finance at this time. There were 68,000 foreclosures in the United States in 1926.[84] By 1929, the number of nonfarm foreclosures had risen to 135,000. By 1933, there were 252,000.[85] When the Department of Commerce surveyed a set of cities in 1934, it found that 45 percent of owner-occupied mortgaged homes were in default.[86]

The nation's mortgage markets were complex. American real estate ranged from big-city apartments to suburban homes to western farms, all spread out over a continent. Country banks offered mortgages in the West, mutuals dominated in the Northeast, and mortgage bonds funded big commercial buildings nationwide. Thrifts operated nationally and had reached 38 percent of the residential market by 1930, but the same proportion of loans was held by non-institutional lenders.[87]

Each of these markets had distinct problems that unfolded at their own pace. The general housing market stalled in 1926, but mortgage bonds continued to rise until 1932. The mortgage bond market had to deal not only with overbuilding but also with systematic financial mismanagement and its ensuing controversy. That, however, was not the issue for the better-managed S&L loans, which instead faltered when their unemployed borrowers defaulted or when banks that held their deposits closed.[88]

The New Deal housing programs offered patchwork solutions for this patchwork market: First, the Federal Home Loan Bank System was established in 1932 to support the S&Ls. The next year, the Home Owners Loan Corporation bought up and refinanced troubled mortgages. The following year, the National Housing Act created FHA mortgage insurance to support the flailing mortgage brokerage business. The two parts of this response that endured—home loan banks for the S&Ls and mortgage insurance for the brokers—would become the backbone of the postwar golden age of American housing.

The housing programs fine-tuned the use of credit support as a way to stimulate the entire economy, not only because credit could be talked about in the inoffensive language of "market corrections," as historian David Freund convincingly argues, but also through its many other benefits: it was cheap, it was almost entirely off-budget, it avoided the veto-ridden appropriations system, and it could broadly stimulate industry and consumer markets.[89]

SAVING THE SAVINGS AND LOANS: THE FEDERAL HOME LOAN BANK SYSTEM

Back in August of 1931, President Hoover had gathered housing experts for the Conference on Home Building and Home Ownership.[90] This first major national response to the housing market crash was an exercise in associational statecraft on a massive scale. The conference's program drew from housing, real estate, economics, and zoning experts. With 3,700 attendees, its planning committee alone included 34 industry leaders and six coordinating committees, while the event included 25 fact-finding committees and generated 11 volumes of reports.

At this time, the banks had credit support through the Federal Reserve system, and the farms had credit support through the farm loan system. Now the S&Ls planned their own system of credit support. A modified version of a plan from their trade association, the USBLL, rose to the top: the creation of a network of 12 banks, capitalized at $5 million, with half drawn from members' subscriptions and the rest from the federal government. The Federal Home Loan Bank (FHLB) system officially opened on October 15, 1932, and started issuing loans in December of the same year.[91] In 1934 the National Housing Act further shored up this system by creating the Federal Savings and Loan Insurance Corporation (FSLIC) to back its deposits.

A group of bureaucratically minded S&Ls that dominated the USBLL quickly took over control of the Federal Home Loan Bank system. Two USBLL executives were installed on the five-member FHLB board in Washington, D.C. USBLL members also filled nearly 70 percent of the seats on the 12 regional banks' 11-member boards of directors. This allowed USBLL members to protect their markets by, for example, only allowing new federal charters for applicants that would not hurt an existing association.[92] Under 20 percent of the 11,000 building and loans in the United States in 1933 entered the FHLB system. Nearly 4,000 more joined in the next four years. Snowden found that this initial group of FHLB members came to dominate the industry and held 92 percent of all S&L assets by 1950.[93]

THE HOLC MOPS UP THE MORTGAGE MARKET

The Federal Home Loan Banks took care of the long-term needs of the S&Ls, but much of the damage to the housing market continued to unfold. Hoover had, in fact, tried another temporary fix: the Emergency Relief and Construction Act of 1932 authorized the RFC to lend money to companies that agreed to build low-income housing in slums. But because of a clash between the legislation and state tax laws, the program never got off the ground. The housing market continued to worsen.

Roosevelt's Home Owners' Loan Corporation (HOLC), created in 1933, was a more decisive response. Funded with $200 million from the Treasury, the HOLC traded government-guaranteed, tax-exempt bonds for mortgages held by troubled lenders. Mortgage purchases provided lenders with much-needed liquidity.[94] Because the HOLC refinanced those mortgages, the program also helped families facing foreclosure.[95]

With 400 offices and a staff of 20,000, the HOLC was large. Forty percent of Americans with mortgages applied to the system for help within three years.[96] By 1936, a fifth of the nation's nonfarm mortgages had been converted into HOLC's long-term (15-year), low-interest (5 percent) amortizing loans.[97] Over a three-year period the Corporation purchased or issued a million loans.[98] Not all Americans benefited equally from the program, however. Instead, the HOLC reproduced a set of racist underwriting standards that benefited white families in white neighborhoods.[99]

MORTGAGE BROKERS IN THE NEW ERA: THE NATIONAL HOUSING ACT OF 1934

While the FHLBs took care of the long-term needs of the S&Ls and the HOLC interceded in the collapsing mortgage market, the future of the nation's mortgage brokers—the group that had specialized in the essential work of moving money across both geographic regions and financial sectors—remained unresolved. With the rise of Wall Street, this work was more important than ever. The brokers, however, were deeply damaged and mired in controversy.

The National Housing Act (NHA) of 1934 looked to shore up the market for the millions of mortgages sold outside of the S&Ls. It did so by building a new national system of mortgage insurance through the Federal Housing Administration. FHA insurance was designed to be a staid, reliable system that could appeal to skittish investors. As a form of risk management for mortgages, this insurance was far more conservatively designed than, say, the shaky guarantees sold in the 1920s.

Like the farm loan system before it, the FHA threw the weight of the government behind the use of the long-term amortized mortgage. The Depression had shown how short-term mortgages left families vulnerable during economic downturns.[100] Mortgages issued outside of S&Ls tended to be 3 to 10 years in length. Down payments typically covered 40 to 60 percent of the value of the property. Families often took out smaller second and third mortgages to cover the additional costs. The principal of the loan was due in one large bullet or balloon payment at the end, while earlier payments went toward paying down the interest. If borrowers did not have the money to pay off the large final bill, they would take out a new loan. However, in a crisis like the Great Depression, when families could not pay off their first loan lenders simply refused to offer new loans.[101]

For families, a longer repayment period and a lower down payment lessened the risk of foreclosure during market crises and eliminated the need for second or third mortgages. For lenders, insurance managed the risk of default. For the Roosevelt administration, it was a low-cost way to promote lending for new homes and repairs for the estimated 13 million homes in need of improvements in 1934.[102]

For investors, however, there was a downside: FHA insurance protected against credit risks, but its long-term mortgages tied up funds for 15 or so years. This created a significant liquidity problem, and it heightened the need for a working secondary market where investors could offload their mortgages.[103] That is, before investors purchased an FHA mortgage, they wanted some assurance that, if need be, they could access the value of the mortgage before the long term of the loan was up. This was further complicated, however, by the fact that the mortgage bond crisis had taken out the secondary market along with the primary one.

Fannie Mae: A Backstop for a Backstop

The origins of Fannie Mae lay in investors' worries about the long tenure of the FHA-insured mortgages. Title II of the 1934 National Housing Act created charters for private national associations to invest in FHA mortgages. If investors could resell the mortgages whenever they liked they would worry less about their long tenure. The attempt to set up a private secondary market at this time failed: no private national associations were ever formed under the act.[104] After a delayed start in setting rules and regulations, officials repeatedly revised the program's requirements in order to make the effort more attractive.[105] They tried lowering capital requirements for the associations from $5 million to $2 million. They tried increasing the leverage ratio from 1:10 to 1:12 and then 1:20. They granted national associations broad exemptions from federal and state taxes. They authorized the RFC to buy stock in the national associations and authorized the national associations to originate FHA loans. None of these strategies worked. The market was too broken, and conservative investors too wary. The only applications the FHA did receive were rejected.

The Roosevelt administration decided to use the RFC to demonstrate the viability of a secondary market for FHA mortgages and to shore up the housing market in the meantime. In 1935 the RFC Mortgage Company was formed with $10 million.[106] It started its efforts with the broken commercial real estate sector. Targeting income-producing big buildings and properties (whose mortgages had previously been peddled by the failed bond houses), the company focused on the especially devastated markets of Detroit, Chicago, and Florida. (Relatively little needed to be done in California, Jones later noted, because there the already RFC-rescued Bank of America had stayed in the mortgage business.[107])

With the success of the entire FHA insurance program predicated on the existence of a secondary mortgage market *that did not actually function*, Congress created Fannie Mae to step into the gap. Initially named the National Mortgage Association after the charters authorized under the NHA, Fannie Mae in 1938 was authorized to buy and sell FHA mortgages.[108] Within the year, it had been renamed the Federal National Mortgage Association (FNMA). Almost immediately traders started calling the company "Fanny May," a derivation of its initials.[109] (In the 1970s the organization patented the spelling of the name as "Fannie Mae" to avoid confusion with the Chicago-based candy company Fanny May.[110])

Fannie bought its first mortgage on May 5, 1938.[111] While the RFC Mortgage Company continued to buy mortgages for older homes and buildings, Fannie Mae was only authorized to buy mortgages on new houses. By supporting and brokering the FHA mortgages (17 percent of which Fannie bought in 1938), Fannie helped promote federal mortgage insurance. By the end of 1938 it housed $80 million in FHA mortgages, $34 million of which had been transferred from the RFC. By 1947 Fannie had spent over $271 million to purchase nearly 67,000 mortgages.[112] Although the actual amount of its early purchases was not particularly large when you consider the total of the entire mortgage market—Jones and Grebler later estimated that Fannie's purchases constituted less than 1 percent of all nonfarm housing loans before World War II—Fannie Mae did provide a degree of assurance for FHA investors.[113]

In 1948, the charter for the private national mortgage associations was revoked. Although the government demonstration had been successful, the private associations had never really materialized, and the few early applications for them had been rejected.[114] Moreover, as Fannie Mae accrued profits, it demonstrated its usefulness as a revenue-generating entity not just to private companies, but also to government officials, who had their own set of fiscal concerns. Jesse Jones tells a story of Jimmy Moffet, a former FHA head and friend of Roosevelt, who inquired about buying Fannie Mae after its first year. "With an invested capital of $11,000,000 and an annual profit in the millions," Jones wrote, "we were not interested in selling it to Mr. Moffett or to anyone else."[115] By 1947, the RFC Mortgage Company, reorganized that year into the RFC, had netted $6 million in profits; Fannie netted another $23 million.[116] As time went on, private companies worried about market failure became concerned instead with market competition. After all, how could they compete with a government corporation with superior credit that allowed it to borrow more cheaply?

Fannie Mae was the last piece of the puzzle for the New Deal housing programs. Construction on new homes rose from 93,000 in 1933 to 619,000 in 1941.[117] After World War II, the emergency programs—the Home Owners' Loan Corporation and the RFC Mortgage Company—were dissolved, but the Federal Home Loan Banks (backed by FSLIC insurance) and FHA insurance (backed by Fannie Mae) remained to prop up a golden age of mortgage finance and housing in the postwar era.

The Political Economy of the Credit Programs

The housing programs were never just about housing. Government officials were learning through them how to use housing *to manage the entire economy*, a strategy that would remain in place long after the housing crisis receded. Such a strategy was possible because of the particular political advantages of credit: its capacity to broadly stimulate economic growth, the way it could be justified as a small market correction, and its low fiscal outlays relative to alternatives.

Credit was a form of stimulus. The NHA was not just designed as a way to support families struggling to keep their homes. It was also intended to address unemployment and stimulate economic growth.[118] Consider what Marriner Eccles later wrote about the NHA:

> The significance of a new housing program that could revive the economy was not lost on President Roosevelt. He knew that almost a third of the unemployed were to be found in the building trades, and housing was by

far the most important part of that trade. A program of new home construction, launched on an adequate scale, not only would gradually help put those men back to work *but would act as the wheel within the wheel to move the whole economic engine.* It would affect everyone, from the manufacturer of lace curtains to the manufacturer of lumber, bricks, furniture, cement, and electrical appliances. The mere shipment of these supplies would affect the railroads, which in turn would need the produce of steel mills for rails, freight cars, and so on.[119]

Eccles's metaphor of housing as a "wheel within the wheel to move the whole economic engine" is revealing. In the postwar era, housing credit was used to prime the pump of the U.S. economy.[120] Officials also knew that if they could use housing to speed up the economy, they could also use it to slow the economy down. Greta Krippner details how the housing industry became the center of a set of "levers and pulleys" to alternately speed up and slow down economic growth.[121] Building on this, Monica Prasad has characterized postwar U.S. economic policy as a kind of "Mortgage Keynesianism."[122] In the U.S. context, a large proportion of economic growth would be assured specifically through credit-fueled homeownership.

Credit also had a kind of market appeal. Historian David Freund points out that using credit as a policy tool had the advantage of keeping the myth of well-functioning free markets alive. He makes this case through a careful analysis of the creation of the FHLBs. The savings and loans, Freund notes, argued in the 1930s that the real problem with the nation's mortgage market was not that lenders were "structurally incapable of supporting affordable loans and widespread homeownership" (in Freund's words) but rather that it was hampered by a mixture of corruption and technical market inefficiencies.[123] From this foundation, the S&Ls could frame the creation of government credit support as a mere technical tweak, a claim supported by the public–private nature of the FHLBs and the purportedly temporary nature of the government's involvement with them. This all allowed government officials to insist that they were bolstering commerce without directing it, that this massive governmental reshuffling of risks was no real challenge to free markets.[124]

Freund explains how this all served to mask how important the government's activities were for the mortgage market:

> To hear Bodfish and others describe it, federal discount operations would not alter existing market mechanisms and thus posed no threat to the free enterprise system. It was "distinctly not proposed that the Federal Government itself act directly," explained the committee on Slums, Large Scale Housing, and Decentralization in their endorsement of the [U.S. Building and Loan League] proposal. The government would merely "set up enabling machinery and establish general policies." Most importantly

(and technically true), the proposed federal banks would not "directly lend money." In what became a common refrain at the conference and in Depression-era debates over federal selective credit programs, the committee described the government's new role as that of intermediary, as a force that would correct and free up sluggish markets, without disrupting or changing them. They also described federal improvement as temporary, necessary only until industry resumed its normal operations and consumers regained their confidence.[125]

Just as the farm loan system framed government credit—distributed through partnerships with private actors—as a means to help farmers help themselves, so now did the home loan system purport to help markets correct themselves. The language had changed from an emphasis on paternalism to an emphasis on "intervention," from a focus on individuals to a focus on the efforts of companies, but the reasoning was analogous: objections to government action should not apply *in this case* because the policy was cooperative, temporary, and involved credit. It was a formulation with wide appeal, because it allowed the government to be massively consequential while also openly deferring to the model of political restraint and free markets.

One group not buying the idea that credit was a mere tweak to the market was the fiscal conservatives. Lending money and paying to purchase loans was expensive work. The use of guarantees (like the RFC guarantees of refinanced municipal bonds or FHLB debt) did not require actual expenditures, but it was no less problematic in the minds of men like Lew Douglas: as inflationary extensions of the U.S. government's credit, guarantees could drive up borrowing costs, scare away careful lenders, and degrade the value of American savings. Treasury Secretary Morganthau was reported to bitterly resent the RFC, disliking both its profligate lending and, on a more personal level, Jones's continued support from Roosevelt.[126]

Defenders of the credit programs, like Jesse Jones, countered that fiscal conservatives failed to make the proper distinction between credit and other forms of government spending. "So far as the budget is concerned," wrote Jones, "Secretary of Treasury Morganthau did not seem to know the difference between the RFC lending money and Henry Hopkins giving it away—the difference between disbursing funds which would be repaid, and dishing out doles and grants."[127] Jones's point was that income-generating programs *should* be treated differently on the budget than other kinds of government expenditures. Yet the United States had no capital budget at the time: spending for loans, if done through the Treasury, appeared the same as spending for grants.

For all their outlays and liabilities, credit programs retained considerable advantages: some could be set up at low cost, and others could be removed from the budget. The FHA's mortgage program was not only a way to help reduce unemployment; it was designed to be a cheap means of doing so. The FHA's fees covered its costs, making it a comparatively inexpensive way for the government to encourage growth in single-family homeownership—and, through that, encourage growth in housing construction, industry, and consumption. These low costs were especially advantageous in the years before the Keynesian revolution, when most Americans believed that budgetary balance was an unassailable principle of good governance.

At the onset of fiscal year 1934 (which had a start date of July 1, 1933), the Treasury distinguished "emergency" from "general" expenditures in its daily reports, a step toward reporting the emergency expenditures outside of the administrative budget at year-end. Emergency spending included construction costs and the operation of the RFC, which, after its $500 million capitalization from the Treasury, had operated totally off-budget. Roosevelt and his defenders justified this change as a reasonable response to the economic crisis, one with precedents in wartime spending and preferable to the previous system, which had excluded the RFC altogether.[128] Fiscal conservatives saw the accounting move as a first step toward budgetary shenanigans and a violation of the principle of budgetary unity.[129] They were not wrong.

The use of corporate forms like the RFC had additional advantages when it came to government costs and accounting. The RFC had a good deal of autonomy even after it was included in the emergency budget in 1933. It could issue its own government-guaranteed debt directly to capital markets. Its loan repayments went into a revolving fund that financed further activities. By 1937, with the commercial banks shored up, farm lending stabilized, and the home loan system in place, the RFC was sending money back to the Treasury.[130] Its techniques were later used by federal credit programs to direct and incentivize private activities, including partnerships, repurchase agreements, and brokerage.

Credit programs could effect change without costing a great deal, or at least without appearing to do so on the budget, but fiscal conservatives who rejected Keynesian thinking warned that government credit was no less problematic because it was caused by the crisis or because it was off-budget. The importance of credit programs for fiscal conservatives was not that selective credit appealed to them, but that it lessened the extent to which they could use the budget deficit to embarrass Roosevelt.

An additional advantage to the credit programs was that they also provided a pathway around the veto-ridden appropriations process. As Federal Reserve Board secretary Chester Morrill noted:

> It became apparent almost immediately, to many Congressman and Senators, that here was a device which would enable them to provide for activities that they favored for which government funds would be required, but

without any apparent increase in appropriations, and without passing an appropriations bill of any kind to accomplish its purposes. After they had done that, there need be no more appropriations and its activities could be enlarged indefinitely, as they were almost fantastic proportions.[131]

Congress understood well that taking programs off budget reduced the pathways available for cutting their funding. The RFC's ability to issue its own debt mattered not only because the RFC appeared to be low-cost, but also because outside sources of funding protected it from the kind of committee politics that would kill the National Resource Planning Board after the war.

Freeing programs from veto points meant detaching them from political control and oversight. Arthur Schlesinger, Jr., calls the RFC "the most enduring stronghold of government-business cooperation" of the New Deal.[132] Public–private partnerships further complicated matters of political accountability. The RFC shared loans with banks. The Commodity Credit Corporation's operations were organized through local warehouses. The federal housing programs similarly relied extensively on partnerships; it was the S&Ls, after all, that took the lead in designing the FHLB system.

This delegated authority necessarily skewed lines of political influence. The report of the Finance Committee of the landmark 1931 Homeownership Conference contained a prescient comment by Howard Kissell, the president of the National Association of Real Estate Boards: "The members of this committee seem to have considered the entire home financing problem not from the point of view of the home buyer, but from the point of view of the investor who is worried about his security."[133] Government programs that rely on business partnerships may present themselves as being more respectful of free markets, but they also give control over public resources to private actors and allow those actors to disproportionately influence the framing of political issues.[134] Furthermore, researchers have shown that the ability to set the terms of a political debate is itself an important vector of political influence.[135]

Another serious problem loomed, one that had to do with administrative control of government credit policy. Keynesianism required the government to carefully watch and adjust the economy. In 1938, economist Gerhard Colm observed that "fiscal policy must be integrated with the whole economic policy, and the budget procedure must be adapted to this new task of governmental policy."[136] This presumed that the government actually could measure the economy and control government activities. Yet many of the qualities that made credit an especially effective political tool—its ability to spur growth, its manifold forms, its budgetary flexibility—were also qualities that made credit programs hard to coordinate and limit.

For all that Keynesian theory modeled the effects of fiscal policy, it did not offer much in the way of political advice for how to deal with a sprawling decentralized government in which many programs were off-budget and implemented through corporations, insurance, and guarantees. This was not much of a problem during the Depression, when economic growth was so desperately needed, but at the end of the postwar era, as inflation mounted, officials complained loudly that the sprawling nature and conflicting agendas of the credit programs created a serious impediment to proper economic adjustment.

Credit Policy Trade-offs

At the start of the 1930s, credit support was still a relatively constrained policy form. By the end of the decade, it sat at the center of America's convoluted, piecemeal, consumption-driven version of a developmental state. Never before had such a variety of credit forms been used on such a large scale, or been so fully institutionalized, by the federal government.

The New Deal programs evince the many advantages of credit support, as well as the associated trade-offs. Credit programs got around the coordination problems that doomed national planning by being targeted and decentralized, but this also made them hard to direct and control. Credit programs relieved worries about government intervention, but this meant ceding control and influence over public resources to private companies. Credit programs had relatively low costs and could be taken off budget, saving them from controversy and veto points, but this compromised transparency and democratic accountability. The credit programs were like a magic spell that could only be enacted by sacrificing some precious thing: transparency, or accountability, or control. But what the nation got in exchange was considerable indeed. Credit compensated for the failures of economic planning. It reached across fraught ideological divides. In the end, credit programs worked not because they resolved the problems that plagued American political life—the fierce ideological disagreements, the cumbersome veto points—but because they circumvented them.

From the point of view of a borrower, credit brings the heavy burden of debt. But for lawmakers, credit can have an amazing quality of airiness. In the New Deal, credit allocation floated past the sticking points that bogged down other kinds of programs. Across generational and ideological divides, American politicians continued to use credit not merely to address specific inefficiencies in the credit markets, but to manage a wide swath of political concerns. And perhaps because sociologists when studying the New Deal have tended to look at the very things that credit policy was used to get around—the biggest controversies, the largest expenditures, the most significant expansions of administrative capacities—the dramatic expansion of credit programs has tended to float right past us as well.

8

Off-Budget and Decentralized

In 1963, the U.S. House of Representatives conducted a survey of federal credit agencies. It identified 74 credit aid programs, 51 of which issued loans directly. As of June 1962, the government held $30 billion in assets and insured or guaranteed another $70 billion; three-quarters of the latter derived from the Federal Housing Administration and the Veterans Administration.[1] Combined, the $100 billion was the equivalent of nearly 15 percent of all outstanding private borrowings in the United States at the time.[2] And these totals excluded loans from the U.S. Agency for International Development and Commodity Credit Corporation, on the grounds that their terms were so forgiving as to effectively make them grant programs.

The resulting report concluded that "the credit programs extended to every segment of the American economy—financial institutions, agriculture, business, private housing, state and local government, international trade, and individual households."[3] The politics of credit had come a long way from the nineteenth-century debates about nationwide mortgage credit distribution. Credit support was no longer reserved for special occasions. It was more like a Swiss army knife, with many components that could be used for many tasks.

This chapter outlines the growth of credit programs from the Second World War through the postwar era. This period saw a surge in wartime credit, the end of the RFC, and the emergence of government support for venture capital and school loans. As postwar credit programs moved capital and pioneered new ways of lending, they shaped how and where U.S. companies lent money. They also helped lift a generation of white families and systematically exclude African Americans. Discriminatory and decentralized, off-budget and complex, the credit programs were a key component of America's peculiar developmental state.

War, Scandal, and Reorganization at the RFC

As the institutional seat of many of the nation's credit programs, the Reconstruction Finance Corporation fluctuated in political favor in the 1930s. Budget hawks like Secretary of Treasury Henry Morgenthau, Jr., nearly convinced Franklin Roosevelt to kill the Corporation just before the recession of 1937–1938 led the president to expand its use. The RFC again faced possible shutdown when the Second World War reversed its fortunes. As the nation prepared for war in the summer of 1940, Congress gave RFC head Jesse Jones carte blanche to support the production and acquisition of weapons, plants, and critical materials.[4]

A new generation of government corporations sprang up to support the war.[5] The Petroleum Oil Reserve Company stockpiled oil and gasoline, while the Rubber Reserve Company stockpiled rubber. By 1945, the government managed over 50 synthetic rubber plants. The Metals Reserve Company spent $3.75 billion in four years acquiring or producing metals and minerals. The Defense Homes Corporation lent money to provide housing for workers, and the War Damage Corporation insured property against enemy attack. By 1945, the RFC had dispersed $9.2 billion through the Defense Plant Corporation to finance the construction of large plants, plus another $2.2 billion through the Smaller War Plants Corporation, $9.3 billion through the Defense Supplies Corporation for materials that ranged from wool to sodium nitrate, and $4.4 billion in small business loans for defense contracts.

The firms who leased the RFC's plants during this time represent a who's who of American corporations: Union Carbide, General Motors, U.S. Steel, B. F. Goodrich, Dow Chemical, and more. For these partners, the work was motivated by more than just a sense of patriotism. Washington generally absorbed the financial risks while sharing the profits. The institutions and places that wartime support built became the foundation for a strong set of linkages between industrial development, university research, and financial support that would be vitally important for the postwar economy.[6]

Despite its resurgence during the Second World War, the RFC's days were numbered. A series of scandals unfolded after Jesse Jones exited the Corporation in 1945, leading to a congressional review of questionable loans in 1949 that was soon followed by an investigation of kickbacks and other abuses of power. One RFC loan applicant was accused of bribing a loan examiner's wife, herself a White House stenographer, with a $10,000 mink coat that was worth more than the loan examiner's salary.[7] The mink was one of many "very succulent tidbits" received by the loan examiner, according to Senator J. William Fulbright, who headed up the investigation.[8] Framed as a symbol of pervasive corruption in the Truman administration, the "mink coat incident" became a talking point of the 1952 election. The RFC scandal eventually tainted both the Democratic and Republican National Committees when investigators found that the chairs of both parties had tried to influence RFC loan decisions.[9]

The RFC's problem was not just accusations that it had become a slush fund for patronage politics. With the nation's worst economic crisis resolved, critics targeted its very reason for being. Some on the Left saw the RFC as a symbol of corporate welfare, a bank that disproportionately benefited large and wealthy businesses. Critics on the Right derided the RFC as an example of government overreach and socialist state capitalism. Eisenhower, elected in 1952, did not wait long to address the scandal-ridden office. The RFC's liquidation was the second item on his 10-point reorganization plan submitted to Congress in 1953.[10] Its breakup started in 1953 and finished in 1957. This was not the end of the RFC programs, but it was a meaningful change. Importantly, it meant that key programs like the Export-Import Bank and loans to small businesses were shifted back onto the budget.

Changes in the Postwar Credit Programs

This section reviews postwar credit programs by major policy arena, but I do so with a caveat. Credit programs frequently transcended narrow policy areas and worked through multiple institutional pathways. This is very clear if we consider the example of disaster relief. Long before the Carter administration created the Federal Emergency Management Agency in 1978, agencies like the SBA and FHA were part of a more decentralized system of disaster relief that included loans and guarantees to fund repairs, the construction of buildings, and the establishment of new businesses in disaster-struck locations.[11] A disaster program might forgive the principal on a loan, allow for deferred payments, or waive normal government lending caps. Under a 1970 law, for example, the secretary of agriculture could provide disaster relief through adjusted payments or 40-year extensions of the Rural Electrification Administration loans.[12] Alternately, loans to local governments could help prevent disaster in the first place. A 1965 provision lent federal money to states for forest and grass fire prevention. Other credit programs, like those offering subsidized mortgage insurance in flood zones, encouraged building in disaster-prone areas. Or consider the ramifications of Cold War military priorities: we will see that they bled into school loan programs, plans to provide credit support for the venture capital industry, and decisions about the provision of development loans to other nations. So while this chapter breaks down credit allocations by major sector—business programs; foreign and military loans; and education, farm, and housing credit programs—it is helpful to keep in mind that an array of economic and social agendas are interwoven throughout.

BUSINESS PROGRAMS, VENTURE CAPITAL,
AND COLD WAR CREDIT

To end the RFC, Congress had to grapple with what, if any, kinds of credit support for business should remain. For years Democrats had advocated for government loans to small businesses while Republicans had called for the RFC to be closed.[13] In 1953 the two sides struck a compromise: the same legislation that closed the RFC also established the Small Business Administration on a temporary basis. The new SBA's staff even included RFC loan officers.[14]

The new agency had three tasks: to provide disaster relief, to help small firms secure government contracts, and to provide business loans through a revolving fund.[15] The name of the agency was always something of a misnomer, because early SBA assistance also went to medium-size and growing businesses—manufacturers with 1,000 employees, retailers with sales of up to $1 million. Nevertheless, support for the SBA remained a way for politicians on both sides of the aisle to signal support for the little guy.[16] In 1958 Congress created the SBA on a permanent basis.

The SBA quickly moved into the field of venture capital.[17] In fact, small business and venture capital shortages had been debated together for decades. Both small businesses and riskier firms had lacked access to long-term capital since the 1930s. Corporations created their own in-house labs for research and development. Guggenheim, Rockefeller, Whitney, Mellon, and Rothschild money made riskier bets in fields like aviation, but this funding stream was more like a patronage relationship than an institutionalized market niche.[18] The capital shortage for small and risky firms was partly a hangover from the 1920s—investors remained risk averse long after the Great Depression—and partly the consequence of New Deal regulations and tax regimes. Glass-Steagall drew a line between commercial and investment banking. Commercial banks could not invest in companies. The investment banks, meanwhile, preferred larger and safer bets and tax-advantaged investments like municipal bonds. In theory the RFC could have stepped in to help both small businesses and riskier firms, but the RFC dealt only with less risky medium-sized firms and manufacturers. Since the late 1930s Congress had weighed policy solutions to this problem ranging from capital credit banks to government-backed investment pools to deregulation. None gained much traction.

The problem of venture capital grew more pronounced as new research opened new opportunities for commercialization. Wartime military programs like the Manhattan Project had generated massive breakthroughs. But in the absence of a working venture capital industry, how would those new technologies become commercialized? In Boston, a team of luminaries from academia, finance, and industry in 1946 formed American Research Development (ARD), which is generally considered the first successful modern venture capital firm. Not coincidentally, ARD's founders included the president and treasurer of MIT, the university that had received half of the Office of Scientific Research and Development's research funds during the war.[19] It was the start of an industry, but a slow one. By one count, the 1940s ended with fewer than 25 operating venture capital firms.[20]

After years of debate about venture capital, it was *Sputnik* that finally spurred Congress into action. The Soviets' show of technological prowess raised pointed questions about the state of U.S research and development. Less than a year passed between *Sputnik*'s 1957 launch and the passage of the Small Business Investment Act of 1958. During that time Congress considered what a reasonable U.S. policy might look like. The Senate Banking and Currency Committee called for a program that was "private and profitable."[21] The main concern was that government efforts to fight the Soviets not come across as themselves socialist in bent. Government stock ownership in private firms and "anything resembling" it was a potential sign of state ownership.[22] In this context, credit programs and partnerships proved crucial. Loans allowed lawmakers to support venture capital at a comfortable distance. The SBA could inject funds into investment groups that would in turn provide long-term debt financing to growing firms.

Small Business Investment Corporations (SBICs) were the result. The SBICs provided small businesses with unsecured long-term (5- to 20-year) loans, with some of the loans convertible to equity.[23] Before they could make investments, the SBICs needed a capitalization of $300,000, but only half of that had to be raised privately. The rest could be borrowed from the SBA.[24] After the initial $300,000 was distributed, a company could apply for more government funds. Tax expenditures further supported the program. Investors in SBICs could write off losses to stock sales against regular income, for example. To strictly guard against state capitalism, no SBIC could own more than 20 percent of the equity of a supported business. To further mark the limits of federal power, the SBAs were chartered through states. Texas representative Wright Patman called the program a way "to help free-enterprise help itself."[25] Then still a senator, Lyndon Johnson proclaimed that the structure did "no violence to free enterprise" because it neither competed with nor sought control over private business.[26]

Problems immediately emerged with the SBICs. Smaller SBICs found that their returns did not cover the considerable expense associated with finding and vetting companies. The larger SBICs did better financially but tended to ignore the smallest businesses. Some SBICs focused on real estate rather than industry and retail, while others were run by neophyte or corrupt investors. These issues led both the media and the SBA to took a closer look at the SBICs in the 1960s. Subsequent investigations exposed extensive rule violations, fraud, expected losses, and even some connections to organized crime. In response, the SBA ramped up regulations and clamped down on rules, which put more pressure on the remaining SBICs. Within a decade, 36 of the 50 publicly traded Corporations had closed.[27] Meanwhile, private West Coast firms had started using limited partnerships to make equity investments in private firms, which turned out to be a far more successful organizational form.[28] By 1988, the SBICs represented about 7 percent of the venture capital business, a far cry from the 75 percent share they had held in the early 1960s.[29]

Before the extent of these problems was revealed, however, the SBICs represented three-quarters of the venture capital industry between 1959 and 1963.[30] These early SBICs acted like a catalyst or "transitional institution" that helped attract a "critical mass" of firms.[31] Before the SBICs, much venture capital work had been done quietly and on the margins. In contrast, SBICs spread familiarity with the fledgling industry while also developing expertise.[32] The commercial and investment banks that had started some SBICs helped train new venture capital investors.[33] In his book on how government programs fail, economist Josh Lerner argues that despite their problems, the early SBICs built the modern venture capital industry's infrastructure: "Many of the early venture capital funds and leading intermediaries in the industry—such as law firms and data providers," he writes, "began as organizations oriented to the SBIC funds, and then gradually shifted their focus to independent venture capitalists."[34] Lerner points out that the premier reporting firm for the venture capital industry, Venture Economics, started in 1961 as the SBIC reporting service. Since the 1960s, SBIC funds have flowed to Costco and Staples, FedEx and Tesla, Apple and Intel, Jenny Craig and Outback Steakhouse.

Today's SBICs look very different from the first generation of these entities. Over time the SBICs' size increased and the restrictions placed on them were loosened. A 1970 law clarified that the SBA could guarantee third-party loans to SBICs, which allowed the program to move away from direct loans. By September of 2016, according to the SBA's webpage, 313 SBICs managed $28 billion in assets, and "all at *ZERO* cost to taxpayers."[35]

Loans for business programs were not limited to the SBA. In fact, credit support for business continues to flow through many other federal offices and agencies: the Department of Commerce offers loans to fisheries; the Department of Energy offers loans for innovative technology; the Department of the Interior guarantees loans to Indian-owned businesses. Bailouts of troubled firms can also be a form of credit support: $250 million in loans were made to Lockheed in 1971, and a $1.5 billion guarantee was extended to Chrysler eight years later.[36] In 2010 the Obama administration created a $30 billion fund for small businesses. These loans operate alongside other programs, like National Science Foundation research grants, DARPA contracts, and dozens of state-level programs. Even venture capital efforts themselves are not limited to the SBICs. One review of government programs that supported venture capital between 1958 and 1997 identified over 20 programs across federal agencies and dozens of state governments.[37]

In addition to the programs that directly supply loans and guarantees to *producers*, other credit programs support U.S. companies through loans to *consumers*. As the previous chapter discussed, the housing programs were designed to support industry by driving up demand for homebuilding materials and consumer goods. As the next section will show, many federal loans and guarantees abroad were designed to support U.S. business as well.

LOANS AS FOREIGN AND MILITARY POLICY

The federal government has long used loans and guarantees to promote U.S. interests abroad.[38] This effort goes far beyond the massive wartime mobilizations of the War Finance Corporation and the RFC. Credit allocation has also repeatedly served as a tool of demobilization and foreign policy. After World War I, the United States used loans to Cuba, Nicaragua, and Argentina to sell off excess war supplies and encourage trade.[39] After World War II, the Marshall Plan combined $13 billion in loans over four years (about 5 percent of 1948's GDP) with generous loan forgiveness to help rebuild war-devastated Europe.[40] The $3.75 billion loan issued to Britain in 1947 and run through the Department of Treasury, for instance, would be worth $34 billion in 2016.[41] Since the 1990s, the United States has provided guarantees for $23.8 billion of other nations' sovereign debt. In 2017, for example, Iraq was offered a $1 billion issuance that was fully backed by the U.S. government.[42] USAID has directly issued loans for development purposes from its inception in 1961, and it also manages federal guarantees of other nations' sovereign debt.[43]

Foreign aid has also regularly been used to sell or distribute U.S. goods. In 1933 the RFC lent $15.4 million (and committed to lend up to $50 million) to the government of China to buy wheat, flour, and cotton.[44] In the 1930s the federal government also made loans to American exporters to sell cotton in Russia, wheat and flour in the Philippines, and prunes in Germany (where "prune butter" was reportedly popular).[45] In 1954 the Food for Peace program began unloading government stores of commodities abroad, either directly through gifts to famine-struck countries or indirectly through loans with low interest rates and long maturities.

Spun off from the RFC in 1953 and tasked with financing the sale of expensive commodities like airplanes and energy equipment, the Export-Import Bank was authorized to issue $5 billion in loans by 1955.[46] In 1969 alone, over $1 billion worth of American commodities were purchased abroad using USAID financing.[47] Today the Export-Import Bank, USAID, and the Overseas Private Investment Corporation are major institutional centers for international credit programs. Loans and guarantees also flow through the Treasury,

Defense, and State Departments, as well as the USDA.[48] Loan programs made up about a tenth of the $1.7 trillion in U.S. military and economic aid that flowed overseas between 1946 and 2016.[49]

SCHOOL LOANS

School loans emerged as a new arena of U.S. credit policy in the second half of the twentieth century. The federal government's first foray into tuition support came in the form of grants offered through the Servicemen's Readjustment Act, or G.I. Bill.[50] Those grants established a role for the federal government in helping individuals afford higher education, but their mandate was narrow: to reintegrate soldiers after the war.[51] As with the SBA's venture capital programs, *Sputnik* proved the catalyst for the emergence of educational loan programs in 1958. In order to boost professional knowledge in defense-related science, technology, engineering, and mathematics (STEM) fields as well as foreign languages, the National Defense Education Act of 1958 provided student loan funds to be managed by colleges.[52]

Student loans made the leap from defense to social policy under Lyndon Johnson, who saw college loans as essential for combating inequality (many progressives at the time, however, objected to the choice of loans over free education or grants as a policy tool).[53] The Higher Education Act of 1965 provided $15 million for school loans and used federal guarantees and subsidies to promote bank lending to students.[54] The federal government would pay all interest on loans for students while they attended school and part of the interest after graduation.[55]

In the 1970s, student loans shifted from an antipoverty program to a middle-class entitlement. The Education Amendments of 1972 introduced the Pell Grants and established the Student Loan Marketing Association (known as Sallie Mae).[56] Like Fannie Mae, Sallie Mae provided a secondary market for government-insured school loans (it was privatized in 2007). One government report noted that "by 1979, every American family, without regard to income, was eligible for a subsidized loan to aid in financing postsecondary education."[57] This expansion ended in the Reagan era, when budget battles resulted in the use of means-testing and origination fees to reverse the trend. As grant money dwindled, loan policies emerged as a viable path forward.[58] The average student in 1975 received five times more grant money than loans. A decade later, the average loan amount was equal to the grant received.[59] This reliance on guarantees continued until the school loan programs were entirely restructured as a direct loan program under the Obama administration (a point to which the chapter will return later).

Total outstanding U.S. student loan debt surpassed $1 trillion in 2012 and continued to grow.[60] That debt is overwhelmingly owned or guaranteed by the federal government. As of 2017, the Department of Education's direct loan program owned nearly $1 trillion in outstanding loans (about 80 percent of all government direct loans) and guaranteed nearly $200 billion of loans from earlier programs.[61]

FARM CREDIT

In the postwar era farm credit developed through two main pathways. On one hand, the Farm Credit Administration oversaw the nation's great farm lending systems: the land banks for agricultural mortgages, the Federal Intermediate Credit Banks for medium-term borrowing, and the Banks for Cooperatives (now CoBank), which supported the farm cooperatives. In 1968 Farm Credit Administration representatives proudly presented the government with two oversized checks to mark their final repayment of the initial government capitalization. A crisis in the mid-1980s, however, led to a later bailout and recapitalization.[62] Today the Farm Credit System Insurance Corporation continues to insure debt issued by the Farm Credit System, which helped secure about 40 percent of all farm loans by 2016.[63]

On the other hand, the Department of Agriculture oversaw a set of programs that incorporated credit allocation into the normal policy work of supporting rural life. Here, as elsewhere, credit support took multiple forms as it was incorporated into the policy spheres of price supports, subsidies, relief efforts, and development initiatives. Some programs helped entire communities, such as those that provided financing for water facilities and community centers. Others offered loans to individual families to purchase homes; manage the day-to-day business of farming; and recover from disasters like floods, cattle disease, or crop loss.[64] The Farmers Home Administration, created in 1946 and consolidated with the Farm Service Agency in 1994, took over the rural antipoverty work of the New Deal's Resettlement Administration and dealt in rural mortgages.[65] As a price support program, the Commodity Credit Corporation's farm subsidies generated a great reserve of goods owned by the federal government. School lunch, food stamp, and foreign aid programs have all served as outlets for this surplus.[66]

At one point in the 1980s, when farm prices plummeted, over half of all U.S. agricultural loans were supported in some way by the government credit programs.[67] In 1987 Congress chartered the Federal Agricultural Mortgage Corporation (known as Farmer Mac) in the model of Fannie Mae and Sallie Mae to provide a secondary market for farm mortgages. Its total outstanding loan volume in 2017 was $18.6 billion.[68] Today the Farm Service Agency (the most central of the farm loan programs) owns $70 billion in loans and another $140 billion in guarantees.[69]

The Postwar Housing Programs

The federal government's housing programs sat at the center of this sprawling web of postwar credit programs. Throughout the Second World War, less essential industries like homebuilding stagnated while the nation's credit, materials, and labor flowed toward military needs. Unlike the situation during the First World War, in the 1940s credit support for housing was already a well-established policy tool. As the FHA continued to insure mortgages, the G.I. Bill authorized the VA to guarantee mortgages for veterans. Between the end of the war and 1952, the VA guaranteed 2.5 million mortgages. This proved a massive boon for veterans: over 4 million men, or 28 percent of all World War II veterans, used the VA home loan program.[70] By 1955, 41 percent of the nation's mortgages were backed by the FHA or VA.[71]

The VA guarantees and FHA insurance combined with high incomes, tax breaks, and lower transportation to push homeownership rates to new heights. Previous generations of Americans had achieved the dream of homeownership with age, after years of saving up a large down payment.[72] A new generation assisted by the government-guaranteed, low–down payment, long-term mortgage could expect to own a home earlier in life. In the two-decade span between 1940 and 1960 nonfarm homeownership rates rose by a half, from 44 percent to 62 percent.[73] As I will discuss in more detail later, these increases overwhelmingly benefited white families.

As rates of homeownership rose, the homebuilding industry consolidated. Whereas earlier generations of developers had operated on a smaller scale and sought to quickly turn over lots, now builders could utilize access to stable mortgage credit in order to operate on a much larger scale.[74] Large-tract developers focused on building subdivisions in the model of Levittown.[75] In 1945, the median homebuilder constructed fewer than five houses a year. By 1949, 10 percent of firms were building 70 percent of all new homes.[76] Unsurprisingly, the housing industry sought to flex its political power. In this effort the National Association of Home Builders operated alongside the National Association of Real Estate Boards, the Mortgage Bankers Association, the American Bankers Association, the National Association of Mutual Savings Banks, and the United States Savings and Loan League. These groups made the housing industry into one of the nation's most influential lobbies.[77]

This great expansion in homeownership was financed by a compartmentalized group of lenders (see table 8.1), each of which was connected to some kind of governmental support. On one side were the S&Ls, which moved money from families into nearby homes. The S&Ls' reserves were supported by the Federal Home Loan Bank System (which could issue tax-exempt bonds), and S&L deposits were backed by the Federal Savings and Loan Insurance

Corporation.[78] In 1940, the S&Ls held about 11 percent of the nation's total mortgage debt. That amount nearly tripled by 1970.[79] If you combine the S&Ls with the savings banks (which steadily held about 12 percent of U.S. housing debt between 1940 and 1970), the postwar era thrifts held 45 percent of all U.S. mortgages by 1970.[80] The S&Ls rarely used FHA loans and in fact had resisted the entire FHA program when it was created, not wanting the added competition in the market. The S&Ls overwhelmingly invested in mortgages, and their mortgages were mostly conventional loans. When they did deal in government-backed loans, they tended to choose VA over FHA loans.[81] S&Ls' dealings with Fannie Mae were limited. Generally, the S&Ls took advances from the Federal Home Loan Bank Board (FHLBB) when they needed additional funds.

On the other side of the market were the mortgage brokers, insurance companies, and some commercial banks. The mortgage brokers were the organizational descendants of the fast-and-loose mortgage companies of the 1920s, the ones that had survived by effectively becoming the lending arms of larger institutional investors like life insurance companies and commercial banks. Humbled in the 1930s, the brokerages now minimized risks by issuing mortgages *after* some other institutional investor made a commitment to purchase. What they did, then, was more like contract work than the creation of a true resale or secondary market, and their profits came mainly from servicing fees.[82] This side of the market had its own federal credit support in the form of FHA insurance, with Fannie Mae acting as a secondary market.[83] It traded *conforming* loans that adhered to FHA and VA standards. The brokers did not hold on to mortgages, but their impact is revealed in part by the third of U.S. residential mortgages held by life insurance companies in 1970 (see table 8.1 and figure 8.1).

As for the commercial banks, they held around 15 to 20 percent of the market in the postwar era (and tended, by the end of the period, to have about that

TABLE 8.1. Mortgage Debt by Type of Holder, Selected Years, 1940–1970 (in Billions)

Year	S&Ls	Mutual Banks	Commercial Banks	Life Insurance Companies	Federal Govt.	Individuals & Other	Total	Total (1960 Dollars)
1940	11%	13%	13%	16%	13%	33%	$36.5	$78.4
1945	15%	12%	14%	19%	7%	34%	$35.5	$59.8
1950	19%	11%	19%	22%	4%	25%	$72.8	$92.6
1955	24%	13%	16%	23%	4%	19%	$130.1	$145.9
1960	29%	13%	14%	20%	6%	18%	$207.6	$207.6
1965	33%	13%	15%	18%	4%	17%	$333.6	$311.2
1970	32%	12%	16%	16%	8%	17%	$474.4	$524.8

Source: Kenneth Snowden, "Table Dc929-949: Mortgage Debt, by Type of Property, Holder, and Financing: 1939–1999," in *Historical Statistics of the United States*. These figures include farm, nonfarm, residential, and commercial mortgages.

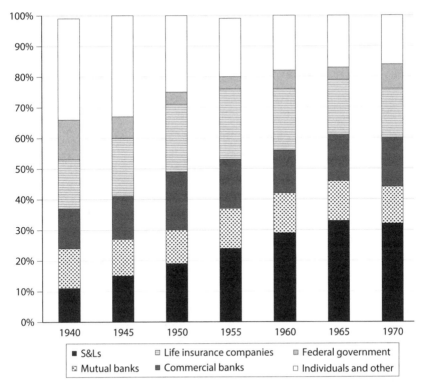

FIGURE 8.1. Mortgage Debt by Type of Holder, 1940–1970
Source: Kenneth Snowden, "Table Dc903–928: Debt on Nonfarm Structures, by Type of Debt, Property, and Holder: 1896–1952," in *Historical Statistics of the United States*. Numbers include farm, nonfarm, residential, and commercial mortgages.

much of their aggregate portfolios invested in mortgages).[84] As it had earlier in U.S. history, the role of postwar era commercial banks varied a great deal.[85] Some banks stayed entirely out of the mortgage business. Smaller country banks that dealt in mortgages for single-family homes often dealt in both conventional and conforming loans. Very few of the nation's largest banks dealt in family mortgages, though the size of the large banks meant that the exceptions to the rule could have a large impact in a given state. The larger banks tended to specialize in financing for larger construction efforts (like subdivisions or multifamily homes) or provide shorter-term financing for mortgage brokers.[86]

The other main institutional trend in mortgage finance during this period was the decline of the individual small investor. Individuals were not allowed to own FHA loans, and as the terms of long-term amortized loans got longer, mortgages stopped being a regular investment of the small saver.[87] In 1940, the "non-institutional" investor still held a third of the nation's loans. By 1970, the non-institutional investor category was down by almost a half and consisted more of smaller organizations that operated at the edges of the mortgage market, such as credit unions, personal trusts, and fraternal orders.[88]

A thicket of government regulations and tax laws generally kept the market segments distinct, although it is important not to overstate the degree of division: all of the groups overlapped at points and contained outliers and exceptions. That said, S&Ls were specialty banks that dealt in residential mortgages. They were limited in how many of their loans they could resell and what kinds of investments they could make; the flip side to these restrictions was that the S&Ls were exempt from some regulations applied to commercial banks and had access to advances from the Federal Home Loan Bank system. Mortgage brokers could sell all the loans they liked, but they did not have equivalent FSLIC protections for their investors. They used the relatively low-risk market for FHA and VA loans to attract financing. On the whole, FHA and VA conforming mortgages were not as profitable as conventional S&L loans because they had various limitations and associated costs, but the banks and insurance companies that held those mortgages could count the loans like government debt when calculating their capital requirements. For institutional investors, this capacity to free up capital reserves compensated for the lower returns.[89]

The divide between the S&Ls and the mortgage brokers was known for being particularly unfriendly. While they competed for mortgages in a general sense, the two camps dealt in fundamentally distinct niches. They had different investors, different loyalties, and different concerns. The S&Ls were local, the brokers national. The S&Ls were financed by family savers, the brokers by financial institutions. Even the S&Ls' conventional mortgages differed from the brokers' FHA and VA conforming mortgages. One result of this divide was a general stability in the field of mortgage finance: each group carefully monitored the regulatory environment so as to prevent any potentially disadvantageous change.[90] The homebuilders and financiers who dominated the housing lobby were not shy about promoting their disparate interests, but they also shared an interest in making sure that housing policy stayed a market-oriented national priority.[91] None of them wanted to see publicly constructed and managed housing.[92] As the government's primary partners in the all-important housing industry, lenders and builders held a great advantage in policy debates. If housing was a top priority for the nation and market systems were best for housing, then what was best for builders and lenders was best for the nation.

This conflation of housing industry and the public interest had organizational ramifications for policy implementation. Private interests did not just help design policy; they also implemented it.[93] Fannie Mae was an extreme version of this phenomenon. When Congress reorganized the agency in 1954 under Eisenhower, one branch of Fannie Mae, the secondary market office, was turned into a quasi-private corporation.[94] The Treasury retained all preferred voting stock in the branch, authorized its debt issuances, and was permitted to lend Fannie up to $1 billion. The head of the Housing and Home Finance Agency chaired Fannie's board and appointed its members.[95] But private citizens were also seated on the board, and companies that dealt with Fannie Mae were required to purchase its common stock, which amounted to $73 million by 1960.[96] Meanwhile, two other branches of Fannie Mae were simply government agencies: the Management and Liquidation branch warehoused Fannie's existing portfolio of loans, while the Special Assistance Functions branch boosted the market by purchasing residential loans to pump funds into the market during downturns.[97] The Special Assistance Functions branch also dealt in mortgages for disaster relief construction, low-income housing, and military housing.[98]

Fannie Mae, in other words, was internally complex and heavily reliant on partnerships. It had a confusing structure. Many of the credit programs did.

Racial Inequality and the Credit Programs

A large body of research shows that postwar credit programs were engines of inequality, highly effective at advancing racial hierarches and highly ineffective at counteracting them. One way to understand this characteristic of the system is through a juxtaposition of postwar housing and business programs.[99]

HOUSING PROGRAMS AND THE BLACK-WHITE WEALTH GAP

An extensive body of research has detailed how the housing credit programs promoted racial inequality.[100] Housing markets had long been discriminatory, hostile, and dangerous for black families. Racial covenants, real estate brokers, and banks together worked to keep families of color out of white neighborhoods. Prospective black homeowners faced a gauntlet of financial traps. Denied access to the array of financial services available to white families, many black homebuyers relied on speculators who offered financing on exploitative terms. Historian Arnold Hirsch's famous study found that these speculators on average raised the cost of homebuying in postwar Chicago by 75 percent (and in some cases up to 115 percent, more than doubling the cost of homebuying).[101] Worse, speculators used land contracts in lieu of mortgages, stripping the homebuyer of equity and key protections. Once they did manage to become homeowners, black purchasers were much more likely to be subject to violations of their property rights—through the use of eminent domain, for example.[102] For those who succeeded in running this gauntlet, one last financial inequity remained. Fearing that black neighbors would drive down their property values and often egged on by fearmongering real estate agents, white homeowners would rush to leave the neighborhood and sell their properties at depressed prices to do so. Instead of seeing the neighborhood's plummeting property values as a self-fulfilling prophecy wrought by white racism and their own behavior, white homeowners blamed the declining values on the black newcomers. In sum, black homeowners had to do much more to get and retain their property than white families, and they gained far less in return.

This is not to say that the risks for black families in housing markets were only financial. When these legal and market barriers failed to exclude black families, white homeowners and renters resorted to harassment and violence to protect residential segregation. Historical accounts are full of examples of white families driving away black families while the police looked on: salted lawns and picketed houses, invectives and threats left overnight in notes or launched in person, paroxysms of violence, beatings, bombings, fires, and riots.[103] Black families who left the South en masse starting in World War I as part of the Great Migration too often found themselves in northern cities where white racism left them with no alternative but to cram into overpriced, overcrowded, and decayed rentals.[104]

The housing credit programs put the force of the government behind residential segregation in housing markets. Famously, the HOLC and the FHA both used redlined maps that flagged mixed-raced neighborhoods as unacceptably risky and privileged newly built homes in suburbs. As a result, the vast majority of FHA loans between 1934 and 1968 went to white families. This financed white flight and shut a large number of African American families out of the same postwar housing boom that lifted a generation of working-class white families up the social ladder. While some people of color purchased homes on the edges of cities and in the suburbs, establishing an important foothold for a rising black middle class, poorer families remained locked in highly segregated urban ghettos.[105]

The credit programs not only helped white families buy homes at unprecedented levels but encouraged those families to see their upward mobility in terms of neutral market outcomes. Historian David Freund has detailed how credit support shaped the nature of northern white racism.[106] Since the New Deal, homebuilders and mortgage lenders had insisted that the wholesale bolstering of American mortgage finance through credit support was best thought of as a set of technical tweaks to fix market inefficiencies, rather than as a strategy of market making built on risk taking, relationship building, and entrepreneurial vision. If it were true that the credit programs were an adjustment and not an innovation, then the families who reaped the windfall of government housing credit support had not, say, hoarded a precious game-changing resource or accepted government aid, but instead had pulled themselves up by their bootstraps.

Unlike white families, who generally ignored the role of the state in the process of securing their home (and with it, the main source of wealth for a typical middle-class family), many black activists openly recognized and decried the racist policies of the housing programs.[107] Political scientist Chloe Thurston has shown that African American organizing in response to this exclusion from FHA programs "date[s] almost to the agency's founding."[108] In 1938, the National Association for the Advancement of Colored People (NAACP) entreated the FHA to rethink its racist lending practices: "Colored people have been branded as slum-dwellers without ambition to live in good houses and yet when they seek better housing, they are told by the government that they must remain within certain areas."[109] It was a fight that the NAACP, the Urban League, and other advocates would wage for years. These groups did eventually win crucial victories, like getting the FHA to withdraw its support for redlining and racial covenants in the 1950s and spurring the creation of the 1954 Voluntary Home Mortgage Credit Program, which provided loans for prospective borrowers who had twice been denied them. This movement also broke a path for later legislative gains like President Kennedy's 1962 executive order that banned discrimination within government housing programs and the 1968 Fair Housing Act.[110]

While acknowledging these victories and gains, the long-term effects of discrimination within the housing credit programs have been especially pernicious. Because the family home is the largest source of wealth for the average family, homeownership remains "the largest driver of the racial wealth gap."[111] Around 70 percent of white households are owner-occupied today, compared to around 45 percent of black and Latino households.[112] That means that white individuals are not just still much more likely to be homeowners; they are also more likely to pass along wealth in the form of an inherited family home, which means that their children are more likely to own homes and, thanks to enduring residential segregation, more likely to have homes with higher returns on their value. One study from 2015 found that the median white household held over $111,000 in wealth holdings, while the median black household held about $7,000. Digging into the causes of that gap, the authors concluded that about 36 percent of it derived from differences in homeownership rates and another 16 percent resulted from differences in returns on value. The study concluded that equalizing disparities in homeownership would cut the black–white racial wealth gap in half.[113] Moreover, since neighborhoods are linked to school quality, social networks, and job opportunities, these trends in homeownership have helped lock in vast gains in income and education for white families.[114]

THE SBA'S MINORITY OWNERSHIP PROGRAMS

If the housing sector speaks to how credit programs deepened racial inequality, the business sector provides insight into why credit programs have often failed as a tool to fight racial inequality. Like other credit programs, the SBA overwhelmingly lent to white borrowers. In the landmark book *Black Power*, Kwame Ture (formerly Stokely Carmichael) and Charles Hamilton condemned the SBA for virtually shutting out black borrowers in its first decade of existence.[115] Under the Kennedy administration, however, the SBA took some steps to lend money to a broader set of Americans. In 1964 the agency set nondiscrimination requirements for all loan applicants, which established a precedent that would later be adopted by other agencies.[116] To promote loans to black borrowers and women—two groups that were less likely to have collateral to borrow against—the SBA experimented with various qualifications for borrowing, like character-based evaluations of creditworthiness. The agency offered 6 × 6 loans ($6,000 lent at 6 percent interest) and created the larger Equal Opportunity Loan program (which guaranteed loans for amounts up to $25,000 without collateral).[117] The Nixon administration continued down this path. Small loans fit well with Nixon's campaign trail emphasis on "black capitalism" as a low-cost solution to racial inequality. As legal scholar Mehrsa Baradaran notes, Nixon's black capitalism rhetoric twisted the black power movement's emphasis on self-sufficiency into something that placed responsibility for economic inequality squarely onto the shoulders of black entrepreneurs. Nixon's focus on black capitalism had the added benefit of deflecting attention away from the more divisive matters of integration and wealth redistribution.[118]

To understand the problems associated with the implementation of these SBA programs, consider the Equal Opportunity Loan program. This program was designed to use careful oversight in lieu of traditional collateral requirements—but staffing caps from the Bureau of the Budget meant that it never received the personnel needed to properly vet and oversee borrowers. Timing was another problem. In 1960 a majority of black Americans lived in cities, and every major American city was losing jobs.[119] Industries were moving to the suburbs, where labor was easier to control and where firms could benefit from tax cuts designed to reduce the nation's vulnerability to concentrated losses from air strikes.[120] Postwar research grants and housing programs further shunted opportunities and white families out of the cities. As jobs and wealth flowed into the suburbs, urban centers became sites of concentrated working poverty. This too undermined the minority-owned business programs, insofar as they focused on neighborhoods where residents lacked the spending power needed to sustain anything but very small businesses.[121] Many of the minority-owned firms that successfully repaid their loans eventually closed because they never generated enough in profits to support a small business owner.[122] In the end, the SBA overwhelmingly provided affirmative action for white borrowers. A full 85 percent of the agency's $550 million in approved loans in 1969 went to businesses with white owners.[123]

When juxtaposed with the housing programs, the limits of the SBA minority-owned business programs are thrown into sharp relief. The success of any credit program depends on its size, the quality of its implementation, and the context in which it is applied. The United States' largest, best-managed, least controversial, and most fortuitously timed programs were also those that privileged white borrowers and regularly excluded borrowers of color. Programs that specifically sought to help borrowers of color were later, limited, and understaffed.

Off-Budget and Decentralized:
The Messy Politics of Postwar Credit

The 1963 congressional survey of credit programs found that the U.S. government offered a wide array of loan, insurance, and guarantee programs. The CCC's non-recourse loans were basically grants. The likelihood of default for USAID's $12 billion in noncommercial loans was completely unknown.[124] (The latter were so unusual as loans, in fact, that the congressional survey bracketed them entirely in its figures.) The Export-Import Bank and Fannie Mae dealt in commercial loans. Between the extremes were various subsidies and benefits: below-market interest rates, longer-term loans, smaller down payments, easy deferrals, refinancing options, and even loan forgiveness.[125]

One-time president of the Minneapolis Federal Reserve Bruce MacLaury warned in the 1970s that this proliferation of programs had resulted in a confusing proliferation of government debts. The obligations of some entities, like the Export-Import Bank, were "virtually indistinguishable in credit standing from direct obligations of the U.S. Government itself."[126] Other government obligations—like the SBA's guarantees of the debentures of the Small Business Investment Corporations—were not as secure as government debt, but not quite private debt either. In between rested "every sort and description of instrument." MacLaury explained that they were "distinguished by differing degrees of access to the Treasury in case of default, of insurance coverage as to interest and principal, of marketability based on size of issue, minimum denomination, etc., and differing degrees of explicitness in the extent to which the obligations are guaranteed, if at all."[127]

The postwar credit programs were also remarkably inconsistent in their accounting and financial management.[128] Each government agency used its own methods to determine its reserves: the FHA conservatively calculated its reserves to cushion against a Depression era–level crisis, but five other programs were operating without any reserves. While many of the 74 credit programs had limits on monetary ceilings or the number of grants they could give out, 15 agencies, among them the FHA and the VA, had no statutory limits whatsoever. When the Congressional Budget Office reviewed the credit programs in 1978, it determined that reporting was so inconsistent and incomplete that even estimating losses incurred from defaults was impossible.[129] Dennis Ippolito, a political scientist and expert on the credit programs, has argued that the credit programs were purposefully dysfunctional in this regard: "The budgetary distortions and evasions relating to federal credit accounting are products of design, not accident." Off-budget accounting and other gimmicks protected programs from being cut and shielded them from oversight.[130]

Within the credit programs, budget rules influenced the types of credit support used. Programs that directly issued or purchased loans often made money in the long run, but before 1992 they showed up on the administrative budget as direct expenditures. A $100,000 loan that would be repaid over time was recorded in the same way as a $100,000 grant. In contrast, insurance and guarantee programs cost almost nothing at the moment of issuance, though they could become terrifically expensive following a default. An actuarially sound loan insurance program like the FHA was able to generate enough in fees to cover even its operating expenses for long periods of time.

MacLaury has proposed that government programs move through a "typical life cycle," wherein the support of a given program moves increasingly off the budget as grants give way to direct loans, which then give way to guarantee programs. "Indeed," MacLaury concludes, "there is little doubt that the single most important factor that explains the growth and proliferation of Federal credit assistance is the desire to see programs funded with a minimum use of scarce budget dollars."[131] By the 1960s congressional reports openly worried that the credit programs were being set up to minimize their appearance on the budget, regardless of whether that particular design would be most effective on the ground or the least expensive option for the government in the long run.[132]

The same low costs that make credit programs attractive at their moment of creation also help them survive over time, detaching them from higher immediate taxes, the single most important mechanism that works against government expansion. Dennis Ippolito notes that once established, these programs create a group of people with very concrete reasons to protect and extend them and force opponents to make more abstract arguments about contingent risks and long-term costs.[133] Historically, this all made the credit programs remarkably useful for government officials, who were expected to avoid excessive deficits even as they ensured steady growth and well-being.

Because credit programs were such useful political tools, they were also sites of political conflict. Debates over proper accounting for these programs occurred fairly regularly and sometimes escalated into high-stakes political showdowns, as the next chapter will show in some detail. For now it is enough to note that these budgetary treatments were frequently contested. For instance, when the U.S. House threatened to close the Export-Import Bank in

1971, the Senate and president moved to protect it by taking it off budget; a later scandal about loans to Communist countries led Congress to put the Export-Import Bank back on the budget, on the grounds that it was "a tool of foreign policy" and so demanded congressional oversight.[134]

Federal credit accounting was modernized and standardized with the Federal Credit Reform Act of 1990, but even after this legislation problems remained: accounting is not entirely consistent, some programs continue to be excluded from budget totals, and data collection remains unreliable.[135] Moreover, changing the design of existing programs, even in a new accounting context, can be difficult. The Obama administration's overhaul of the school loan program is illuminating in this regard. The switch to direct loans in 2010 was feasible because after 1990 loans could be accounted for on an accrual basis; before that change, each loan would have counted in its entirely as an outlay, which would have rendered the program politically unfeasible. However, it is important to note the two-decade lag between the accounting rule change and the new policy. Suzanne Mettler argues that multiple forces had to align—media attention, policy problems, and a larger number of student voters—to create a window of opportunity for the change to direct loans to occur.[136] Accounting shapes the organizational design of credit programs, but it is far from the only factor taken into consideration and is likely to have an especially large impact at the moment of founding.

This complexity and decentralization also have ramifications for macroeconomic policy. Credit programs can help speed up and slow down the economy. Some of the actions taken by Fannie Mae's Special Assistance Functions branch were specifically countercyclical. From 1957 to 1959, Fannie Mae spent over $2.5 billion in order to offset an economic downturn.[137] But not all of Fannie's activities were coordinated with the Federal Reserve or federal fiscal policy. In 1950, while the nation rationed credit in other sectors so that capital and manufacturing could be directed toward the Korean War effort, Fannie Mae purchased over $1 billion in FHA and VA loans, a boon to the housing industry that went directly against the anti-inflationary wartime policy.[138] Fannie's various functions sometimes clashed, and this laid the groundwork for a showdown over priorities. This too will be discussed in more detail in the following chapter.

Debating Economic Costs and Benefits

How should we think of the overall economic effect of the credit programs? The same data and accounting problems that have protected credit programs from government oversight have also thwarted researchers, but scholars have worked around this hurdle by focusing on specific periods or case studies. Many experts see a place for credit programs in the promotion of public goods or markets in which private investors might not have otherwise invested but from which society at large benefits (in other words, investments with positive externalities). Credit support also, most agree, has a place in markets where information costs and asymmetries lead to underinvestment (the farm loans were an early example of this) or during times of crisis.[139] Economist Deborah Lucas has begun modeling the overall effect of federal credit policies on the economy. In times of crisis, she argues, credit programs have a big multiplier that can give them a large "bang-for-the-buck." Whereas more typical fiscal stimulus efforts lead to $1.50 output for every $1 of spending, Lucas estimates that in 2010 the credit programs generated $5.27 of stimulus for every $1 of taxpayer cost.[140]

Many economists, including Lucas, warn against the rampant overuse of credit programs. Government credit support can skew incentives and promote inappropriate risk taking (a phenomenon called moral hazard). Credit programs often outlive the problem that led to their creation, at which point they can "crowd out" private firms.[141] Some economists decry the danger of "substituting political judgments for the discipline of the market."[142] To the extent that misplaced credit programs drive up interest rates or disrupt macroeconomic policy, they hurt the entire economy.[143] By this logic, credit programs are an inefficient system for redistributing credit that potentially raises prices instead of expanding markets.[144] The most strident free-market advocates argue that credit programs are inherently ineffective and counterproductive: any of the programs' institutional advances would have happened through private channels at a more appropriate time.

Even many scholars who see the development of credit programs after the 1970s as inflationary or counterproductive concede that they played a significant role in developing American credit markets throughout the postwar period.[145] A review of this era suggests that credit programs were key institution builders and pioneers, adopting and popularizing new lending techniques and practices and demonstrating how new kinds of lending could be successful.[146] Earlier in this chapter I detailed how the Small Business Investment Corporations were an important step in the institutional development of the venture capital industry. This is only one of many examples. Before the creation of the RFC, bankers relied on promissory notes that were either paid in a lump sum in a year or else renewed; the RFC showed that small, amortizing business loans could turn a reliable profit.[147] The Export-Import Bank did the same for medium- and long-term loans abroad.[148] Louis Hyman's research has shown that FHA home improvement loan programs helped promote consumer credit.[149]

The modern mortgage contract is perhaps the most famous example of this kind of institution building. Some S&Ls used long-term (10- to 15-year), low-value loans before the HOLC and FHA embraced them, but these institutions only held about a fifth of residential mortgages in 1934. Most Americans

TABLE 8.2. Mortgages for Existing Homes by Maturity and Loan-to-Value Ratio, Selected Years

Year	Maturity			Loan-to-Value Ratio		
	FHA (Average)	VA (Average)	Conventional (Median)	FHA (Average)	VA (Average)	Conventional (Median)
1950	20.2	19.7	12.3	76.4	86.4	64.6
1954	20.1	21.4	14.6	77.8	86.8	65.2
1958	24.2	22.3	15.5	88.1	87.4	68.9
1962	27.4	26.6	18.8	92.1	94.9	75.1
1966	28.4	27.8	22.2	93	96.8	74.5

Source: Kenneth Snowden, "Table Dc1192-1209: Terms on Nonfarm Home Mortgages, by Type of Mortgage and Holder: 1920–1967," *Historical Statistics of the United States*.

at that time still dealt in short-term (three- to five-year) nonamortizing loans with bullet payments at the end, high down payments (50 or 60 percent of the value), and second or third mortgages.[150] Table 8.2 shows that from 1950 to 1966, the FHA and VA consistently offered loans with longer maturities and lower down payments (resulting in a higher loan-to-value ratio) than the S&Ls' conventional loans did.[151] A similar transformation occurred in the agricultural sector, with farm mortgages and production loans increasingly having lower interest rates, longer tenures, and looser terms.[152] For lenders, those contracts had the benefit of standardization, which significantly lowered information and transaction costs and so helped draw them into the mortgage market.[153] In this sense, the postwar credit programs are consistent with Mazzucato's insight that the government, as a creative market participant, specializes in taking big risks with huge payoffs.[154]

A Peculiar Developmental State

Each major crisis of the early twentieth century—the First World War, the Great Depression, the Second World War—saw an expansion of the credit programs. Some of the biggest changes in the economic development of the nation were accompanied by new types of credit support: farm loans gave way to home loans in the consumer's republic; home loans were joined by education loans in the knowledge economy. The general trend though the postwar era was not the shrinking of credit programs, but the transformation in the type of credit programs used: a move from direct loans to guarantees. By the time the RFC closed in 1953, the nation had already moved toward a reliance on guarantees rather than direct loans (figure 8.1). During the postwar era, this trend continued (figures 8.2 and 8.3).

The point here is not that credit programs are unassailably good or bad. They can be inflationary and chaotic. They privilege business partners and

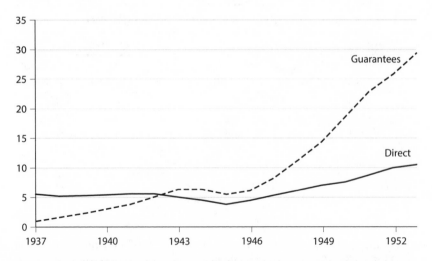

FIGURE 8.2. Government Outstanding Direct vs. Guaranteed Loans, 1932–1950 (in Billions)
Sources: R. J. Saulnier, H. O. Halcrow, and N. H. Jacoby, *Federal Lending and Loan Insurance* (Princeton, N.J.: Princeton University Press, 1958); Appendix A; "Final Report on the Reconstruction Finance Corporation" (Washington, D.C.: Government Printing Office, 1969), tables in appendix. Note: This excludes loans from the off-budget "federally sponsored agencies"—the Farm Credit System, the FDIC, and the Federal Reserve—as well as some programs for which annual data were not available, loans for certain defense purposes that the authors considered "incidental," and loan-based programs that they considered effectively grants (like advances to Alaska for public works). For details, see Saulnier, Halcrow, and Jacoby, *Federal Lending and Loan Insurance*, ch. 2, n. 1.

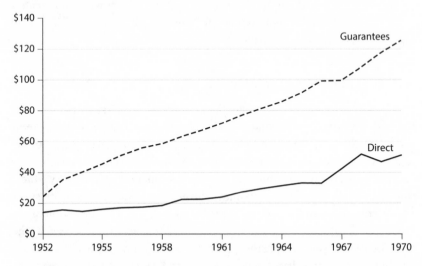

FIGURE 8.3. Growth of Outstanding Direct and Guaranteed Loans, 1952–1970 (in Billions)
Source: "Federal Credit Program: A Statistical Compilation" in *Loan Guarantees: Current Concerns and Alternatives for Control*, ed. Congressional Budget Office (Washington, D.C.: Government Printing Office, 1978).

sidestep congressional oversight, which is antidemocratic.[155] They have a terrible record of racial inequality. Their history is peppered with scandals and failures. They have also built key credit institutions and played an expansive role in U.S. economic development. The point is simply to note the role they have played in the U.S. political economy, both for better and for worse. We must stop neglecting credit allocation in accounts of development and social policy or talking about credit programs as if they are temporary exceptions to the rule, limited to specific sectors or time periods. Credit programs are not aberrations in the system. They are a core aspect of how the system works.

9

A Return to Securitization

In the period following the Second World War, a 25-year stretch from 1945 to 1970, the United States saw one of the greatest bursts of economic growth in world history.[1] With European and Japanese producers decimated by the war and global currencies pegged to the dollar under Bretton Woods, America's already-strong manufacturing sector reaped a windfall.[2] By the late 1940s, the U.S. produced half of the world's total manufacturing output—including four-fifths of the world's automobiles—and held 42 percent of global wealth. All of this benefited a mere 7 percent of the world's population.[3] Technological dominance resulted in high levels of productivity, measured both historically and in comparison to other nations.[4] GNP rose by 37 percent over the course of the 1950s and then increased by another 35 percent by 1966.[5]

It was the heyday of New Deal growth liberalism. Defense contracts represented about 10 percent of GNP for the second half of the 1950s, and "well into the 1960s," political scientists Jacob Hacker and Paul Pierson note, "the federal government spent more than the combined total of all R&D spending by governments and businesses outside the United States."[6] The legacy of governmental investments in research, development, and education can be seen in many of the leading industries of the era: electrical and chemical engineering, pharmaceuticals and processed foods, transistors and computers. Radar, satellites, global positioning systems, semiconductors, integrated circuits, radio and microwaves, plastics and metallurgy, and penicillin all benefited from government support of some kind.[7] Early in the Kennedy administration, signs saying "What have you done for Growth [sic] today?" were placed on every desk in the Department of Commerce.[8] The field of economics was dominated by Keynesians who advised the government and sought full employment and stable economic growth through, as sociologist Stephanie Mudge puts it, "a combination of scientific know-how and cooperative bargaining."[9]

In the political economy of this "Golden Age," housing finance played a central role in both distributional politics and economic stabilization.[10] Securitization existed at the margins of the economy. Private firms experimented with it but never successfully launched a profitable market. Meanwhile, government officials used securitization in the credit programs as a mode of off-budget finance, first sparingly, and then more aggressively.

This chapter discusses the distributional politics of mortgage markets and securitization in the postwar era and explains their transformation in the 1960s as Fannie Mae was "spun off" from the government and authorized to finance itself by issuing a new kind of government-guaranteed mortgage-backed security. In the second half of the decade, a series of crises marked the end of one era and the beginning of a long transition into a new one marked by scarcity, neoliberalism, and financialization.

The end of postwar affluence created a distributional struggle over which social groups would pay for what, and that process played out through the highly contentious and veto-ridden world of budget politics. Housing credit was doubly implicated in these fights, first because it was hit hard and early in market corrections, and second because its credit programs could be used for off-budget accounting. For all that the new approach to securitization reflected a changing relationship between the state and the market, the modern mortgage-backed security continued to reflect the institutional logic of the credit programs: the use of state-promoted financial development and risk redistribution as an alternative to more direct forms of wealth redistribution.

The Architecture of Postwar Affluence

Homeownership was always a central pillar of postwar growth liberalism. As chapter 7 noted, Franklin Roosevelt understood that the construction industry consumed resources and created jobs.[11] Once built, homes were giant boxes that Americans filled with things: TVs and radios, toys and clothes, refrigerators and toasters. The era's (mostly) low interest rates meant that Americans could rely on cheap credit to buy homes and purchase goods. Between the 1950s and 1970, household debt jumped from 25 to 50 percent of GNP.[12] Family purchasing power grew by 30 percent in the 1950s.[13] Disposable income rose 15 percent between the end of the 1940s and the early 1970s.[14] With the rise of credit cards, consumer debt rose as well.[15] "These were above all years of nearly unimaginable consumption of goods," writes historian James Patterson.[16] By the end of the 1960s nearly 80 percent of Americans owned cars.[17] Homes, consumerism, and increased productivity combined to propel growth.[18] There was nothing inevitable about this. Prasad points out that many European nations at the time had a political economy that prioritized exports over domestic consumption. In Europe, wage caps kept production costs low to promote exports. Labor agreed to lower wages in exchange for more welfare state protections. Regressive taxation helped fund the welfare state. These policies discouraged domestic consumption.[19]

Perpetual growth carried with it the promise of widespread opportunity that came without the need for European levels of economic redistribution. As historian Lizabeth Cohen writes, the postwar consumers' republic held the promise of using liberal means for progressive ends, in that it "promised the socially progressive end of economic equality without requiring politically progressive means of redistributing existing wealth." Consumerism did this by pledging to "expand the overall pie without reducing the size of any of the portions."[20] The power of growth as a mode of distributional politics is evident in Lyndon Johnson's War on Poverty. In 1964 the great public intellectual Walter Lippman remarked that "a generation ago it would have been taken for granted that a war on poverty meant taxing money away from the haves and . . . turning it over to the have nots." Now "a revolutionary idea has taken hold. The size of the pie can be increased by invention, organization, capital investment, and fiscal policy, and then a whole society, not just one part of it, will grow richer."[21] This was not just a matter of rhetoric. Unlike the New Deal's jobs programs, the War on Poverty offered school loans and job training. These programs were designed to bring the poor into the fold—to offer a "hand up, not a hand out," to open "doors to opportunity."[22]

To a great extent the postwar boom's gains were widely shared across economic classes. Low unemployment and strong unions kept wages high. Regressive taxes left over from the war limited accumulation among the wealthiest Americans and funded research and development investments and programs like the G.I. Bill, Social Security, the construction of new highways, expansions in education, and grants to state and local governments.[23] Before the Second World War, the top 10 percent of earners captured around 40 to 45 percent of the nation's total income, but from 1945 to 1970 the top decile held steady at a little over 30 percent of the nation's income share.[24] Ninety-two percent of Americans born in 1940 would go on to earn more than their parents (only about half of the children born in 1984 can expect the same). Between 1940 and 1970, the proportion of Americans living below the poverty line fell from 40 to 10 percent, and the quality of life for the poorest Americans increased substantially.[25] Economists Claudia Goldin and Robert Margo call this trend the "Great Compression."[26] Historian Jefferson Cowie has argued that the level of equality was actually a "Great Exception" to the United States' otherwise long history of economic inequality.[27]

Postwar distributional politics played out not just on the national level, but also in local fights over who could get which jobs and who could live in what neighborhoods.[28] Excluded from many unions and subject to job and wage discrimination, a black male worker in 1960 could expect to earn about 40 to 60 cents on the dollar earned by a white man depending on the region.[29] African Americans also had higher rates of unemployment and poverty than whites.[30] And while black families made gains in homeownership after the 1940s, the racial homeownership gap nevertheless widened because white families became homeowners at an even faster pace: between 1940 and 1960, homeownership among white families increased from 40 to 66 percent, while homeownership among black families rose from 19 to 37 percent.[31] Twenty years into one of the greatest economic surges the world has ever seen, black residents still had not reached the level of homeownership that white families had enjoyed at the start. Asian and Latinx Americans as well as Native Americans all faced discrimination in labor, home, and credit markets.[32] People of color organized, mobilized, and made gains, but vast inequality nevertheless ensured that the rising economic tide lifted white families first and highest.

THE CENTRALITY OF MORTGAGE CREDIT
FOR GROWTH LIBERALISM

The problem with growth is the potential for instability. Postwar policymakers were well aware that it was possible for an economy to overheat.[33] Consequently, through fiscal and monetary policy, lawmakers periodically slowed growth to counteract business cycles. Over time, expansions grew longer and recessions grew shorter. Banking regulations were a key reason why. New Deal lawmakers had looked upon the excesses of the 1920s and concluded that unchecked financial markets were dangerous. The banking laws and regulations of the 1930s broke financial markets into segments: Investment banks could continue to seek high returns with big bets, but they could not do so with the savings of everyday families. Instead, family savings were safeguarded in smaller depository institutions: commercial banks, mutuals, and S&Ls. None of these depository institutions were allowed to offer high returns to depositors for fear that high rates would encourage speculation, so the Federal Reserve used a policy called Regulation Q to set rate ceilings for commercial bank deposits. The FHLBB was responsible for setting ceilings for S&Ls.[34] Higher ceilings for these institutions gave them a competitive advantage in attracting deposits, which helped ensure the flow of capital into mortgage markets.

The regulations that divided depository institutions also acted like automatic economic stabilizers. As sociologist Greta Krippner has explained, these regulations, dismantled and reformed in the 1970s and 1980s, were incredibly important "levers and pullies" that government officials used to control economic growth.[35] As the "wheel within the wheel" to move the economy, mortgage credit allocation could speed up growth or slow it down. If the Federal

Reserve let short-term rates rise above the regulatory ceilings for deposits, savers responded by moving money out of the commercial banks and S&Ls and over to government and corporate bonds. This caused an outflow of deposits that forced banks and S&Ls to limit their lending activity. The result was that the economy cooled, interest rates dropped back below the ceilings, money flowed back into banks and S&Ls, and lending resumed.[36] In this system, the burden of the sacrifice for systemwide stability fell disproportionally on the housing sector. When interest rates were high, the housing credit programs were expected to give up growth in the housing sector in exchange for overall stability in the nation's economy.[37]

Homeownership helped families build wealth and save over the life course (see chapter 7). Homebuilding boosted industry, promoted consumption, promised a bright and fair future, and upheld racial hierarchies. It was also a central lever of economic management. Housing meant growth, steady growth, and all of the promise that entailed.

PRIVATE MARKETS

Securitization existed on the margins of this highly managed economy. On one hand, private firms experimented with mortgage-backed debt but failed to build a successful secondary mortgage market around it. On the other hand, government officials used asset pools as a form of off-budget financing for the credit programs.

Oliver Jones was an economist who would later go on to become an executive in the Mortgage Bankers Association of America. In his 1961 dissertation, he sought an answer to the question of why the nation's private secondary mortgage market was not more successful. Jones examined the market of the 1950s and found that the aggressive dealers of the 1930s had grown into conservative brokers, most of whom did not buy mortgages until a third party, like an insurance company or bank, first agreed to purchase them.[38] Facing legal hurdles, startup costs, and big swings in market value related to mortgage regulations, the brokers retreated to the "shelter of the advance commitment," which made them "in fact, if not in law, an agent of the buyer."[39]

An example can clarify why private firms failed to build a more successful securitization market in the postwar era. The Institutional Securities Corporation was owned by a group of New York savings banks that used it to purchase out-of-state mortgages.[40] In 1957, the Corporation formed a subsidiary, Instlcorp, to sell FHA mortgage-backed collateral trust notes to pension funds. To clear the way for the sales, the FHA repealed a prohibition against owning a partial share of an FHA mortgage (a repeal that was negotiated by Adolf Berle's old law firm).[41] The bonds quickly ran into trouble, however, because a separate FHA rule change about how mortgages could be priced in the first place lowered the expected profits and rendered the subsidiary's structure financially unviable.[42]

Instlcorp's story reveals some key trends. First, it shows a new effort to target pension funds as a source of funds in housing markets. Between 1940 and 1960 the assets held by private and public pension plans skyrocketed from $6 billion to $108.6 billion, but only $9.3 billion of that ended up invested in mortgages.[43] Pension fund managers, most of whom came from the banking world, preferred lower-maintenance investments that did not have to be continually managed. The main benefit of the collateral trust notes was that they could allow pension fund managers to sit back and receive payments while Instlcorp did the nitty-gritty work of servicing the mortgages.

Instlcorp's use of FHA mortgages also speaks to the importance of the mortgage brokers and FHA loans for the nascent securitization market. The S&Ls dealt mostly in conventional loans, operated under the conservative FHLB, and originated loans with the expectation of holding them until repayment. At the same time, FHA mortgages were widely considered the best bet for establishing a real secondary market because they were insured and uniform. In the postwar era, much as in earlier periods, most of the experiments with securitization were carried out by brokers who often serviced loans they did not own.

Finally, the Instlcorp case illustrates how legal restrictions stymied the development of a securitization market. Across the nation, state laws created a mix of usury limits, foreclosure rules, and extra "doing business" fees for out-of-state dealers. These rules impeded the flow of credit from capital-rich states to the capital-hungry Sun Belt. New York's restriction on out-of-state investments in savings banks is why Instlcorp's parent company existed in the first place. Then there were federal regulations, like FHA rules about the ownership and resale of insured mortgages.[44] But restrictions like the FHA's prohibition on owning partial shares, while certainly a hurdle, did not seem particularly hard to overcome.

The much bigger problem was the FHA's rules about the mortgages it would insure in the first place, particularly regarding how expensive the insured mortgage could be, which depended on the cost of the house and the interest charged. These regulations were hard to change because they went to the heart of the FHA's mission.[45] Lawmakers generally did not want to be in the business of insuring houses for wealthy families, and lawmakers also did not want to encourage high long-term interest rates. The FHA price restrictions were the crux of the secondary market problem: when the nation's interest rates were low, mortgages were competitive with other kinds of investments and brokers had access to plenty of funds. Conversely, when interest rates were high, brokers were motivated to innovate to attract new investors, but that was precisely when the FHA caps made returns on mortgages unattractive relative to other bonds. When brokers could afford to make a profit on securitization, they did not need it, and they worried in any case about how market corrections would hit their profits. In congressional hearings on mortgage credit in the late 1950s, speakers discussed the innovation of a new instrument or debenture backed by mortgages that could be sold by mortgage brokers or the FNMA or the S&Ls. They noted that a real secondary market should bring down the cost of mortgages overall. But FHA and VA ceilings were the far more pressing matter, because they generally impeded profits overall.[46]

By 1968, Oliver Jones had concluded that the federal government would have to lead the way in developing the market for "a security that can be substituted for a mortgage."[47] Only the government could trade in the large amounts needed to bring down the costs enough to make a mortgage-backed security competitive with corporate bonds.[48] A government program, organized through Fannie Mae or a similar entity, would appeal to investors, absorb startup costs, and, importantly, familiarize investors with the business. "These events could not be accomplished overnight," Jones wrote, "but once accomplished the way would be clear for the private market to take over, to issue a mortgage-backed security."[49]

There was good reason to think this plan would work. Fannie Mae was selling something like this already.

GOVERNMENT ASSET SALES

As the credit programs grew, the federal government accumulated a large portfolio of loans. Government officials regularly sold these loans and sometimes used loan pools to do so. In this way, forms of securitization became a means of off-budget finance for the credit programs.

Why were asset sales a form of off-budget finance? Because the main administrative budget was operated on a cash account basis, which meant that any time the government purchased or issued a loan, the entire cost showed up on the budget as an expenditure. The flip side of this accounting standard was that when loans were sold or paid off, the revenue could be directly counted *against* expenditures. If enough money came in through repayments or sales, the revenue could offset the cost of a credit program altogether. For policymakers, selling off loans was therefore a very useful policy tool. The problem was that someone had to want to buy the loans. The majority of early sales had been through the Export-Import Bank and Fannie Mae, agencies that dealt in plain "vanilla" loans.[50] Unusual loans, those with atypical terms and below-market interest rates, were harder to unload, and managing the sales demanded man-hours and expertise.[51] Officials wanted a better way to unload less profitable loans, so running parallel to the direct sale of assets they organized a series of experiments using asset pools, options, and guarantees to construct bonds with wider appeal.[52] Government offices sold more and more loans, both through pools and individually: $364 million under Truman, $1.78 billion under Eisenhower.[53] Reported expenditures fell accordingly.[54]

An early example of government securitization deals were the loan pools that helped unwind the RFC. When it closed, the RFC's foreign loans moved to the Export-Import Bank, its disaster loans went to the Small Business Administration, and its mortgages went to Fannie Mae. Some 2,848 smaller loans, totaling $73.4 million, were left over. These were collected into a pool of loans that collateralized certificates bearing a 3 percent interest rate.[55] That same year, the Commodity Credit Corporation used a similar structure as an emergency response to a budget overage of over $1 billion; the government repurchased the certificates at a loss the next year, with the difference effectively being a price subsidy to farmers.[56] In 1962 the Export-Import Bank adapted the pooling technique to issue participation certificates (see chapter 6 on their history). In this instance, pooling was useful because anonymity mitigated any potential political embarrassment that could come from the U.S. government offloading the debt of another nation.[57]

The sale of certificates backed by pools of government-held assets moved to the housing programs in the mid-1960s. Housing acts in 1964 and 1965 authorized Fannie Mae to sell participation certificates (PCs) backed by assets held by Fannie and the VA.[58] To enable the sale of loans with below-market interest rates through the pools, the acts also authorized appropriations to cover the difference between the government rate and the market rate.[59] The *Wall Street Journal* reported that this sale "concentrated the benefit" of repayments on those loans and offset $300 million in spending in 1964.[60] Within a couple of years, this program would dramatically expand and then ignite a controversy.

THE SOCIAL LOGIC OF SECURITIZATION
UNDER GROWTH LIBERALISM

Financial markets were carefully controlled under postwar growth liberalism. The federal government oversaw the allocation of credit across sectors through banking regulations and the federal credit programs. Insurance of mortgages (through the FHA) and of deposits (through the FSLIC and FDIC) contained and managed risks. To move money across regions, the Federal Home Loan Banks issued advances to S&Ls, and Fannie Mae supported brokers. Private experiments with securitization both were constrained by and relied upon government insurance programs. At a time when the federal government self-consciously managed the economy, that involvement was reflected in the limits and form of the nascent securitization market.

Government involvement in financial markets transformed not just private markets, but also how the state managed its own accounts. Here we see that when governments run banking and insurance operations, they become an institutional pathway for creative engagement with financial innovation and techniques. As organizations with budgets, governments have their own interest in financial instruments. With the credit programs, government activities went far beyond the basics of taxing, borrowing, and spending. Government postwar securitization reveals that as bureaucrats used financial techniques, they transposed that knowledge to the management of the general accounts of the state. As the next section will show, they also may have promoted the circulation of those techniques within the market.

Governmental use of securitization was not extensive in the postwar period, especially before the 1960s. However, securitization did provide an emergency funding option when the demands of the credit programs ran up against the constraints of the federal budget or market shortfalls. As a funding mechanism, then, securitization was part of a larger mobilization of the credit programs as a low-cost, low-controversy approach to economic developmental and social policy.

The End of an Era

In retrospect, we know that the postwar era of affluence was rapidly coming to an end by the mid-1960s. U.S. manufacturers faced increasing competition as Europe and Japan recovered from the war.[61] In the second half of the 1960s, U.S. labor productivity declined, and the nation's trade surplus faded.[62] While it was not entirely clear at the time, the mid-1960s was the starting point of a painful and protracted transformation of the political economy.

What happens to distributional politics based on the promise of growth when that growth stops? Sociologist Greta Krippner addresses this question in her study of how the United States transitioned to a new era of financialization. By the 1960s a quarter century of economic gains and activist government had primed citizens to expect a great deal from Washington and for their futures.[63] As a new period of scarcity settled in, these rising demands ran into the problem of shrinking resources.[64] Lawmakers who happily took credit for the economy when the size of the overall pie was growing now were faced with dividing up a shrinking one. This meant deciding whose portions would be reduced, and by how much. Krippner shows that over the course of decades, lawmakers progressively dismantled the regulations they had once used to control the economy in order to plausibly abdicate political responsibility for economic outcomes. When government officials controlled interest rate ceilings, constituents could blame them for credit shortages. In a deregulated market, in contrast, if a homeowner with good credit could not find a loan, it was understood to be *the market* that denied him or her access to credit, not a withholding regulator or a politician who could be voted out of office. Mortgage markets would be at the forefront of this transition because they were hit early and hard during times of credit shortage under growth liberalism.

CRISIS IN MORTGAGE MARKETS

Even before the late 1960s, U.S. mortgage markets showed signs of strain. One problem was finding funds to create better housing in city centers. A quarter century of suburbanization and racism had created concentrated poverty in city centers. These neighborhoods contained dilapidated housing stock, were largely cut off from job opportunities and credit markets, and were predominantly populated by black families. By mid-decade, social unrest had boiled over. Years later the Kerner Commission would blame racial discrimination and poor housing stock as the ultimate causes of the urban riots that erupted in the second half of the decade.[65] Even before then, Johnson recognized that the War on Poverty and Great Society were incomplete without urban housing improvements—an acknowledgment of what African American activists had been saying for decades.[66] Johnson elevated the Housing and Home Finance Agency to a cabinet-level Department of Housing and Urban Development (HUD) in 1965, making agency head Robert Weaver the nation's first African American cabinet member in the process.[67] An economist who had come up through the New Deal, Weaver had written a 1948 book entitled *The Negro Ghetto* that critiqued government housing programs for encouraging segregation and made the early case that white racism—not black neighbors—was bad for property values.[68] Headed by Weaver, HUD was positioned to make changes to the urban housing problem. But updating urban housing stock, rehabilitating cities, and providing fair credit access for families of color would all cost money.

Housing credit for middle-class suburban families also faced challenges. The fact that pension fund trustees wanted little to do with mortgage markets was a worsening problem as American pension and deferred savings plans grew from $33.1 billion to $51.9 billion between 1963 and 1967 alone.[69] As highways, air-conditioning, and government funding drew families into the Sun Belt, the need to move mortgage credit across the continent once again became a real concern, and some complained that the conservative Federal Home Loan Bank Board was failing to move enough credit across regions.[70] Experts looked at these trends and wondered how the existing system could accommodate the growing needs of the baby boomers as they settled down and had children.[71]

These trends, while bothersome, were not necessarily catastrophic when short-term interest rates were low, which was the case for much of the 1950s. Commercial banks offered rates below the Regulation Q ceilings for most of the decade, and S&Ls offered much higher returns for depositors in their savings accounts.[72] In the tight credit markets of the late 1950s, however, banks worried that they were losing business clients and looked to attract more deposit funds to lend out through the marketing of new instruments like commercial paper and negotiable certificates of deposit.[73] The growing business in Eurodollars (U.S. dollars held in Europe) allowed the banks to get around U.S. regulations entirely.[74] As banks worked to attract more capital, the Federal Reserve helped them along by periodically raising their regulatory ceilings on domestic accounts. S&Ls were suddenly "locked in competitive battle with high-flying capital market instruments."[75] By the early 1960s the rate difference between the S&Ls and banks had narrowed considerably.[76] S&Ls complained that they could not compete with banks indefinitely. By law and by mission, their investments were tied up in low-interest loans, and if brought into competition with the banks, their only choices were driving up interest rates, lowering the quality of their loans, or investing more outside of mortgages.

These long-term problems were common concerns in the housing market, and various options were discussed for addressing them.[77] But not much changed until the market faced real instability in the second half of the decade.

CREDIT CRUNCH: AN ECONOMIC CRISIS
HITS THE HOUSING MARKET

The Council of Economic Advisers celebrated in the summer of 1965. Johnson had passed Kennedy's tax proposal almost as soon as he had entered office, and the $11.5 billion cut had resulted in a $7 billion influx in government revenues from an expanded tax base by the second quarter of 1965.[78] For the fifth year in a row real GNP increased by over 5 percent.[79] The economy neared full employment. It all seemed a triumph of Keynesian policy. Yet even as members of the Council celebrated, Johnson authorized the deployment of more troops to Vietnam.[80] With the costs of war added to an economy already operating at full capacity, markets started to overheat. By the end of 1965 the Council and the budget director had called for a tax increase to combat inflation. Johnson refused to pursue a politically unpopular tax before the midterm elections, especially one he claimed would not pass Congress. As inflation rose, the Fed let interest rates increase, hoping to cool the economy.[81]

By spring of 1966 the commercial banks were offering higher interest rates on deposits than the S&Ls. In response, American families pulled their savings out of the S&Ls and sought higher returns offered elsewhere. The S&Ls were hit with $722 million in withdrawals in April.[82] Over the next year the Federal Reserve worked to regain control of the commercial banks and the economy by adjusting regulatory ceilings and interest rates (as part of this effort, Regulation Q was extended to the S&Ls).[83] The changes helped, but only for a time, and only after much damage had already been done. By year-end, deposits at S&Ls were down 58 percent from 1965.[84] Construction on new homes dropped to a 20-year low.[85] Economist Hyman Minsky called the 1966 credit crunch the "first serious financial disruption of the postwar era."[86] The disruptions of 1966 would loom over housing market discussions for years.[87]

Once it was clear that the mortgage markets were in real trouble, why did the housing credit programs fail to intervene? In theory, they existed to prevent exactly this sort of problem from occurring and could have mobilized to force other markets—like business loans and municipal bonds—to take some of the hit from the credit crunch. The problem was that all of the main options for helping the housing markets came with dangerous economic or political side effects. The government could have helped the housing sector compete for credit by allowing the S&Ls to offer higher returns, for instance, or by allowing the FHA to insure home loans with higher mortgage interest rates. But most policymakers did not want "a policy of houses at any price" and worried that forcing up mortgage rates would be inflationary over the long term.[88] Lawmakers were not yet ready to give up the use of credit rationing to control the economy.

Alternatively, the housing agencies could have issued bonds to raise money to fund mortgage lenders. But there was no way to ensure that the money raised would not draw from funds that *would have gone to housing in any case*. No matter what, agency bond issuances would exacerbate the underlying credit shortage, especially since international capital flows were still highly regulated. In September 1966, Johnson announced that government agencies should only issue enough debt to cover operating expenses, lest the additional pull on funds worsen the credit shortage.[89] Ray Lapin, who became president of Fannie Mae in 1967, compared the Corporation at this time to "a fire department that had plenty of water except when there was a real conflagration."[90]

A third potential response to the credit crunch was to have Fannie Mae's Special Assistance Functions branch purchase FHA and VA mortgages, which would have supplied brokers with more funds. The problem here was not just inflation, but also the federal budget. The Special Assistance Functions branch was on-budget, which meant that this option would contribute to a worsening of the budget problem. Recall that Johnson had not previously asked for a tax increase (which would have slowed inflation in the first place) even as the costs of Vietnam and the Great Society programs mounted. Without the tax increase the Treasury was forced to borrow to fund government expenditures. As the budget neared the debt limit, Republicans threatened not to raise it, using the limit as leverage to force cuts in domestic spending.

In the middle of 1966, every political response to the credit crunch threatened to create a bigger problem than it solved. Housing was at the center of a much larger set of national-level fights about who would go without— without credit, without taxes, without government expenditures. As housing became part of this larger set of negotiations, the New Deal housing system, especially Fannie Mae, would become a pawn in a much larger fight about U.S. budget politics.

Budget Battles

In her analysis of the financial turn in the U.S. political economy, Krippner discusses the inflationary pressures of the era. [91] Inflation, she notes, is famously described as "too much money chasing too few goods." But she also stresses that another tradition views inflation as a symptomatic flare-up of a society that has not used political means to decide who must go without either money or goods. Lyndon Johnson's policies between 1966 and 1968 are a textbook case of this brand of political indecision. In 1966 Johnson refused to sacrifice either guns or butter, to cut military or social spending, and failed to push for raising taxes.[92] Inflation rose. But Johnson could only put off making hard distributional decisions for so long. In the U.S. system, governance is shared, Congress holds spending authority, and the budget process contains numerous opportunities for opponents to force some kind of compromise. Between 1966 and 1968 a series of budget battles unfolded in which Johnson resisted making cuts to domestic spending while Republicans and fiscally conservative Democrats like Wilbur Mills used political means—not just votes, but also control over committees and the budget ceiling—to force a compromise on domestic spending. It makes sense that budget battles intensified at this moment: the national budget is the official word on who gets what from the government and who pays what to that government. The budget is, in the famous formulation, "the skeleton of the state stripped of all misleading ideologies."[93]

On one hand, the budget battles of the 1960s played out in fights over taxation. By the time Johnson proposed a surcharge in 1967 to pay for the war, the midterm elections had eroded the Democratic majority. Johnson now faced a cohort of Republicans who campaigned on the deficit, had little interest in compromise, and had powerful allies in the fiscally conservative Southern Democrats. Mills, a Democrat from Arkansas and head of the Ways and Means Committee, stood in Johnson's way, believing that the country could not afford to raise living standards at home, fight expensive wars overseas, and pursue other policies like space exploration and foreign aid.[94] Mills held up hearings and refused to advance a tax increase without promises for simultaneous spending cuts.

On the other hand, the budget battles included fights over the debt limit. With taxes on hold and expenses high, the Treasury continued to borrow to cover expenditures. The debt limit was raised 13 times between 1960 and 1970; most of those were adjustments to a temporary debt limit (see figure 9.1). By 1966, the official limit had reached $285 billion, and the budget hawks were

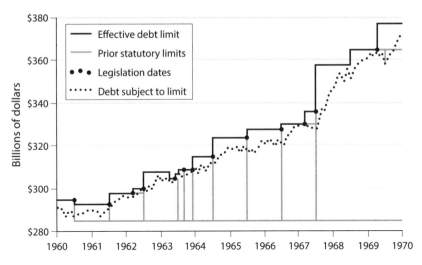

FIGURE 9.1. Effective Limit Adjustments in the 1960s

Sources: "Temporary Debt Limit Raised Three Times," in *CQ Almanac 1963* (Washington, D.C.: Congressional Quarterly, 1964), 569–72; "Debt Limit," in *CQ Almanac 1966* (Washington, D.C.: Congressional Quarterly, 1967), 714. During these years, the statutory debt limit would fall to a lower level on June 30 (the last day of the fiscal year).

also using it to put pressure on Johnson to cut domestic spending. In March of 1967 Johnson would announce that he would not seek or accept the party nomination and would then pursue the tax increase and negotiate with Congress over spending cuts. But in 1966 Johnson was still seeking to salvage the Great Society programs and privileged them over warnings about inflation. To that end, he pursued ways around his political opponents.

It was in this context of worsening budget battles and mounting inflation that Johnson turned to securitization as a partial solution to his problem. In its original form, the Participation Sales Act would have authorized Fannie Mae to sell all $33 billion in loans held by the government (although Johnson assured Congress that he only planned to sell $3.2 billion in the following year). Johnson framed this move as a substitution of private funds for public credit and a simple rationalization of existing practices. However, the deeper budgetary implications were clear to everyone involved at the time. Johnson and Congress were negotiating over temporary budget limit increases in $2 billion to $6 billion increments. Selling the PCs would provide substantial leeway. In fact, the strategy was part of an overall trend of reliance on asset sales as a form of off-budget finance: by 1966, special analyses of the budget reported that such sales were expected to completely offset $9 billion in future costs.[95] By 1968 nearly three-fourths of the loan programs' income came from asset sales.[96] A later government report said that Johnson saw this strategy as "a tremendous breakthrough in the financial management of Federal lending programs" and that it potentially was seen as a key element of his Great Society agenda because it provided a means of financing policy outside of budgeting constraints.[97]

Budget hawks were incensed. Their case rested on the fact that the PCs were issued with a guarantee of payment of principal and interest from the government. This meant that the Treasury was financially responsible for the loans. By their logic, if the government serviced the loans and retained their risks, it had not really sold the assets, and if this was not a real sale then it was a way of raising money. They concluded that the government had not reduced expenditures but had done the opposite: it had issued a new kind of debt. Instead of spending less, it now owed more. First in committee and later on the floor, Republicans branded PCs as a dangerous budgetary trick designed to camouflage the full extent of the administration's spending and as a kind of "backdoor" accounting that bypassed the appropriations process while concentrating power in the hands of the president. They warned against inflationary consequences and decried the high costs of the PCs: since Fannie Mae could not issue debt as cheaply as the Treasury, and since the government would subsidize some of the deals, the PCs meant the government would pay a premium to hide the size of the budget, making this a costly form of refinancing.[98] For the $3.2 billion in sales that Johnson actually planned for fiscal year 1967, the refinancing cost amounted to $10 to $14 million.[99]

Republicans insisted that they would have supported a true sale of assets, but that this was not a true sale, since the government serviced the loans and held the titles. Moreover, the PC holder received payments at a predetermined rate, like a bondholder, rather than as a *pro rata* share of the pool. Because these bonds had government guarantees, the issuing agencies bore the default risk.[100] Republicans further warned that the credit protection ran into moral hazard problems: since any bad debts were backed with credit protection from the government, they would sell at the same price as good debt.

Rejecting the notion that the PCs were a true sale, Republicans branded them as an inflationary and expensive form of debt refinancing and a dangerous budgetary gimmick:

> It makes no difference as to what the quality of these assets are. It makes no difference as to whether maturities are "short" or "long." It makes no difference what the rate of interest on the asset is. The poorest of them and the most desirable from an investment point of view could be pooled and participations sold against them. They would be just as readily marketable and they would sell at the same rate of interest as participations sold against a pool of the best of these assets. The reason for this is that the investment quality of the participations is established by the FNMA

[Fannie Mae] guarantee of the participations, in turn backed by an un-
limited draw on the U.S. Treasury, rather than by whatever the quality
of the assets pooled.

This is a neat gimmick. Indirectly government credit could be used to
effect a reduction in the Federal debt.

The miracles of bookkeeping are indeed marvelous![101]

Some Democrats conceded that PCs mattered for the budget, but they also
argued that the primary impetus behind the bill was to bring private funds
into the market[102]:

The Participation Sales Act of 1966 will permit us to conserve our budget
resources by substituting private for public credit while still meeting ur-
gent credit needs in the most efficient and economical manner possible. It
will enable us to make the credit market stronger, more competitive, and
better able to serve the needs of our growing economy. But above all, the
legislation will benefit millions of taxpayers and the many vital programs
supported by Federal credit. The Act will help us move this nation forward
and bring a better life to all the people.

Private statements of Democrats were sometimes more candid. In a letter
to Johnson's special assistant Barefoot Saunders, Democratic representative
Brock Adams explained, "The deficit is so bad that many of us who believe that
these assets should be used either for emergencies or for long-term benefits
and not to simply cover operating deficits have supported them because of the
emergency caused by the Viet Nam spending."[103]

For his part, Johnson argued that he was simply rationalizing an existing
practice, that this was a reasonable and advisable way to manage the costs
of the credit programs, and that he was following precedent. If that was the
case, it was the Republicans who were being politically opportunistic. Johnson
accused his opponents of trying to push the deficit above Eisenhower's 1959
peacetime record of $12.4 billion in an attempt to embarrass him. "I'm a good
country girl. I can feel it when you do it to me," Johnson told House Minority
Leader Gerald Ford in a phone call. "I've been doing it to y'all all these years.
And I know it. What you do is run my deficit up past Eisenhower's. Now I ain't
going to let you do that."[104]

The final version of the Participation Sales Act, passed in May of 1966,
allowed Fannie Mae to broker $11 billion worth of loans from six agencies
but required sales to receive congressional approval through the appropriations process.[105] While providing substantially less in funding and flexibility
than initially proposed, the measure provided a degree of budgetary relief.
The following year, Raymond H. Lapin was installed as the new president of
Fannie Mae, replacing J. Stanley Baughman. A former mortgage broker from

California who was supported by the National Association of Home Builders, Lapin would encourage the PC sales.[106]

The asset sales could ease Johnson's debt limit problem, but not his inflation problem. Fannie Mae had purchased over $4 billion worth of mortgages in the course of the 1966 credit crunch. Johnson was eager to offset this, even in part, by selling these mortgages, but selling PCs threatened to divert funds from private investments, making money even tighter.[107] The housing industry objected, and the Treasury sent a memo to the president telling him to avoid issuing PCs until market conditions changed.[108] Johnson now had to choose between what was best for the housing market and what was best for his budget. In a game of "financial chicken," the White House agreed to delay sales in hope of improved market conditions, but only until the middle of 1967 so that the sales could count toward the budget.[109]

During these deliberations, the administration considered selling all the PCs back to the government trusts to reduce the impact of the sale on the housing market, but Johnson's advisors worried that this would cause political embarrassment and instead settled on a plan to have the trusts invest in a smaller portion of the PCs.[110] Since the trusts could only invest in government debt, the attorney general ruled that the PCs were backed by the federal government. Contrary to Johnson's statements about bringing private funds into the housing market, in 1967 the president tried to minimize capital market investment in PCs and reasserted their connection to the Treasury. This decision would come back to haunt him. Republicans would subsequently argue that as obligations of the federal government, the PCs should count toward the debt limit.

THE PRESIDENT'S COMMISSION ON BUDGETARY CONCEPTS

Johnson's victory on the PC issue was fraught and temporary. Republicans continued to fight the PC sales. In August, they launched a failed attempt to stop authorization of a sale of PCs and then again raised the issue in January's hearings for another temporary debt limit increase. At a time when Johnson's continual restatement of budget numbers was raising accusations of a "credibility gap," Democrats and Republicans explicitly debated the PCs as a budget trick used to avoid the hard choice between Vietnam and the Great Society.

In a phone call to the president, Treasury head Henry "Joe" Fowler argued to Johnson that the best way to handle this conflict was to openly address the budget issue: "No sense in your getting blamed for what Kennedy did, Eisenhower did, Truman did." Fowler warned Johnson that the Republicans planned to continue to call attention to the PCs and urged the president to get ahead of the matter: "I think the best answer to the Republicans on this is to say, 'We're perfectly ready to go by the book if someone will write the book. But the book hasn't been written.'"[111]

Early in 1967, Fowler sent a memo to the White House explaining that debates over the budget were becoming increasingly heated and acrimonious, citing the Participation Sales Act as a "prime example" of the growing hostility.[112] A staff paper later stated that the PC accounting scandal had "perhaps done more to undermine public and congressional confidence in the integrity of budget totals than any single other issue."[113] Fowler recommended that the president convene a special committee to review the budget, arguing that the political advantages of a more transparent budget outweighed the potential downside of less flexibility. In a phone conversation with Johnson, Fowler warned that the Republicans would continue to use the issue to "try to make some great common cause out of this budget gimmickry business."[114]

In line with Fowler's logic, Johnson worked the idea of a budget review into the resulting 1967 debt limit compromise bill. Hawks insisted that they would not raise the limit unless the PCs were counted toward it. When Johnson spoke to Ford about the issue in February of 1967, he opened with a vigorous defense of the sales: "You all ought not to play recommittal and partisan on this debt limit bill. This is one we need and we need in a hurry." Reminding Ford that Eisenhower had sold assets, Johnson offered a compromise: Fannie Mae's PCs would count toward the debt limit for the next year. In exchange for a raise of the permanent debt limit, a bipartisan commission would review the national budget procedures and determine the right way to account for asset sales.[115]

Three months later the White House announced that it had appointed the President's Commission on Budgetary Concepts. Headed by banker David Kennedy, its members included the heads of the Treasury, the Bureau of the Budget, and the General Accounting Office; members of the Appropriations Committee; and private economists and experts.[116] This budget commission led to the most significant changes in federal budgeting since the executive budget had been created in 1921.[117] The commission took a holistic look at the budget, examining trade-offs between transparency and complexity and grappling with how its decisions would matter for political control and economic policy. Of all the issues before the commission, members considered the accounting of government loans and the participation certificates to be especially important and especially difficult. Because they possessed qualities of both loan sales and government debt, the participation certificates were complex entities.[118] Economist Arthur Okun of the Council of Economic Advisers argued that the PCs effectively just converted direct loans into government guarantees of loans, and so, like other government loan guarantees, they should be excluded from the budget.[119] Most everyone else on the commission disagreed and instead believed that the PCs were government debt.[120] This would become the final position of the President's Commission.

Laying out the logic for a new unified budget that would include a more comprehensive treatment of lending programs, its members reached consensus on everything *except* PCs.[121] Over the objections of Treasury Secretary Henry Fowler and Budget Director Charles Schultze, the group concluded that PCs were *not* a true sale of assets:

> In one sense, the sale of shares in a pool of loans is but a short, logical step beyond the sale of the asset itself; but it is a crucial step. When an asset is sold, the Federal Government retains no equity in it although it usually guarantees the loans it sells. When it is pooled, however—and participation certificates sold in the pool—the ownership (though not the beneficial equity) is still retained by the federal government. Interest payments on the loan continue to flow to the Government and the Government continues not only to incur servicing costs but also to assume fully the risk of default on any individual loan as far as the investor in the participation certificate is concerned.[122]

Commission members concluded that if the government serviced the loans and held the risk, then the government owned those mortgages. This ruling did more than merely prevent PCs from being used as budgetary reductions; it also ensured that PCs, now considered a liability, would add to the deficit.

The Turning Point: The Fannie Mae Spin-Off and Mortgage-Backed Securities

The budget commission's decision was a problem for the Johnson administration: now none of Fannie Mae's mortgage purchases could be offset from asset sales.[123] His advisors warned that disregarding the conclusions of his commission, given the deal he had made around it, would be a "political impossibility"[124] and a "major tactical mistake."[125]

The commission's decision immediately raised the prospect of a spin-off. The idea was far from new. Fannie itself had been created in 1938 only after an attempt to charter private versions of it had failed. Even then, Fannie had been supposed to be a temporary proof of concept for investors still skittish from the collapse of the nation's housing market during the Depression.[126] It persisted as a government agency, but so did questions about its status as a government agency, which again became a topic of debate during the 1954 organizational redesign.

With new budget rules changing the political calculus around Fannie Mae, the Johnson administration embraced privatization. At this point things moved quickly. An intra-agency committee on mortgage finance had been meeting since 1966. Headed by James Duesenberry of the Council of Economic Advisers and Sherman Maisel of the Federal Reserve, this group, known as the

Mortgage Finance Task Force, included representatives from the Bureau of the Budget and Treasury and worked on an array of issues and solutions related to housing finance problems, from FHA regulations to Fannie Mae's system for mortgage purchases. The task force had previously dismissed the possibility of privatizing Fannie, a decision consistent with the centrality of housing in the postwar political economy.[127] Now that there was a strong push to spin off Fannie, the group would need to devise a way to fund it.

Securing adequate financing for Fannie meant grappling with the credit and liquidity problems that had repelled investment bankers from the program in the first place. The task force discussed how it might adjust the PC to make it more appealing. At a meeting in May of 1967, a representative of the Erie County Savings Bank suggested that the government look into private companies already issuing mortgage bonds. The comment is itself revealing: it speaks to how government officials had been thinking about the practice in terms of the PCs, rather than about nascent private efforts.[128]

The device the task force eventually settled on to replace the PC as a mechanism for financing Fannie Mae would take the form of the pass-through certificate, which experts have called the first modern mortgage-backed security.[129] In debates about the Participation Sales Act, the fact that PC holders received payments at predetermined rates had been cited as evidence that PCs were debt obligations rather than true sales of assets. For the new instruments, repayments were to flow directly to investors on a *pro rata* basis. Allowing funds to "pass through" the structure helped establish that this was a bona fide sale of assets. Another argument leveled against the PCs-as-sales was that Fannie Mae—and not investors—retained the title to the loans in the pool.[130] The new mortgage-backed securities placed titles in a special trust, clarifying that Fannie Mae was not the real owner and helping to legitimate their transfer as a real sale.

To help secure the success of the new system, task force members met with private companies and bankers about their plans. When discussing the new mortgage-backed security, bankers argued that investors would rather buy Treasury securities than this new instrument and asserted that they would only invest in it with some kind of government guarantee.[131] A second guarantee was therefore added to the pools. In addition to the FHA and VA guarantees of loans going into the pools, the return of principal and interest of the pool itself would be guaranteed by the U.S. government. One government official later boasted, "The double federal guarantee should produce a virtually riskless security with broad market acceptability."[132] The Senate Housing and Currency Committee noted that if private companies started using them in large amounts, the new mortgage-backed securities could help attract capital to mortgage markets.[133]

Title VII of the Housing and Urban Development Act of 1968 split Fannie Mae in two. The secondary mortgage operations were spun off, meaning that the Treasury sold off its preferred shares for that branch. The Government National Mortgage Association (Ginnie Mae) was formed as a new agency within the government to house the old Management & Liquidation and Special Assistance Functions branches. Ginnie was authorized to guarantee mortgage-backed securities that were issued by Fannie and approved by private companies, as long as those securities were backed by mortgages already insured by the FHA, VA, and Farmers Home Loan Administration.

In exchange for agreeing to help promote the nation's secondary mortgage market, the new Fannie Mae was granted special privileges, including the tax exemption of its bonds, regulatory oversight through HUD rather than the SEC, and a $2.25 billion line of credit. Administrative control over the new agency was shared between the government and stockholders, but not evenly: after a transition period, Fannie would have a 15-member board of directors, 5 appointed by the U.S. president and the rest elected by shareholders.

This new system of housing finance was highly leveraged from the start. The planning committee argued that Fannie Mae should not be hindered by any debt-to-equity ratio requirements; if that met resistance, members suggested a ratio of 25 to 1.[134] The justification for this was that the FHA and VA loans that Fannie brokered were unusually low-risk investments, a logic partially belied by discussions already underway about how Fannie Mae could also deal in non-insured "conventional" loans.[135] Because Fannie Mae's mortgage-backed securities were held in a trust through which funds passed on the way to the new owners of the debt, the reconfigured Fannie Mae did not have to count the securities toward its debt-to-equity ratio. The loans were officially off Fannie Mae's balance sheet.

In the end, the main risks associated with this highly leveraged Fannie Mae were shifted to taxpayers. Ginnie Mae's guarantee of the mortgage-backed securities and a $2.25 billion line of credit meant that the Treasury was financially responsible in the event of a default within these pools. Yet even though the government maintained close ties with Fannie Mae and absorbed much of its risk, Fannie Mae was officially no longer part of the U.S. government, which meant that $1.4 billion of its planned expenditures would not be included on the federal budget totals for the next year.[136]

Ginnie Mae and Fannie Mae were authorized to contract work for each other, which created a new way to offset Ginnie Mae's costly Special Assistance Functions branch on the federal budget. Through a new "Tandem Plan," Ginnie Mae could direct Fannie Mae to purchase private mortgages with below-market interest rates (that is, subsidized mortgages for lower-income homes). Ginnie would then pay the difference between the lower purchase price and the market rate to Fannie. In this way, only the federal subsidy cost would show up on the budget for Ginnie Mae. Because the federal government never actually owned the mortgages, the Tandem Plan stuck to the letter of the rules set by the President's Commission on Budgetary Concepts. Such arrangements became an important pathway for the now spun-off Fannie Mae to provide off-budget financing for more highly subsidized mortgage support for low-income housing, like the Section 235 program that for a few years subsidized interest payments on mortgages for low-income families.[137]

THE AFTERMATH

The Housing and Urban Development Act of 1968 passed with remarkably little controversy. This may have been because the budget hawks had already realized significant gains. PCs would no longer be used across multiple agencies to circumvent the debt limit, and the administration had followed the budget commission's proposed rules with the redesign, even though measures like the second guarantee and the Tandem Plan stretched the limits of credibility.

Republicans also had other reasons to support the housing bill by the summer of 1968. The year before, they along with conservative Democrats had publicly ridiculed a pest control bill that they had defeated, which they called the "rat bill." This backfired. "The press gave them holy hell for being so heartless," Weaver later explained, "because really this involves children's being bitten and diseases being carried."[138] Beyond the chance to recover some lost political capital, the omnibus housing bill included a host of other provisions that appealed to voters across the political spectrum, including an array of public–private partnerships for housing development. The massive deal accomplished what von Hoffman has called "a kind of social policy logrolling" that incorporated big businesses as agents of housing development. A Republican aide said that the "sheer enormity of the bill made it difficult to defeat."[139]

These inconsistencies indicate that just as the PCs' sales were about budget politics, so too were many of the objections to them. The Republican attack on the PCs was part of an effort to use the debt limit to pressure the Johnson administration, force cuts, and gain political advantage. We should not interpret this effort as an uncompromising rejection of budget gimmickry or asset sales; after all, no political party has a monopoly on budget gimmickry, and PCs had been sold under Eisenhower, who had run up a budget deficit as large as Johnson's in 1967.[140] Strategies on both sides shifted when it advantaged the players.

Congress created Freddie Mac (the Federal Home Loan Mortgage Corporation) in the model of Fannie Mae in 1970. It was Freddie Mac and Ginnie Mae that took the lead in developing mortgage-backed securities in the 1970s. Within a decade, a quarter of all home loans in the United States were financed through $40 billion in mortgage-backed securities, mostly through Fannie and Freddie, as private firms worked to adapt the structure.[141]

Political contests over Fannie Mae, asset sales, and budget gimmickry continued after the spin-off. The Nixon administration would later tell the *Wall Street Journal* that Fannie Mae was effectively a shadow government agency that had been privatized only to hide the size of the federal budget.[142] In 1971 a memo from the Federal Reserve proposed that the government reclassify Ginnie Mae–guaranteed securities in order to include them in the budgetary outlay totals. This was intended as a step toward putting all of the government's $25 billion insured and guaranteed securities, including the FHA and VA loans, on the official budget accounts (in comparison, the mortgage-backed securities in 1971 would add only $2 billion annually to the budget). The Treasury, the Office of Management and Budget, and HUD strenuously objected to the proposal.[143] Moreover, with Fannie Mae now spun off from the government, other agencies like the SBA returned to selling their own assets and all the problems that entailed. In 1974 the Federal Financing Bank was created as a new off-budget institution that would do what Fannie Mae had originally been supposed to do under the Participation Sales Act: broker and coordinate the sale of assets from other credit programs.[144] The Federal Financing Bank also purchased government-guaranteed loans, effectively turning them into off-budget direct loans.[145]

The Social Logic of the New Mortgage-Backed Security

The pass-throughs, as the first of a new generation of mortgage-backed securities, were a creature of the credit programs. They reflected a larger political project in which the government worked to stabilize and develop national markets, sometimes by promoting new lending strategies and frequently by absorbing and redistributing market risks. Faced with a fiscal crisis, the Johnson administration did not simply cut spending or refrain from influencing the economy. Instead, the administration creatively moved money and exerted influence outside of the budget rules that constrained it. In doing so, the administration drew on the government's authority to set and recognize property rights and the capacity of the federal credit programs to buy, sell, guarantee, and insure loans. Furthermore, it drew on the capacity of the state to normalize business practices simply by using them: Fannie Mae's use of the mortgage-backed security in this way was part of a tradition that went back to the farm credit programs' use of the long-term amortizing loan.

None of this means that private actors did not matter for the transformation of U.S. housing finance. Bankers and mortgage brokers controlled the financial resources that the government sought to direct and had a long history of policy influence. Bankers testified at congressional hearings and were well represented in meetings of the Mortgage Finance Task Force and groups like the President's Commission on Budgetary Concepts. A mortgage broker, Ray

Lapin, ran Fannie Mae starting in 1967. Much as they had during the creation of the federal housing credit system in the 1930s, lenders' concerns dominated the discussion and set the terms of debate. But if you look *only* at those points of influence, you will miss how mid-level political institutions like budget rules shaped the selection, timing, and design of the policies that emerged. If a new financial class mobilized power in the 1970s, as many scholars have suggested, it did so by taking advantage of political problems that had existed since the start of the nation and that posed a particularly difficult set of problems for lawmakers at the time. Members of this class also accomplished this mobilization through adjustments to a set of partnerships and credit supports that had long been active in the housing sector.

Krippner's study of financialization found that processes like this played out multiple times over the course of the 1970s and 1980s: mounting inflation caused a clash over resources, government officials tried various solutions, and eventually they turned to deregulation or reorganization to avoid directly rationing resources. Krippner concludes that these periods of deregulation set key conditions for the rise of finance: a focus on the free flow of funds through all sectors of the economy, the removal of New Deal laws that kept the power and resources of financial markets in check, and an emphasis on rising interest rates that attracted savings from around the world.[146] The ultimate outcome of booming financial markets was neither intended nor expected. What seemed far more likely at the time was that high prices and high interest rates would eventually force most people out of the market, causing a painful period of austerity that would lessen consumption and and lower expectations. But, much to the surprise of government officials, the deregulation of global financial flows in the 1970s enabled a flood of global savings into the United States, which kept the American consumer rich in credit. U.S. household debt and financial profits both increased. As the financial sector gained power it was able to use more political influence to protect its position and gains.

In the 1950s and 1960s, the financial sector held a roughly 15 percent share of the nation's profits. By 2000, it held about 40 percent of profit share (peaking at 45 percent in 2007), with even nonfinancial firms capturing more of their profits from financial income.[147] On one hand, the reorganization of housing finance in 1968 reflected major trends associated with the rise of finance: privatization, the rising power and influence of financial firms, the rollback of government controls, high levels of leverage, and transfers of risk from Wall Street to Main Street. Viewed this way, we can see the spin-off of Fannie Mae and the turn to mortgage-backed securities as a kind of vanguard moment of the financial turn. Financialization is associated, above all, with the accumulation of profits among financial elites and the proliferation of new risks—including risks of systemwide instability—that are shunted onto taxpayers and borrowers.[148] It is part of what sociologist Wolfgang Streeck has called "the revolt of capital against the postwar mixed economy."[149] Securitization is the ideal property right for a financialized world where one class increasingly retains profits and another retains risks, because, as a machine for the reorganization of property rights, it can isolate various components of profit and risk produced by an asset.[150]

On the other hand, a close look at the emergence of modern securitization also calls attention to *continuities* between the financialized economy and earlier stages of the U.S. economy: an uninterrupted commitment to the expansion of homeownership, a reliance on credit as a tool of economic and social policy, the substitution of risk for the direct allocation of wealth, and the enduring participation of government officials as creative actors in the economy. In 1968 the federal government rearranged its involvement in the market, deferring more control and profits to private firms, but we should not confuse this shift with the government taking a truly hands-off approach to the market. Government officials worked to ensure the success of the new system, a process that involved the continued socialization of market risk.[151]

10

What We Owe One Another

This book has looked at U.S. credit allocation on two levels: the macro level of the political economy, as revealed by the credit programs, and the more micro level of specific financial exchanges, as revealed through securitization deals. Each chapter has showed people using credit to solve problems, including the problem of governing in a complex and fractured political landscape. Government officials have repeatedly turned to credit and housing in an elusive search for economic opportunities that come with minimal political conflict or open wealth redistribution. This pattern started with the use of credit to sell land to pay off Revolutionary War debt and continued with grants of land and credit support to build the transcontinental railroads. This pattern was later transformed with the advent of the farm loan system. The use of credit and property ownership as tools of statecraft expanded in the New Deal and postwar eras, and persists today.

Credit allocation, especially for mortgages, has mattered in different ways at different times. In the nineteenth century, everyday people regularly participated in mortgage markets, not just as borrowers but also as lenders and investors. In the nineteenth century, widespread distrust of credit and government served as a powerful check on the more extensive use of credit policies. Finance is always a part of capitalism, but as many other scholars have noted, at many other times financial markets were subordinated to other kinds of markets and were expected to act more like a public utility and less like a profit center.[1]

This conclusion restates the main points of the book, points out areas for future research, and draws connections with later developments in securitization and credit programs leading up to the crash of 2007–2008. It ends with a reflection on the role of the government in crises past and crises perhaps yet to come.

Redistributing Risk, Redistributing Wealth

The United States is a large and complex nation with a sprawling and frag-mented political system. This political fragmentation complicates both gov-ernance and dispute resolution and encourages the use of land and credit dis-tribution as political tools. In this rocky political terrain, government officials have repeatedly turned to finance as a means to resolve political disputes. By supporting and directing financial markets, government officials have sought to induce change in off-budget and noncontroversial ways. In making this case, I have worked to clarify the properties of credit allocation that make it particu-larly valuable as a political device. Credit policy yields results for low costs. Credit programs are easily taken off budget. Credit exchanges can represent different things to different people and are reasonably justified through a vari-ety of logics. In the complex and conflicted U.S. political landscape, these core characteristics, which I call the lightness of credit, have been especially useful.

The long view shows that U.S. land and credit policy have traveled down a structurally reinforced path. Political fragmentation is a problem that has confronted each generation of government officials anew. But each generation has faced this problem in ways that have been influenced by past events and armed with solutions generated by previous generations. This is sociologist Jeffrey Haydu's insight about institutions as instances of iterative problem solv-ing.[2] Earlier periods create new possible problems and new resources for later groups of people. In the nineteenth century, credit was mainly a supplement and support for land policy. After the Federal Farm Loan Act, and especially after the New Deal, credit was more readily available as a tool of statecraft.

In all, this book shows that the use of credit as a policy tool emerged earlier, and more expansively, than many existing accounts suggest. As pathbreaking institution builders that promoted financial technologies (like securitization) and fledging markets (like the venture capital industry after World War II), credit programs ensured lending to key groups and sectors. FHA home im-provement loans helped pave the way for an increase in consumer credit.[3] The RFC showed that small, amortizing business loans could turn a reliable profit, and the Export-Import Bank pioneered medium- and long-term loans abroad.[4] The Federal Farm Loan Act and FHA championed the use of long term, amortized loans domestically. In each of these cases, the federal govern-ment used its capacity to absorb risk to popularize a particular way of lending, with large downstream consequences.

These findings provide strong support for claims that the United States does in fact have a developmental, entrepreneurial state in which government officials act as creative market participants, albeit in ways that look very dif-ferent from the more centralized planning seen in other nations. The findings from these chapters also provide strong support for the idea that the United

States has a credit- and housing-heavy welfare state. *American Bonds* adds to that literature by providing a more comprehensive account of the policies and programs behind this trend and theorizing with more detail the qualities of credit that have encouraged this pattern.

Official discourse about credit programs often relies on the neutral-sounding language of "risk absorption" and "market correction," but as David Freund has noted when looking at the housing programs, we should not let such dry terms blind us to the importance of these programs for the ongoing work of the state.[5] A review of the credit programs suggests that extensive developmental support may proliferate in even the most advanced liberal capitalist economies, and that land and credit have long served as key facets of American social policy.

The history of credit programs further shows that veto points and budget-ary constraints are not just paralyzing, but also things that generate creative political strategies. Sociologist Isaac Martin has argued that political fragmen-tation "may actually increase the rate of policy innovation."[6] Martin's insight is that veto points can also provide little windows of opportunity for various publics to exert influence. My account shows a different but complementary pathway of policy innovation that results from political fragmentation: faced with limited resources or political roadblocks, officials can and do seek capital and influence through means not already precluded by existing rules. In this way, contentious politics can compel the adoption of financial policies.

The usefulness of credit as a policy tool means that government officials have a strong incentive to define any number of problems as *financial* problems that can be addressed with financial solutions. These include social policies that might otherwise be organized through government grants or direct expendi-tures. This reliance on credit is perhaps not all bad, insofar as it can allow for key political efforts that might otherwise be thwarted. Perhaps if the choice is between credit policy and no policy, there are many cases in which credit policy is the best option. On the other hand, as chapter 8 discussed in some detail, the proliferation of credit programs can create problems of transpar-ency, control, and democratic accountability.

In the wake of the crisis of 2007–2008, we can add financial instability to the list of problems associated with the credit programs. We have seen that financial markets have internal structures that lead to destabilizing and pain-ful booms and busts. The fiscal crisis of 1968 led to the spin-off of Fannie Mae from the federal government and a reinvigorated securitization market, which helped set the stage for the crisis of 2007–2008, which led to a bailout and later fiscal crisis, culminating in a budget shutdown of the government in 2013. This series of events suggests a cycle wherein adversarial political contexts compel government officials to embrace financial techniques that may be difficult to control in later years, setting a path for later fiscal crises and more financial policies. Put more simply: political battles can encourage financial policies that introduce instability that causes later political problems.

When contentious politics compel the adoption of financial policies, government accounting rules and institutions can shape the organizational design of the resulting financial systems through a process that organizational scholars call imprinting.[7] The key insight here is that moments of organizational founding are especially consequential for organizational structures. One of the lessons of the Fannie Mae spin-off is that when programs are designed to get around budget constraints, the federal budget rules set initial conditions that have especially powerful and enduring effects for organizational structure. In other words, budget constraints influence the design of the policies they help generate. Contests over issues like off-budget forms of borrowing and spending not only impact fiscal outcomes but can have especially large financial ramifications by shaping domestic and global capital flows.

To say that risk redistribution might be a substitute for wealth redistribution as a policy is not to imply that risk redistribution does not ultimately affect the distribution of wealth. On the contrary, the housing programs are a powerful reminder that the redistribution of risks in credit markets can have profound long-term economic consequences. Historically, to be excluded from the HOLC and FHA housing credit programs was to be excluded from the main opportunity for wealth building available to the average American family. For families of color, exclusion from the great postwar housing programs compounded systems of discrimination and produced lasting disadvantages in access to homes, schools, and jobs. As a time machine, credit carries more than economic value across decades. The later gains and repayments that accompany it bring the inequalities of the past into the present and will help carry today's inequities into the future. Whether credit programs promote coal or clean energy will have large impacts on the trajectory of those industries, their profits and market shares, and the people who live in the world they create.

This history of credit can help us understand how U.S. history could contain such vibrant strands of progressive and statist approaches to markets at the same time that the United States became famous for its love of markets and widespread distrust of central government. In a fragmented and veto-ridden system, a subset of market-loving, state-hating Americans has long used the array of veto points to slow or redirect state action.[8] In that context, simple pragmatic problem solving can lead officials to discover how a variety of government capacities—guarantees, tax expenditures, incentives, regulations, authority over property rights, and the state's own position as a consumer of goods—to move money and exert influence by other means. For officials who must govern under severe constraints, finance offers a viable path forward. Still, as scholars like Marc Sheinberg, Michael Schwartz, and Gerald Berk have argued, this overall pattern should not blind us to the many populist, statist, progressive cooperatives that run through American history.[9] So, too, when we recognize that U.S. markets did not have the central planning of European counterparts, we should take care not to confuse that with the notion that American markets actually developed largely without help from the government.

Sociologist Seymour Lipset wrote that "America has been the purest example of a society which has followed market norms."[10] I believe he is correct, but perhaps not in the sense he intended. One of the enduring lessons from Karl Polanyi is that laissez-faire was always a utopian dream; the separation of the market from the state was at most approximated, never achieved.[11] Governments protect local economies. Attempts to move into a laissez-faire world mean deregulation, which inevitably causes instability, crisis, and human suffering, leading people to demand protection from the government. Polanyi teaches us that the point is not to *be* laissez-faire so much as to profess a commitment to laissez-faire principles and then go about having the state protect and stablize the economy. "Free markets," in other words, is essentially a rhetorical device that businesses use to push back against regulations they do not like while accepting support that they do. If the United States is the most capitalist of countries, the most frequently thought of as laissez-faire, it is perhaps because no other nation has so successfully managed this contradiction of having extensive government involvement in markets while also generally dismissing the importance of those policies for market development so well. Credit was part of how this was accomplished.

Finally, this book has sought to show how understandings of community and nation are written deep into the structure of debt instruments. Comparisons over time show how Americans have devised lending systems in accordance with much broader principles of social and political obligation. Louisiana mortgage bonds in the 1830s reflected the social logic of nineteenth-century developmental banking in the Cotton South: government activities were organized on a subnational level, while planters' risks were socialized (through state guarantees) and displaced onto black bodies (through collateral and mortgage contracts). This system was very different from those that produced the state support of railway bonds (reflecting the early industrial focus of a growing national government); the laissez-faire mortgage bonds of the western brokers in the 1870s or the city bond houses of the 1920s; the cooperative agreements built into the Farmers' Alliance joint-note plan; or the emergent financialized logic of Fannie Mae's pass-throughs, in which the federal government used a mix of privatized profits and socialized risks to ensure the flow of funds into the nation's housing markets.

Understandings of the limits and possibilities of what people owe to each other and can expect from the state are written into the designs of financial instruments. These understandings help determine the distribution of profits and risks within specific financial transactions. This matters because the distributional politics of credit plays out simultaneously on the level of how credit fits within a political economy and on the level of specific exchanges and loans. The issue, in other words, is not just whether the people of a nation generally use credit to pay for housing or college, but the terms built into those loans: if you or the lender will end up covering the costs of rising interest rates, if the borrower can declare bankruptcy on student loans, if the investor's repayment is guaranteed by the government, either whole or in part. What people do in financial markets, what those financial markets are expected to do—together these dynamics make up the social life of credit in a nation.

Areas for Future Research

These findings have implications for areas of future research. While this book is a study of the United States, there are good reasons to believe that the core relationships posited here matter elsewhere, although we should expect them to play out differently in other nations given their different institutional contexts. New research shows that the European Union is moving toward capital market integration built around the securitization market. Research on this effort suggests that, much like the Johnson administration did in the late 1960s, the European Central Bank sees in securitization the promise of an economic jolt large enough to obviate the need for more costly and divisive political solutions.[12] Englen and Glasmacher conclude that this effort is "an attempt to indirectly spur economic growth in a political conjuncture where direct public support for economic growth through budgetary expansion is blocked."[13]

Other research has shown the importance of budgeting for outcomes like fiscal targets and deficit spending in other nations; my work predicts that the same dynamics should also encourage financial liberalization and expansion.[14] Again, there is some empirical support for this hypothesis. When the United States imposed requirements for budgetary balance on Japan after the Second World War, Japan developed the off-budget Fiscal Investment Loan Program to encourage economic growth through financial policy tools.[15] Financialization in China was spurred in part by budget problems caused by declining tax revenues and bad investments.[16]

Another area for future research concerns state-level policies in the United States. Scholars of American political development have called attention to the centrality of subnational governments in the United States. There is much to be gained from combining a focus on state-level governance with a focus on credit politics. While economic historians have noted that nineteenth-century state governments aggressively pursued developmental banking policies, much of that literature remains focused on the history of capital markets and banking rather than more general matters of political and institutional development.

Similarly, sociologist Josh Pacewicz has analyzed how state and local governments are securitizing tax revenues. Identifying and theorizing patterns on the subnational level will yield a more complete and multilayered account of the role of finance in U.S. political and economic institutions.[17]

A third area of future research concerns the circulation of financial instruments through political and private spaces. Governments are always also financial entities, with their own interest in financial techniques and internal systems that generate expertise. Chapter 9 suggests that financial tools can gain legitimacy through the state's authority over property rights, but they can also become vulnerable to political controversy. When analyzing the policies of states that set the conditions of possibility for financial markets, it is crucial that we attend to how a government's own finances affect its orientation to financial markets and how financial forms are transformed as they move through the official domain of government usage (what Pierre Bourdieu calls the "bureaucratic field").[18] More generally, this book indicates that a closer look at budget politics and political institutions may allow for a more fine-tuned understanding of how financial policies are selected and designed at different moments in time. A recent study by Benjamin Braun, for example, has found that the European Central Bank has favored financial policies when it depends on them to meet some other kind of political goal but has been more strict with derivatives markets that it does not think it needs for the purposes of governance.[19] In other words, a closer look at political institutions can help us better understand the emergence of specific policies at specific times and the interaction of government forces with private efforts.

A Prehistory of a Crisis

The basic form of the modern mortgage-backed security was in place by 1970: An issuer (like Fannie Mae or a bank) works with a company (called the originator) to combine a group of its assets (like mortgages) within a shell company, called a special purpose vehicle (SPV). The issuer arranges some kind of credit protection for the pool (like a government guarantee) and then sells bonds (or similar debt instruments, like certificates) against the pool of assets.[20] The SPV is what makes the transfer of the assets from the originator a true sale and so differentiates the mortgage-backed security from on–balance sheet obligations. Without the SPV, what you have is just a group of mortgages held by a company. Sociologist Gerald Davis has written that securitization helped usher in a new era in which the American economy revolved around financial markets instead of manufacturing. He called it a Copernican revolution in markets.[21]

For the purposes of this conclusion, I want to highlight a few trends that allow us to situate the eventual role of securitization in the crisis of 2007–2008.

In doing so, I draw on more extensive treatments of changes in housing and financial markets since the 1960s.[22]

The first thing to note is that as securitization developed, a wave of deregulation made borrowing much riskier for families. This deregulation, as Krippner and others have argued, can be understood as a further expression of the desire of lawmakers to avoid political responsibility for distributional outcomes in a time of mounting scarcity.[23] A 1980 federal law overrode state usury laws that limited interest rates on mortgages.[24] Two years later another law overrode state-level restrictions on adjustable-rate mortgages.[25] Since the New Deal, the long-term mortgage had placed interest rate risk squarely in lenders' hands: when interest rates rose, borrowers kept paying the low rates of earlier periods. Lenders thus previously hesitated to make long-term investments in things like mortgages lest they miss out on a chance to receive higher returns later. However, with an adjustable-rate mortgage, if rates rose, families simply paid a higher rate. By 1989, half of the mortgages owned by the thrifts were adjustable-rate mortgages.[26] This shift of risks from elites to nonelites has been widely noted as one of the hallmarks of financialization and neoliberalism.[27]

A second important trend to note is that before the private market could fully succeed, investors had to trust that the bonds' underlying mortgage risks were in fact appropriately resolved by the securitization structure.[28] Until potential buyers believed this, the burgeoning securitization market was dependent on guarantees from Ginnie, Fannie, or Freddie. Many of the key financial innovations before the 1990s worked to build risk management techniques that freed the market from its reliance on these three agencies' guarantees. Some companies experimented with overcollateralization, meaning that they placed more mortgages into a pool than was required to meet expected cash flows. (This approach was effective but expensive; every additional mortgage in the pool was a mortgage not sold for profit.) Later protections come in the form of bond insurance and credit default swaps.

A breakthrough came in 1983 when First Boston, Salomon Brothers, and Freddie Mac divided up mortgage pools into different "tranches" (or slices) that allowed bondholders to be paid at different rates. Potential investors in securitized bonds now had a choice between buying more expensive, higher-rated bonds backed by the tranches and with surefire returns (meaning the bonds that had dibs on the first group of payment flows through the pool) or purchasing subordinated bonds that were less expensive, lower rated, and riskier. This technique helped the $30 billion market for mortgage-backed securities in 1982 jump to a $265 billion market in 1986.[29]

Securitization had succeeded in transforming mortgages from an idiosyncratic, hard-to-sell, long-term commitment into an easily traded homogenous product.[30] In the process securitization was also fine-tuned as a new kind of property right, one capable of turning any anticipated revenue stream into a bond.[31] The market spread, moving beyond mortgages in the 1980s. School loans, auto loans, credit card debts—all were securitized. The bonds created in these cases are called asset-backed securities. Eventually issuers securitized more exotic revenue streams, like Italian social security delinquent receivables and French champagne bottles. Bowie bonds securitized revenues from David Bowie's music, and Bond bonds securitized revenues from James Bond movies.[32] By combining securitization with derivatives (which were also on the rise in the 1980s and 1990s), financial engineers found that they could tailor deals to the tastes of investors around the globe. With increasing precision, the risks and revenues associated with American debts were identified, catalogued, isolated, and sold.

As waves of deregulation did away with rules limiting banking, the nature of mortgage lending underwent a profound transformation. Historically, banks held loans until they were repaid, so they were extremely careful with the risks they accepted. In the postwar era, getting a loan from a bank marked the beginning of a relationship that would last for years. In this context personal relationships, local knowledge, and reputation guided economic transactions. If the mortgage was resold, it usually ended up held by an insurance company or mutual bank. After the 1960s, this changed. New technologies like credit scores collected and disseminated detailed information about individuals, making it easier to make loans in faraway markets. Securitization allowed bankers to resell loans into pools that telegraphed the revenues from individual loans to investors around the globe. Banks replaced the slow cultivation of relationships and profits with the rapid generation of fees by making loans and then funneling them into SPVs. Lending became more distant, impersonal, and transient—and, as we now know, much riskier.[33]

Home prices rose with the securitization market, increasing most quarters between 1975 and 2007, and never dipping a single quarter during a nearly 16-year span that started in 1991. Prices subsequently rose 80 percent between 1996 and 2006.[34] In 1993, 64 percent of Americans owned homes; at the height of the housing bubble in 2005, homeownership rates hovered just under 70 percent.[35] Yet these trends did not translate to direct gains in wealth for American families, because debt rose as well: between 1980 and 2007 household debt surged from 48 percent to 99 percent of GDP, driven mostly by mortgages and home equity loans.[36] Families were growing not wealthier, but more highly leveraged, meaning that they had a great deal more debt relative to any equity they built up in their homes.

Securitization was at the center of these trends. The size of the mortgage-backed securities market tripled between 1995 and 2006, from $2.4 trillion to $7.1 trillion in outstanding bonds. By 2005, over two-thirds of new home loans were securitized.[37] Now so much money was pouring into American homes that lenders hustled to find new borrowers. The year 2003 was the fulcrum of this change.[38] Before then, the regulated mortgage giants Fannie Mae and Freddie Mac dominated the securitization market. After 2003, there was a rapid rise of securitizations of riskier mortgages that Fannie and Freddie could not legally offer under their existing regulations. That parallel market for "private label" securitization took three main forms: "jumbo" loans for very expensive mortgages; "Alt-A" loans to highly leveraged borrowers; and "subprime" loans to riskier borrowers with credit scores under 660, recent delinquencies, or even bankruptcy within the past five years.[39]

The private label market skyrocketed from $377 billion in 2000 to nearly $2 trillion in 2007 (in the same time period, agency mortgage-backed securities nearly doubled, from $2.6 trillion to $4 trillion).[40] In 2001, under half of subprime and Alt-A mortgages were securitized; by 2007, over 90 percent were.[41] Between 2000 and 2007 the amount of total outstanding subprime mortgage-backed securities increased from $81 billion to $730 billion, quadrupling in market share from 3 to 12 percent.[42] New subprime bonds increased from 6 to 20 percent of the market between 2002 and 2006.[43] Economists estimate that all the gains in homeownership during the main years of the bubble were owed to securitized loans for subprime borrowers.[44] All the while, as sociologist Donald MacKenzie has noted, Wall Street failed to adjust for the fact that its own behaviors ran counter to the assumptions built into its formulas.[45] And all the while, lawmakers lauded and encouraged the expansion of homeownership, seeing it as a sign of economic vibrancy and the expansion of the American Dream.

In 2007, rising interest rates triggered an increase in adjustable-rate mortgages at the same time that housing prices started to drop. This meant homeowners could no longer sell or refinance to manage their debts. Defaults rose. Lenders pulled out of the market. Between 2006 and 2009 home prices dropped by 30 percent.[46] A recent report estimates that there were 7.8 million foreclosures nationally between 2007 and 2016. In Florida, the foreclosure rate topped 12 percent in June 2011; at its worst, in February of 2011, nearly a fifth of mortgages in the Miami metropolitan area were in foreclosure.[47]

For collateralized mortgage obligations issued in 2006, prices for AAA-rated bonds dropped by a fifth, and lower-rated bonds dropped by 70 percent.[48] Two massive hedge funds at Bear Stearns that specialized in risky housing bonds collapsed in June of 2007. That year Standard & Poor's ratings agency downgraded 1,400 subprime issuances.[49] In 2008, private label issuances plummeted to 5 percent of the market's 2006 peak.[50] Fannie Mae and Freddie Mac's own highly regulated issuances were in good shape, but both corporations had purchased riskier private label securitizations, and eventually the decline in housing values hit their own deals as well. By one estimate, Fannie and Freddie had lost $45 billion by the middle of 2008.[51]

The housing crisis ricocheted through the economy. As Mian and Sufi have shown, high levels of debt meant that a 20 percent decline in the value of a home for a family that had paid less than 20 percent of the home value wiped out *all* of its wealth. As these families reined in their spending, they stopped purchasing other goods.[52] The U.S. Bureau of Labor Statistics reports that the unemployment rate of 5 percent in 2007 had doubled to 10 percent by 2009; for African Americans, the unemployment rated topped 15 percent.[53] The crash did not just wipe out mortgage lenders like Countrywide and Indymac; it brought down entire investment banks—Bear Stearns, Lehman Brothers, and Merrill Lynch.[54] The United States had entered the Great Recession.

The crash revealed that racial inequality in American mortgage markets had not been resolved in the boom years but had transformed from a system based on exclusion to a system based on exploitation.[55] During the boom, mortgage lending had finally opened up for many borrowers of color who had historically been shut out of mortgage markets.[56] Minority homeownership increased by 30 percent between 1988 and 1998, a trend that caused some to hail the lending boom as a "civil rights crusade" and the "democratization" of credit.[57] The crash gave the lie to such claims. One study found that black and Latino families with good credit were three times more likely to be given a subprime loan than white counterparts, even controlling for income.[58] Those subprime loans had low teaser rates that converted into volatile adjustable-rate mortgages and were more likely to contain penalties for prepayments.[59] After the crash, black and Latino borrowers were more likely to be foreclosed on than white borrowers and more likely to have gains in wealth wiped out completely.[60] Studies of foreclosure patterns have found evidence that sub-prime lenders specifically targeted communities of color, and that foreclosure rates spiked in formerly redlined neighborhoods.[61] The market had only fully opened up to borrowers of color after deregulation had made borrowing riskier and more expensive for them.[62]

As with other crises, the government stepped in as a risk manager of last resort. In 2009, the special inspector general for the Troubled Asset Relief Program (TARP) testified to Congress that the total potential exposure of the federal government through its extensive guarantees, in a worst-case scenario and combining all of its programs, was $23.7 trillion—the equivalent of 150 percent of the GDP.[63] It was a number that makes the more realistic estimated exposure of $6.3 trillion seem modest in comparison.[64] Deemed too important to let fail, Fannie and Freddie were both placed under government conservatorship in September of 2008.

At the heart of the financial bailout was TARP's 13 programs, which extensively used credit support.[65] Recent Congressional Budget Office estimates say that $445 billion of the $700 billion pledged through the program will be spent.[66] Former SEC secretary Jonathan Katz reminds readers that TARP was "a small piece of a very large pie" of government guarantees and secondary market assistance.[67] The Federal Reserve alone housed another 18 programs for this purpose. Additional supports existed in the FDIC, the housing agencies, and the Departments of Education and Treasury.

While libertarians have objected that the bailout increased the likelihood of future bad behavior, observers on the Left have decried the bailout's unequal protection of Wall Street and Main Street. Relief for struggling homeowners has been widely viewed as weak and ineffective.[68] The Home Affordable Modification Program, inspired by the New Deal mortgage refinancing programs, started with a goal of helping up to 4 million homeowners but had only assisted a tenth of that by 2010.[69] By year-end 2016, the total of 1.6 million homeowners who had received these loan modifications still fell far short of the initial goals.[70]

BLAME JOHNSON?

Does this all mean that the federal government is to blame for the crisis? Sometimes I am asked this question when I present this research. After all, as Mian and Sufi note, the government played a central role in keeping credit cheap, and cheap credit fueled the crisis.[71] While it is a fair question, I nevertheless worry that it is a misleading one. It is obviously bad policy for a government to hit the accelerator on financial markets while also removing the brakes. Aside from the issue of whether this question deflects responsibility from Wall Street (after all, the history of credit markets is hardly a story of general serenity and stability that came to an end when misguided regulations incentivized bad choices), it carries the unspoken assumption of a world where advanced capitalist markets somehow exist without extensive governmental participation. Of course the state helped cause the crisis. Under what conditions would we expect it not to? A breakdown of this scale requires systemic failures. Moreover, as Levitin and Wachter note, the real problem was not regulation but overzealous deregulation.[72]

I sometimes imagine the troubled housing market of the late 1960s as a mobile home perched on a flatbed trailer. In this scenario, the mounting interest rates of the era were like a hill that government officials wanted to haul that trailer over. Lawmakers turned to securitization in pursuit of a financial engine strong enough for the job. There was a very different world on the hill's other side, however. Interest rates eventually fell, investors from around the world poured money into American housing, and lending increased. Deregulation raised the speed limit and took the police off the road. Credit agencies and regulators that were supposed to police the markets failed to adequately evaluate risks. Aided by computers, mathematical breakthroughs, and complex derivatives, securitization itself became turbo-charged. Given these changes, we might not wonder that such a strong engine, revved up and without any checks, would eventually crash.

Although the debates of the late 1960s had identified the dangers of securitization (at least from the point of view of the late 1960s), when government officials were plying bankers with guarantees to make mortgage bonds attractive, it may have been difficult to foresee the full extent of the devastation that could be wrought from the eventual securitization of toxic debts. There seems to have been no awareness that the same fiscal pressures and focus on homeownership that had inspired the 1968 policies would, in time, also promote waves of deregulation and change the financial context entirely.

I do not think the Johnson administration could necessarily have foreseen all of these changes, but I do believe that in the midst of the subprime crisis, the same things that made the mortgage-backed securities such an efficient solution for Johnson—a capacity to parse risk and ownership, the ability to move unwanted assets off a company's balance sheet, a level of obscurity that rendered these deals unintelligible to the layperson, and, most of all, a structure that justified high levels of leverage—all served to fuel the subprime bubble. If the balance sheets of banks became a mess, it is in part because they followed the lead of the federal budget. If we find today that securitization makes it difficult to measure what risks companies hold or encourages companies to assume a higher ratio of obligations to equity, we would do well to remember that securitization has done that from the first. Moreover, if Americans were quick to believe that homeownership, secured through easy credit, was a path to widespread economic well-being, we should remember that a history of housing policy, embraced by politicians on both sides of the aisle, long ago laid the groundwork for that as well.

Looking Ahead

As I write, the White House website is promoting a new infrastructure plan that purports to turn a $100 billion government investment into a $1 trillion gain for infrastructure. It promises to do this by "unleash[ing] private sector capital and expertise," in part by "slashing regulations" and encouraging local "self help." The proposal indicates that a combination of federal loans, tax expenditures, and public–private partnerships will accomplish this outcome. For businesses, it is a chance to lock in profits while having taxpayers cover the risks. For government officials, it is a chance for a massive developmental effort that will be mostly off-budget and can be discussed in terms of self-help and deregulation.

This is, of course, the same volatile combination of cheap credit and deregulation that preceded the housing bubble—and, prior to that, the same mix of economic need and political gridlock.[73] The proposed infrastructure plan is likely to lead to massive corporate profits, transfers of expenses and risks to consumers, and, eventually, large economic failures requiring government bailouts. The alternative is for the nation to let its infrastructure continue to decay or else somehow find a way to raise taxes at a time of extreme political polarization. The wheel keeps turning.

With each crisis, Americans face anew the question of how to organize finance. With each crisis, choices are guided by long-established institutions. And with each crisis, there nevertheless exists the potential for something new to emerge. Whatever lies ahead, the organization of credit—and the social bonds that it entails—will be decided on two levels: the specific exchanges we allow and how we delimit the role of finance in the political economy. A clear-eyed look at both means that in considering any credit policy we must ask: Should this issue be resolved through finance? And if it is resolved through finance, what divisions of profits and risks, and what divisions of opportunities and obligations, should be built into those structures?

NOTES

Chapter 1: The Problem and Promise of Credit in American Life

1. For contemporary homeownership rates, see U.S. Bureau of the Census, "Homeownership Rate for the United States [Rhorusq156n]" (Federal Research Economic Database [FRED], Federal Reserve Bank of St. Louis, 2018). For estimates for farm households in 1890, see Richard Sutch, "Before the American Dream: The Early Years of Urban Home Ownership, the United States, 1850–1940" (Departments of Economics and History, University of California, Riverside, 2011), table 1. Kenneth Jackson notes that such early high levels of ownership rates were similar in other land-rich settler colonies like Canada and Australia but far outstripped levels in Europe, which only caught up after the Second World War. Kenneth T. Jackson, *Crabgrass Frontier: The Suburbanization of the United States* (New York: Oxford University Press, 1985), 7.

2. In making this point, I draw from the insights of Miles Colean, who stressed the importance of moving capital across the frontier into mortgage markets as a significant problem for the young nation. Colean was an architect of the National Housing Act of 1934 who later became the Federal Housing Administration's chief economist, served as an advisor for the Mortgage Bankers Association, and coined the phrase "urban renewal." In his book *The Impact of Government on Real Estate Finance in the United States*, Colean points out that while the early federal government set out to increase the demand for property ownership, it failed to provide a means of financing the purchase of land. Colean believed that this was a policy fundamentally at odds with itself, and it resulted in frequent spasms of land speculation. Miles Lanier Colean, *The Impact of Government on Real Estate Finance in the United States* (New York: National Bureau of Economic Research, 1950). See also Federal Housing Administration, *The FHA Story in Summary, 1934–1959* (Washington, D.C.: Federal Housing Administration, 1959); David M. Freund, *Colored Property: State Policy and White Racial Politics in Suburban America* (Chicago: University of Chicago Press, 2007), 124; Jackson, *Crabgrass Frontier*, 203.

3. On the historical limits of commercial banks in housing markets, see chapter 2. See also Daniel Immergluck, *Credit to the Community: Community Reinvestment and Fair Lending Policy in the United States*, Cities and Contemporary Society (Armonk, N.Y.: M.E. Sharpe, 2004); Eugene White, "Banking and Finance in the Twentieth Century," in *Cambridge Economic History of the United States: The Twentieth Century*, ed. Robert E. Gallman and Stanley L. Engerman (Cambridge: Cambridge University Press, 2000).

4. I take this definition from William N. Goetzmann, *Money Changes Everything: How Finance Made Civilization Possible* (Princeton, N.J.: Princeton University Press, 2016), 382.

5. Robin Greenwood and David Scharfstein, "The Growth of Finance," *Journal of Economic Perspectives* 27, no. 2 (2013): 21.

6. For more on the early days and subsequent rise of the current securitization market, see Michael Lewis, *Liar's Poker: Rising Through the Wreckage on Wall Street* (New York: Norton, 1989), 136; Gerald F. Davis, *Managed by the Markets: How Finance Reshaped America* (New York:

Oxford University Press, 2009); Louis Hyman, *Debtor Nation: The History of America in Red Ink* (Princeton, N.J.: Princeton University Press, 2011); Richard K. Green and Susan M. Wachter, "The American Mortgage in Historical and International Context," *Journal of Economic Perspectives* 19, no. 4 (2005); Atif Mian and Amir Sufi, *House of Debt: How They (and You) Caused the Great Recession, and How We Can Prevent It from Happening Again* (Chicago: University of Chicago Press, 2014). On the implications of this for understanding the importance of states for creating liquidity in markets, see Bruce G. Carruthers and Arthur L. Stinchcombe, "The Social Structure of Liquidity: Flexibility, Markets, and States," *Theory and Society* 28, no. 3 (1999); Natalya Vinokurova, "How Mortgage-Backed Securities Became Bonds: The Emergence, Evolution, and Acceptance of Mortgage-Backed Securities in the United States, 1960–1987," *Enterprise & Society* 19, no. 3 (2018).

7. Hyman, *Debtor Nation*, 222.

8. U.S. Office of Management and Budget, "Analytical Perspectives, Budget of the United States Government, Fiscal Year 2018" (Washington, D.C.: Government Printing Office, 2017), table 19-1.

9. Board of Governors of the Federal Reserve, "Financial Accounts of the United States," 2018, table L2.11.

10. Mariana Mazzucato and L. Randall Wray, "Financing the Capital Development of the Economy: A Keynes-Schumpeter-Minsky Synthesis," Working Paper No. 837 (Levy Economics Institute of Bard College, 2015), 23–24.

11. Joint Committee on Taxation, "Background Information on Tax Expenditure Analysis and Historical Survey of Tax Expenditure Estimates (JCX-15-11)," report prepared for the Senate Committee on Finance, February 28, 2011. Available at http://www.jct.gov.

12. Federal Housing Administration, "The Federal Housing Administration (FHA)," 2018, https://www.hud.gov/program_offices/housing/fhahistory.

13. For book-length treatments of federal credit, see Douglas J. Elliott, *Uncle Sam in Pinstripes: Evaluating U.S. Federal Credit Programs* (Washington, D.C.: Brookings Institution, 2011); Barry Bosworth, Andrew S. Carron, and Elisabeth Rhyne, *The Economics of Federal Credit Programs* (Washington, D.C.: Brookings Institution, 1987); Dennis S. Ippolito, *Hidden Spending: The Politics of Federal Credit Programs* (Chapel Hill: University of North Carolina Press, 1984).

14. See, e.g., Gail Radford, *The Rise of the Public Authority: Statebuilding and Economic Development in Twentieth-Century America* (Chicago: University of Chicago Press, 2013); Daniel T. Rodgers, *Atlantic Crossings: Social Politics in a Progressive Age* (Cambridge, Mass.: Belknap Press, 1998).

15. Suzanne Mettler, *The Submerged State: How Invisible Government Policies Undermine American Democracy* (Chicago: University of Chicago Press, 2011); Christopher Howard, *The Hidden Welfare State: Tax Expenditures and Social Policy in the United States* (Princeton, N.J.: Princeton University Press, 1997); Freund, *Colored Property*.

16. For reviews of sociological work on the role of governments in markets, see especially Fred Block and Peter B. Evans, "The State and the Economy," in *The Handbook of Economic Sociology*, ed. Neil J. Smelser and Richard Swedberg (Princeton, N.J.: Princeton University Press, 2003); Neil Fligstein, "Markets as Politics: A Political-Cultural Approach to Market Institutions," *American Sociological Review* 61, no. 4 (1996).

17. On developmental states, see especially Peter B. Evans, *Embedded Autonomy: States and Industrial Transformation*, Princeton Paperbacks (Princeton, N.J.: Princeton University Press, 1995); Alexander Gerschenkron, *Economic Backwardness in Historical Perspective: A Book of Essays* (Cambridge, Mass.: Belknap Press of Harvard University Press, 1962); Meredith Woo-Cumings, *The Developmental State*, Cornell Studies in Political Economy (Ithaca, N.Y.: Cornell University Press, 1999). On why governments are so important for solving certain kinds of risk

management problems, see David A. Moss, *When All Else Fails: Government as the Ultimate Risk Manager* (Cambridge, Mass.: Harvard University Press, 2002). On governments and the institutional foundations of markets, see Douglass C. North, *Institutions, Institutional Change, and Economic Performance* (New York: Cambridge University Press, 1990); Douglass C. North and Barry R. Weingast, "Constitutions and Commitment: The Evolution of Institutions Governing Public Choice in Seventeenth-Century England," *Journal of Economic History* 49, no. 4 (1989). For a fascinating look at how efforts to build capitalist markets can fail without the proper state institutional support, see Vadim Volkov, *Violent Entrepreneurs: The Use of Force in the Making of Russian Capitalism* (Ithaca, N.Y.: Cornell University Press, 2002).

18. Greta Krippner, *Capitalizing on Crisis: The Political Origins of the Rise of Finance* (Cambridge, Mass.: Harvard University Press, 2011).

19. This summary of financial regulations finance is especially indebted to D'Arista's excellent review, *The Evolution of U.S. Finance*, 2 vols., Columbia University Seminar Series (Armonk, N.Y.: M.E. Sharpe, 1994), 118–51. D'Arista notes that the principles of good financial regulation are well known and sometimes are in conflict with one another. In particular, a commitment to fairness, which can justify allocation, can conflict with the notion that the government should take a neutral stance on credit distribution.

20. Viviana A. Rotman Zelizer, *The Social Meaning of Money* (New York: Basic Books, 1994); Bruce G. Carruthers, *City of Capital: Politics and Markets in the English Financial Revolution* (Princeton, N.J.: Princeton University Press, 1996); Marion Fourcade, *Economists and Societies: Discipline and Profession in the United States, Britain, and France, 1890s to 1990s*, Princeton Studies in Cultural Sociology (Princeton, N.J.: Princeton University Press, 2009).

21. William J. Novak, "The Myth of the 'Weak' American State," *American Historical Review* 113, no. 3 (2008).

22. Stephen Skowronek, *Building a New American State: The Expansion of National Administrative Capacities, 1877–1920* (New York: Cambridge University Press, 1982), 23–27.

23. Byron E. Shafer, "'Exceptionalism' in American Politics?," *PS: Political Science and Politics* 22, no. 3 (1989); Monica Prasad, *The Politics of Free Markets: The Rise of Neoliberal Economic Policies in Britain, France, Germany, and the United States* (Chicago: University of Chicago Press, 2006); Novak, "Myth"; Ellen M. Immergut, "Institutions, Veto Points, and Policy Results: A Comparative Analysis of Health Care," *Journal of Public Policy* 10, no. 4 (1990); Sarah A. Binder, *Stalemate: Causes and Consequences of Legislative Gridlock* (Washington, D.C.: Brookings Institution Press, 2003).

24. Elizabeth M. Sanders, *Roots of Reform: Farmers, Workers, and the American State, 1877–1917* (Chicago: University of Chicago Press, 1999); James Belich, *Replenishing the Earth: The Settler Revolution and the Rise of the Anglo-World, 1783–1939* (New York: Oxford University Press, 2009).

25. Binder, *Stalemate*; Francis Fukuyama, *Political Order and Political Decay: From the Industrial Revolution to the Globalization of Democracy* (New York: Farrar, Straus and Giroux, 2014).

26. Michael J. Sandel, *Democracy's Discontent: America in Search of a Public Philosophy* (Cambridge, Mass: Belknap Press of Harvard University Press, 1996); Gary Gerstle, *Liberty and Coercion: The Paradox of American Government from the Founding to the Present* (Princeton, N.J.: Princeton University Press, 2015).

27. Eric Schickler, *Disjointed Pluralism: Institutional Innovation and the Development of the U.S. Congress*, Princeton Studies in American Politics (Princeton, N.J.: Princeton University Press, 2001).

28. Damon Mayrl and Sarah Quinn, "Defining the State from Within: Boundaries, Schemas, and Associational Policymaking," *Sociological Theory* 34, no. 1 (2016). On how historical changes in the structure of collaborations results in different styles of local politics, see Josh Pacewicz,

Partisans and Partners: The Politics of the Post-Keynesian Society (Chicago: University of Chicago Press, 2016). For more on partnerships in U.S. history, see especially Elisabeth Clemens and Doug Guthrie, *Politics and Partnerships: The Role of Voluntary Associations in America's Political Past and Present* (Chicago: University of Chicago Press, 2010); Eldon J. Eisenach, *The Lost Promise of Progressivism* (Lawrence: University Press of Kansas, 1994); Gail Radford, *The Rise of the Public Authority: Statebuilding and Economic Development in Twentieth-Century America* (Chicago: Univeristy of Chicago Press, 2013). On more contemporary uses of partnerships, see especially Kimberly J. Morgan and Andrea Louise Campbell, *The Delegated Welfare State: Medicare, Markets, and the Governance of Social Policy*, Oxford Studies in Postwar American Political Development (New York: Oxford University Press, 2011); Colin Crouch, *The Strange Non-Death of Neo-Liberalism* (Malden, Mass.: Polity, 2011), 71–96; Jamila Michener, *Fragmented Democracy: Medicaid, Federalism, and Unequal Politics* (New York: Cambridge University Press, 2018).

29. See Howard, *Hidden Welfare State.*

30. Richard H. Thaler and Cass R. Sunstein, *Nudge: Improving Decisions About Health, Wealth, and Happiness* (New Haven, Conn.: Yale University Press, 2008).

31. Subcommittee on the Social and Behavioral Sciences Team, "Social and Behavioral Sciences Team Annual Report," ed. National Science and Technology Council Executive Office of the President (Office of Science and Technology Policy, 2016).

32. See, for example, Elisabeth Clemens, "From City Club to Nation State: Business Networks in American Political Development," *Theory and Society* 39, no. 3 (2010).

33. See, for example, Crouch, *Strange Non-Death.*

34. Howard, *Hidden Welfare State.*

35. Thaler and Sunstein, *Nudge*, 5.

36. Novak, "Myth"; Frank Dobbin and John R. Sutton, "The Strength of a Weak State: The Rights Revolution and the Rise of Human Resources Management Divisions," *American Journal of Sociology* 104, no. 2 (1998); Brian Balogh, *A Government out of Sight: The Mystery of National Authority in Nineteenth-Century America* (New York: Cambridge University Press, 2009); Kimberly J. Morgan and Ann Shola Orloff, *The Many Hands of the State: Theorizing Political Authority and Social Control* (New York: Cambridge University Press, 2016).

37. Mettler, *Submerged State.*

38. Steven M. Teles, "Kludgeocracy in America," *National Affairs* 17 (2013).

39. Elisabeth Clemens, "Lineages of the Rube Goldberg State: Building and Blurring Public Programs, 1900–1940," in *Rethinking Political Institutions: The Art of the State*, ed. Ian Shapiro, Stephen Skowronek, and Daniel Galvin (New York: New York University Press, 2006), 187; Novak, "Myth."

40. Laura Jensen, *Patriots, Settlers, and the Origins of American Social Policy* (New York: Cambridge University Press, 2003).

41. William N. Goetzmann, *Money Changes Everything: How Finance Made Civilization Possible* (Princeton, N.J.: Princeton University Press, 2016).

42. U.S. Office of Management and Budget, "Special Analyses, Budget of the United States Government," (Washington, D.C.: Executive Office of the President, 1963), 305.

43. Hybrid forms of property, for the purposes of this analysis, include participation loans, which allow banks to issue or own part of a much larger loan, and deferred participation loans, in which the government agrees to later purchase a portion of a loan on demand. See U.S. House Subcommittee on Domestic Finance and Committee on Banking and Currency, "A Study of Federal Credit Programs" (Washington, D.C.: Government Printing Office, 1964).

44. Sarah Quinn, "'The Miracles of Bookkeeping': How Budget Politics Link Fiscal Policies and Financial Markets," *American Journal of Sociology* 123, no. 1 (2017).

45. Ippolito, *Hidden Spending.*

46. While people often think of credit as a derivation of money, historians and anthropologists have shown that the opposite is true: money emerged as a way of tracking credit. For more on debt as a promise and its history, see Craig Muldrew, *The Economy of Obligation: The Culture of Credit and Social Relations in Early Modern England*, Early Modern History (New York: St. Martin's Press, 1998); David Graeber, *Debt: The First 5,000 Years* (Brooklyn, N.Y.: Melville House, 2011); Bruce G. Carruthers and Laura Ariovich, *Money and Credit: A Sociological Approach* (Cambridge: Polity, 2010); Friedrich Wilhelm Nietzsche, *The Birth of Tragedy and the Genealogy of Morals*, ed. Francis Golffing (New York: Anchor Books, 1990).

47. A group of scholars who study both culture and states have explained why the government's ability to classify is so important. Government classifications ultimately determine what counts as law, who gets to be a citizen and who qualifies for benefits, and which businesses are regulated. The state, however much it is disliked or critiqued, has acquired massive amounts of symbolic power through its ability to officially name and categorize things and people. Maps, censuses, statistics, records—these are all part of symbolic power. Consider the idea that men are heads of the family. It is, of course, an old notion. The New Deal welfare programs incorporated it into a system that provided entitlements for mostly male breadwinners, creating a powerful institutional mechanism that locked in female dependence on their husbands and left single mothers to a much more stigmatized and stingy system of support widely seen as a form of charity. Pierre Bourdieu, *On the State: Lectures at the College de France, 1989–1992* (Malden, Mass.: Polity Press, 2014), 9; Morgan and Orloff, *Many Hands*; Ann Orloff, "Gender in the Welfare State," *Annual Review of Sociology* 22 (1996).

48. Carruthers and Stinchcombe, "Social Structure of Liquidity."

49. Padgett and Ansell coined the term "robust action" to describe how skilled social actors strategically exploit ambiguity; John F. Padgett and Christopher K. Ansell, "Robust Action and the Rise of the Medici, 1400–1434," *American Journal of Sociology* 98, no. 6 (1993).

50. Freund, *Colored Property*, ch. 4.

51. U.S. Office of Management and Budget, "Analytical Perspectives, Budget of the United States Government, Fiscal Year 2017," (Washington, D.C.: Government Printing Office, 2016).

52. Mayrl and Quinn, "Defining the State."

53. On the foundational nature of boundaries in social life, see Mary Douglas, *Purity and Danger: An Analysis of Concepts of Pollution and Taboo*, Routledge Classics (New York: Routledge, 2005); Eviatar Zerubavel, *Social Mindscapes: An Invitation to Cognitive Sociology* (Cambridge, Mass.: Harvard University Press, 1997); Geoffrey C. Bowker and Susan Leigh Star, *Sorting Things Out: Classification and Its Consequences* (Cambridge, Mass.: MIT Press, 1999). On the positive and negative consequences of category transgression, see Greta Hsu, "Jacks of All Trades and Masters of None: Audiences' Reactions to Spanning Genres in Feature Film Production," *Administrative Science Quarterly* 51, no. 3 (2006); Greta Hsu, Özgecan Koçak, and Michael T. Hannan, "Multiple Category Memberships in Markets: An Integrative Theory and Two Empirical Tests," *American Sociological Review* 74, no. 1 (2009); Gabriel Rossman, "Obfuscatory Relational Work and Disreputable Exchange," *Sociological Theory* 32, no. 1 (2014).

54. This is a rapidly growing literature. See especially Balogh, *Government out of Sight*; Radford, *Rise of the Public Authority*; Jacob S. Hacker and Paul Pierson, *American Amnesia: How the War on Government Led Us to Forget What Made America Prosper* (New York: Simon & Schuster, 2016); Novak, "Myth"; Moss, *When All Else Fails*; John Lauritz Larson, *Internal Improvement: National Public Works and the Promise of Popular Government in the Early United States* (Chapel Hill: University of North Carolina Press, 2001); William J. Novak, *The People's Welfare: Law and Regulation in Nineteenth-Century America* (Chapel Hill: University of North Carolina Press, 1996); Fred L. Block and Matthew R. Keller, *State of Innovation: The U.S. Government's Role in Technology Development* (Boulder, Colo.: Paradigm Publishers, 2010); Mariana Mazzucato,

The Entrepreneurial State: Debunking Public vs. Private Sector Myths (New York: Anthem Press, 2013); Robert C. Hockett and Saule T. Omarova, "Public Actors in Private Markets: Toward a Developmental Finance State," *Washington University Law Review* 93 (2015).

55. Fred Block, "Swimming Against the Current: The Rise of a Hidden Developmental State in the United States," *Politics & Society* 36 (2008); Block and Keller, *State of Innovation*. See also Novak, "Myth."

56. Mazzucato, *Entrepreneurial State*. See also Mariana Mazzucato and L. Randall Wray, "Financing the Capital Development of the Economy: A Keynes-Schumpeter-Minsky Synthesis" (Annandale-on-Hudson, N.Y.: Levy Economics Institute, 2015).

57. Hockett and Omarova, "Public Actors in Private Markets."

58. U.S. Department of Housing and Urban Development, "The Federal Housing Administration (FHA)," http://www.hud.gov/program_offices/housing/fhahistory.

59. U.S. Office of Management and Budget, "Analytical Perspectives, Budget of the United States Government, Fiscal Year 2019" (Washington, D.C.: Government Printing Office, 2018), 249.

60. Office of the Special Inspector General for the Troubled Asset Relief Program, "Quarterly Report to Congress," October 26, 2016, https://www.sigtarp.gov/Quarterly%20Reports/October_26_2016_Report_To_Congress.pdf. See also Jonathan G. Katz, "Who Benefited from the Bailout?," *Minnesota Law Review* 95, no. 5 (2011).

61. John Zysman, *Governments, Markets, and Growth: Financial Systems and the Politics of Industrial Change*, Cornell Studies in Political Economy (Ithaca, N.Y.: Cornell University Press, 1983), 133.

62. Ibid., 76–77.

63. Jensen, *Patriots, Settlers*.

64. Francis G. Castles, "The Really Big Trade-Off: Home Ownership and the Welfare State in the New World and the Old," *Acta Politica* 33, no. 1 (1998); Edwin Amenta and Theda Skocpol, "Taking Exception: Explaining the Distinctiveness of American Public Policies in the Last Century," in *The Comparative History of Public Policy*, ed. Francis G. Castles (Cambridge: Polity Press, 1989); Jim Kemeny, "Comparative Housing and Welfare: Theorising the Relationship," *Journal of Housing and the Built Environment* 16, no. 1 (2001); Herman Schwartz, "Housing, the Welfare State, and the Global Financial Crisis: What Is the Connection?," *Politics & Society* 40, no. 1 (2012); Waltraud Schelkle, "In the Spotlight of Crisis: How Social Policies Create, Correct, and Compensate Financial Markets," *Politics & Society* 40, no. 1 (2012). Note that this is somewhat consistent with—although a significant extension of—Esping-Anderson's observation that U.S. welfare programs have always followed a market logic. Gøsta Esping-Andersen, *The Three Worlds of Welfare Capitalism* (Princeton, N.J.: Princeton University Press, 1990).

65. Gunnar Trumbull, "Credit Access and Social Welfare: The Rise of Consumer Lending in the United States and France," *Politics & Society* 40, no. 1 (2012); idem, *Consumer Lending in France and America: Credit and Welfare* (New York: Cambridge University Press, 2014).

66. Monica Prasad, *The Land of Too Much: American Abundance and the Paradox of Poverty* (Cambridge, Mass.: Harvard University Press, 2012); Trumbull, *Consumer Lending*.

67. Wolfgang Streeck, "The Crises of Democratic Capitalism," *New Left Review* 71 (2011); idem, "The Politics of Public Debt: Neoliberalism, Capitalist Development and the Restructuring of the State," *German Economic Review* 15, no. 1 (2014); Crouch, *Strange Non-Death*; Teresa A. Sullivan, Elizabeth Warren, and Jay Lawrence Westbrook, *The Fragile Middle Class: Americans in Debt* (New Haven, Conn.: Yale University Press, 2000).

68. The argument about the ideological lightness of credit as a social policy is consistent with and elaborates on arguments that the "market-ness" of credit programs can render them invisible. However, in calling out how the nature of market obligations sublimates the gifts entailed in credit transfers, I am specifically invoking Mauss's theory of the gift exchange. In his famous

essay, Mauss details how gifts work by an analogous, but opposite, logic: with a gift exchange, it is the obligation that is sublimated by the nominally voluntary and spontaneous nature of the exchange; Marcel Mauss, *The Gift: Forms and Functions of Exchange in Archaic Societies* (Glencoe, Ill.: Free Press, 1954). See also Mettler, *Submerged State*; Freund, *Colored Property*.

69. On ownership and economic citizenship, see Greta Krippner, "Democracy of Credit: Ownership and the Politics of Credit Access in Late Twentieth-Century America," *American Journal of Sociology* 123, no. 1 (2017).

70. Chloe N. Thurston, "Policy Feedback in the Public–Private Welfare State: Advocacy Groups and Access to Government Homeownership Programs, 1934–1954," *Studies in American Political Development* 29, no. 2 (2015). On racial discrimination in housing and lending markets, see Guy Stuart, *Discriminating Risk: The U.S. Mortgage Lending Industry in the Twentieth Century* (Ithaca, N.Y.: Cornell University Press, 2003); Devah Pager and Hana Shepherd, "The Sociology of Discrimination: Racial Discrimination in Employment, Housing, Credit, and Consumer Markets," *Annual Review of Sociology* 34, no. 1 (2008).

71. Melvin L. Oliver and Thomas M. Shapiro, *Black Wealth, White Wealth: A New Perspective on Racial Inequality*, 10th anniversary ed. (New York: Routledge, 2006); Pager and Shepherd, "Sociology of Discrimination."

72. Freund, *Colored Property*.

73. Lizabeth Cohen, *A Consumers' Republic: The Politics of Mass Consumption in Postwar America* (New York: Knopf, 2003), 127.

74. Krippner, *Capitalizing on Crisis*.

75. Raghuram Rajan, *Fault Lines: How Hidden Fractures Still Threaten the World Economy* (Princeton, N.J.: Princeton University Press, 2010); Crouch, *Strange Non-Death*; Streeck, "Crises of Democratic Capitalism"; idem, "Politics of Public Debt."

76. Marion Fourcade, "Cents and Sensibility: Economic Valuation and the Nature of 'Nature,'" *American Journal of Sociology* 116, no. 6 (2011).

77. Theda Skocpol, *Vision and Method in Historical Sociology* (Cambridge, Mass.: Cambridge University Press, 1984).

78. Paul Pierson, *Politics in Time: History, Institutions, and Social Analysis* (Princeton, N.J.: Princeton University Press, 2004).

79. Jeffrey Haydu, "Making Use of the Past: Time Periods as Cases to Compare and as Sequences of Problem Solving," *American Journal of Sociology* 104, no. 2 (1998).

Chapter 2: The Credit Frontier

1. I thank Fred Block for this turn of phrase.

2. Paul Frymer, "'A Rush and a Push and the Land Is Ours': Territorial Expansion, Land Policy, and U.S. State Formation," *Perspectives on Politics* 12, no. 1 (2014).

3. Bonnie Martin, "Neighbor-to-Neighbor Capitalism: Local Credit Networks and the Mortgaging of Slaves," in *Slavery's Capitalism: A New History of American Economic Development* (Philadelphia: University of Pennsylvania Press, 2016). See also Edward E. Baptist, *The Half Has Never Been Told: Slavery and the Making of American Capitalism* (New York: Basic Books, 2014).

4. Under colonial law, Massachusetts, Connecticut, New York, Virginia, North and South Carolina, and Georgia had land rights stretching to the Mississippi River. Of the seven states without a claim to public lands, Maryland was the most populated and most insistent that those lands rightfully belonged to the entire nation. Maryland refused to sign the Articles of Confederation until the other states agreed to cessation, withholding its agreement until 1781. Due to Maryland's insistence, it would be Congress, and not the seven public land states, that controlled the public domain. The process of actually ceding the land took many years, with the state of Georgia making

its final cessation of lands in 1802. While public land states kept rights to lands in and outside their official borders, they ceded a total of 237 million acres to the public domain. Paul Wallace Gates, *History of Public Land Law Development*, ed. U.S. Public Land Law Review Commission, Management of Public Lands in the United States (New York: Arno Press, 1979), 55. Congress had no right to issue taxes under the Articles of Confederation, however. On the assumption of state debt, see Edwin J. Perkins, *American Public Finance and Financial Services, 1700–1815*, Historical Perspectives on Business Enterprise Series (Columbus: Ohio State University Press, 1994), 213–15. See also Chester W. Wright, *Economic History of the United States*, 2nd ed. (New York and London: McGraw-Hill, 1948), 211. On the cession of public lands, see Gates, *History of Public Land*, 49–57. On the distribution of the public lands, see Benjamin Horace Hibbard, *A History of the Public Land Policies* (Madison: University of Wisconsin Press, 1965); Gates, *History of Public Land*; Payson J. Treat, *The National Land System, 1785–1820* (New York: E. B. Treat, 1910); Malcolm J. Rohrbough, *The Land Office Business: The Settlement and Administration of American Public Lands, 1789–1837* (Belmont, Calif.: Wadsworth, 1990); Murray Reed Benedict, *Farm Policies of the United States, 1790–1950: A Study of Their Origins and Development* (New York: Twentieth Century Fund, 1953); Daniel Feller, *The Public Lands in Jacksonian Politics* (Madison: University of Wisconsin Press, 1984); Roy Marvin Robbins, *Our Landed Heritage: The Public Domain, 1776–1936* (Princeton, N.J.: Princeton University Press, 1942); Milton Conover, *The General Land Office: Its History, Activities, and Organization*, Service Monographs of the United States Government (Baltimore: Johns Hopkins Press, 1923); Gary D. Libecap, "Property Rights and Federal Land Policy," in *Government and the American Economy: A New History*, ed. Price Van Meter Fishback (Chicago: University of Chicago Press, 2007); Jeremy Atack, Fred Bateman, and William Parker, "Northern Agriculture and the Westward Movement," in *The Cambridge Economic History of the United States*, vol. 2: *The Long Nineteenth Century*, ed. Robert E. Gallman and Stanley L. Engerman, Cambridge Economic History of the United States (Cambridge: Cambridge University Press, 2000); Thomas Donaldson, *The Public Domain, Its History with Statistics*, ed. U.S. Public Land Commission, History of American Economy (New York: Johnson Reprint Corp., 1884).

5. Richard Sylla, "Experimental Federalism: The Economics of American Government, 1789–1914," in *The Cambridge Economic History of the United States*, ed. Stanley L. Engerman and Robert E. Gallman (New York: Cambridge University Press, 1996), 498. Of the total dent, $18 million was assumed from the states. Davis Rich Dewey, *Financial History of the United States* (New York: Longmans, Green and Co., 1934), 56.

6. Feller, *Public Lands in Jacksonian Politics*, 3–13; Rohrbough, *Land Office Business*, 6. The use of land sales for revenue and to compensate soldiers was not limited to the United States, of course. In early seventeenth-century England, for example, the Stuarts sold land to make up shortfalls before turning to new "impositions," forced loans, the sale of peerage and titles, and property seizures—actions that ultimately led to the Glorious Revolution. See North and Weingast, "Constitutions and Commitment." Treat, *National Land System*, notes that in 1772 the British Board of Trade was developing a plan to sell off colonial lands at a fixed price.

7. Laura Jensen, *Patriots, Settlers, and the Origins of American Social Policy* (New York: Cambridge University Press, 2003).

8. Frymer, "Rush and a Push," 121.

9. Jefferson quoted in Gates, *History of Public Land*, 62.

10. Ibid., 61–68.

11. Ibid., 765.

12. Pelatiah Webster, quoted in Treat, *National Land System*, 16.

13. On early land policy, see Benedict, *Farm Policies*, 6–16. Hibbard, *History of the Public Land*, 33–81. Under the New England system of township planning, a survey laid out townships of six square miles in an orderly grid of 640-acre lots, with land set aside for public schools.

14. On the military and squatters, see Gates, *History of Public Land*, 123. On squatters and disputes over land claims from other governments, see ibid., 87–120. On the administrative potential of the private companies, see ibid., 71.

15. Ibid., 121; Wright, *Economic History*, 216.

16. Gates, *History of Public Land*, 121; Wright, *Economic History*, 216.

17. Howard Bodenhorn, *State Banking in Early America: A New Economic History* (New York: Oxford University Press, 2003), 3. The Bank of New York had operated since 1784 but did not receive its charter until the next year. Bray Hammond, *Banks and Politics in America, from the Revolution to the Civil War* (Princeton, N.J.: Princeton University Press, 1957), 65.

18. Accounts of the credit system can be found in Hibbard, *History of the Public Land*, 82–100; Gates, *History of Public Land*, 121–83; idem, *The Farmer's Age: Agriculture, 1815–1860*, Economic History of the United States (New York: Holt, Rinehart and Winston, 1960), 51–69; Treat, *National Land System*, 66–161; Robbins, *Our Landed Heritage*, 20–34.

19. Benedict, *Farm Policies*, 13.

20. Gates, *History of Public Land*, 132.

21. Ibid., 127; Rohrbough, *Land Office Business*, 49.

22. Hibbard, *History of the Public Land*, 84–86.

23. Ibid., 84; Benedict, *Farm Policies*, 15; Treat, *National Land System*, 110.

24. Hibbard, *History of the Public Land*, 88.

25. Cited in ibid., 90.

26. Feller, *Public Lands in Jacksonian Politics*, 26.

27. Dewey, *Financial History*, 216–17; Gates, *History of Public Land*, 134–37.

28. Charles Poor Kindleberger and Robert Z. Aliber, *Manias, Panics and Crashes: A History of Financial Crises*, 5th ed., Wiley Investment Classics (Hoboken, N.J.: John Wiley & Sons, 2005), 90. For more recent work on whether credit cycles are best thought of as ultimate causes or mechanisms of change, see Alan M. Taylor, "Credit, Financial Stability, and the Macroeconomy," *Annual Review of Economics* 7, no. 1 (2015). See also Ben S. Bernanke, "The Financial Accelerator and the Credit Channel," paper presented at the Credit Channel of Monetary Policy in the Twenty-First Century conference, Atlanta, Georgia, June 15, 2007; Nobuhiro Kiyotaki and John Moore, "Credit Cycles," *Journal of Political Economy* 105, no. 2 (1997). On the relationship between boom-bust cycles and Kuznet's theory of business cycles, see James Belich, *Replenishing the Earth: The Settler Revolution and the Rise of the Anglo-World, 1783–1939* (New York: Oxford University Press, 2009), 95–98.

29. Kindleberger and Aliber, *Manias, Panics and Crashes*, 110.

30. Irving Fisher, "The Debt-Deflation Theory of Great Depressions," *Econometrica* 1 (1933): 341.

31. Gates, *The Farmer's Age*, 57.

32. Murray Newton Rothbard, *The Panic of 1819: Reactions and Policies*, Kindle ed. (n.p.: Ludwig von Mises Institute, 2007), location 154. Gates, *Farmer's Age*, 87.

33. Charles Sellers, *The Market Revolution: Jacksonian America, 1815–1846* (New York: Oxford University Press, 1991), 133–34.

34. Gates, *History of Public Land*, 138.

35. Sellers, *Market Revolution*, 126.

36. Hibbard, *History of the Public Land*, 78; Gates, *History of Public Land*, 136.

37. Ibid., location 309; Sellers, *Market Revolution*, 135.

38. Rothbard, *Panic of 1819*, location 309.

39. Daniel Walker Howe, *What Hath God Wrought: The Transformation of America, 1815–1848*, Oxford History of the United States (New York: Oxford University Press, 2007), 142–47; Sellers, *Market Revolution*, 132–36.

40. Gates, *Farmer's Age*, 60–63.

41. Rothbard, *Panic of 1819*, locations 356–62.

42. Sellers, *Market Revolution*, 137.

43. Rothbard, *Panic of 1819*, locations 345–46.

44. Gates, *History of Public Land*, 136. See also Treat, *National Land System*, 142–57.

45. Gates, *Farmer's Age*, 63–64.

46. Quoted in Earl Sylvester Sparks, *History and Theory of Agricultural Credit in the United States* (New York: Thomas Y. Crowell Company, 1932), 231.

47. Quoted in Aaron M. Sakolski, *The Great American Land Bubble: The Amazing Story of Land-Grabbing, Speculations, and Booms from Colonial Days to the Present Time* (Mansfield Center, Conn.: Martino Publishing, 2011), 178; see also Sellers, *Market Revolution*, 138.

48. Sellers, *Market Revolution*, 171–201.

49. Rothbard, *Panic of 1819*, locations 796–1647.

50. Representatives from the West also pushed for preemption rights that would allow settlers to retain land that they had improved but faced opposition from a variety of fronts: eastern farmers were wary of western competition, budding eastern industrialists worried that westward migration would raise their labor costs, some in Congress resisted the rise of western influence, and still others were committed to using land as a source of revenue. Many of these sectional divides would also serve to slow the process of railroad and other internal developments. See George M. Stephenson, *The Political History of the Public Lands, from 1840 to 1862: From Preemption to Homestead*, Studies in American History (Boston: R. G. Badger, 1917), 24.

51. Feller, *Public Lands in Jacksonian Politics*, 27.

52. Jane Knodell, "Rethinking the Jacksonian Economy: The Impact of the 1832 Bank Veto on Commercial Banking," *Journal of Economic History* 66, no. 3 (2006).

53. In addition to table 2.2, see also Sylla, "Experimental Federalism," 521–22; Dewey, *Financial History*, 168–69.

54. "By the end of Andrew Jackson's presidency (1829–1836)," writes historian John Laritz Larson, "as new technologies matured and the popular demand for public works approached its zenith, politicians at the federal level found that designs or programs for internal improvements engendered such negative fantasies of consolidation, corrupt, and anti-democratic manipulation as to make them virtually unsupportable." Larson, *Internal Improvement*, 5.

55. For instance, while Adams lost to Jackson in the election of 1828, historian Daniel Walker Howe warns against drawing undue conclusions about the unpopularity of the American System from a campaign that was "probably the dirtiest in American history." See Howe, *What Hath God Wrought*, 278, 357–410.

56. Stephen Minicucci, "Internal Improvements and the Union, 1790–1860," *Studies in American Political Development* 18, no. 2 (2004): 166.

57. Howe, *What Hath God Wrought*, 270–84.

58. Stephen Minicucci, "Internal Improvements," 160.

59. Stephen Minicucci, "Internal Improvements," 162.

60. Feller, *Public Lands in Jacksonian Politics*, 152. Within-region disagreements about policies contributed to the complexity of political alliances related to early developmental policy. The American System proposed (among other things) using land sales to fund internal improvements. Many settlers in the western states objected to this on the grounds that the land should be distributed for free. But some settlers in the West thought better transportation would have a bigger payoff than free land. Many southerners decried the internal improvement plans of republican nationalists as a kind of northern imperialism, but a few noted that the American System's proposed land sales might offset the need for much-hated tariffs. Many northeastern conservatives, who had long advocated for the expansion of the frontier and its markets, supported the

American System proposal. But there were also eastern manufacturers who feared that labor costs would rise if too many workers moved west and eastern farmers who saw western farms as competition.

61. Hibbard, *History of the Public Land*; Stephenson, *Political History*; Howe, *What Hath God Wrought*; Eric Foner, *Free Soil, Free Labor, Free Men: The Ideology of the Republican Party Before the Civil War* (New York: Oxford University Press, 1995).

62. Minicucci, "Internal Improvements," 161–62.

63. Brian Balogh, *A Government out of Sight: The Mystery of National Authority in Nineteenth-Century America* (New York: Cambridge University Press, 2009).

64. Many states received a share of the proceeds of sales of federal land within their borders (6 states got 3 percent of those proceeds, and 24 got 5 percent), which were nominally supposed to be put toward improvements or education: however, this policy had no actual teeth for enforcement. With preemption in 1841, Congress granted 500,000 acres (roughly the equivalent of 780 square miles) to public land states. Minicucci, "Internal Improvements," 167.

65. Carter Goodrich, *Government Promotion of American Canals and Railroads, 1800–1890* (Westport, Conn.: Greenwood Press, 1974), 201–2.

66. Sakolski, *Great American Land Bubble*, 282; Atack, Bateman, and Parker, "Northern Agriculture," 302.

67. Carter Goodrich, *Government Promotion*, 170–71.

68. Alfred D. Chandler, *The Visible Hand: The Managerial Revolution in American Business* (Cambridge, Mass.: Belknap Press, 1977).

69. Richard White, *Railroaded: The Transcontinentals and the Making of Modern America* (New York: W. W. Norton & Co., 2011), 21.

70. Ibid., 17; Goodrich, *Government Promotion*, 182–83.

71. Chandler, *Visible Hand*; idem, "Patterns of American Railroad Finance, 1830–50," *Business History Review* 28, no. 3 (1954).

72. The extent to which this granting of rights represents a subsidy or a savvy exchange has been debated by historians. In return for support for the railways, the federal government secured free shipping and was permitted to set prices for mail delivery, a privilege that later ended up being very valuable, though it is not clear that anyone at the time could have foreseen how much money it would eventually save the government. See Vernon Rosco Carstensen, *The Public Lands: Studies in the History of the Public Domain*, general ed. (Madison: University of Wisconsin Press, 1963), 121–73, which includes arguments of eight separate historians on the matter. See also Donaldson, *Public Domain*; White, *Railroaded*, 17–36.

73. Ronald E. Shaw, *Canals for a Nation: The Canal Era in the United States, 1790–1860* (Lexington: University Press of Kentucky, 1990), 225.

74. Here the railway acted as creditor, with rates that ranged from a low of 2 percent to a high of 10 percent and often easy terms, including no down payments and generous extensions on repayments. One company reported in 1924 that its land sales for the year had added up to $136 million, far surpassing the $70 million it had spent building its railroad. Hibbard, *History of the Public Land*, 260.

75. White, *Railroaded*, 22.

76. Historian Richard White in his book *Railroaded* points out that the deal ended up much sweeter for the railroads than Congress had initially intended for two reasons. First, the railways went to court over the ambiguously written laws to argue that the federal government, and not railways, was responsible for paying interest on the bonds in the 30-year period before they matured; the court ruled in favor of the railways, which granted them what amounted to an additional $43 million subsidy. Second, while the 1862 law specified that the bonds constituted a first mortgage on all the railroad's property—meaning that the national government had the first

claim on the railway's property in case of default—after 1864 other bondholders were allowed to take precedence in case of a crisis. White, *Railroaded*, 17–36.

77. The creation of a national banking system directed even more funds to the railways, albeit through circuitous and unintended means. The National Banking Acts of 1863 and 1864 were passed to help finance the Civil War. Among other things, these acts created charters for federal banks that were supported by a reserve system with a pyramid structure that shunted the nation's capital to New York, where banks lent money to traders under terms that allowed banks to quickly recall their loans. The influx of cash from the banks, paired with an influx of government bonds issued to pay for the war, was a shot in the arm for New York's stock market. When the war ended and the federal government started returning its debt by buying back bonds, financiers like Jay Cooke, working with the money shunted through the banking system and the funds from repaid Civil War debt, turned to the railways. Richard Franklin Bensel, *Yankee Leviathan: The Origins of Central State Authority in America, 1859–1877* (New York: Cambridge University Press, 1990); Gerald Berk, *Alternative Tracks: The Constitution of American Industrial Order, 1865–1917* (Baltimore: Johns Hopkins University Press, 1994).

78. Dale L. Flesher, Gary J. Previts, and William D. Samson, "Early American Corporate Reporting and European Capital Markets: The Case of the Illinois Central Railroad, 1851–1861," *Accounting Historians Journal* 33, no. 1 (2006); Chandler, "Patterns of American Railroad Finance"; Lance E. Davis and Robert E. Gallman, *Evolving Financial Markets and International Capital Flows: Britain, the Americas, and Australia, 1865–1914* (New York: Cambridge University Press, 2001), 9.

79. Bensel, *Yankee Leviathan*, 251.

80. For comparison, Davis and Gallman add that the total investment as of 1898 in U.S. rail was $5.2 billion. Davis and Gallman, *Evolving Financial Markets*, 252.

81. Sylla, "Experimental Federalism," 556.

82. White, *Railroaded*, 84.

83. Berk, *Alternative Tracks*, 36.

84. Frank Dobbin, *Forging Industrial Policy: The United States, Britain, and France in the Railway Age* (New York: Cambridge University Press, 1994), 83.

85. Andrew Shonfield, *Modern Capitalism: The Changing Balance of Public and Private Power* (New York: Oxford University Press, 1965). See also William G. Roy, *Socializing Capital: The Rise of the Large Industrial Corporation in America* (Princeton, N.J.: Princeton University Press, 1997); Berk, *Alternative Tracks*; Adolf A. Berle and Gardiner C. Means, *The Modern Corporation and Private Property* (New Brunswick, N.J.: Transaction Publishers, 2009).

86. Sven Beckert, *Empire of Cotton: A Global History* (New York: Alfred A. Knopf, 2014), 222.

87. Bodenhorn, *State Banking in Early America*, 254.

88. On the cotton factor, see Harold D. Woodman, *King Cotton and His Retainers: Financing and Marketing the Cotton Crop of the South, 1800–1925* (Lexington: University of Kentucky Press, 1968); Richard Holcombe Kilbourne, *Debt, Investment, Slaves: Credit Relations in East Feliciana Parish, Louisiana, 1825–1885* (Tuscaloosa: University of Alabama Press, 1995).

89. Calvin Schermerhorn, *The Business of Slavery and the Rise of American Capitalism, 1815–1860* (New Haven, Conn.: Yale University Press, 2015), 108.

90. Baptist, *Half Has Never Been Told*, 245.

91. Martin, "Neighbor-to-Neighbor Capitalism."

92. John J. Clegg, "Credit Market Discipline and Capitalist Slavery in Antebellum South Carolina," *Social Science History* 42, no. 2 (2018); Sven Beckert and Seth Rockman, *Slavery's Capitalism: A New History of American Economic Development*, Early American Studies (Philadelphia: University of Pennsylvania Press, 2016); Bonnie Martin, "Slavery's Invisible Engine: Mortgaging Human Property," *Journal of Southern History* 76, no. 4 (2010); Schermerhorn, *Business of Slavery*, 122.

93. In the colonial era, property banks and loan offices used land as collateral to issue notes and loans. This was considered a way to "melt down" property and render its value liquid. But these property banks were frequently unstable and prone to failure, and so they soon fell out of favor. Fritz Redlich, *The Molding of American Banking: Men and Ideas*, 2 vols., History of American Economy (New York: Johnson Reprint Corporation, 1968), 1:206–7; Theodore Thayer, "The Land-Bank System in the American Colonies," *Journal of Economic History* 13, no. 2 (1953).

94. Baptist, *Half Has Never Been Told*, 245–54; Emile Grenier, "Property Banks in Louisiana" (Ph.D. diss., Louisiana State University, 1942); Irene D. Neu, "J. B. Moussier and the Property Banks of Louisiana," *Business History Review* 35, no. 4 (1961); Bodenhorn, *State Banking in Early America*, 249–50; Schermerhorn, *Business of Slavery*, 95–123.

95. Irene Neu's account of Moussier supposes that the inspiration might have come from earlier domestic experiments with land banks or some kind of exposure to Prussian *Landschaften* (which I will discuss in some detail in chapter 4). Redlich argues that the organizational form adopted suggests that the colonial property banks and land offices were the actual precedents; Redlich, *Molding of American Banking*, 1:206–7.

96. Ibid., 207n.20.

97. Bodenhorn, *State Banking in Early America*, 245.

98. Redlich, *Molding of American Banking,* 1:208.

99. Bodenhorn, *State Banking in Early America*, 259.

100. Redlich, *Molding of American Banking*, 1:206.

101. Baptist, *Half Has Never Been Told*, 256.

102. On the developmental projects of southern state banks, see Bodenhorn, *State Banking in Early America*; Woodman, *King Cotton*, 98.

103. Grenier, "Property Banks in Louisiana," 186.

104. Contemporaries blamed speculation and mismanagement. More recently, Howard Bodenhorn, in *State Banking in Early America,* has argued that they were effectively doomed because they did not have enough time to establish themselves before the market took a downturn.

105. Bodenhorn, *State Banking in Early America,* 258–60.

106. Hammond, *Banks and Politics in America*, 280; Atack, Bateman, and Parker, "Northern Agriculture," 311–15; Clarence H. Danhof, "Farm-Making Costs and the 'Safety Valve': 1850–60," *Journal of Political Economy* 49, no. 3 (1941).

107. On preemption, see Gates, who notes that the passage was largely a symbolic victory, since claims associations and a series of earlier acts had already made preemption effectively active: Gates, *History of Public Land*, 218–47.

108. George Ade, quoted in Gates, *Landlords and Tenants on the Prairie Frontier: Studies in American Land Policy* (Ithaca, N.Y.: Cornell University Press, 1973), 175.

109. Idem, *Farmer's Age*, 420.

110. Idem, *Landlords and Tenants*, 311; Jeremy Atack, "Farm and Farm-Making Costs Revisited," *Agricultural History* 56, no. 4 (1982); Danhof, "Farm-Making Costs."

111. Juliet E. K. Walker, *The History of Black Business in America: Capitalism, Race, Entrepreneurship*, Twayne's Evolution of Modern Business Series (New York: MacMillan Library Reference USA, 1998), 95.

112. Miles Lanier Colean, *The Impact of Government on Real Estate Finance in the United States* (New York: National Bureau of Economic Research, 1950), 15–16; Allan G. Bogue, *Money at Interest: The Farm Mortgage on the Middle Border* (Ithaca, N.Y.: Cornell University Press, 1955); Gates, *Landlords and Tenants*.

113. On the problems of enforcing long-distance mortgage contracts, see especially Kenneth Snowden, "The Evolution of Interregional Mortgage Lending Channels, 1870–1940: The Life Insurance-Mortgage Company Connection," in *Coordination and Information: Historical Perspectives on the Organization of Enterprise*, ed. Naomi R. Lamoreaux and Daniel M. G. Raff,

National Bureau of Economic Research Conference Report (Chicago: University of Chicago Press, 1995).

114. Marc A. Weiss, "Marketing and Financing Home Ownership: Mortgage Lending and Public Policy in the United States, 1918–1989," *Business and Economic History* 18 (1989); Richard K. Green and Susan M. Wachter, "The American Mortgage in Historical and International Context," *Journal of Economic Perspectives* 19, no. 4 (2005); Michael S. Carliner, "Development of Federal Homeownership 'Policy,'" *Housing Policy Debate* 9, no. 2 (1998).

115. Bogue, *Money at Interest*, 220.

116. The main exception was the national thrifts, which are discussed in chapter 5. On the rise of community lending, see Kenneth A. Snowden, "Building and Loan Associations in the U.S., 1880–1893: The Origins of Localization in the Residential Mortgage Market," *Research in Economics* 51, no. 3 (1997); Henry Morton Bodfish, *History of Building and Loan in the United States* (Chicago: United States Building and Loan League, 1931); David Lawrence Mason, *From Buildings and Loans to Bail-Outs: A History of the American Savings and Loan Industry, 1831–1995* (New York: Cambridge University Press, 2004).

117. Leo Grebler, Louis Winnick, and David Mordecai Blank, *Capital Formation in Residential Real Estate: Trends and Prospects*, Studies in Capital Formation and Financing (Princeton, N.J.: Princeton University Press, 1956), 191; Marc A. Weiss, *The Rise of the Community Builders: The American Real Estate Industry and Urban Land Planning* (New York: Columbia University Press, 1987).

118. Kenneth Snowden, "Table Dc903–928: Debt on Nonfarm Structures, by Type of Debt, Property, and Holder: 1896–1952," *Historical Statistics of the United States, Earliest Times to Present*, Millennial ed. (2006), http://dx.doi.org/10.1017/ISBN-9780511132971.Dc903–1288.

119. For a detailed review of earlier case studies and surveys of farm mortgage lending, see Allan G. Bogue, "Land Credit for Northern Farmers, 1789–1940," *Agricultural History* 50, no. 1 (1976).

120. Martin, "Neighbor-to-Neighbor Capitalism," 114.

121. Many states—including the financial behemoth New York—banned life insurance companies from investing in out-of-state mortgages in the 1870s and 1880s. This meant that by the time life insurance companies were well established in the 1870s, many were unable to issue mortgages across state lines. By the early 1890s insurance companies held around 6.5 percent of the total mortgages in the country. Raymond J. Saulnier, *Urban Mortgage Lending by Life Insurance Companies* (New York: National Bureau of Economic Research, 1950), 9; Bogue, "Land Credit for Northern Farmers," 85.

122. Redlich, *Molding of American Banking*, 2:22.

123. Erling A. Erickson, "Money and Banking in a 'Bankless'State: Iowa, 1846–1857," *Business History Review* 43, no. 2 (1969): 171.

124. Carter H. Golembe, *State Banks and the Economic Development of the West* (New York: Arno Press, 1978); Knodell, "Rethinking the Jacksonian Economy."

125. Bodenhorn, *State Banking in Early America*, 289.

126. Richard Sylla, "Federal Policy, Banking Market Structure, and Capital Mobilization in the United States, 1863–1913," *Journal of Economic History* 29, no. 4 (1969): 659; Richard H. Keehn and Gene Smiley, "Mortgage Lending by National Banks," *Business History Review* 51, no. 4 (1977). The national banks had ways of getting around long-term lending restrictions (for example, they could accept a mortgage to secure an existing debt and hold a mortgage for under five years), and regulators were often generous in their interpretation of the restrictions. Keehn and Smiley argue that banks were especially active in agricultural regions and that their participation in the market may be significantly underreported. Still, even if we double estimates from the 1895 Census, commercial banks only represent 6 percent of holdings. Given those numbers,

it seems reasonable to conclude that the 1864 regulations depressed commercial bank mortgage investment.

127. Sylla, "Federal Policy."

128. Hugh Rockoff, "Banking and Finance, 1789–1914," in *The Cambridge Economic History of the United States*, vol. 2: *The Long Nineteenth Century*, ed. Robert E. Gallman and Stanley L. Engerman, Cambridge Economic History of the United States (Cambridge: Cambridge University Press, 2000), 652.

129. Bodenhorn, *State Banking in Early America*, 139–42.

130. Knodell, "Rethinking the Jacksonian Economy," 561.

131. Redlich, *Molding of American Banking*, 1:206–7; Thayer, "Land-Bank System."

132. Bodenhorn, *State Banking in Early America,* 259–60; Knodell, "Rethinking the Jacksonian Economy," 560–61.

133. Bogue, *Money at Interest.*

134. Gates, *Landlords and Tenants*, 58; idem, *Farmer's Age*, 73.

135. Erickson, "Money and Banking"; Kilbourne, *Debt, Investment, Slaves.*

136. Ray Allen Billington, "The Origin of the Land Speculator as a Frontier Type," *Agricultural History* 19, no. 4 (1945): 211.

137. Sakolski, *Great American Land Bubble*, 175.

138. Kenneth T. Jackson, *Crabgrass Frontier: The Suburbanization of the United States* (New York: Oxford University Press, 1985); Bogue, *Money at Interest*, 2; John William Reps, *The Making of Urban America: A History of City Planning in the United States* (Princeton, N.J.: Princeton University Press, 1965).

139. Beardsly, quoted in Gates, *Landlords and Tenants*, 52.

140. Stephen Aron, "Pioneers and Profiteers: Land Speculation and the Homestead Ethic in Frontier Kentucky," *Western Historical Quarterly* 23, no. 2 (1992).

141. Colean, *Impact of Government*; Kiyotaki and Moore, "Credit Cycles."

142. Colean, *Impact of Government.*

143. Jeremy Atack, Fred Bateman, and Will Parker, "The Farm, the Farmer, and the Market," in *The Cambridge Economic History of the United States*, vol. 2: *The Long Nineteenth Century*, ed. Robert E. Gallman and Stanley L. Engerman (Cambridge: Cambridge University Press, 2000), 245–48, 274.

144. Sparks, *History and Theory*, 178; D. M. Frederiksen, "Mortgage Banking in America," *Journal of Political Economy* 2, no. 2 (1894): 206; Kenneth A. Snowden, "Mortgage Rates and American Capital Market Development in the Late Nineteenth Century," *Journal of Economic History* 47, no. 3 (1987): 675.

145. Among economic historians, western markets are seen as a test case for understanding the relationship between the state and the market. If the market was already integrated (putting aside the disruption caused by the Civil War), then federal banking regulations were not needed to fix it, and the idea that markets are capable of rational allocation of resources is supported. Alternatively, if the market was inefficient and segmented and federal intervention *overcame* those problems, the implication is that markets benefit from government oversight. The result has been decades-long debate about the extent to which western markets were integrated with eastern markets and whether higher interest rates in the West represented rational risk allocations or credit rationing. While much of the work on this topic has focused on short-term interest rates, Davis's classic statement considers mortgage rates. Lance E. Davis, "The Investment Market, 1870–1914: The Evolution of a National Market," *Journal of Economic History* 25, no. 3 (1965). For a helpful summary of these debates, see Howard Bodenhorn, "Two Centuries of Finance and Growth in the United States, 1790–1980," NBER Working Paper Series (Cambridge, Mass.: National Bureau of Economic Research, 2016). For a new contribution to the debate, see

Raghuram G. Rajan and Rodney Ramcharan, "Land and Credit: A Study of the Political Economy of Banking in the United States in the Early 20th Century," *Journal of Finance* 66, no. 6 (2011). Regardless of whether one believes that farmers were correct about middlemen (a point to which I will return in the next chapter), it is clear that transaction costs and credit risks drove up their rates, and that secondary markets could address those issues. This would prove important in later experiments for solutions, either via securitization (chapter 3) or through federal credit programs (chapter 4).

146. For an excellent overview of the 10 major American sectors following the Civil War, their economic bases, and their political correlates, see Elizabeth M. Sanders, *Roots of Reform: Farmers, Workers, and the American State, 1877–1917* (Chicago: University of Chicago Press, 1999), 13–29.

147. Hibbard, *History of the Public Land*, 103, 106, 113. Cited in Atack, Bateman, and Parker, "Northern Agriculture," 298.

148. John D. Hicks, *The Populist Revolt: A History of the Farmers' Alliance and the People's Party* (Lincoln: University of Nebraska Press, 1961), 23. For a review of the debates on the relative importance of different staples, especially cotton versus eastern food consumption, as underlying causes of crises, see Belich, *Replenishing the Earth*.

Chapter 3: Three Failures

1. For the sociological study of morality and markets, see Marion Fourcade and Kieran Healy, "Moral Views of Market Society," *Annual Review of Sociology* 33, no. 1 (2007).

2. Monica Prasad, *The Land of Too Much: American Abundance and the Paradox of Poverty* (Cambridge, Mass.: Harvard University Press, 2012), 46–95.

3. Ibid., 54.

4. Murray Reed Benedict, *Farm Policies of the United States, 1790–1950: A Study of Their Origins and Development* (New York: Twentieth Century Fund, 1953), 85.

5. James Belich, *Replenishing the Earth: The Settler Revolution and the Rise of the Anglo-World, 1783–1939* (New York: Oxford University Press, 2009); Elizabeth M. Sanders, *Roots of Reform: Farmers, Workers, and the American State, 1877–1917* (Chicago: University of Chicago Press, 1999); Michael Schwartz, *Radical Protest and Social Structure: The Southern Farmers' Alliance and Cotton Tenancy, 1880–1890* (Chicago: University of Chicago Press, 1988).

6. Charles Postel, *The Populist Vision* (New York: Oxford University Press, 2007).

7. See Jonathan Levy, *Freaks of Fortune: The Emerging World of Capitalism and Risk in America* (Cambridge, Mass.: Harvard University Press, 2012), 170–71; Charles F. Heller, Jr., and John T. Houdek, "Women Lenders as Sources of Land Credit in Nineteenth-Century Michigan," *Journal of Interdisciplinary History* 35, no. 1 (2004).

8. Sanders, *Roots of Reform*, 101.

9. Scholars debate the accuracy of farmers' claims that they were being deliberately fleeced by middlemen, arguing that transaction costs account for these differentials (see chapter 2 for a similar discussion about mortgage rate differentials). See, for example, Peal's discussion of cotton factors in "The Politics of Populism: Germany and the American South in the 1890s," *Comparative Studies in Society and History* 31, no. 2 (1989). I believe there is sufficient historical evidence of rent-seeking, but even if that were not the case, as others before me have noted, what matters most for scholars interested in populism is whether farmers *believed* they were being fleeced. On that question there is broad agreement.

10. For more on the politics of railway rates, see Gerald Berk, *Alternative Tracks: The Constitution of American Industrial Order, 1865–1917* (Baltimore: Johns Hopkins University Press, 1994).

11. In theory, declining prices should have had two benefits for farmers: it should have lowered production costs by driving down the price of supplies, and it should have increased exports. In *Land of Too Much*, Prasad argues that production costs did not decline in step with prices (1) because volatile real interest rates drove up the cost of borrowing, and (2) because farmers glutted global markets to such an extent that there were no further gains in exports to be had. To that I would add that in the South credit and marketing monopolies would likely have distorted the market as well.

12. Prasad, *Land of Too Much*, 72.

13. Sanders, *Roots of Reform*, 109.

14. Gretchen Ritter, *Goldbugs and Greenbacks: The Antimonopoly Tradition and the Politics of Finance in America* (New York: Cambridge University Press, 1997).

15. There is a large literature on the nineteenth-century agrarian movements. In this account, I draw most extensively from Postel, *Populist Vision*; Omar H. Ali, *In the Lion's Mouth: Black Populism in the New South, 1886–1900* (Jackson: University Press of Mississippi, 2010); Lawrence Goodwyn, *Democratic Promise: The Populist Moment in America* (New York: Oxford University Press, 1976); Elisabeth Clemens, *The People's Lobby: Organizational Innovation and the Rise of Interest Group Politics in the United States, 1890–1925* (Chicago: University of Chicago Press, 1997); Sanders, *Roots of Reform*; Robert H. Wiebe, *The Search for Order, 1877–1920* (New York: Hill and Wang, 1967); Richard Hofstadter, *The Age of Reform: From Bryan to F.D.R.*, 1st ed. (New York: Knopf, 1955); John D. Hicks, *The Populist Revolt: A History of the Farmers' Alliance and the People's Party* (Lincoln: University of Nebraska Press, 1961); Solon Justus Buck, *The Agrarian Crusade* (New Haven, Conn.: Yale University Press, 1920); Schwartz, *Radical Protest*.

16. Richard White, *Railroaded: The Transcontinentals and the Making of Modern America* (New York: W. W. Norton & Co., 2011), 111; Sidney Fine, *Laissez Faire and the General-Welfare State: A Study of Conflict in American Thought, 1865–1901* (Ann Arbor: University of Michigan Press, 1956).

17. Clemens, *People's Lobby*; Postel, *Populist Vision*.

18. Clemens, *People's Lobby*. See also Marc Schneiberg, "Toward an Organizationally Diverse American Capitalism?: Cooperative, Mutual, and Local State-Owned Enterprise," *Seattle University Law Review* 34 (2013); Marc Schneiberg, Marissa King, and Thomas Smith, "Social Movements and Organizational Form: Cooperative Alternatives to Corporations in the American Insurance, Dairy, and Grain Industries," *American Sociological Review* 73 (2008); Heather A. Haveman, "Between a Rock and a Hard Place: Organizational Change and Performance Under Conditions of Fundamental Environmental Transformation," *Administrative Science Quarterly* 37, no. 1 (1992).

19. Clemens, *People's Lobby*.

20. See Sanders, *Roots of Reform*.

21. For overviews of the historiographies of liberalism and republicanism in the United States, see Daniel T. Rodgers, "Republicanism: The Career of a Concept," *Journal of American History* 79, no. 1 (1992); Cécile Laborde, "Republicanism," in *The Oxford Handbook of Political Ideologies*, ed. Michael Freeden and Marc Stears (Oxford University Press, 2012); Michael J. Sandel, *Democracy's Discontent: America in Search of a Public Philosophy* (Cambridge, Mass.: Belknap Press of Harvard University Press, 1996).

22. Fine, *Laissez Faire*.

23. Marc A. Weiss, *The Rise of the Community Builders: The American Real Estate Industry and Urban Land Planning* (New York: Columbia University Press, 1987); Allan G. Bogue, *Money at Interest: The Farm Mortgage on the Middle Border* (Ithaca, N.Y.: Cornell University Press, 1955); Glenn H. Miller, Jr., "The Hawkes Papers: A Case Study of a Kansas Mortgage Brokerage Business, 1871–1888," *Business History Review* 32, no. 3 (1958).

24. Gleed, quoted in Levy, *Freaks of Fortune*, 164.

25. Bogue, *Money at Interest*; Kenneth A. Snowden, "Covered Farm Mortgage Bonds in the United States During the Late Nineteenth Century," *Journal of Economic History* 70, no. 4 (2010).

26. Note that NPR's well-regarded "Giant Pool of Money" report offered a strikingly similar analysis of the securitization boom of the 1990s, noting that declines in U.S. Treasury yields similarly led investors to turn to American mortgages as a supposedly safe investment with more attractive returns. See Alex Blumberg and Adam Davidson, "The Giant Pool of Money," in *This American Life*, ed. WBEZ Alliance and Ira Glass (n.p.: Public Radio International, 2008); H. Peers Brewer, "Eastern Money and Western Mortgages in the 1870s," *Business History Review* 50, no. 3 (1976).

27. Brewer, "Eastern Money and Western Mortgages."

28. Levy, *Freaks of Fortune*.

29. Earl Sylvester Sparks, *History and Theory of Agricultural Credit in the United States* (New York: Thomas Y. Crowell Company, 1932), 178–79; Lance E. Davis, "The Investment Market, 1870–1914: The Evolution of a National Market," *Journal of Economic History* 25, no. 3 (1965): 385.

30. Snowden, "Covered Farm Mortgage Bonds"; D. M. Frederiksen, "Mortgage Banking in America," *Journal of Political Economy* 2, no. 2 (1894): 216.

31. Sparks, *History and Theory*, 180–81.

32. See, for example, this account from 1889: "For years, say up to 1885, the success of the mortgage-loan business was marvelous. Seldom did the lender lose a dollar. The reason was plain: Land increased in value regularly every year, and loans, although they may have been excessive at the time they were made, were given a safe margin by the increase in the value of the security. This led the people of the east to demand more and more of these mortgages. They wanted more than were to be had." W. F. Mappin, "Farm Mortgages and the Small Farmer," *Political Science Quarterly* 4, no. 3 (1889): 438.

33. Snowden, "Covered Farm Mortgage Bonds."

34. Sprankle, quoted in Bogue, *Money at Interest*, 142.

35. Sparks, for instance, reports that in 1887 the state of Connecticut responded to the farm mortgage craze by creating a commissioner of foreign mortgage companies. See Sparks, *History and Theory*. Also see Allan Bogue, "Land Credit for Northern Farmers, 1789–1940," *Agricultural History* 50, no. 1 (1976): 84n.24.

36. See Blumberg and Davidson, "Giant Pool of Money."

37. Jonathan Levy, "The Freaks of Fortune: Moral Responsibility for Booms and Busts in Nineteenth-Century America," *Journal of the Gilded Age and Progressive Era* 10, no. 4 (2011): 436. For Levy, the mortgage bond represented a financial structure that severed traditional lending relationships and thus transformed farmers' experience of themselves as bearers of debt in a more abstract sense. Overall, I find his general argument about changing notions of risk in the nineteenth century deeply illuminating and incisive, especially as it pertains to his analyses of insurance markets. That said, I do not agree with his conclusion that the nineteenth-century mortgage bond market itself was a catalyst of dramatic psychological change. The mortgage bond market was destabilizing, but it seems to have hardly displaced traditional forms of lending on a large scale, since it seems to have represented only one-tenth of western debt (according to the same data from Snowden that Levy draws from). So while the mortgage bond market is a useful *example* of how farmers could embrace laissez-faire and corporate organizational repertoires, I find it less likely that the nineteenth-century mortgage bond was transformative to the extent that Levy suggests.

38. Ibid.

39. Fine, *Laissez Faire*.

40. Berk, *Alternative Tracks*; William G. Roy, *Socializing Capital: The Rise of the Large Industrial Corporation in America* (Princeton, N.J.: Princeton University Press, 1997); Richard

Franklin Bensel, *Yankee Leviathan: The Origins of Central State Authority in America, 1859–1877* (New York: Cambridge University Press, 1990); Richard Sylla, "Federal Policy, Banking Market Structure, and Capital Mobilization in the United States, 1863–1913," *Journal of Economic History* 29, no. 4 (1969).

41. For an elegant discussion of this, see Roy, *Socializing Capital*.

42. David Ciepley, "Beyond Public and Private: Toward a Political Theory of the Corporation," *American Political Science Review* 107, no. 1 (2013): 145.

43. Fine, *Laissez Faire*.

44. Adolf A. Berle and Gardiner C. Means, *The Modern Corporation and Private Property* (New Brunswick, N.J.: Transaction Publishers, 2009); Frank Dobbin, *Forging Industrial Policy: The United States, Britain, and France in the Railway Age* (New York: Cambridge University Press, 1994).

45. Fine, *Laissez Faire*.

46. Ibid., 104–9.

47. Berk and Roy offer particularly useful and sociologically relevant analyses of the considerable political jockeying and intellectual gymnastics that underlay the rise of the corporation. Berk notes that courts bailed out large railroads and let smaller ones fail, further bolstering the large and nonlocal corporation against the objections of Americans who supported smaller, local alternatives. Berk and Roy both show how it was not just the courts that promoted the growth of the corporation, but also midcentury financial policies, which set corporate-friendly financial infrastructures and conditions. Both note that this troubles Chandler's assertion that corporations emerged as an efficient response to new demands of capital in the age of the railroad. See Berk, *Alternative Tracks*; Ciepley, "Beyond Public and Private"; Roy, *Socializing Capital*; Alfred D. Chandler, *The Visible Hand: The Managerial Revolution in American Business* (Cambridge, Mass.: Belknap Press, 1977).

48. Berle and Means, *Modern Corporation*, 8.

49. W.E.B. Du Bois, *Black Reconstruction in America: Toward a History of the Part Which Black Folk Played in the Attempt to Reconstruct Democracy in America, 1860–1880*, Kindle ed. (n.p.: Oxford University Press, 2007 [1935]), location 13,933–36.

50. Ibid., location 14,348–49.

51. Matthew Jaremski, "State Banks and the National Banking Acts: Measuring the Response to Increased Financial Regulation, 1860–1870," *Journal of Money, Credit and Banking* 45, nos. 2–3 (2013).

52. The rise of the railroads further resulted in the replacement of the cotton factor with the furnishing merchant (financed by northern manufacturers), which further degraded the existing system of southern credit distribution. See Roger L. Ransom and Richard Sutch, "Debt Peonage in the Cotton South After the Civil War," *Journal of Economic History* 32, no. 3 (1972); Howard Bodenhorn, "Capital Mobility and Financial Integration in Antebellum America," *Journal of Economic History* 52 (1992).

53. Schwartz, *Radical Protest*, 34.

54. Ransom and Sutch, "Debt Peonage."

55. Bensel, *Yankee Leviathan*. The classic discussion of how northern greed undermined the promise of Reconstruction is offered by Du Bois, *Black Reconstruction in America*.

56. Harold D. Woodman, *New South, New Law: The Legal Foundations of Credit and Labor Relations in the Postbellum Agricultural South*, Walter Lynwood Fleming Lectures in Southern History (Baton Rouge: Louisiana State University Press, 1995).

57. W.E.B. Du Bois, "The Economics of Negro Emancipation in the United States," *Sociological Review* 4, no. 3 (October 1911): 309.

58. Ibid., 105. Woodman warns against overstating the coherence of this system. The first generation of laws was largely unsuccessful, generating competing claims on the mortgaged

crops that led to conflicts between landowners, merchant-suppliers, and workers, who often all had a claim on the crop, which was not itself large enough to meet all of those claims. In later years, the law subordinated the claims of workers to those of lenders and employers.

59. Roger L. Ransom and Richard Sutch, *One Kind of Freedom: The Economic Consequences of Emancipation*, 2nd ed (New York: Cambridge University Press, 2001), table D3.

60. Schwartz, *Radical Protest*, 5.

61. Robert C. McMath, *Populist Vanguard: A History of the Southern Farmers' Alliance*, Norton Library (New York: Norton, 1977); Hicks, *Populist Revolt*.

62. Postel, *Populist Vision*, 39–40.

63. Ali, *In the Lion's Mouth*.

64. Schwartz, *Radical Protest*, 201–15.

65. William Edward Spriggs, "The Virginia Colored Farmers' Alliance: A Case Study of Race and Class Identity," *Journal of Negro History* 64, no. 3 (1979); William F. Holmes, "The Demise of the Colored Farmers' Alliance," *Journal of Southern History* 41, no. 2 (1975); idem, "The Leflore County Massacre and the Demise of the Colored Farmers' Alliance," *Phylon* 34, no. 3 (1973); Omar Ali, "Reconceptualizing Black Populism in the South," in *Populism in the South Revisited: New Interpretations and New Departures*, ed. James M. Beeby (Jackson: University Press of Mississippi, 2012).

66. Holmes, "Demise of the Colored Farmers' Alliance," 169.

67. Schwartz, *Radical Protest*.

68. This section draws from the following accounts of the Southern Farmers' Alliance and the Farmers' Exchange: Ralph A. Smith, "'Macuneism,' or the Farmers of Texas in Business," *Journal of Southern History* 13 (1947); Hicks, *Populist Revolt*; Goodwyn, *Democratic Promise*; Schwartz, *Radical Protest*; Donna A. Barnes, *Farmers in Rebellion: The Rise and Fall of the Southern Farmers Alliance and People's Party in Texas* (Austin: University of Texas Press, 1984).

69. Quoted in Barnes, Farmers in Rebellion, 82.

70. Smith, "'Macuneism'"; Goodwyn, *Democratic Promise*, 126.

71. Goodwyn, *Democratic Promise*, 216–17.

72. Schwartz, *Radical Protest*, 218.

73. Smith, "'Macuneism'"; Goodwyn, *Democratic Promise*, 126.

74. Barnes, *Farmers in Rebellion*.

75. Goodwyn, *Democratic Promise*, 129.

76. Noting the undercapitalization of the Exchange, Heather Barnes argues that the banks' refusals of credit were in line with local risk management and lending practices, and that even some farmers believed that poor management on the part of the Alliance was the reason the exchanges failed. By April of 1888 the Alliance had collected only $20,215 in fees but had issued $200,975 in joint notes. The $78,000 collected was not even one-fifth of the planned original capitalization. In contrast, Michael Schwartz argues that the banks set more stringent standards for the Exchange than for other merchants. Barnes, *Farmers in Rebellion*; Schwartz, *Radical Protest*, 229–32. For my purposes here, what matters is farmers' own beliefs about what caused the failures and how that shaped their later political mobilizations.

77. Knapp reports that the Georgia Exchange was open until 1893. See Joseph Grant Knapp, *The Rise of American Cooperative Enterprise: 1620–1920* (Danville, Ill.: Interstate Printers & Publishers, 1969).

78. Clemens, *People's Lobby*, 158.

79. Goodwyn, *Democratic Promise*, 134–42.

80. Ibid., 139.

81. Postel, *Populist Vision*.

82. Ibid., 118.

83. Quoted in Knapp, *Rise of American Cooperative Enterprise*, 65.

84. On the corporation as socialized property, see Roy, *Socializing Capital*.

85. Postel is careful to note, however, that the commitment to democratic principles did not extend to free speech, since certain forms of religious, political, and oppositional speech were constrained. See Postel, *Populist Vision*.

86. Knapp, *Rise of American Cooperative Enterprise*, 60.

87. Postel, *Populist Vision*, 166.

88. Goodwyn, *Democratic Promise*. For discussions of the other influences on this idea, see James C. Malin, "The Farmers' Alliance Subtreasury Plan and European Precedents," *Mississippi Valley Historical Review* 31, no. 2 (1944); Hicks, *Populist Revolt*, 188–89.

89. Hicks, *Populist Revolt*, 192–93.

90. Goodwyn, *Democratic Promise*, 166–67.

91. Ibid.

92. Postel, *Populist Vision*, 160.

93. Goodwyn, *Democratic Promise*, 243. See also Postel, *Populist Vision*, 153–71.

94. Fine, *Laissez Faire*, 204–6.

95. Clemens, *People's Lobby*, 148.

96. Postel, *Populist Vision*; Knapp, *Rise of American Cooperative Enterprise*; Clemens, *People's Lobby*.

97. For more on the nineteenth century's patchwork state, see Stephen Skowronek, *Building a New American State: The Expansion of National Administrative Capacities, 1877–1920* (New York: Cambridge University Press, 1982); Bensel, *Yankee Leviathan*.

98. Sylla, "Federal Policy."

99. Sanders, *Roots of Reform*.

Chapter 4: Credit as a Tool of Statecraft

1. Gail Radford, *The Rise of the Public Authority: Statebuilding and Economic Development in Twentieth-Century America* (Chicago: University of Chicago Press, 2013).

2. Simone Polillo, "Money, Moral Authority, and the Politics of Creditworthiness," *American Sociological Review* 76 (2011).

3. For these exceptions, see Elizabeth M. Sanders, *Roots of Reform: Farmers, Workers, and the American State, 1877–1917* (Chicago: University of Chicago Press, 1999); Radford, *Rise of the Public Authority*; Stuart William Shulman, "The Origin of the Federal Farm Loan Act: Agenda Setting in the Progressive Era Print Press" (Ph.D. diss., University of Oregon, 1999); Daniel T. Rodgers, *Atlantic Crossings: Social Politics in a Progressive Age* (Cambridge, Mass.: Belknap Press, 1998).

4. George E. Putnam, "The Federal Farm Loan Act," *American Economic Review* 6, no. 4 (1916); Radford, *Rise of the Public Authority*, 48–50.

5. Thomas Bentley Mott, *Myron T. Herrick, Friend of France: An Autobiographical Biography* (Garden City, N.Y.: Doubleday, Doran & Company, 1929), ch. 6.

6. Myron T. Herrick, *Preliminary Report on Land and Agricultural Credit in Europe* (Washington, D.C.: Government Printing Office, 1912), 23.

7. Joseph Grant Knapp, *The Rise of American Cooperative Enterprise: 1620–1920* (Danville, Ill.: Interstate Printers & Publishers, 1969).

8. Wilbert M. Schneider, *The American Bankers Association, Its Past and Present* (Washington, D.C.: Public Affairs Press, 1956).

9. Radford, *Rise of the Public Authority*, 49; Paul Studenski and Herman Edward Krooss, *Financial History of the United States: Fiscal, Monetary, Banking, and Tariff, Including Financial*

Administration and State and Local Finance, 2nd ed. (Washington, D.C.: Beard Books, 2003), 261–62.

10. Within three years, $45.7 million in loans had been issued to farmers from commercial banks. See Studenski and Krooss, *Financial History*, 262.

11. Walter B. Palmer, "The Federal Farm Loan Act," *Publications of the American Statistical Association* 15, no. 115 (1916): 292–93.

12. David B. Danbom, *The Resisted Revolution: Urban America and the Industrialization of Agriculture, 1900–1930* (Ames: Iowa State University Press, 1979); idem, *Born in the Country: A History of Rural America*, Revisiting Rural America (Baltimore: Johns Hopkins University Press, 1995).

13. Radford, *Rise of the Public Authority*, 44–45.

14. Knapp, *Rise of American Cooperative Enterprise*; Rodgers, *Atlantic Crossings*.

15. For a useful introduction to the thin historical literature on the Country Life Commission, see Scott J. Peters and Paul A. Morgan, "The Country Life Commission: Reconsidering a Milestone in American Agricultural History," *Agricultural History* 78, no. 3 (2004).

16. Rodgers, *Atlantic Crossings*, 334.

17. United States Country Life Commission, *Report of the Country Life Commission* (Washington, D.C.: Government Printing Office, 1909), 48.

18. Christopher W. Shaw, "'No Place for Class Politics': The Country Life Commission and Immigration," *Agricultural History* 85, no. 4 (2011).

19. Country Life Commission, *Report*, 59.

20. Rodgers, *Atlantic Crossings*.

21. Shulman, "Origin."

22. In response to the Panic of 1907, the National Monetary Commission issued an extended report on the German *Landschaft* system that also stoked interest in mortgage credit. See Putnam, "Federal Farm Loan Act." See also S. Clayton Ellsworth, "Theodore Roosevelt's Country Life Commission," *Agricultural History* 34, no. 4 (1960); Shulman, "Origin," 69–75; L. H. Bailey, "Country Life Commission, 1908–09," *Agricultural History* 45, no. 3 (1971); Elisabeth Clemens, *The People's Lobby: Organizational Innovation and the Rise of Interest Group Politics in the United States, 1890–1925* (Chicago: University of Chicago Press, 1997).

23. Kassis tells this story of Lubin: As a baby, he was burned on his cheek from the wayward wick of a Sabbath candle. His mother, at the encouragement of a rabbi, took this as a sign of predestined greatness. See Annette Kassis, *Weinstock's: Sacramento's Finest Department Store* (Charleston, S.C.: History Press, 2012), 14. For more on Lubin, see Rodgers, *Atlantic Crossings*, 336–37; Council of the Food and Agricultural Organization of the United States, "David Lubin (1849–1919): An Appreciation," Library of the Food and Agricultural Organization of the United States (1969), http://www.fao.org/library/about-library/general-information/david-lubin-an-appreciation/en/.

24. Grace Larsen, "A Progressive in Agriculture: Harris Weinstock," *Agricultural History* 32, no. 3 (1958): 122; Knapp, *Rise of American Cooperative Enterprise*.

25. Rodgers, *Atlantic Crossings*, 336; Southern Commercial Congress, *American Commission for the Study of the Application of the Cooperative System to Agricultural Production, Distribution, and Finances in European Countries* (Washington, D.C.: Government Printing Office, 1913).

26. Rodgers, *Atlantic Crossings*; Southern Commercial Congress, *American Commission*, 125.

27. David Lubin, quoted in Knapp, *Rise of American Cooperative Enterprise*, 126.

28. Rodgers, *Atlantic Crossings*, 337.

29. Rodgers, *Atlantic Crossings*.

30. United States Commission and American Commission, *Agricultural Cooperation and Rural Credit in Europe* (Washington, D.C.: Government Printing Office, 1913).

31. "Italy Greets Americans," *New York Times*, May 11, 1913; "Study Farmers' Credits," *New York Times*, May 13,

1913; "Decides to Visit Spain," *New York Times*, May 15, 1913.

32. Knapp, *Rise of American Cooperative Enterprise*, 337.

33. Rodgers, *Atlantic Crossings*, 269.

34. Note that this was after a 1729 rural credits scheme in Prussia had failed. It was also 100 years before Bismarck set up Germany's pathbreaking welfare state programs. United States Commission and American Commission, *Agricultural Cooperation and Rural Credit*, 363, 381.

35. Ibid., 439.

36. Ibid., 21.

37. Ralph Metcalf and Clark G. Black, *Rural Credit, Cooperation and Agricultural Organization in Europe* (Olympia, Wash.: F. M. Lamborn, 1915), 382.

38. United States Commission and American Commission, *Agricultural Cooperation and Rural Credit*, 360.

39. Ibid., 365.

40. Ibid., 364, 384.

41. Dr. Brodnitz circa 1914, quoted in ibid., 355. Other quotes from ibid., 58.

42. Ibid., 10.

43. United States Commission to Investigate and Study in European Countries Cooperative Land-Mortgage Banks, Cooperative Rural Credit Unions, and Similar Organizations and Institutions Devoting Their Attention to the Promotion of Agriculture and the Betterment of Rural Conditions (hereafter U.S. Commission), *Agricultural Credit: Land Mortgage or Long Term Credit* (Washington, D.C.: Government Printing Office, 1914), 15, 19.

44. Ibid., 23.

45. Ibid., 22.

46. Ibid., 31.

47. Ibid., 663.

48. Ibid., 647.

49. Ibid., 230.

50. Henry Wolff, quoted in Metcalf and Black, *Rural Credit*, 226.

51. Ibid.

52. United States Commission and American Commission, *Agricultural Cooperation and Rural Credit*, part II, 8.

53. Ibid.

54. Stephen Skowronek, *Building a New American State: The Expansion of National Administrative Capacities, 1877–1920* (New York: Cambridge University Press, 1982). For more on the USDA, see Theda Skocpol and Kenneth Finegold, "State Capacity and Economic Intervention in the Early New Deal," *Political Science Quarterly* 97, no. 2 (1982).

55. Daniel P. Carpenter, *The Forging of Bureaucratic Autonomy: Reputations, Networks, and Policy Innovation in Executive Agencies, 1862–1928* (Princeton, N.J.: Princeton University Press, 2001).

56. Adam D. Sheingate, *The Rise of the Agricultural Welfare State: Institutions and Interest Group Power in the United States, France, and Japan*, Princeton Studies in American Politics (Princeton, N.J.: Princeton University Press, 2001).

57. Carpenter, *Forging of Bureaucratic Autonomy*.

58. "Bill for Farm Loan Bureau," *New York Times*, January 20, 1914; "Would Aid Farmers by Federal Loans," *New York Times*, January 5, 1913; Radford, *Rise of the Public Authority*, 53.

59. "Fight over Rural Credits," *New York Times*, January 31, 1914.

60. "Wilson for Farm Banks," *New York Times*, January 29, 1914; Radford, *Rise of the Public Authority*, 12; Arthur Stanley Link, *Wilson: The New Freedom* (Princeton, N.J.: Princeton University Press, 1956).

61. H. M. Hanson, *Proceedings of the Fourth Annual Convention of the Farm Mortgage Bankers Association of America Held in Minneapolis, Minnesota, September 11–13, 1917* (Chicago: Farm Mortgage Bankers Association of America, 1917), 17.

62. Ibid.

63. Wilson, quoted in Link, *Wilson*, 263. See also Radford, *Rise of the Public Authority*; "Rural Credit Plan Shelved," *New York Times*, May 13, 1914.

64. Radford, *Rise of the Public Authority*; "House Filibuster over Rural Credits," *New York Times*, May 5, 1914.

65. Reorganized in 1927 following some bank failures, the Federal Farm Loan Board was designed to ensure political balance. The Secretary of the Treasury would be on it, and the six other members would be appointed by the president, with the stipulation that no more than three would be from one party. See Link, *Wilson*, 115–16; Earl Sylvester Sparks, *History and Theory of Agricultural Credit in the United States* (New York: Thomas Y. Crowell Company, 1932); Studenski and Krooss, *Financial History*.

66. Limits on the size of loans were removed, however, in 1959, and larger farms have come to benefit from this system. See chapter 8.

67. Here I follow Jones and Grebler: while these land banks provided credit support, they were not technically serving as a secondary market for farm mortgages so much as they constituted a central mortgage bank. See Oliver Jones and Leo Grebler, *The Secondary Mortgage Market: Its Purpose, Performance, and Potential* (Los Angeles: Real Estate Research Program, Graduate School of Business Administration, University of California, Los Angeles, 1961), 108–9.

68. Federal Farm Loan Bureau, "New Mortgages for Old: A Story Illustrating the Practical Application of the Federal Farm Loan Act" (Washington, D.C.: Government Printing Office, 1916).

69. Robert J. Bulkley, "The Federal Farm-Loan Act," *Journal of Political Economy* 25, no. 2 (1917); Sparks, *History and Theory*, 116–17.

70. Sparks, *History and Theory*, 111.

71. Maureen O'Hara, "Tax-Exempt Financing: Some Lessons from History," *Journal of Money, Credit and Banking* 15, no. 4 (1983).

72. *Smith v. Kansas City Title & Trust Co.*, 255 U.S. 180.

73. Hanson, *Proceedings*.

74. Jones and Grebler, *Secondary Mortgage Market*.

75. For legal scholars, this case is largely interesting for the jurisdictional issues it raised: while the case hinged on the constitutionality of the tax exemption, Smith argued that the trust violated Missouri state law, so it was unclear if federal courts had jurisdiction. The Supreme Court ruled that the federal court did have jurisdiction, which left the tax exemption in place. "Mr. Smith Goes to Federal Court: Federal Question Jurisdiction over State Law Claims Post-Merrell Dow," *Harvard Law Review* 115, no. 8 (2002).

76. "Tests Farm Loan Bank Act," *New York Times*, October 15, 1920; O'Hara, "Tax-Exempt Financing."

77. Howard H. Preston, "The Federal Farm Loan Case," *Journal of Political Economy* 29, no. 6 (1921): 436.

78. Ibid., 441.

79. Ibid., table 6.

80. Willard O. Brown and Harold T. Lingard, *Interest Charges Payable on Farm Indebtedness in the United States, 1910–40*, ed. United States Department of Agriculture (Washington, D.C.: n.p., 1942), https://catalog.hathitrust.org/Record/009077916.

81. Victor W. Bennett, "Joint Stock Land Banks in Retrospect," *Journal of Farm Economics* 20, no. 4 (1938); Studenski and Krooss, *Financial History*.

82. According to Jones and Grebler, this was in part because the land banks' investors were reassured by the government's support and in part because the joint-stock banks suffered from more fraud and less investor confidence. According to O'Hara, the joint-stock banks were crowded out by the stronger land banks and doomed by regulatory limits. See Jones and Grebler, *Secondary Mortgage Market*, 110–11; O'Hara, "Tax-Exempt Financing."

83. Frank Dobbin, *Forging Industrial Policy: The United States, Britain, and France in the Railway Age* (New York: Cambridge University Press, 1994), 92.

84. Andrew Shonfield, *Modern Capitalism: The Changing Balance of Public and Private Power* (New York: Oxford University Press, 1965); Dobbin, *Forging Industrial Policy*.

85. Ibid.

86. N. Leon Lindberg and John L. Campbell, "The State and the Organization of Economic Activity," in *Governance of the American Economy*, ed. John L. Campbell, J. Rodgers Hollingsworth, and N. Leon Lindberg (New York: Cambridge University Press, 1991), 57.

87. George E. Putnam, "The Federal Farm Loan System," *American Economic Review* 9, no. 1 (1919).

88. Radford, *Rise of the Public Authority*.

89. Christopher Howard, *The Hidden Welfare State: Tax Expenditures and Social Policy in the United States* (Princeton, N.J.: Princeton University Press, 1997).

90. Damon Mayrl and Sarah Quinn, "Beyond the Hidden American State: Classification Struggles and the Politics of Recognition" (Universidad Carlos III de Madrid and the University of Washington, 2015).

91. Eviatar Zerubavel, *Social Mindscapes: An Invitation to Cognitive Sociology* (Cambridge, Mass.: Harvard University Press, 1997); Mary Douglas, *Purity and Danger: An Analysis of Concepts of Pollution and Taboo*, Routledge Classics (New York: Routledge, 2005); Émile Durkheim and Marcel Mauss, *Primitive Classification* (Chicago: University of Chicago Press, 1963).

92. Greta Hsu, "Jacks of All Trades and Masters of None: Audiences' Reactions to Spanning Genres in Feature Film Production," *Administrative Science Quarterly* 51, no. 3 (2006); Ezra W. Zuckerman, "The Categorical Imperative: Securities Analysts and the Illegitimacy Discount," *American Journal of Sociology* 104, no. 5 (1999); Pierre Bourdieu, *Distinction: A Social Critique of the Judgement of Taste* (Cambridge, Mass.: Harvard University Press, 1984).

93. Elizabeth G. Pontikes, "Two Sides of the Same Coin: How Ambiguous Classification Affects Multiple Audiences' Evaluations," *Administrative Science Quarterly* 57, no. 1 (2012); Michael T. Hannan, "Partiality of Memberships in Categories and Audiences," *Annual Review of Sociology* 36 (2010); Greta Hsu, Özgecan Koçak, and Michael T. Hannan, "Multiple Category Memberships in Markets: An Integrative Theory and Two Empirical Tests," *American Sociological Review* 74, no. 1 (2009); Martin Ruef and Kelly Patterson, "Credit and Classification: The Impact of Industry Boundaries in Nineteenth-Century America," *Administrative Science Quarterly* 54, no. 3 (2009).

94. Russell J. Funk and Daniel Hirschman, "Derivatives and Deregulation: Financial Innovation and the Demise of Glass–Steagall," *Administrative Science Quarterly* 59, no. 4 (2014).

95. Wendy Griswold, "The Fabrication of Meaning: Literary Interpretation in the United States, Great Britain, and the West Indies," *American Journal of Sociology* 92, no. 5 (1987).

96. John F. Padgett and Christopher K. Ansell, "Robust Action and the Rise of the Medici, 1400–1434," *American Journal of Sociology* 98, no. 6 (1993).

97. Studenski and Krooss, *Financial History*, 337–38.

98. Jones and Grebler, *Secondary Mortgage Market*, 111.

99. Randal R. Rucker and E. C. Pasour, Jr., "The Growth of U.S. Farm Programs," in *Government and the American Economy: A New History*, ed. Price Van Meter Fishback (Chicago: University of Chicago Press, 2007); Sheingate, *Rise of the Agricultural Welfare State*, 16.

100. For a more extensive summary of these events, see Theodore Saloutos, *The American Farmer and the New Deal* (Ames: Iowa State University Press, 1982), ch. 1; Rucker and Pasour, "Growth of U.S. Farm Programs," 460–61; Sheingate, *Rise of the Agricultural Welfare State*.

Chapter 5: From a Nation of Farmers to a Nation of Homeowners

1. For more on urban and rural property values, see Richard Sutch, "Before the American Dream: The Early Years of Urban Home Ownership, the United States, 1850–1940" (Departments of Economics and History, University of California, Riverside, 2011).

2. Jackson explains that with the exception of a few real estate syndicates in urban areas, it was the small developers who bought land, commissioned civil engineers to design streets and lots, and then constructed roads or lobbied the local municipality to do so. The developer would often keep a lot for his own use and then sell off the rest of the land. It was the land buyers who then built houses for their use or resale. Sam Bass Warner, in his study of Boston, found that speculators mortgaged their land to make improvements like roads. On changing homeownership rates, see Kenneth T. Jackson, *Crabgrass Frontier: The Suburbanization of the United States* (New York: Oxford University Press, 1985), 46, 129–35; Kenneth A. Snowden, "Construction, Housing, and Mortgages," *Historical Statistics of the United States, Earliest Times to the Present: Millenial Edition* 4 (2006). On the rise of urban construction, see Gail Radford, *Modern Housing for America: Policy Struggles in the New Deal Era*, Historical Studies of Urban America (Chicago: University of Chicago Press, 1996), 7. On mortgage markets and the settlement of Boston suburbs, see Sam Bass Warner, Jr., *Streetcar Suburbs: The Process of Growth in Boston, 1870–1900*, Publications of the Joint Center for Urban Studies (Cambridge, Mass: Harvard University Press, 1978), 117–52.

3. Paul Pierson, *Politics in Time: History, Institutions, and Social Analysis* (Princeton, N.J.: Princeton University Press, 2004).

4. Quoted in Michael J. Sandel, *Democracy's Discontent: America in Search of a Public Philosophy* (Cambridge, Mass.: Belknap Press of Harvard University Press, 1996), 144.

5. The eighteenth-century U.S. political economy had as its central goal the creation of a thriving nation through the cultivation of *civic virtues*. Like any grand tradition, this one contained multiple strands. In the Jacksonian era, some supporters of manufacturing made the case that paid labor was consistent with the republican ideal as long as men had the opportunity to one day become economically independent; others turned to the Millsian liberal tradition to argue that true freedom was founded not in economic independence but in the ability to make choices, such as the choice to enter into a labor contract. See ibid.

6. Ibid., 124–67.

7. Ibid.

8. Ananya Roy, "Paradigms of Propertied Citizenship: Transnational Techniques of Analysis," *Urban Affairs Review* 38 (2003): 464

9. Julia C. Ott, *When Wall Street Met Main Street: The Quest for an Investors' Democracy* (Cambridge, Mass.: Harvard University Press, 2011), 10.

10. Margaret Marsh, "From Separation to Togetherness: The Social Construction of Domestic Space in American Suburbs, 1840–1915," *Journal of American History* 76, no. 2 (1989).

11. Seymour Dexter, *A Treatise on Co-operative Savings and Loan Associations* (1889), cited in Heather A. Haveman and Hayagreeva Rao, "Structuring a Theory of Moral Sentiments:

Institutional and Organizational Coevolution in the Early Thrift Industry," *American Journal of Sociology* 102, no. 6 (1997).

12. Jackson, *Crabgrass Frontier*; Gwendolyn Wright, *Building the Dream: A Social History of Housing in America* (Cambridge, Mass.: MIT Press, 1983), 89.

13. John F. Bauman, Roger Biles, and Kristin M. Szylvian, *From Tenements to the Taylor Homes: In Search of an Urban Housing Policy in Twentieth-Century America* (University Park: Pennsylvania State University Press, 2000), 6–11; Marsh, "From Separation to Togetherness."

14. Dolores Hayden, *Redesigning the American Dream: The Future of Housing, Work, and Family Life* (New York: W. W. Norton, 1984), 32–33.

15. Ibid., 32.

16. John A. Fitch, *The Steelworkers* (New York: Russell Sage Foundations, 1910), quoted in Michael R. Haines, "Homeownership and Housing Demand in Late Nineteenth Century America: Evidence from State Labor Reports" (Department of Economics, Colgate University, 2011), 2.

17. David Lawrence Mason, *From Buildings and Loans to Bail-Outs: A History of the American Savings and Loan Industry, 1831–1995* (New York: Cambridge University Press, 2004), 27–28.

18. Daniel D. Luria, "Wealth, Capital, and Power: The Social Meaning of Home Ownership," *Journal of Interdisciplinary History* 7, no. 2 (1976).

19. Becky M. Nicolaides, *My Blue Heaven: Life and Politics in the Working-Class Suburbs of Los Angeles, 1920–1965* (Chicago: University of Chicago Press, 2002).

20. Andrew Wiese, *Places of Their Own: African American Suburbanization in the Twentieth Century* (Chicago: University of Chicago Press, 2004), 5.

21. Wright, *Building the Dream*, 89–100.

22. Jackson, *Crabgrass Frontier*, 108.

23. Wright, *Building the Dream*, 41.

24. Wright, *Building the Dream*, 22.

25. Hayden, *Redesigning the American Dream*, 81.

26. Quoted in Jackson, *Crabgrass Frontier*, 50.

27. Richard Sutch, "Immigrant Homeownership, Economic Assimilation, and Return Migration During the Age of Mass Migration to the United States" (Departments of Economics and History, University of California, Riverside, 2013); idem, "Before the American Dream"; Haines, "Homeownership and Housing Demand."

28. Sutch, "Before the American Dream."

29. Based on this, Sutch concludes that there was a massive transition in how Americans made choices about finances and families over their life cycle during this time. Starting in the 1830s, families stopped counting on grown children to take care of them at the end of life and instead relied on the resources invested in their homes. Ibid.

30. Kenneth Snowden, "Table Dc903–928: Debt on Nonfarm Structures, by Type of Debt, Property, and Holder: 1896–1952," *Historical Statistics of the United States, Earliest Times to Present*, Millennial ed. (2006), http://dx.doi.org/10.1017/ISBN-9780511132971.Dc903–1288.

31. One consequence of this was the increased construction of multifamily buildings, which made up one-third of new units built between 1900 and 1907. Radford, *Modern Housing for America*.

32. Nicolaides, *My Blue Heaven*, 20, 29.

33. Warner, *Streetcar Suburbs*, 118.

34. Snowden, "Table Dc903–928."

35. Idem, "Building and Loan Associations in the U.S., 1880–1893: The Origins of Localization in the Residential Mortgage Market," *Research in Economics* 51, no. 3 (1997).

36. Raymond J. Saulnier, *Urban Mortgage Lending by Life Insurance Companies* (New York: National Bureau of Economic Research, 1950), 11.

37. Haveman and Rao, "Structuring a Theory," 1608; Henry Morton Bodfish, *History of Building and Loan in the United States* (Chicago: United States Building and Loan League, 1931), 14, 25, 29; William Howard Steiner, "Mutual Savings Banks," *Law and Contemporary Problems* 17, no. 1 (1952).

38. Haveman and Rao, "Structuring a Theory," 1609; Miles Lanier Colean, *The Impact of Government on Real Estate Finance in the United States* (New York: National Bureau of Economic Research, 1950), 60–61; Bodfish, *History of Building and Loan*, 5–14; Leon T. Kendall, *The Savings and Loan Business: Its Purposes, Functions, and Economic Justification*, Commission on Money and Credit (Englewood Cliffs, N.J.: Prentice-Hall, 1962), 4.

39. Leo Grebler, Louis Winnick, and David Mordecai Blank, *Capital Formation in Residential Real Estate: Trends and Prospects*, Studies in Capital Formation and Financing (Princeton, N.J.: Princeton University Press, 1956), 195–98.

40. Haveman and Rao, "Structuring a Theory"; Kendall, *Savings and Loan Business*, 32–72; Bodfish, *History of Building and Loan*.

41. Haveman and Rao, "Structuring a Theory," 1608; Bodfish, *History of Building and Loan*, 14, 25, 29.

42. Snowden, "Building and Loan Associations," 228.

43. Bodfish, *History of Building and Loan*, 136; Haveman and Rao, "Structuring a Theory," 1609.

44. Mason, *From Buildings and Loans*.

45. Kenneth A. Snowden, "Mortgage Lending and American Urbanization, 1880–1890," *Journal of Economic History* 48, no. 2 (1988).

46. Ibid.

47. W.E.B. Du Bois, *The Philadelphia Negro: A Social Study* (Philadelphia: University of Pennsylvania Press, 1996), 78. For more on urban black real estate investment, see Juliet E. K. Walker, *The History of Black Business in America: Capitalism, Race, Entrepreneurship*, Twayne's Evolution of Modern Business Series (New York: MacMillan Library Reference USA, 1998), 96–99, 171–72, 196–200.

48. Snowden, "Building and Loan Associations," 226; idem, "Mortgage Lending"; Bodfish, *History of Building and Loan*.

49. On women and thrifts, see Mason, *From Buildings and Loans*, 29–32.

50. Bodfish, *History of Building and Loan*, 64.

51. Mason, *From Buildings and Loans*, 29–30.

52. Bodfish, *History of Building and Loan*, 362.

53. Mason, *From Buildings and Loans*, 62.

54. "Women's Federal Savings Bank," in *The Encyclopedia of Cleveland History* (1987), http://ech.case.edu/cgi/article.pl?id=WFSB.

55. Mason, *From Buildings and Loans*, 28–29.

56. Ibid.

57. Bodfish, *History of Building and Loan*, 136; Kendall, *Savings and Loan Business*, 9.

58. Note that the trade organization was originally named the National Association of Real Estate Exchanges but changed its name in 1916. See Mason, *From Buildings and Loans*.

59. Other reformers, professionals, and scholars organized to influence housing policy. In 1909, the National Conference of City Planners was formed, and by the 1920s it had become a locus of organizing among planners and housing economists. That same year Lawrence Veiller, a leader of the City Planning movement, formed the progressive National Housing Association. See Alexander Von Hoffman, "Enter the Housing Industry, Stage Right: A Working Paper on the History of Housing Policy" (Joint Center for Housing Studies, Harvard University, 2008); Kevin Fox Gotham, "Racialization and the State: The Housing Act of 1934 and the Creation of the Federal Housing Administration," *Sociological Perspectives* 43, no. 2 (2000).

60. David M. Freund, *Colored Property: State Policy and White Racial Politics in Suburban America* (Chicago: University of Chicago Press, 2007).

61. Bodfish, *History of Building and Loan*, 16.

62. Haveman and Rao, "Structuring a Theory."

63. Haveman and Rao, "Structuring a Theory," 47.

64. Bodfish, *History of Building and Loan*.

65. For a review of the structures of the thrifts, see Mason, *From Buildings and Loans*; Snowden, "Building and Loan Associations"; Bodfish, *History of Building and Loan*.

66. Snowden, "Building and Loan Associations," 18–21.

67. Heather A. Haveman, Hayagreeva Rao, and Srikanth Paruchuri, "The Winds of Change: The Progressive Movement and the Bureaucratization of Thrift," *American Sociological Review* 72, no. 1 (2007); Haveman and Rao, "Structuring a Theory."

68. Snowden, "Building and Loan Associations."

69. Mason, *From Buildings and Loans*; Snowden, "Building and Loan Associations."

70. Snowden, "Building and Loan Associations," 219.

71. Haveman and Rao, "Structuring a Theory," 1639; Bodfish, *History of Building and Loan*, 100.

72. Bodfish, *History of Building and Loan*, 107.

73. Ibid.

74. Snowden, "Building and Loan Associations."

75. Haveman, Rao, and Paruchuri, "Winds of Change," 37.

76. Mason, *From Buildings and Loans*.

77. See, for example, Wood, *Recent Trends*.

78. Charles Tilly, *Coercion, Capital, and European States, A.D. 990–1990*, Studies in Social Discontinuity (Oxford: Blackwell, 1990).

79. Gerald Berk, *Alternative Tracks: The Constitution of American Industrial Order, 1865–1917* (Baltimore: Johns Hopkins University Press, 1994); Richard Franklin Bensel, *Yankee Leviathan: The Origins of Central State Authority in America, 1859–1877* (New York: Cambridge University Press, 1990).

80. Jerry W. Markham, "World War I," in *A Financial History of the United States*, vol. 2: *From J. P. Morgan to the Institutional Investor (1900–1970)* (Armonk, N.Y.: M. E. Sharpe, 2002), 69–79, http://link.galegroup.com/apps/doc/CX3460100064/GVRL?u=wash_main&sid=GVRL&xid=aeef3279; William Edward Leuchtenburg, *The Perils of Prosperity, 1914–1932*, 2nd ed. (Chicago: University of Chicago Press, 1993), 35, 255.

81. Mason, *From Buildings and Loans*, 15.

82. Ibid., 52.

83. Radford, *Modern Housing for America*, 16.

84. William J. Williams, "Accommodating American Shipyard Workers, 1917–1918: The Pacific Coast and the Federal Government's First Public Housing and Transit Programs," *Pacific Northwest Quarterly* 84, no. 2 (1993): 15.

85. Karen Dunn-Haley, "The House That Uncle Sam Built: The Political Culture of Federal Housing Policy, 1919–1932" (Ph.D. diss., Stanford University, 1995), 15.

86. Radford, *Modern Housing for America*, 62; Roy Lubove, "Homes and 'a Few Well Placed Fruit Trees': An Object Lesson in Federal Housing," *Social Research* 27, no. 4 (1960); Eric J. Karolak, "'No Idea of Doing Anything Wonderful': The Labor-Crisis Origins of the National Housing Policy and the Reconstruction of the Working-Class Community, 1917–1919," in *From Tenements to the Taylor Homes: In Search of an Urban Housing Policy in Twentieth-Century America*, ed. John F. Bauman, Roger Biles, and Kristin M. Szylvian (University Park: Pennsylvania State University Press, 2000).

87. Lubove, "Homes."

88. Paul C. Luken and Suzanne Vaughan, "'. . . Be a Genuine Homemaker in Your Own Home': Gender and Familial Relations in State Housing Practices, 1917–1922," *Social Forces* 83, no. 4 (2005).

89. Quote from Edward M. Hurley in memorandum to the Senate Committee on Commerce in Emergency Fleet Corporation U.S. Shipping Board, "Hearings on S. 170, Directing the Committee on Commerce to Investigate All Matters Connected with the Building of Merchant Vessels Under the Direction of the United States Shipping Board Emergency Fleet Corporation, and Report Its Findings to the Senate, Together with Its Recommendations Thereon," in *Committee on Commerce* (Washington, D.C.: Government Printing Office, 1918), 362.

90. Williams, "Accommodating American Shipyard Workers."

91. Ibid.; Luken and Vaughan, "'. . . Be a Genuine Homemaker'"; Janet Hutchison, "Building for Babbitt: The State and the Suburban Home Ideal," *Journal of Policy History* 9 (1997); Christian Topalov, "Scientific Urban Planning and the Ordering of Daily Life: The First 'War Housing' Experiment in the United States, 1917–1919," *Journal of Urban History* 17, no. 1 (1990): 16.

92. Wood, *Recent Trends*, 66–67.

93. Quoted in Topalov, "Scientific Urban Planning," 470.

94. See Wood, *Recent Trends*, 67.

95. Ibid.

96. Karolak, "'No Idea of Doing.'"

97. For more on these mortgages, see Lubove, "Homes," 68.

98. Williams, "Accommodating American Shipyard Workers." Congress later authorized another $20 million in loans to transportation companies to help get the workers to the shipyards.

99. Wood, *Recent Trends*, 71.

100. John L. Tierney, "War Housing: The Emergency Fleet Corporation Experience," *Journal of Land & Public Utility Economics* 17, no. 2 (1941): 153; Wood, *Recent Trends*, 17.

101. Radford, *Modern Housing for America*, 307.

102. Steven Andrachek, "Housing in the United States: 1890–1929," in *The Story of Housing*, ed. Gertrude Sipperly Fish and Federal National Mortgage Association (New York: Macmillan, 1979), 172; Tierney, "War Housing," 69.

103. Radford, *Modern Housing for America*.

104. Topalov, "Scientific Urban Planning."

105. Karolak, "'No Idea of Doing,'" 69–70.

106. Topalov, "Scientific Urban Planning." See also Dunn-Haley, "House That Uncle Sam Built."

107. Lubove, "Homes"; Wood, *Recent Trends*.

108. Andrachek, "Housing in the United States," 172; Wood, *Recent Trends*, 77.

109. Williams, "Accommodating American Shipyard Workers," 71–88.

110. Quoted in Wood, *Recent Trends*, 305.

111. For a good example of this, see Frederick Law Olmsted, "Lessons from Housing Developments of the United States Housing Corporation," *Monthly Labor Review* 8, no. 5 (1919). For a discussion, see Wood, *Recent Trends*, 79.

112. Wood, *Recent Trends*, 74.

113. Tierney, "War Housing," 486.

114. Karolak, "'No Idea of Doing.'"

115. Ibid.

116. There were some victories on the state level, including a land bank in New York created under Governor Alfred Smith.

117. Williams, "Accommodating American Shipyard Workers."

118. Karolak, "'No Idea of Doing,'" 63; Lubove, "Homes," 60–80.

119. Radford, *Modern Housing for America*.

120. Ellis W. Hawley, "Herbert Hoover, the Commerce Secretariat, and the Vision of an 'Associative State,' 1921–1928," *Journal of American History* 61, no. 1 (1974).

121. Elizabeth Lebas, Susanna Magri, and Christian Topalov, "Reconstruction and Popular Housing After the First World War: A Comparative Study of France, Great Britain, Italy and the United States," *Planning Perspectives* 6, no. 3 (1991).

122. Hawley, "Herbert Hoover."

123. Wood, *Recent Trends*, 78.

124. Hutchison, "Building for Babbitt," 196.

125. Freund, *Colored Property*, 74; Wright, *Building the Dream*, 196; Hawley, "Herbert Hoover," 125; Luken and Vaughan, "'. . . Be a Genuine Homemaker.'"

126. Hutchison, "Building for Babbitt," 191; Dunn-Haley, "House That Uncle Sam Built."

127. Hawley, "Herbert Hoover," 139.

128. Hutchison, "Building for Babbitt," 202; Louis Hyman, *Debtor Nation: The History of America in Red Ink* (Princeton, N.J.: Princeton University Press, 2011).

Chapter 6: Mortgage Bonds for the Small Investor

1. Quoted in Rosemarie Haag Bletter, "The Invention of the Skyscraper: Notes on Its Diverse Histories," *Assemblage*, no. 2 (1987): 116.

2. William N. Goetzmann and Frank Newman, "Securitization in the 1920's," National Bureau of Economic Research Working Paper Series (2009), http://www.nber.org/papers/w15650.pdf.

3. Kenneth A. Snowden, "The Anatomy of a Residential Mortgage Crisis: A Look Back to the 1930s" (Bryan School of Business and Economics, University of North Carolina, Greensboro, 2009).

4. Goetzmann and Newman, "Securitization in the 1920's," 4.

5. Alan Rabinowitz, *The Real Estate Gamble: Lessons from 50 Years of Boom and Bust* (New York: AMACOM, 1980), 33; J. Carson Webster, "The Skyscraper: Logical and Historical Considerations," *Journal of the Society of Architectural Historians* 18, no. 4 (1959); Bletter, "Invention of the Skyscraper."

6. For Wolner, the new generation of skyscrapers was not so much an effort to jettison an agricultural past as it was an effort to translate that past's most valued attributes—tenacity, hard work, upward mobility, and the "myth of the 'self-made' man"—into a new urban landscape. See Edward W. Wolner, "The City-within-a-City and Skyscraper Patronage in the 1920's," *Journal of Architectural Education* 42, no. 2 (1989).

7. Snowden, "Anatomy of a Residential Mortgage Crisis."

8. Robert Alexander Halliburton, *The Real Estate Bond House: A Study of Some of Its Financial Practices* (Franklin, Ind.: Edwards Brothers, 1939), 24–26.

9. Julia C. Ott, *When Wall Street Met Main Street: The Quest for an Investors' Democracy* (Cambridge, Mass.: Harvard University Press, 2011).

10. House Select Committee to Investigate Real Estate Bondholders' Reorganizations, "Investigation of Real Estate Bondholders' Reorganizations," June 19, 1936, 1.

11. Halliburton, *Real Estate Bond House*, 17–19; Snowden, "Anatomy of a Residential Mortgage Crisis," 10. (This was a First Mortgage Fee Corporation Bond.)

12. Halliburton, *Real Estate Bond House*, 3; Rabinowitz, *Real Estate Gamble*, 43.

13. George William Alger, *Report to His Excellency Herbert H. Lehman, Governor of the State of New York* (New York: State of New York, 1934), 109.

14. Kenneth Snowden, "Table Dc903–928: Debt on Nonfarm Structures, by Type of Debt, Property, and Holder: 1896–1952," *Historical Statistics of the United States, Earliest Times to*

Present, Millennial ed. (2006), http://dx.doi.org/10.1017/ISBN-9780511132971.Dc903-1288. But see Rabinowitz for alternate estimates: the Securities and Exchange Commission in 1936 estimated that the market size had been slightly over $5 billion in 1931, and the Investment Bankers Association estimated that bonds had represented 17.2 percent of national mortgage debt the same year; Rabinowitz, *Real Estate Gamble*, 43.

15. Leo Grebler, Louis Winnick, and David Mordecai Blank, *Capital Formation in Residential Real Estate: Trends and Prospects*, Studies in Capital Formation and Financing (Princeton, N.J.: Princeton University Press, 1956), 446; cited in Snowden, "Anatomy of a Residential Mortgage Crisis," 9.

16. The other cities were Detroit, Los Angeles, Philadelphia, San Francisco, Washington, D.C., Boston, and Cleveland. Due to the limitations of available data, Johnson looked at long-term securities (that is, those with maturities of five years or longer) and large issues ($1 million or larger), which he estimated to represent 70 percent of the national mortgage securities market. Focusing on larger issues with longer denominations, he estimated that between 1919 and 1934, bond sales were a $4 billion market. See Ernest A. Johnson, "The Record of Long-Term Real Estate Securities," *Journal of Land & Public Utility Economics* 12, no. 1 (1936): 44.

17. Goetzmann and Newman, "Securitization in the 1920's."

18. We know this from the aftermath: more than a dozen states passed laws specifically in response to the insolvency of mortgage guarantee companies by 1934, and a later congressional investigation identified 29 states where defaulted bonds were being managed by New York– and Chicago-based protective committees; this was very likely a lowball estimate, for the investigators had focused on states east of the Mississippi. "Present Problems in New York Guaranteed Mortgages," *Columbia Law Review* 34, no. 4 (1934).

19. "S. W. Straus & Co.," *Bankers Magazine* 104, no. 1 (January 1922).

20. Goetzmann and Newman, "Securitization in the 1920's," 6.

21. Ibid., 16.

22. Alger, *Report to His Excellency*, 8.

23. Ibid.

24. Glenn B. Canner and Wayne Passmore, "Private Mortgage Insurance," *Federal Reserve Bulletin* 80, no. 10 (1994): 884; Alger, *Report to His Excellency*.

25. "Summary of Moreland Commisioner Alger's Report on Mortgage Investigation," *New York Times*, October 8, 1934, 10–11.

26. Lawrence Chamberlain and George William Edwards, *The Principles of Bond Investment*, rev. and enlarged ed. (New York: Holt, 1927), 305–25.

27. Chamberlain and Edwards also refer to these instruments as "Real Estate First Collateral Trust Certificates" and compare them to English Investment Trust certificates. See ibid.

28. Alger, *Report to His Excellency*, 11.

29. Participation certificates at this time were more commonly used to finance railway equipment. See Hastings Lyon, *Corporations and Their Financing* (Boston: D. C. Heath and Company, 1938), 276.

30. Chamberlain and Edwards, *Principles of Bond Investment*, 455.

31. Halliburton, *Real Estate Bond House*.

32. Alger, *Report to His Excellency*, 11–12.

33. Ibid., 147.

34. Halliburton, *Real Estate Bond House*, 4–6; Alger, *Report to His Excellency*, 103.

35. Excerpted in Alger, *Report to His Excellency*, 103–4.

36. U.S. House of Representatives, "Investigation of Real Estate Bondholders' Reorganizations" (Washington, D.C.: Government Printing Office, 1934), 23.

37. "New York Guaranteed Mortgages: The Second Phase," *Columbia Law Review* 35, no. 6 (1935).

38. Herbert S. Swan, "Land Values and City Growth," *Journal of Land & Public Utility Economics* 10, no. 2 (1934): 193.

39. U.S. House of Representatives, "Investigation of Real Estate Bondholders' Reorganizations," 1.

40. Ott, *When Wall Street Met Main Street*, 55–57.

41. Ibid., 54.

42. Ibid., 1.

43. Ibid., 171.

44. "Advice to Investors, Bond Stocks and Mortgages," *McClure's*, February 1921, 54.

45. Alger, *Report to His Excellency*, 104–5.

46. Halliburton, *Real Estate Bond House*, 24–25. Senate Committee on the District of Columbia, ed., "Real Estate, Mortgage, and Security Situation in the District of Columbia, to Accompany Senate Resolution 58" (Washington, D.C.: Government Printing Office, 1931).

47. Mary Riis, "Women Who Invest," *Woman's Home Companion*, October 1922. However, the article did warn that "investors should be sure that they are not based on too high values. When buildings and real estate are high, as at present, their mortgages may be based on temporary high values."

48. G. L. Miller and Co., "Changeless Security and a 7% Yield," *World's Work Advertiser*, circa 1923.

49. Alger, *Report to His Excellency*, 105.

50. Halsey, Stuart, & Co., Inc., "Bonds to Fit the Investor" (1930), print advertisement (author's personal collection).

51. See, for example, Alger, *Report to His Excellency*, 12.

52. G. L. Miller and Co., "Changeless Security."

53. Halliburton, *Real Estate Bond House*, 8.

54. Unnamed letter writer quoted in U.S. House of Representatives, "Investigation of Real Estate Bondholders' Reorganizations," 53.

55. Ibid.

56. James Grant, *Money of the Mind: Borrowing and Lending in America from the Civil War to Michael Milken* (New York: Farrar Straus Giroux, 1992); Halliburton, *Real Estate Bond House*, 24–25.

57. Goetzmann and Newman, "Securitization in the 1920's," 17–18.

58. Eugene White, "Lessons from the Great American Real Estate Boom and Bust of the 1920s," National Bureau of Economic Research Working Paper Series (2009), http://www.nber.org/papers/w15573.pdf.

59. "Realty Bond Houses Adopt New Rules," *New York Times*, February 7, 1927.

60. U.S. House of Representatives, "Investigation of Real Estate Bondholders' Reorganizations", 30.

61. Rabinowitz, *Real Estate Gamble*, 27.

62. Snowden, "Anatomy of a Residential Mortgage Crisis," 11–12.

63. Goetzmann and Newman, "Securitization in the 1920's," 17–18.

64. Ibid.

65. William W. Bartlett and Françoise Dearden, *Mortgage-Backed Securities: Products, Analysis, and Trading* (New York: New York Institute of Finance, 1989), 5; Richard K. Green and Susan M. Wachter, "The American Mortgage in Historical and International Context," *Journal of Economic Perspectives* 19, no. 4 (2005), 94–95.

66. Kevin Fox Gotham, "Racialization and the State: The Housing Act of 1934 and the Creation of the Federal Housing Administration," *Sociological Perspectives* 43, no. 2 (2000): 296–97.

67. Bartlett and Dearden, *Mortgage-Backed Securities*, 5; Green and Wachter, "American Mortgage," 94–95.

68. Alger, *Report to His Excellency*, 19. See also Thomas Hertzog, "History of Mortgage Finance with an Emphasis on Mortgage Insurance" (2009), https://www.soa.org/library /monographs/finance/housing-wealth/2009/september/mono-2009-mfi09-herzog-history -comments.pdf.

69. Halliburton, *Real Estate Bond House*, 33; Hertzog, "History of Mortgage Finance," 16.

70. Alger, *Report to His Excellency*, 17–23.

71. Snowden, "Anatomy of a Residential Mortgage Crisis," 14–15.

72. See, for example, U.S. House of Representatives, "Investigation of Real Estate Bond-holders' Reorganizations," 105.

73. Ibid., 48.

74. Halliburton, *Real Estate Bond House*, 7, 35; Alger, *Report to His Excellency*, 12.

75. Alger, *Report to His Excellency*, 110.

76. U.S. House of Representatives, "Investigation of Real Estate Bondholders' Reorganizations," 44.

77. Halliburton, *Real Estate Bond House*, 7, 47.

78. Ibid., 33.

79. Ibid., 44.

80. U.S. House of Representatives, "Investigation of Real Estate Bondholders' Reorganizations," 56.

81. Alger, *Report to His Excellency*, 17–18.

82. Halliburton, *Real Estate Bond House*, 7.

83. Alger, *Report to His Excellency*, 109.

84. Ibid., 108.

85. Halliburton, *Real Estate Bond House*, ch. 9.

86. Carrie Maude Jones, "Apartment House Bonds: Some Plans for Reorganizing Defaulted Issues," *Journal of Land & Public Utility Economics* 9, no. 4 (1933).

87. House Select Committee to Investigate Real Estate Bondholders' Reorganizations, *Investigation of Real Estate Bondholders' Reorganizations*, January 29, 1935.

88. Ibid., 66.

89. Ibid.

90. Both quotes are excerpts from unnamed letter writers in ibid., 2.

91. The Martin Act was broadly written antifraud legislation that gave the attorney general power to "regulate, investigate and take action against securities fraud, including seeking monetary remedies." See "New York State's Martin Act: A Primer," *Financial Services* (2004), https:// www.dechert.com/files/Publication/a4def5dd-77bf-48ae-bead-491bfcb9142c/Presentation /PublicationAttachment/dbeb2852-2e00-49d6-971f-4c2db9674658/FS_2004-04.pdf.

92. "Asks More Reform in Realty Bonds," *New York Times*, February 8, 1927. Despite press claims that these were "drastic reforms," the recommendations did not cause substantial improvements in the behavior of real estate bond companies. Even at the time, a *New York Times* article noted that leaders of some insurance and bond corporations thought the reforms should go further by requiring an independent trustee for all bond issues, not just those in which bond houses had a material interest. "Urge Trustee Plan for Realty Bonds," *New York Times*, February 9, 1927.

93. "Lehman Orders Inquiry," *Wall Street Journal*, December 16, 1933.

94. John E. Burton, "Guaranteed Certificated Mortgages in New York," *Journal of Land & Public Utility Economics* 12, no. 2 (1936).

95. This was preceded by an investigation of the $100 million mortgage market by the Senate Subcommittee on Insurance and Banks of the Committee of the District of Columbia: see Senate Subcommittee on Insurance and Banks, "Real Estate, Mortgage, and Security Situation."

96. The Securities Act did not cover intra-state transactions, however, so in-state mortgage bonds could theoretically still be issued without registration.

97. The Securities Exchange Act of 1934 created the SEC and initiated the SEC investigation into protective committees. The SEC was given broad oversight of securities and security-trading organizations and was empowered to take disciplinary action. The act also requires public reporting for any company with more than $10 million in assets and 500 or more owners.

98. David A. Skeel, *Debt's Dominion: A History of Bankruptcy Law in America* (Princeton, N.J.: Princeton University Press, 2014).

99. Rabinowitz, *Real Estate Gamble.*

100. "Ban on Guaranteed Mortgage Companies Recommended by Legislative Committee," *New York Times*, March 21, 1937.

101. Senate Subcommittee on Insurance and Banks, "Real Estate, Mortgage, and Security Situation."

102. Skeel, *Debt's Dominion.*

103. Ibid., 117. For example, after New York's Shackno and Mortgage Commission Acts allowed government agencies to take over and resolve failed mortgage insurers, Samuel Untermyer reacted angrily to the idea that the government could force bondholders to submit to its agencies' plans, saying, "The wanton arrogant destruction of individual property rights has no precedent in history. It is virtual confiscation." "Untermyer Hits Mortgage Bill," *New York Times*, April 17, 1934.

104. Grant, *Money of the Mind*, 167.

105. David Saperstein, "Real Estate Bond Issues of the Future," address delivered to the National Mortgage Board of the National Association of Real Estate Boards, Atlantic City, N.J., October 23, 1935, https://www.sec.gov/news/speech/1935/102335saperstein.pdf.

106. Ibid., 1.

107. Ibid., 2.

108. Antonio Gramsci, *Selections from the Prison Notebooks of Antonio Gramsci*, trans. Quintin Hoare and Geoffrey Nowell-Smith (London: Lawrence & Wishart, 1971).

109. Saperstein, "Real Estate Bond Issues," 3.

110. Ibid., 4.

111. Saul B. Klaman, *The Postwar Residential Mortgage Market* (Princeton, N.J.: Princeton University Press, 1961), 239–80.

112. Ernest M. Fisher, "Changing Institutional Patterns of Mortgage Lending," *Journal of Finance* 5, no. 4 (1950): 109.

Chapter 7: The Rise of Federal Credit Programs

1. Karl Polanyi, *The Great Transformation: The Political and Economic Origins of Our Time* (Boston: Beacon Press, 1957). See also Fred L. Block and Margaret R. Somers, *The Power of Market Fundamentalism: Karl Polanyi's Critique* (Cambridge, Mass.: Harvard University Press, 2014).

2. See Christopher Leman, "Patterns of Policy Development: Social Security in the United States and Canada," *Public Policy* 25 (1977); Theda Skocpol, "A Society Without a 'State'?: Political Organization, Social Conflict, and Welfare Provision in the United States," *Journal of Public Policy* 7, no. 4 (1987); G. John Ikenberry and Theda Skocpol, "Expanding Social Benefits: The Role of Social Security," *Political Science Quarterly* 102, no. 3 (1987); Jill Quadagno, "Creating a Capital Investment Welfare State: The New American Exceptionalism: 1998 Presidential Address," *American Sociological Review* 64, no. 1 (1999); Margaret Weir, Ann Shola Orloff, and Theda Skocpol, *The Politics of Social Policy in the United States*, Studies from the Project on the Federal Social Role (Princeton, N.J.: Princeton University Press, 1988).

3. Katznelson characterizes the outcome as a "procedural" state in which political procedures remain easily influenced by interest groups; Mayrl refers to the government as having an
enduring quality of "permeability" to private actors who influence and participate in policy. See
Ira Katznelson, *Fear Itself: The New Deal and the Origins of Our Time* (New York: Liveright Publishing Corporation, 2013); Damon Mayrl, *Secular Conversions: Politics, Institutions, and Religious Education in the United States and Australia, 1800–2000* (New York: Cambridge University
Press, 2016).

4. But see David M. Freund, *Colored Property: State Policy and White Racial Politics in Suburban America* (Chicago: University of Chicago Press, 2007).

5. Price Van Meter Fishback, "The New Deal," in *Government and the American Economy: A
New History*, ed. Price Van Meter Fishback (Chicago: University of Chicago Press, 2007), 418–19.

6. Ellis Wayne Hawley, *The New Deal and the Problem of Monopoly: A Study in Economic
Ambivalence* (New York: Fordham University Press, 1995), vii.

7. Hawley is careful to point out that there were many differences within these three groups,
as well as various exceptions and intersections that complicate this neat typology. See ibid. On
how New Dealers' different diagnoses of the economic problem led to different proposed cures,
see Arthur M. Schlesinger, *The Politics of Upheaval, 1935–1936: The Age of Roosevelt*, 1st Mariner
Books ed. (Boston: Houghton Mifflin, 2003), 232–35, 385–409.

8. For the clash of economic ideologies in the New Deal, see Hawley, *New Deal and the
Problem*.

9. Arthur M. Schlesinger, *The Coming of the New Deal*, American Heritage Library (Boston:
Houghton Mifflin, 1988), 423.

10. See Katznelson, *Fear Itself*; Hawley, *New Deal*; Schlesinger, *Coming of the New Deal*.

11. Hawley, *New Deal*, 146.

12. Ibid., 272–74.

13. Monica Prasad, *The Land of Too Much: American Abundance and the Paradox of Poverty*
(Cambridge, Mass.: Harvard University Press, 2012).

14. Katznelson, *Fear Itself*. See also Julian E. Zelizer, "The Forgotten Legacy of the New Deal:
Fiscal Conservatism and the Roosevelt Administration, 1933–1938," *Presidential Studies Quarterly* 30, no. 2 (2000).

15. For more on the "crazy quilt" of American welfare programs and the Southern Democrats, see Katznelson, *Fear Itself*, 163. See also idem, *When Affirmative Action Was White: An Untold History of Racial Inequality in Twentieth-Century America* (New York: W. W. Norton, 2005);
Jill S. Quadagno, *The Color of Welfare: How Racism Undermined the War on Poverty* (New York:
Oxford University Press, 1994).

16. Katznelson, *Fear Itself*.

17. Zelizer, "Forgotten Legacy."

18. Douglas, cited in ibid., 334.

19. Ibid.

20. Katznelson, *Fear Itself*, 375–77.

21. Ibid., 377.

22. Hawley, *New Deal*, 492.

23. Mayrl, *Secular Conversions*; Dorit Geva, "Selective Service, the Gender-Ordered Family, and the Rational Informality of the American State," *American Journal of Sociology* 121, no. 1
(2015); Quadagno, *Color of Welfare*.

24. Mayrl, *Secular Conversions*; Katznelson, *Fear Itself*. On the persistence of partnerships and brokerage as an American style of governance, see Fred Block, "Swimming Against
the Current: The Rise of a Hidden Developmental State in the United States," *Politics & Society* 36 (2008); Kimberly J. Morgan and Andrea Louise Campbell, *The Delegated Welfare State:*

Medicare, Markets, and the Governance of Social Policy, Oxford Studies in Postwar American Political Development (New York: Oxford University Press, 2011); Damon Mayrl and Sarah Quinn, "Defining the State from Within: Boundaries, Schemas, and Associational Policymaking" (Universidad Carlos III de Madrid and the University of Washington, 2015); Jennifer Klein, *For All These Rights: Business, Labor, and the Shaping of America's Public-Private Welfare State*, Politics and Society in Twentieth-Century America (Princeton, N.J.: Princeton University Press, 2003); Freund, *Colored Property*; Elisabeth Clemens, "Lineages of the Rube Goldberg State: Building and Blurring Public Programs, 1900–1940," in *Rethinking Political Institutions: The Art of the State*, ed. Ian Shapiro, Stephen Skowronek, and Daniel Galvin (New York: New York University Press, 2006).

25. James Stuart Olson, *Saving Capitalism: The Reconstruction Finance Corporation and the New Deal, 1933–1940* (Princeton, N.J.: Princeton University Press, 1988), 116.

26. Kenneth T. Jackson, *Crabgrass Frontier: The Suburbanization of the United States* (New York: Oxford University Press, 1985); Douglas S. Massey and Nancy A. Denton, *American Apartheid: Segregation and the Making of the Underclass* (Cambridge, Mass.: Harvard University Press, 1993).

27. Barry Bosworth, Andrew S. Carron, and Elisabeth Rhyne, *The Economics of Federal Credit Programs* (Washington, D.C.: Brookings Institution, 1987), 81, citing Paul Studenski and Herman Edward Krooss, *Financial History of the United States: Fiscal, Monetary, Banking, and Tariff, Including Financial Administration and State and Local Finance*, 2nd ed. (Washington, D.C.: Beard Books, 2003).

28. Joseph R. Mason, "The Evolution of the Reconstruction Finance Corporation as a Lender of Last Resort in the Great Depression," in *Bailouts: Public Money, Private Profit*, ed. Robert E. Wright (New York: Columbia University Press, 2010), 72.

29. Olson, *Saving Capitalism*, 3.

30. Jesse H. Jones and Edward Angly, *Fifty Billion Dollars: My Thirteen Years with the R.F.C. (1932–1945)* (New York: Da Capo Press, 1975), 40; Mason, "Evolution."

31. For Hoover's associational alternative, see Olson, *Saving Capitalism*, 9–11; Mason, "Evolution."

32. On the RFC, see Schlesinger, *Coming of the New Deal*; Jones and Angly, *Fifty Billion Dollars*; Mason, "Evolution"; idem, "Do Lender of Last Resort Policies Matter?: The Effects of Reconstruction Finance Corporation Assistance to Banks During the Great Depression," *Journal of Financial Services Research* 20, no. 1 (2001); Olson, *Saving Capitalism*; Fishback, "New Deal."

33. Olson, *Saving Capitalism*, 15. The War Finance Corporation itself is not well studied, and its use even in World War I was limited. See Gerald T. White, "Financing Industrial Expansion for War: The Origin of the Defense Plant Corporation Leases," *Journal of Economic History* 9, no. 2 (1949): 156.

34. Ibid., 14.

35. Mason, "Do Lender of Last Resort Policies Matter?"; idem, "Evolution," 82.

36. Olson, *Saving Capitalism*, 68.

37. Fishback, "New Deal," 394; Schlesinger, *Coming of the New Deal*, 427; Olson, *Saving Capitalism*, 8.

38. Jones and Angly, *Fifty Billion Dollars*; Olson, *Saving Capitalism*, 17–18.

39. On this transition, see Olson, *Saving Capitalism*, 17–19.

40. Hoover, quoted in Schlesinger, *Coming of the New Deal*, 427.

41. Olson, *Saving Capitalism*, 84–103.

42. Ibid., 47.

43. Schlesinger, *Coming of the New Deal*, 426.

44. Olson, *Saving Capitalism*, 42.

45. Jones and Angly, *Fifty Billion Dollars*. On the relationship between Jones and Roosevelt, see Olson, *Saving Capitalism*, 60–62.

46. Walter L. Buenger, "Between Community and Corporation: The Southern Roots of Jesse H. Jones and the Reconstruction Finance Corporation," *Journal of Southern History* 56, no. 3 (1990).

47. Jones and Angly, *Fifty Billion Dollars*, 231.

48. Ibid., 236.

49. Ibid., 236–37.

50. Ibid., 9.

51. Olson, *Saving Capitalism*, 44, 49.

52. On Berle, see ibid., 87–88.

53. Berle, quoted in ibid.

54. For more on Berle's vision for the state and credit, see ibid., 86–91, 118–20, 35–40; Jordan A. Schwarz, *Liberal: Adolf A. Berle and the Vision of an American Era* (New York: Free Press, 1987).

55. Olson, *Saving Capitalism*, 84–86.

56. Schlesinger, *Coming of the New Deal*, 428; Jones and Angly, *Fifty Billion Dollars*.

57. Mason, "Evolution"; Ronnie J. Phillips, "An End to Private Banking: Early New Deal Proposals to Alter the Role of the Federal Government in Credit Allocation," *Journal of Money, Credit and Banking* 26, no. 3 (1994): 554; Olson, *Saving Capitalism*, 79–83.

58. Mason, "Do Lender of Last Resort Policies Matter?"

59. Schlesinger, *Coming of the New Deal*, 430.

60. Jones and Angly, *Fifty Billion Dollars*, 39.

61. Ibid., 40.

62. Prasad, *Land of Too Much*.

63. Randal R. Rucker and E. C. Pasour, Jr., "The Growth of U.S. Farm Programs," in *Government and the American Economy: A New History*, ed. Price Van Meter Fishback (Chicago: University of Chicago Press, 2007), 461.

64. Farm Credit Administration, "History of the F.C.A. and F.C.S.," https://www.fca.gov/about/history/historyFCA_FCS.html.

65. The act also turned the Federal Farm Loan Board into the Federal Farm Board.

66. Jerry W. Markham, "Commodity Market Reforms," in *A Financial History of the United States: From J. P. Morgan to the Institutional Investor (1900–1970)* (Armonk, N.Y.: M. E. Sharpe, 2002).

67. Schlesinger, *Coming of the New Deal*, 43; Jess Gilbert and Carolyn Howe, "Beyond 'State vs. Society': Theories of the State and New Deal Agricultural Policies," *American Sociological Review* 56, no. 2 (1991); Tom Fulton, *The United States Senate Committee on Agriculture, Nutrition, and Forestry 1825–1998: Members, Jurisdiction, and History* (Washington, D.C.: Government Printing Office, 1998).

68. Farm Credit Administration, "History of the F.C.A. and F.C.S."; Howard H. Preston, "Our Farm Credit System," *Journal of Farm Economics* 18, no. 4 (1936).

69. Schlesinger, *Coming of the New Deal*.

70. Theodore Saloutos, *The American Farmer and the New Deal* (Ames: Iowa State University Press, 1982), 269; Fishback, "New Deal," 402; William I. Myers, "Important Issues in Future Farm Credit Administration Policy," *Journal of Farm Economics* 19, no. 1 (1937): 121–46.

71. Jones and Angly, *Fifty Billion Dollars*, 92–93.

72. Ibid., 92.

73. Ibid., 93.

74. Ibid.

75. Ibid., 103.

76. U.S. Department of Agriculture, "About the Commodity Credit Corporation," https://www.fsa.usda.gov/about-fsa/structure-and-organization/commodity-credit-corporation/index.

77. Ronald C. Tobey, *Technology as Freedom: The New Deal and the Electrical Modernization of the American Home* (Berkeley: University of California Press, 1996); U.S. House Subcommittee on Domestic Finance and Committee on Banking and Currency, "A Study of Federal Credit Programs" (Washington, D.C.: Government Printing Office, 1964).

78. Of all the RFC programs, it was the disaster loans program that suffered the most major losses, accruing $2 million in defaults, primarily due to job loss or death, before it closed in June 1945. See Jones and Angly, *Fifty Billion Dollars*, 199.

79. Studenski and Krooss, *Financial History*.

80. Fishback, "New Deal," 394–95.

81. Jones and Angly, *Fifty Billion Dollars*, 171.

82. Ibid., 183.

83. Ibid., 184.

84. Adam Gordon, "The Creation of Homeownership: How New Deal Changes in Banking Regulation Simultaneously Made Homeownership Accessible to Whites and Out of Reach for Blacks," *Yale Law Journal* 115, no. 1 (2005): 192. See also Jackson, *Crabgrass Frontier*.

85. Jonathan D. Rose, "The Incredible H.O.L.C.?: Mortgage Relief During the Great Depression," *Journal of Money, Credit and Banking* 43, no. 6 (2011): 1077.

86. Ibid.

87. Kenneth Snowden, "Table Dc903–928: Debt on Nonfarm Structures, by Type of Debt, Property, and Holder: 1896–1952," *Historical Statistics of the United States, Earliest Times to Present*, Millennial ed. (2006), http://dx.doi.org/10.1017/ISBN-9780511132971.Dc903-1288.

88. Idem, "The Anatomy of a Residential Mortgage Crisis: A Look Back to the 1930s" (Bryan School of Business and Economics, University of North Carolina, Greensboro, 2009), 21. The USBLL had previously lobbied *against* deposit insurance for S&Ls, believing that it posed a moral hazard problem and so would encourage careless risk management and speculation. However, since commercial banks now benefited from FDIC deposit insurance, the USBLL concluded that its members needed similar protections to compete.

89. Freund, *Colored Property*.

90. For the Conference on Home Building and Home Ownership, see ibid., 103–4; Jackson, *Crabgrass Frontier*, 194–96; Oliver Jones and Leo Grebler, *The Secondary Mortgage Market: Its Purpose, Performance, and Potential* (Los Angeles: Real Estate Research Program, Graduate School of Business Administration, University of California, Los Angeles, 1961), 113; Gertrude Sipperly Fish, *The Story of Housing* (New York: Macmillan, 1979), 178–82.

91. J. E. McDonough, "The Federal Home Loan Bank System," *American Economic Review* 24, no. 4 (1934); Snowden, "Anatomy of a Residential Mortgage Crisis."

92. Snowden, "Anatomy of a Residential Mortgage Crisis," 21n.28.

93. Ibid.

94. Freund, *Colored Property*, 114–15.

95. Rosalind Tough, "The Life Cycle of the Home Owners' Loan Corporation," *Land Economics* 27, no. 4 (1951).

96. Snowden, "Anatomy of a Residential Mortgage Crisis," 19; Freund, *Colored Property*, 112.

97. Freund, *Colored Property*, 111–12.

98. Rose, "Incredible H.O.L.C.?," 1073.

99. For more on the history of redlining and its legacy, see Freund, *Colored Property*; Jackson, *Crabgrass Frontier*; Massey and Denton, *American Apartheid*.

100. Richard K. Green and Susan M. Wachter, "The American Mortgage in Historical and International Context," *Journal of Economic Perspectives* 19, no. 4 (2005), 94; William W. Bartlett and Françoise Dearden, *Mortgage-Backed Securities: Products, Analysis, and Trading* (New York: New York Institute of Finance, 1989), 4.

101. Snowden, "Anatomy of a Residential Mortgage Crisis"; Freund, *Colored Property*, 104, 106; Green and Wachter, "American Mortgage"; Marc A. Weiss, "Marketing and Financing Home Ownership: Mortgage Lending and Public Policy in the United States, 1918–1989," *Business and Economic History* 18 (1989); Michael S. Carliner, "Development of Federal Homeownership 'Policy,'" *Housing Policy Debate* 9, no. 2 (1998); Jackson, *Crabgrass Frontier*, 204; Rabinowitz, *Real Estate Gamble*, 65; Jones and Grebler, *Secondary Mortgage Market*; Henry Morton Bodfish, *History of Building and Loan in the United States* (Chicago: United States Building and Loan League, 1931).

102. Studenski and Krooss, *Financial History*; U.S. House Subcommittee on Domestic Finance and Committee on Banking and Currency, "Study of Federal Credit Programs."

103. Jones and Grebler, *Secondary Mortgage Market*, 115; Federal National Mortgage Association (FNMA), "Background and History of the Federal National Mortgage Association" (Washington, D.C.: FNMA, 1966).

104. See, for example, the discussion in Jones and Grebler, *Secondary Mortgage Market*, 115.

105. For details on the failure of the national mortgage associations, see ibid., 116–17.

106. Snowden, "Anatomy of a Residential Mortgage Crisis," 23.

107. On the RFC mortgage company, see Jones and Angly, *Fifty Billion Dollars*, 150.

108. By 1966 Fannie Mae was allowed to purchase uninsured mortgages under the conditions that they were first mortgages and that they were worth 60 percent of the appraised value. See FNMA, "Background and History," 10. In 1948, Fannie Mae's secondary market operations were limited to purchasing new (as of April 30, 1948) insured or guaranteed mortgages. See ibid., C1.

109. John Broderick, "Bonds and Bond Men," *Wall Street Journal*, March 22, 1938.

110. "Business Briefs: Senate Gets Rail-Nationalization Bill, Fannie Mae Name Protected by Patent, G. M. Saves It Shuns Money Speculation, House Extends Equalization Tax," *New York Times*, February 28, 1973.

111. FNMA, "Background and History," 9. For details on the early effects of Fannie Mae, see Jones and Grebler, *Secondary Mortgage Market*, 118–21.

112. Jones and Angly, *Fifty Billion Dollars*, 152.

113. Jones and Grebler, *Secondary Mortgage Market*, 122.

114. Ibid., 116–17.

115. Jones and Angly, *Fifty Billion Dollars*, 244; Jones and Grebler, *Secondary Mortgage Market*, 122.

116. Jones and Angly, *Fifty Billion Dollars*, 152.

117. Jackson, *Crabgrass Frontier*, 205.

118. Ibid., 203; Fish, *Story of Housing*, 200.

119. Eccles, quoted in Fish, *Story of Housing*, 200 (emphasis added).

120. Lizabeth Cohen, *A Consumers' Republic: The Politics of Mass Consumption in Postwar America* (New York: Knopf, 2003), 73.

121. Greta Krippner, *Capitalizing on Crisis: The Political Origins of the Rise of Finance* (Cambridge, Mass.: Harvard University Press, 2011), 83–89. Specifically, officials would use Regulation Q, which set a limit on the interest rates that S&Ls could pay on deposits.

122. Prasad, *Land of Too Much*.

123. Freund, *Colored Property*, 119.

124. Ibid., 106.

125. Ibid., 108.

126. Olson, *Saving Capitalism*.

127. Jones and Angly, *Fifty Billion Dollars*, 266.

128. J. Wilner Sundelson, "The Emergency Budget of the Federal Government," *American Economic Review* 24, no. 1 (1934).

129. See, for example, discussions in Gerhard Colm, "Comment on Extraordinary Budgets," *Social Research* 5, no. 2 (1938); Harry F. Byrd, "Expenditures of the Federal Government," *Proceedings of the Academy of Political Science* 17, no. 4 (1938).

130. Jones and Angly, *Fifty Billion Dollars*, 267.

131. Morrill, quoted in Olson, *Saving Capitalism*, 43.

132. Schlesinger, *Coming of the New Deal*, 132.

133. Quoted in Fish, *Story of Housing*, 180.

134. See also Kevin Fox Gotham, "Racialization and the State: The Housing Act of 1934 and the Creation of the Federal Housing Administration," *Sociological Perspectives* 43, no. 2 (2000): 303; Freund, *Colored Property*.

135. Rachel Kahn Best, "Disease Politics and Medical Research Funding: Three Ways Advocacy Shapes Policy," *American Sociological Review* 77, no. 5 (2012); Daniel Hirschman and Elizabeth Popp Berman, "Do Economists Make Policies?: On the Political Effects of Economics," *Socio-Economic Review* 12, no. 4 (2014); Joseph R. Gusfield, *The Culture of Public Problems: Drinking-Driving and the Symbolic Order* (Chicago: University of Chicago Press, 1981).

136. Colm, "Comment on Extraordinary Budgets."

Chapter 8: Off-Budget and Decentralized

1. U.S. House Subcommittee on Domestic Finance and Committee on Banking and Currency, "A Study of Federal Credit Programs" (Washington, D.C.: Government Printing Office, 1964); President's Commission on Budgetary Concepts, "Report of the President's Commission on Budgetary Concepts" (Washington, D.C.: Government Printing Office, 1967).

2. Council of Economic Advisers, "Economic Report of the President: 1964" (Washington, D.C.: Government Printing Office, 1964), C52.

3. U.S. House Subcommittee on Domestic Finance and Committee on Banking and Currency, "Study of Federal Credit Programs."

4. James Stuart Olson, *Saving Capitalism: The Reconstruction Finance Corporation and the New Deal, 1933–1940* (Princeton, N.J.: Princeton University Press, 1988), 216.

5. Data on the wartime RFC efforts from ibid., 217–20.

6. Margaret Pugh O'Mara, *Cities of Knowledge: Cold War Science and the Search for the Next Silicon Valley*, Politics and Society in Twentieth-Century America (Princeton, N.J.: Princeton University Press, 2005).

7. "E. Merl Young Gets Perjury Sentence," *New York Times*, May 1, 1953; "RFC Problems," in *CQ Almanac 1951* (Washington, D.C.: Congressional Quarterly, 1950).

8. "RFC 'Influence' Investigation," in *CQ Almanac 1951* (Washington, D.C.: Congressional Quarterly, 1952).

9. "Boyle, Gabrielson, and R.F.C.," in *CQ Almanac 1951* (Washington, D.C.: Congressional Quarterly, 1952).

10. "President's Reorganization Plans," in *CQ Almanac 1953* (Washington, D.C.: Congressional Quarterly, 1954).

11. On the creation of FEMA, see Saundra K. Schneider, "Reinventing Public Administration: A Case Study of the Federal Emergency Management Agency," *Public Administration Quarterly* 22, no. 1 (1998).

12. Details of SB 3619, the Disaster Relief Act of 1970, from "Federal Disaster Assistance," in *CQ Almanac 1970* (Washington, D.C.: Congressional Quarterly, 1971).

13. Jonathan J. Bean, *Big Government and Affirmative Action: The Scandalous History of the Small Business Administration* (Lexington: University Press of Kentucky, 2001), 8–9.

14. Ibid., 13.

15. The SBA's revolving fund for loans was authorized at $150 million when it was created in 1953 and raised to $650 million in 1958 when the SBA was made permanent. "Small Business Loans," in *CQ Almanac 1963* (Washington, D.C.: Congressional Quarterly, 1962).

16. Bean, *Big Government*, 12.

17. For the Small Business Investment Corporations, see especially Joshua Lerner, *Boulevard of Broken Dreams: Why Public Efforts to Boost Entrepreneurship and Venture Capital Have Failed and What to Do About It*, Kauffman Foundation Series on Innovation and Entrepreneurship (Princeton, N.J.: Princeton University Press, 2009), 39–41; Martin Kenney, "How Venture Capital Became a Component of the U.S. National System of Innovation (1847203)" (Department of Human and Community Development, University of California, Davis, 2011); Bean, *Big Government*; Martha Louise Reiner, "The Transformation of Venture Capital: A History of Venture Capital Organizations in the United States" (University of California, Berkeley, 1989); Paul A. Gompers, "The Rise and Fall of Venture Capital," *Business and Economic History* 23, no. 2 (1994); Paul Gompers and Josh Lerner, "The Venture Capital Revolution," *Journal of Economic Perspectives* 15, no. 2 (2001). On early debates over how to address the problem of venture capital and small business financing, see Reiner, "Transformation of Venture Capital"; Sarah Quinn, Mark Igra, and Selen Guler, "'A Modern Financial Tool-Kit': Lessons from Berle for a More Democratic Financial System," paper for the Real Utopias Project Conference on Democratizing Finance (Department of Sociology, University of Washington, 2018); Ronnie J. Phillips, *The Chicago Plan and New Deal Banking Reform* (Armonk, N.Y.: M. E. Sharpe, 1995).

18. Kenney, "How Venture Capital."

19. On the creation of ARD, see Reiner, "Transformation of Venture Capital," 166–67. On MIT funding, see Elizabeth Popp Berman, *Creating the Market University: How Academic Science Became an Economic Engine* (Princeton, N.J.: Princeton University Press, 2012), 19–20.

20. Reiner, "Transformation of Venture Capital," 133.

21. Ibid., 300.

22. Ibid., 285, 303.

23. For the early SBICs, a small business was defined as one having annual sales of under $500,000 and earnings of under $150,000, as well as debt that converted into equity. To preserve the power of state governments, the federal government would only grant charters in cases in which states were unable to, and even then, only within a three-year window. William John Martin and Ralph J. Moore, "The Small Business Investment Act of 1958," *California Law Review* 47, no. 1 (1959): 146.

24. George Melloan, "Rise of the SBIC's," *Wall Street Journal*, September 28, 1960.

25. Bean, *Big Government*, 18.

26. Johnson, quoted in Kenney, "How Venture Capital," 25.

27. Ibid., 27–28.

28. Reiner, "Transformation of Venture Capital," 303–7.

29. Gompers, "Rise and Fall," 8.

30. Ibid.

31. Reiner, "Transformation of Venture Capital," 276, 301.

32. Ibid., 308.

33. Ibid., 317–18, 323.

34. Lerner, "Venture Capital Revolution," 39.

35. U.S. Small Business Administration, "Program Overview," https://www.sba.gov/sbic/general-information/program-overview (emphasis in original).

36. See Barry Bosworth, Andrew S. Carron, and Elisabeth Rhyne, *The Economics of Federal Credit Programs* (Washington, D.C.: Brookings Institution, 1987); Brian M. Freeman and Allan I. Mendelowitz, "Program in Search of a Policy: The Chrysler Loan Guarantee," *Journal of Policy Analysis and Management* 1, no. 4 (1982). For more on Lockheed, see Public Law 92–70. For more on how the Troubled Asset Relief Program (TARP) includes an array of public–private partnerships, off-budget programs, asset guarantees, and credit support, see Douglas J. Elliott, *Uncle Sam in Pinstripes: Evaluating U.S. Federal Credit Programs* (Washington, D.C.: Brookings Institution, 2011).

37. Josh Lerner, "The Government as Venture Capitalist: The Long-Run Effects of the SBIR Program," *Journal of Business* 72 (1999): table 1.

38. On the U.S. use of foreign aid to support domestic interests, see Michael Hudson, *Super Imperialism: The Origin and Fundamentals of U.S. World Dominance*, 2nd ed. (London and Sterling, Va.: Pluto Press, 2003).

39. Frank A. Fetter, "The Economists and the Public," *American Economic Review* 15, no. 1 (1925).

40. Herbert Stein, *The Fiscal Revolution in America: Policy in Pursuit of Reality*, 2nd rev. ed. (Washington, D.C.: AEI Press, 1996), 6.

41. U.S. Agency for International Development Economic Analysis and Data Services, "U.S. Economic and Miliary Assistance Fiscal Years 1946–2016," in *Greenbook* (Washington, D.C.: USAID Bureau for Legislative and Public Affairs, 2016).

42. USAID, "Agency Financial Report, Fiscal Year 2017," https://www.usaid.gov/sites/default/files/documents/1868/USAIDFY2017AFR.pdf, 50.

43. According to its inaugural 1962 operations report, about 8 percent of USAID's authorizations were for loan programs.

44. Edwin Griswold Nourse, Joseph Stancliffe Davis, and John D. Black, *Three Years of the Agricultural Adjustment Administration* (Washington, D.C.: Brookings Institution, 1937), 191–92.

45. Ibid., 191–94.

46. "Congress Revises Foreign Aid Program," in *CQ Almanac 1961* (Washington, D.C.: Congressional Quarterly, 1961); Bosworth, Carron, and Rhyne, *Economics of Federal Credit Programs*, 81, 97.

47. USAID, "Operations Report" (Washington, D.C.: Office of Program and Policy Coordination, Statistics and Reports Division, 1969), 7.

48. U.S. Office of Management and Budget, "Analytical Perspectives, Budget of the United States Government, Fiscal Year 2018," 320.

49. USAID Economic Analysis and Data Services, "U.S. Economic and Miliary Assistance," 12.

50. Joel Best and Eric Best, *The Student Loan Mess: How Good Intentions Created a Trillion-Dollar Problem* (Berkeley: University of California Press, 2014); Keith W. Olson, *The G.I. Bill, the Veterans, and the Colleges* (Lexington: University Press of Kentucky, 1974).

51. Best and Best, *Student Loan Mess*, 25; Christopher P. Loss, *Between Citizens and the State: The Politics of American Higher Education in the 20th Century*, Politics and Society in Twentieth-Century America (Princeton, N.J.: Princeton University Press, 2012), 117; John R. Thelin, "Higher Education and the Public Trough: A Historical Perspective," in *Public Funding of Higher Education: Changing Contexts and New Rationales*, ed. Edward P. St. John and Michael D. Parsons (Baltimore: Johns Hopkins University Press, 2004), 32; Suzanne Mettler, *Soldiers to Citizens: The G.I. Bill and the Making of the Greatest Generation* (New York: Oxford University Press, 2005), 16; Olson, *G.I. Bill*, 4.

52. Suzanne Mettler, *Degrees of Inequality: How the Politics of Higher Education Sabotaged the American Dream* (New York: Basic Books, 2014), 58; Barbara Barksdale Clowse, *Brainpower for the Cold War: The* Sputnik *Crisis and National Defense Education Act of 1958*, Contributions to the Study of Education (Westport, Conn.: Greenwood Press, 1981), 44; Best and Best, *Student Loan Mess*, 27–30; Elliott, *Uncle Sam in Pinstripes*, 51; Elizabeth Berman and Abby Stivers, "Student Loans as a Pressure on U.S. Higher Education," *Research in the Sociology of Organizations* 46 (2016): 134.

53. Bosworth, Carron, and Rhyne, *Economics of Federal Credit Programs*, 130. Clowse, *Brainpower for the Cold War*.

54. Best and Best, *Student Loan Mess*, 31.

55. Ibid., 32–33; Dennis S. Ippolito, *Hidden Spending: The Politics of Federal Credit Programs* (Chapel Hill: University of North Carolina Press, 1984), 31.

56. Mettler, *Degrees of Inequality*, 63; Berman and Stivers, "Student Loans as a Pressure," 135; Loss, *Between Citizens and the State*, 212.

57. U.S. National Commission on Student Financial Assistance, *Guaranteed Student Loans: A Background Paper* (Washington, D.C.: National Commission on Student Financial Assistance, 1982), 1.

58. Best and Best, *Student Loan Mess*, 81; Mettler, *Degrees of Inequality*, 52–55, 67–68.

59. Mettler, *Degrees of Inequality*, 52–53.

60. Michael Corkery and Stacy Cowley, "For Better or Worse, Debt Reaches New Peak," *New York Times*, May 17, 2017.

61. Rohit Chopra, "Student Debt Swells, Federal Loans Now Top a Trillion" (Consumer Financial Protection Bureau, 2013), https://www.consumerfinance.gov/about-us/newsroom/student-debt-swells-federal-loans-now-top-a-trillion/.

62. Farm Credit Administration, "Farm Credit Administration 85th Anniversary Timeline" (2018), https://www.fca.gov/template-fca/about/2018fcatimeline.pdf.

63. Jim Monke, "Agricultural Credit: Institutions and Issues," ed. Congressional Research Service, RS21977 (Washington, D.C.: 2016), http://nationalaglawcenter.org/wp-content/uploads/assets/crs/RS21977.pdf.

64. U.S. Farmers Home Administration, "A Brief History of FmHA" (Washington, D.C.: Government Printing Office, 1984).

65. This system went through major organizational changes as it grew. It started with the Resettlement Administration (which moved the nation's most desperate farm and migrant workers onto better land), which was reorganized into the Department of Agriculture's Farm Security Administration in 1937, later reshuffled into the Farmers Home Administration (created in 1946), and finally reorganized into the Farm Service Agency (in 1994), with some loans again put under the direct purview of the Rural Development Office of the Department of Agriculture.

66. Randal R. Rucker and E. C. Pasour, Jr., "The Growth of U.S. Farm Programs," in *Government and the American Economy: A New History*, ed. Price Van Meter Fishback (Chicago: University of Chicago Press, 2007), 477.

67. James T. Massey, "Farmers Home Administration and Farm Credit System Update," *Nebraska Law Review* 73 (1994): 187, citing Harold G. Halcrow, Robert G. Spitze, and Joyce E. Allen-Smith, *Food and Agricultural Policy: Economics and Politics*, 2nd ed. (New York: McGraw-Hill, 1994).

68. U.S. Office of Management and Budget, "Analytical Perspectives, Budget of the United States Government, Fiscal Year 2018," 251.

69. Ibid., table 19–1.

70. Lizabeth Cohen, *A Consumers' Republic: The Politics of Mass Consumption in Postwar America* (New York: Knopf, 2003), 141; John Quigley, "Federal Credit and Insurance Programs:

Housing," *Federal Reserve Bank of St. Louis Review* 88 (2006); Mary K. Nenno, "Housing in the Decade of the 1940s—the War and the Postwar Periods Leave Their Marks," in *The Story of Housing*, ed. Gertrude Sipperly Fish (New York: Macmillan, 1979), 252.

71. James T. Patterson, *Grand Expectations: The United States, 1945–1974*, Oxford History of the United States (New York: Oxford University Press, 1996), 72.

72. Kenneth Snowden, "Table Dc903–928: Debt on Nonfarm Structures, by Type of Debt, Property, and Holder: 1896–1952," *Historical Statistics of the United States, Earliest Times to Present*, Millennial ed. (2006), http://dx.doi.org/10.1017/ISBN-9780511132971.Dc903-1288.

73. Daniel K. Fetter, "How Do Mortgage Subsidies Affect Home Ownership?: Evidence from the Mid-Century GI Bills," *American Economic Journal: Economic Policy* 5, no. 2 (2013): 116.

74. Robert Fishman, *Bourgeois Utopias: The Rise and Fall of Suburbia* (New York: Basic Books, 1987), 175–76.

75. Cohen, *Consumers' Republic*, 158; Alexander Von Hoffman, "Enter the Housing Industry, Stage Right: A Working Paper on the History of Housing Policy" (Joint Center for Housing Studies, Harvard University, 2008).

76. Kenneth T. Jackson, *Crabgrass Frontier: The Suburbanization of the United States* (New York: Oxford University Press, 1985), 233.

77. For more on the rise of homebuilders in the 1950s and 1960s, see Rabinowitz, *Real Estate Gamble*, 106–26; Von Hoffman, "Enter the Housing Industry," 4.

78. Note that the mortgage bonds are not themselves resold, so this system has no real secondary market, even though it does have credit support.

79. Snowden, Historical Statistics of the United States, "Table Dc903–928."

80. Note that these numbers are from Snowden, "Table Dc903–928," in *Historical Statistics of the United States*, which is useful here because it disaggregates the S&Ls and mutuals. It is important to note, however, that this series includes farm and nonfarm mortgages for both commercial and residential properties (unlike the data in table 5.1, which looks exclusively at residential mortgage debt). In 1940, the S&Ls and mutuals held only 23 percent of the entire national mortgage debt, but if you just look at home mortgages, in which they specialized, the S&Ls and mutuals held a 40 percent share of the debt. By 1970, the S&Ls and mutuals held 56 percent of mortgage debt for residential homes. For data on the holders of the U.S. residential mortgage market, see "Table Dc950-982" in *Historical Statistics of the United States*.

81. Saul B. Klaman, *The Postwar Residential Mortgage Market* (Princeton, N.J.: Princeton University Press, 1961), 161–65; Harry S. Schwartz, "The Role of Government-Sponsored Intermediaries," *Housing and Monetary Policy*, no. 4 (1970).

82. Unlike their predecessors from the 1920s, these brokers were not in the business of selling to small investors like families—in fact, they were legally prohibited from selling families FHA and VA loans. As Saul Klaman argues, loans with such long maturities were less appealing to individual investors in any case. Klaman, *Postwar Residential Mortgage Market*; Kenneth Snowden, "The Anatomy of a Residential Mortgage Crisis: A Look Back to the 1930s" (Bryan School of Business and Economics, University of North Carolina, Greensboro, 2009).

83. Jones and Grebler estimated in 1961 that four-fifths of Fannie Mae's loans were bought from mortgage companies. See Oliver Jones and Leo Grebler, *The Secondary Mortgage Market: Its Purpose, Performance, and Potential* (Los Angeles: Real Estate Research Program, Graduate School of Business Administration, University of California, Los Angeles, 1961), 34.

84. Schwartz, "Role of Government-Sponsored Intermediaries."

85. Klaman, *Postwar Residential Mortgage Market*, 166–72.

86. Ibid., 165–72.

87. Ibid., 241.

88. On "other" investors, see ibid., 172.

89. Jones and Grebler, *Secondary Mortgage Market*, 47.

90. Ibid., 47, 119.

91. Von Hoffman, "Enter the Housing Industry."

92. Ibid.

93. Damon Mayrl and Sarah Quinn, "Defining the State from Within: Boundaries, Schemas, and Associational Policymaking" (Universidad Carlos III de Madrid and the University of Washington, 2015).

94. Jones and Grebler, *Secondary Mortgage Market*, 131.

95. FNMA, "Background and History," 41–41.

96. First for 3 percent of the amount of the sale, then later for 1 to 2 percent. See Jones and Grebler, *Secondary Mortgage Market*, 36.

97. FNMA, "Background and History," 14.

98. For a detailed account of Fannie Mae's business practices and congressional authorizations in the 1950s and early 1960s, see ibid., 12–25. Also useful are Jones and Grebler, *Secondary Mortgage Market*, 127–28; Leonard Perry Vidger, "The Federal National Mortgage Association, 1938–57," *Journal of Finance* 16, no. 1 (1961); Henry J. Aaron, *Shelter and Subsidies: Who Benefits from Federal Housing Policies?*, Studies in Social Economics (Washington, D.C.: Brookings Institution, 1972), 92; David M. Freund, *Colored Property: State Policy and White Racial Politics in Suburban America* (Chicago: University of Chicago Press, 2007), 192; Michael S. Carliner, "Development of Federal Homeownership 'Policy,'" *Housing Policy Debate* 9, no. 2 (1998): 308.

99. Excellent work has also been done on racial inequality and the farm loan programs. The kind of extensive outreach and education campaign that the USDA had undertaken with the creation of the Farm Loan Associations (see chapter 4) stands in stark contrast to the near-total lack of outreach to African Americans, who had also long been excluded from representation in the public–private farm loan system and faced extensive discrimination from government lenders. See Valerie Grim, "Black Participation in the Farmers Home Administration and Agricultural Stabilization and Conservation Service, 1964–1990," *Agricultural History* 70, no. 2 (1996); Shakara S. Tyler, Louie Rivers III, Eddie A. Moore, and Rene Rosenbaum, "Michigan Black Farm Owners' Perceptions About Farm Ownership Credit Acquisition: A Critical Race Analysis," *Race, Gender & Class* 21, nos. 3/4 (2014); Pete Daniel, *Dispossession: Discrimination Against African American Farmers in the Age of Civil Rights* (Chapel Hill: University of North Carolina Press, 2013); Alec Fazackerley Hickmott, "Black Land, Black Capital: Rural Development in the Shadows of the Sunbelt South, 1969–1976," *Journal of African American History* 101, no. 4 (2016).

100. There is an extensive body of scholarship on the federal housing programs, suburbanization, racial inequality, and segregation. See Ta-Nehisi Coates's famous article for a synthesis: Ta-Nehisi Coates, "The Case for Reparations," *Atlantic* 313, no. 5 (2014). For accounts by historians, see especially Jackson, *Crabgrass Frontier*, 190–230; Thomas J. Sugrue, *The Origins of the Urban Crisis: Race and Inequality in Postwar Detroit*, 1st Princeton Classics ed. (Princeton, N.J.: Princeton University Press, 2014); Arnold R. Hirsch, *Making the Second Ghetto: Race and Housing in Chicago, 1940–1960*, Historical Studies of Urban America (Chicago: University of Chicago Press, 1998); N.D.B. Connolly, *A World More Concrete: Real Estate and the Remaking of Jim Crow South Florida* (Chicago and London: University of Chicago Press, 2014); Ira Katznelson, *When Affirmative Action Was White: An Untold History of Racial Inequality in Twentieth-Century America* (New York: W. W. Norton, 2005), ch. 5. On the history of redlining and racial discrimination in private markets, see Amy E. Hillier, "Residential Security Maps and Neighborhood Appraisals: The Home Owners' Loan Corporation and the Case of Philadelphia," *Social Science History* 29, no. 2 (2005); Guy Stuart, *Discriminating Risk: The U.S. Mortgage Lending Industry in the Twentieth Century* (Ithaca, N.Y.: Cornell University Press, 2003). On housing credit and accumulative disadvantage, see Devah Pager and Hana Shepherd, "The Sociology of Discrimination: Racial

Discrimination in Employment, Housing, Credit, and Consumer Markets," *Annual Review of Sociology* 34, no. 1 (2008). On the various social forces that reproduce patterns of segregation, see Maria Krysan and Kyle Crowder, *Cycle of Segregation: Social Processes and Residential Stratification* (New York: Russell Sage Foundation, 2017). On the enduring legacy of segregation for black neighborhoods, see Mary E. Pattillo, *Black on the Block: The Politics of Race and Class in the City* (Chicago: University of Chicago Press, 2007).

101. Hirsch, *Making the Second Ghetto*, 32.

102. Connolly, *World More Concrete*, 5–9, 144–49.

103. Among the many examples of white harassment and violence against black neighbors in defense of all-white neighborhoods, see Connolly, *World More Concrete*, 254–58; Freund, *Colored Property*, 1–4; Hirsch, *Making the Second Ghetto*; Richard Rothstein, *The Color of Law: A Forgotten History of How Our Government Segregated America* (New York: Liveright Publishing Corporation, 2017), 138–51.

104. On the Great Migration, see Isabel Wilkerson, *The Warmth of Other Suns: The Epic Story of America's Great Migration* (New York: Random House, 2010).

105. Sugrue, *Origins of the Urban Crisis*. On the black middle class in the suburbs, and the conditions under which the FHA did lend to black families, see Andrew Wiese, *Places of Their Own: African American Suburbanization in the Twentieth Century* (Chicago: University of Chicago Press, 2004); Connolly, *World More Concrete*, 139–42.

106. Freund, *Colored Property*.

107. See, for example, Louis Lee Woods II, "Almost 'No Negro Veteran . . . Could Get a Loan': African Americans, the GI Bill, and the NAACP Campaign Against Residential Segregation, 1917–1960," *Journal of African American History* 98, no. 3 (2013); Robert O. Self, *American Babylon: Race and the Struggle for Postwar Oakland* (Princeton, N.J.: Princeton University Press, 2003); Tyler et al., "Michigan Black Farm Owners' Perceptions"; Connolly, *World More Concrete*.

108. Chloe N. Thurston, "Policy Feedback in the Public–Private Welfare State: Advocacy Groups and Access to Government Homeownership Programs, 1934–1954," *Studies in American Political Development* 29, no. 2 (2015), 257.

109. Quoted in ibid.

110. Freund, *Colored Property*, 178, 373–74; Douglas S. Massey and Nancy A. Denton, *American Apartheid: Segregation and the Making of the Underclass* (Cambridge, Mass.: Harvard University Press, 1993), 186–95.

111. Shapiro, quoted in Jim Surowiecki, "The Hidden Cost of Race," *New Yorker* 92, no. 32 (2016).

112. Laura Sullivan, Tatjana Meschede, Lars Dietrich, Thomas Shapiro, Amy Traub, Catherine Ruetschlin, and Tamara Draut, "The Racial Wealth Gap: Why Policy Matters" (Demos and the Institute on Assets and Social Policy, Brandeis University, 2015), 1.

113. Ibid., 1–3, 10–14.

114. For more on homeownership and racial inequality, see Melvin L. Oliver and Thomas M. Shapiro, *Black Wealth, White Wealth: A New Perspective on Racial Inequality*, 10th anniversary ed. (New York: Routledge, 2006); Massey and Denton, *American Apartheid*; Dalton Conley, "A Room with a View or a Room of One's Own?: Housing and Social Stratification," *Sociological Forum* 16, no. 2 (2001); Dalton Conley and Brian Gifford, "Home Ownership, Social Insurance, and the Welfare State," *Sociological Forum* 21, no. 1 (2006); Pager and Shepherd, "Sociology of Discrimination"; Melvin E. Thomas, Richard Moye, Loren Henderson, and Hayward Derrick Horton, "Separate and Unequal: The Impact of Socioeconomic Status, Segregation, and the Great Recession on Racial Disparities in Housing Values," *Sociology of Race and Ethnicity* 4, no. 2 (2017); Robert McClelland and Joint Committee on Taxation, "The Distribution of Asset

Holdings and Capital Gains," ed. Congressional Budget Office (Washington, D.C.: Congressional Budget Office, 2016).

115. Stokely Carmichael and Charles V. Hamilton, *Black Power: The Politics of Liberation in America* (New York: Vintage Books, 1992), 10.

116. Bean, *Big Government*, 42.

117. Ibid., 44.

118. Mehrsa Baradaran, *The Color of Money: Black Banks and the Racial Wealth Gap* (Cambridge, Mass.: Belknap Press of Harvard University Press, 2017), 166.

119. Sugrue, *Origins of the Urban Crisis*, location 1125.

120. See O'Mara, *Cities of Knowledge*; Sugrue, *Origins of the Urban Crisis*.

121. Timothy Bates, "Minority Business Development Programs: Failure by Design," in *Race, Poverty, and Domestic Policy*, ed. C. Michael Henry (New Haven, Conn.: Yale University Press, 2004).

122. Ibid., 703.

123. Bean, *Big Government*, 68.

124. U.S. House Subcommittee on Domestic Finance and Committee on Banking and Currency, "Study of Federal Credit Programs."

125. U.S. Office of Management and Budget, "Special Analyses, Budget of the United States Government" (Washington, D.C.: Executive Office of the President, 1965).

126. MacLaury notes that this was also true for other, non-credit-based government hybrid corporations, like the postal service. See Bruce K. MacLaury, "Federal Credit Programs—the Issues They Raise," paper presented at the Issues in Federal Debt Management Conference Series No. 10, Boston, 1973.

127. Ibid., 92.

128. U.S. House Subcommittee on Domestic Finance and Committee on Banking and Currency, "Study of Federal Credit Programs."

129. Congressional Budget Office, ed., "Loan Guarantees: Current Concerns and Alternatives for Control" (Washington, D.C.: Governmenting Printing Office, 1978).

130. Ippolito, *Hidden Spending*, xiii.

131. MacLaury, "Federal Credit Programs," 211.

132. U.S. House Subcommittee on Domestic Finance and Committee on Banking and Currency, "Study of Federal Credit Programs," xvii.

133. Ippolito, *Hidden Spending*.

134. Congressional Budget Office, quoted in ibid., 71.

135. Elliott, *Uncle Sam in Pinstripes*; Subsidyscope, "Government Subsidies: Revealing the Hidden Budget," *PEW Economic Policy Group* (2009), http://subsidyscope.org/loans/.

136. Mettler, *Degrees of Inequality*, 133–61.

137. Albert Cole, who was head of the Housing and Home Finance Agency (the precursor to the Department of Housing and Urban Development) from 1953 to 1959 noted that "Fannie Mae had a sensitive position in the Executive Branch as its activities played an important part in the monetary and fiscal policy as viewed by the Congress, the Treasury, and the Federal Reserve System. . . . [T]he Administration, by exercising its judgment through the HHFA, had an important stake in FNMA's marketing policy." See Albert M. Cole, "Federal Housing Programs: 1950–1960," in *The Story of Housing*, ed. Gertrude Sipperly Fish (New York: Macmillan, 1979), 292–93.

138. Leonard Perry Vidger, "The Federal National Mortgage Association, 1938–1957" (University of Washington, 1960), 186.

139. Raymond J. Saulnier, Harold G. Halcrow, and Neil H. Jacoby, *Federal Lending: Its Growth and Impact* (New York: National Bureau of Economic Research, 1957), 29, 34.

140. Deborah Lucas, "Credit Policy as Fiscal Policy," *Brookings Papers on Economic Activity*, no. 1 (2016).

141. Herman B. Leonard and Elisabeth H. Rhyne, "Federal Credit and the 'Shadow Budget,'" *Public Interest* 65 (2006): 40; James. T. Bennett and Thomas. J. DiLorenzo, "The Underground Federal Government: Bane of the Balanced Budget?," *Cato Policy Analysis* 19 (1982).

142. See especially Bosworth, Carron, and Rhyne, *Economics of Federal Credit Programs*, 173; Bennett and DiLorenzo, "Underground Federal Government"; Clifford M. Hardin and Arthur T. Denzau, "The Unrestrained Growth of Federal Credit Programs" (Center for the Study of American Business, Washington University, 1981), 1.

143. On the inflationary effects of credit programs, see Saulnier, Halcrow, and Jacoby, *Federal Lending*, 29; MacLaury, "Federal Credit Programs"; Henry Kauffman, "Federal Debt Management: An Economist's View from the Marketplace," in *Issues in Federal Debt Managment, Conference Series*, no. 10 (Boston: Federal Reserve Bank of Boston, 1973); Hardin and Denzau, "Unrestrained Growth"; Edward J. Kane, "Good Intentions and Unintended Evil: The Case Against Selective Credit Allocation," *Journal of Money* 9, no. 1 (1977).

144. On efforts to investigate the outcomes of the credit programs, see Ippolito, *Hidden Spending*; Jacob L. Vigdor, "Liquidity Constraints and Housing Prices: Theory and Evidence from the VA Mortgage Program," *Journal of Public Economics* 90, nos. 8–9 (2006); Hardin and Denzau, "Unrestrained Growth"; Michael Belongia and R. Alton Gilbert, "The Effects of Federal Credit Programs on Farm Output," *American Journal of Agricultural Economics* 72, no. 3 (1990); William Gale, "Economic Effects of Federal Credit Programs," *American Economic Review* 81, no. 1 (1991); Anita M. Schwarz, "How Effective Are Directed Credit Policies in the United States?: A Literature Survey," in *Policy Research Working Papers* (Washington, D.C.: World Bank 1992); Congressional Budget Office, "Loan Guarantees"; Fetter, "How Do Mortgage Subsidies."

145. See, for example, Quigley, "Federal Credit and Insurance Programs"; Bosworth, Carron, and Rhyne, *Economics of Federal Credit Programs*, 84.

146. Saulnier, Halcrow, and Jacoby, *Federal Lending*, 44.

147. Ibid., 44–46.

148. Ibid.

149. Louis Hyman, *Debtor Nation: The History of America in Red Ink* (Princeton, N.J.: Princeton University Press, 2011).

150. Marc A. Weiss, *The Rise of the Community Builders: The American Real Estate Industry and Urban Land Planning* (New York: Columbia University Press, 1987); Carliner, "Development of Federal Homeownership 'Policy.'"

151. Conventional loans in 1950 had a median maturity of 12 years and a loan-to-value ratio of 64 percent. In the same year, a government-guaranteed mortgage had an average maturity that was nearly twice as long (20 years), with substantially higher average loan-to-value ratios: 76 percent through the FHA and 86 percent through the VA. By 1964 conventional loans looked more like the FHA-guaranteed loans issued 14 years earlier, with a median maturity of 20 years and a loan-to-value ratio of 76 percent. By that time the government-guaranteed loans had even looser terms, with an average maturity of nearly 30 years and a loan-to-value ratio of over 90 percent. Snowden, "Table Dc903–928."

152. Saulnier, Halcrow, and Jacoby, *Federal Lending*, 44.

153. Bruce G. Carruthers and Arthur L. Stinchcombe, "The Social Structure of Liquidity: Flexibility, Markets, and States," *Theory and Society* 28, no. 3 (1999).

154. Mariana Mazzucato, *The Entrepreneurial State: Debunking Public vs. Private Sector Myths* (New York: Anthem Press, 2013).

155. See Suzanne Mettler, *The Submerged State: How Invisible Government Policies Undermine American Democracy* (Chicago: University of Chicago Press, 2011).

Chapter 9: A Return to Securitization

1. James T. Patterson, *Grand Expectations: The United States, 1945–1974*, Oxford History of the United States (New York: Oxford University Press, 1996), 61.

2. Ibid., 313. See also Judith Stein, *Pivotal Decade: How the United States Traded Factories for Finance in the Seventies* (New Haven, Conn.: Yale University Press, 2010).

3. Patterson, *Grand Expectations*, 62.

4. For historical comparisons, see ibid., 64; for international comparisons, see Richard R. Nelson and Gavin Wright, "The Rise and Fall of American Technological Leadership: The Postwar Era in Historical Perspective," *Journal of Economic Literature* 30, no. 4 (1992).

5. Patterson, *Grand Expectations*, 312–13.

6. On the defense contracts, see ibid., 314. On the R&D expenditures, see Jacob S. Hacker and Paul Pierson, *American Amnesia: How the War on Government Led Us to Forget What Made America Prosper*, Kindle ed. (New York: Simon & Schuster, 2016), locations 712–13.

7. Ibid., locations 1242–44.

8. Robert M. Collins, *More: The Politics of Economic Growth in Postwar America* (New York: Oxford University Press, 2000), 52.

9. Stephanie L. Mudge, *Leftism Reinvented: Western Parties from Socialism to Neoliberalism*, Kindle ed. (Cambridge, Mass.: Harvard University Press, 2018), location 685. On the political influence of U.S. economists, see also Marion Fourcade, *Economists and Societies: Discipline and Profession in the United States, Britain, and France, 1890s to 1990s*, Princeton Studies in Cultural Sociology (Princeton, N.J.: Princeton University Press, 2009); Daniel Hirschman and Elizabeth Popp Berman, "Do Economists Make Policies?: On the Political Effects of Economics," *Socio-Economic Review* 12, no. 4 (2014).

10. Collins notes that before the 1930s, the federal government was much smaller, and during the cataclysm of the Great Depression, it focused on stability and balance more than expansion. What was new about growth liberalism was not government support for pursuit of market growth, but the means and tools available for such support. Collins also notes that growth has always had its critics, and not just from the anticapitalist tradition—groups like the Puritans, the antimonopolists, the hippies, and the environmental movement have all opposed it at different times. Collins, *More*.

11. Ronald Tobey, Charles Wetherell, and Jay Brigham, "Moving Out and Settling In: Residential Mobility, Home Owning, and the Public Enframing of Citizenship, 1921–1950," *American Historical Review* 95, no. 5 (1990).

12. Eugene White, "Banking and Finance in the Twentieth Century," in *Cambridge Economic History of the United States: The Twentieth Century*, ed. Robert E. Gallman and Stanley L. Engerman (Cambridge: Cambridge University Press, 2000), 777–78.

13. Patterson, *Grand Expectations*, 313.

14. Stein, *Pivotal Decade*, 2.

15. On consumer debt, see especially Louis Hyman, *Debtor Nation: The History of America in Red Ink* (Princeton, N.J.: Princeton University Press, 2011); Leon Glen Calder, *Financing the American Dream: A Cultural History of Consumer Credit* (Princeton, N.J.: Princeton University Press, 1999).

16. Patterson, *Grand Expectations*, 70.

17. Ibid., 316.

18. Lizabeth Cohen, *A Consumers' Republic: The Politics of Mass Consumption in Postwar America* (New York: Knopf, 2003).

19. Monica Prasad, *The Land of Too Much: American Abundance and the Paradox of Poverty* (Cambridge, Mass.: Harvard University Press, 2012).

20. Lizabeth Cohen, *A Consumers' Republic: The Politics of Mass Consumption in Postwar America* (New York: Knopf, 2003), 127.

21. Collins, *More*, 60.

22. Patterson, *Grand Expectations*, 353.

23. W. Brownlee, "The Public Sector," in *The Cambridge Economic History of the United States*, vol. 3: *The Twentieth Century*, ed. Robert E. Gallman and Stanley L. Engerman, Cambridge Economic History of the United States (Cambridge: Cambridge University Press, 2000).

24. Thomas Piketty and Emmanuel Saez, "The Evolution of Top Incomes: A Historical and International Perspective," *American Economic Review* 96, no. 2 (2006): 201. See also Claudia Goldin and Robert A. Margo, "The Great Compression: The Wage Structure in the United States at Mid-Century," *Quarterly Journal of Economics* 107, no. 1 (1992).

25. Stein, *Pivotal Decade*, 1.

26. Goldin and Margo, "Great Compression." See also Stein, *Pivotal Decade*, ch. 1.

27. Robert O. Self, *American Babylon: Race and the Struggle for Postwar Oakland* (Princeton, N.J.: Princeton University Press, 2003).

28. Ibid.

29. Maria Canon and Elise Marifan, "Changes in the Racial Earnings Gap Since 1960," *Regional Economist*, July 2013, https://www.stlouisfed.org/publications/regional-economist/july-2013/changes-in-the-racial-earnings-gap-since-1960.

30. Patterson, *Grand Expectations*, 381.

31. Leah Platt Boustan and Robert A. Margo, "White Suburbanization and African-American Home Ownership, 1940–1980," National Bureau of Economic Research Working Paper Series No. 16702 (2011), table 1. Boustan and Margo found that gains in black homeownership rates owed to black families being able to purchase homes at lower costs in city neighborhoods left by white families headed to the suburbs. They note that the lower home prices likely made homeownership easier for families of color, and that the timing of the Great Migration meant that black families left southern cities where homeownership would have been cheaper had they been able to access it for northern cities where industrial jobs were already in decline and housing discrimination would force them into segregated neighborhoods with the worst housing stock.

32. Patterson, *Grand Expectations*, 375–404.

33. Greta Krippner, *Capitalizing on Crisis: The Political Origins of the Rise of Finance* (Cambridge, Mass.: Harvard University Press, 2011), 61; Collins, *More*, 43–44.

34. The FHLBB ceilings were "unofficial" in that they were not written into law like the Regulation Q authority. However, the FHLBB was not entirely free of coercive mechanisms: it needed permission from the U.S. Treasury to issue bonds (though it did officially have the option of placing some bonds with the Treasury in an emergency situation). Similarly, the FHLBB could not legally compel compliance from its members via its authority to advance, but it had the power to control advances to its members, and any noncompliant S&L could be excluded from the market on the grounds of upholding the FHLBB's charter, which called for the institution to ensure stability and high standards in mortgage lending. Federal Home Loan Bank Board (FHLBB), "Annual Report of the Federal Home Loan Bank Administration" (Washington, D.C.: Government Printing Office, 1966), 47–45; Dwight M. Jaffee, "The Federal Home Loan Bank System Since 1965," *Carnegie-Rochester Conference Series on Public Policy* 4 (1976): 196.

35. Krippner, *Capitalizing on Crisis*.

36. It was not just the outflow of funds from S&Ls that hurt housing; when commercial banks lost funds, they cut off the flow of funds to mortgages first in order to appease larger business clientele. See ibid.

37. Richard W. Bartke, "Fannie Mae and the Secondary Mortgage Market," *Northwestern University Law Review* 66 (1971): 28.

38. Oliver Jones, "The Development of an Effective Secondary Mortgage Market," *Journal of Finance* 17, no. 2 (1962); Saul B. Klaman, *The Postwar Residential Mortgage Market* (Princeton, N.J.: Princeton University Press, 1961), 263.

39. Jones, "Development," 360, 67; see also Oliver Jones and Leo Grebler, *The Secondary Mortgage Market: Its Purpose, Performance, and Potential* (Los Angeles: Real Estate Research Program, Graduate School of Business Administration, University of California, Los Angeles, 1961).

40. Klaman, *Postwar Residential Mortgage Market*.

41. George A. Mooney, "Savings Banks Ask Wider Investment," *New York Times*, January 11, 1948; Clayton Knowles, "Building by Banks Backed at Albany," *New York Times*, February 7, 1948; Ronald S. Foster, "Noninsured Corporate Pension Funds as a Source of Funds for Savings and Loans Associations" (Ph.D. diss., Ohio State University, 1961), 241–47.

42. Discounts are, in fact, a very old form of banking. For example, they were commonly used for nineteenth-century short-term business loans. With a discount, the cost of borrowing is built into the principle of the loan. Borrowers procuring discounted loans might be required to pay back $100 for each $98 they actually received. While it is possible to use the discount rate to calculate the effective rate of interest on a loan, structuring the cost of borrowing in this way was enough of a legal difference to get around the FHA's rate ceilings. Discussing the problems of mortgage credit in the 1950s, mortgage dealer James Rouse noted that mortgage originators and brokers would use discounts to increase the yield on a mortgage in an effort to compete with corporate and government bonds offering higher returns. However, this approach could also decrease sales to insurance companies, which found discounts unseemly, in part because they suspected that the home borrower did not fully understand the transaction. In his testimony to the Senate's Banking and Currency Committee, Rouse explained, "There is something unreal and repelling about extreme discounts." Senate Committee on Banking and Currency, "Study of Mortgage Credit: Does the Decade 1961–70 Pose Problems in Private Housing and Mortgage Markets Which Require Federal Legislation by 1960?" (Washington, D.C.: U.S. Government Printing Office, 1958), 364. On the rule change, see Walter H. Stern, "F.H.A. Clears Use of Pension Funds," *New York Times*, August 18, 1957.

43. Georgetown University Law Center, "A Timeline of the Evolution of Retirement in the United States," *Memos and Fact Sheets* (2010), http://scholarship.law.georgetown.edu/legal/50.

44. Klaman notes that a small number of mortgage brokers sold conventional mortgages to individuals (constituting an estimated 5 percent of sales in 1955). Klaman, *Postwar Residential Mortgage Market*, 246. On the prohibition of FHA sales to individuals, see ibid., 240.

45. See Senate Committee on Banking and Currency, "Study of Mortgage Credit," 280, 286, 362–266.

46. There were other attempts besides that of Instlcorp. Investors Central Management Corporation was a mortgage banker that by 1958 serviced $170 million in mortgages for 16 life insurance companies and 25 savings banks around the nation and sold mortgages to three pension funds; like Instlcorp, it found that no one was interested in investing when market rates went above the FHA ceilings. In Baltimore, the Mortgage Corporation of America issued $4 million in 10- and 20-year collateral trust notes. In 1962, the Realty Collateral Corporation of New York issued $40 million in 20-year collateral trust notes backed by single-family FHA mortgages but only placed $3 million. "40 Million in 5% Realty Notes Offered by Warnecke Concern," *New York Times*, January 12, 1962; Oliver Jones, "Private Secondary Market Facilities," *Journal of Finance* 23, no. 2 (1968). See also Bartke, "Fannie Mae," 15–16. For another proposal, see Senate Committee on Banking and Currency, *Housing Amendments of 1957: Hearings Before a Subcommittee of the Committee on Banking and Currency, United States Senate, Eighty-Fifth Congress, First Session, on Various Bills to Amend the Federal Housing Laws, and Other Bills, March 18, 19, 21, 22, 25, 26,*

27, 28, April 1, 2, and 3, 1957, ed. Subcommittee on Housing (Washington, D.C.: United States Government Printing Office, 1957), 299–300.

47. Jones, "Private Secondary Market Facilities"; "FHA Adopts New Policy on Mortgages," *Los Angeles Times*, June 14, 1959.

48. Jones, "Private Secondary Market Facilities," 364.

49. Ibid., 364–65.

50. U.S. Office of Management and Budget, "Special Analyses, Budget of the United States Government" (Washington, D.C.: Executive Office of the President, 1965).

51. U.S. House Subcommittee on Domestic Finance and Committee on Banking and Currency, "A Study of Federal Credit Programs" (Washington, D.C.: Government Printing Office, 1964). See also Lyndon B. Johnson, "President Johnson to Gerald Ford, 7 February 1967, 4:00p," Tape WH6702.02, Program 3, Citation 11520, Lyndon Baines Johnson Library, Austin, Texas, distributed by the Miller Center of Public Affairs Presidential Recordings Program, Charlottesville, Virginia.

52. One government report claims that the Commodity Credit Corporation sold certificates backed by pools of loans in the 1930s, but it does not provide detail about how or why this occurred. Congressional Budget Office, ed., "Loan Guarantees: Current Concerns and Alternatives for Control" (Washington, D.C.: Governmenting Printing Office, 1978), 83.

53. S. E. Harris, S. H. Slichter, P. A. Samuelson, W. Fellner, E. S. Shaw, H. M. Groves, H. C. Wallich, A. C. Harberger, and N. Goldfinger, "The Economics of Eisenhower: A Symposium," *Review of Economics and Statistics* 38, no. 4 (1956).

54. U.S. House Subcommittee on Domestic Finance and Committee on Banking and Currency, "Study of Federal Credit Programs."

55. Sidney G. Tickton, *The Budget in Transition: A Staff Study Prepared for the NPA Business Committee*, Planning Pamphlets No. 89 (College Park, MD: National Planning Association, 1955), RG51, Box 31, National Archives, Washington, D.C.; Congressional Budget Office, "Loan Guarantees"; U.S. House Subcommittee on Domestic Finance and Committee on Banking and Currency, "Study of Federal Credit Programs."

56. Ibid.

57. On the Export-Import Bank sales, see Christopher Weeks, "Letter on the Export-Import Bank Participation Certificate Sale" (College Park, MD: National Planning Association, 1962), RG51, E37, Box 85, File: "Participation Certificates—1962–1965," National Archives, Washington, D.C. .

58. "Fanny May Plans $300 Million Issue," *New York Times*, October 14, 1964; "New Type of Security Sold to Group by FNMA," *Washington Post*, October 20, 1964. United States President's Commission on Budgetary Concepts, "Staff Papers and Other Materials: Including Proceedings of a Seminar on Budget Concepts for Economic Analysis Sponsored Jointly by the Commission and the Brookings Institution" (Washington D.C.: U.S. Government Printing Office, 1967), 285. The Staff Papers also note (see 309) that the FmHA by this time was selling loans that came with a guarantee in large blocks to financial institutions. Since the FmHA was a government-sponsored enterprise, this was a potential contingent liability of the United States but would have not been included on the budget.

59. "Major Housing Legislation Enacted," in *CQ Almanac 1965* (Washington, D.C.: Congressional Quarterly, 1966).

60. Richard Janssen, "Housing Bill, Signed by President, Lifts Aid to Persons, Cities, Firms," *Wall Street Journal*, September 3, 1964.

61. Raghuram Rajan, "The True Lessons of the Recession: The West Can't Borrow and Spend Its Way to Recovery," *Foreign Affairs* 91, no. 3 (2012). In the three years between 1967 and 1970 alone, Japanese exports to the United States nearly doubled. Stein, *Pivotal Decade*, 36.

62. Stein, *Pivotal Decade*, 30.

63. Here Krippner synthesizes and builds on the work of social theorists like Hirschman and Hirsch and Goldthorp. Krippner, *Capitalizing on Crisis*; Albert Hirschman, "The Social and Political Matrix of Inflation: Elaborations on the Latin American Experience," in *Essays in Trespassing: Economics to Politics and Beyond* (Cambridge: Cambridge University Press, 1980); Fred Hirsch and John H. Goldthorpe, *The Political Economy of Inflation* (Cambridge, Mass.: Harvard University Press, 1978). Patterson's history of the postwar era stresses the importance of rising expectations as the defining characteristic of the time, as does Daniel Bell's work. See Patterson, *Grand Expectations*; Daniel Bell, *The Cultural Contradictions of Capitalism* (New York: Basic Books, 1976).

64. Krippner, *Capitalizing on Crisis*, 21.

65. U.S. National Advisory Commission on Civil Disorders, *Report of the National Advisory Commission on Civil Disorders* (Washington, D.C.: Government Printing Office, 1968).

66. Chloe N. Thurston, "Policy Feedback in the Public–Private Welfare State: Advocacy Groups and Access to Government Homeownership Programs, 1934–1954," *Studies in American Political Development* 29, no. 2 (2015).

67. Robert Clifton Weaver, *The Negro Ghetto* (New York: Harcourt, 1948).

68. James Barron, "Robert C. Weaver, 89, First Black Cabinet Member, Dies," *New York Times*, July 19, 1997; Weaver, *Negro Ghetto*; Cary D. Wintz, "Weaver, Robert C," in *Encyclopedia of African American History: 1896 to the Present*, online ed., ed. Paul Finkelman (Oxford University Press); Williams Zachery, "Davis, John P.," in *Encyclopedia of African American History: 1896 to the Present*, online ed., ed. Paul Finkelman (Oxford University Press); Wendell E. Pritchett, *Robert Clifton Weaver and the American City: The Life and Times of an Urban Reformer* (Chicago: University of Chicago Press, 2008).

69. Elsie K. Goodman, "The Administration of Large Pension Plans," *Monthly Labor Review* 90, no. 10 (1967).

70. On the rise of the Sun Belt and the importance to this process of the military-industrial complex and support for education, see Margaret Pugh O'Mara, *Cities of Knowledge: Cold War Science and the Search for the Next Silicon Valley*, Politics and Society in Twentieth-Century America (Princeton, N.J.: Princeton University Press, 2005); Matthew D. Lassiter, *The Silent Majority: Suburban Politics in the Sunbelt South*, Politics and Society in Twentieth-Century America (Princeton, N.J.: Princeton University Press, 2006). On government investments in highways, see Mark H. Rose, *Interstate: Express Highway Politics, 1939–1989*, rev. ed. (Knoxville: University of Tennessee Press, 1990).

71. Lewis Ranieri, "The Origins of Securitization, Sources of Its Growth, and Its Future Potential," in *A Primer on Securitization*, ed. Leon T. Kendall and Michael J. Fishman (Cambridge, Mass.: MIT Press, 1996); Henry J. Aaron, *Shelter and Subsidies: Who Benefits from Federal Housing Policies?*, Studies in Social Economics (Washington, D.C.: Brookings Institution, 1972), 1.

72. Federal Home Loan Bank Board, "Annual Report," 15.

73. See Krippner, *Capitalizing on Crisis*. In February 1961, the First National Bank of New York sold the first negotiable certificate of deposit; within three years these certificates were a $15 billion business only surpassed by Treasury bills in money markets. Federal Reserve Bank of Richmond, "Negotiable Certificates of Deposit," *Economic Quarterly* (1965), https://fraser .stlouisfed.org/files/docs/publications/frbrichreview/pages/65469_1965-1969.pdf; Krippner, *Capitalizing on Crisis*, 89–99; John J. Redfield, "Savings Banks and Savings and Loan Associations: The Past and the Future," *Business Lawyer* 16, no. 1 (1960).

74. Federal Reserve Bank of Richmond, "Negotiable Certificates of Deposit"; Krippner, *Capitalizing on Crisis*, 89–99; Redfield, "Savings Banks."

75. Saul B. Klaman, "Public/Private Approaches to Urban Mortgage and Housing Problems," *Law and Contemporary Problems* 32, no. 2 (1967): 254.

76. S&Ls offered an average interest rate of 2.7 percent in 1952, which was more than double the commercial banks' average rate of 1.1 percent on deposits. By 1965, the 4.25 percent return from S&Ls was only 13 percent higher than the 3.69 percent rate paid out by commercial banks. Ernest Bloch, "Two Decades of Evolution of Financial Institutions and Public Policy," *Journal of Money, Credit and Banking* 3, no. 2 (1971): 562.

77. Homebuilders and lenders called for various reforms in the early 1960s: Why not devise a standard system for classifying mortgages so investors could quickly gauge their quality? Why not lift FHA lending ceilings that limited the flow of funds out west or lift restrictions on the kinds of mortgages Fannie Mae purchased? Could the government allow insurance companies to invest in riskier, more leveraged loans or allow the S&Ls to purchase more corporate assets? What about requiring S&Ls to hold larger reserves of government bonds so they could have a cushion when the housing market declined? Why not encourage more lending by allowing adjustable-rate mortgages? Over the next decades many of these changes would come to pass. See Robert Weaver, "Future Prospects in Housing Finance," address delivered at the Mortgage Bankers Association of America Annual Convention, Berkeley, California, November 2, 1966. Senate Committee on Banking and Currency, "Study of Mortgage Credit." See also Gordon H. Sellon and Deana Van-Nahmen, "The Securitization of Housing Finance," *Economic Review—Federal Reserve Bank of Kansas City* 73, no. 7 (1988): 100–4; Richard K. Green and Susan M. Wachter, "The American Mortgage in Historical and International Context," *Journal of Economic Perspectives* 19, no. 4 (2005); Cohen, *Consumers' Republic*, 235; Aaron, *Shelter and Subsidies*; Jones, "Development," 358–59; idem, "Private Secondary Market Facilities"; Klaman, "Public/Private Approaches."

78. Lyndon B. Johnson, "Radio and Television Remarks upon Signing the Tax Bill," ed. John T. Woolley and Gerhard Peters (Santa Barbara, Calif.: American Presidency Project, 1964), http://www.presidency.ucsb.edu/ws/?pid=26084; Irving Bernstein, *Guns or Butter: The Presidency of Lyndon Johnson* (New York: Oxford University Press, 1996), 41.

79. Collins, *More*, 53.

80. In 1965 Johnson first lied to his advisors (and everyone else) about how much Vietnam would really cost; it was a feat he could pull off only because military contractors were being paid on a 6- to 18-month delay. Johnson could not long hide the inflationary effect of the war, however, since the contractors secured interim financing from the banks. The military budget for 1965 was expected to rise by $12.8 billion, not the announced $3 billion to $5 billion. See Bernstein, *Guns or Butter*, 363.

81. On Johnson's objection to this increase and debates about it at the Fed, see Robert P. Bremner, *Chairman of the Fed: William McChesney Martin, Jr., and the Creation of the Modern American Financial System* (New Haven, Conn.: Yale University Press, 2004), 186.

82. FHLBB, "Annual Report," 15.

83. On the Fed's early response, see Thomas Mayer, "A Case Study of Federal Reserve Policymaking," *Journal of Monetary Economics* 10, no. 2 (1982). As of December of 1965, the Federal Reserve raised the Regulation Q ceiling on time deposits to 5.5 percent. By spring of 1966, commercial banks were offering 5 percent on one- to three-month certificates of deposits, putting them above the 4 percent (on average) that S&Ls offered on savings deposits. In the fall of that same year, the Fed tried to gain control by raising its own rates above the Regulation Q ceiling, drawing money away from the banks that had themselves drawn money from the S&Ls. The strategy worked to get the banks in line (somewhat) but did not provide relief to housing because the banks cut off mortgages before their business clients. Regulation Q was extended to S&Ls in 1966 with the provision that their ceilings could be set slightly higher than those of the commercial banks to preserve their historical advantage in interest rates on deposit accounts. R. Alton Gilbert, "Requiem for Regulation Q: What It Did and Why It Passed Away," *Review (Federal Reserve Bank of St. Louis)*, February (1986).

84. The inflow of savings into the mutuals was down by over a quarter. Jane F. Nelson, "Disintermediation," *Economic Quarterly* April (1968), https://fraser.stlouisfed.org/files/docs/publications/frbrichreview/rev_frbrich_index_1952-1973.pdf.

85. Green and Wachter, "American Mortgage"; Gertrude Sipperly Fish, *The Story of Housing* (New York: Macmillan, 1979).

86. Minsky, cited in L. Randall Wray, "The 1966 Financial Crisis: Financial Instability or Political Economy?," *Review of Political Economy* 11, no. 4 (1999): 416.

87. See, for example, Lynn A. Stiles, "The Trend of Business: Another 1966 for Homebuilding? (Impact on Housing of the Tight Credit Market in 1969)," *Business Conditions* November (1969), https://fraser.stlouisfed.org/title/5562/item/540281/toc/520833; Bremner, *Chairman of the Fed*, 246.

88. Charles M. Haar, *Federal Credit and Private Housing: The Mass Financing Dilemma* (New York: McGraw-Hill, 1960), 153.

89. That fall the FHLB issued $590 million in new obligations, just enough to cover its maturing bonds. In offering $1.5 billion in advances in 1966, the FHLB had set a new record, but that $1.5 billion was the equivalent of the S&Ls' losses in the single brutal month of July. FHLBB, "Annual Report," 37–40. Nelson, "Disintermediation."

90. Raymond H. Lapin, interview by David G. McComb, November 21, 1968.

91. Krippner, *Capitalizing on Crisis*, 17–18, 63–66.

92. Biographers have tended to account for Johnson's indecision in terms of his psychology: some mix of stubbornness, short-sightedness, ignorance, and denial. Social scientists have tended to offer a more structural analysis of the moment. For a social conservative like Daniel Bell, the problem was a cultural dysregulation in which the American populace was unable or unwilling to reign in its various desires. For a burgeoning neoliberal economist, the problem was Keynesianism itself, which was doomed to fail because government officials were always going to have an impetus to expand the economy but not the backbone to impose fiscal cuts as needed. And for a leftist critic, this moment was a textbook crisis of late capitalism in which the pressure of maintaining global hegemony and demand at home outpaced the capacity of the economy and the ability of the state to generate revenues, sparking a fiscal crisis. Bell, *Cultural Contradictions*; James O'Connor, *The Fiscal Crisis of the State* (New Brunswick, N.J.: Transaction, 2002); Fred Block, "The Fiscal Crisis of the Capitalist State," *Annual Review of Sociology* 7 (1981).

93. Joseph A. Schumpeter, "The Crisis of the Tax State," in *The Economics and Sociology of Capitalism*, ed. Richard Swedberg (Princeton, N.J.: Princeton University Press, 1991 [1918]), 101.

94. Robert M. Collins, "The Economic Crisis of 1968 and the Waning of the 'American Century,'" *American Historical Review* 101, no. 2 (1996): 403–4. Johnson also faced additional pressure for taxation from a worsening situation with the balance of payments, driven by U.S. trade deficits and exacerbated by the spending in Vietnam. A tax increase was a way to signal that the United States was serious about addressing the deficit and in so doing calm worries that the United States would fail to continue to support convertibility to gold. For other discussions of the balance of payments problems in the 1960s, see Stein, *Pivotal Decade*; Aaron Major, *Architects of Austerity: International Finance and the Politics of Growth* (Stanford, Calif.: Stanford University Press, 2014); Collins, *More*.

95. U.S. Department of the Treasury, "Federal Credit Programs: A Report by the Secretary of the Treasury to the Congress" (Washington, D.C.: Government Printing Office, 1967); U.S. House Committee on Banking and Currency, "Sale of Participations in Government Agency Loan Pools," ed. U.S. House of Representatives (Washington, D.C.: Government Printing Office, 1966).

96. Congressional Budget Office, "Loan Guarantees."

97. U.S. Bureau of the Budget, "Staff Paper (Memo to the President's Commission on Budgetary Concepts): Loans, Participation Certificates, and the Financing of Budget Deficits," May

29, 1967, 12, 15, in RG 51, Box 120, Folder: "BOB Comments on PCBC Report—Chapter V," National Archives and Records Administration.

98. U.S. House Committee on Banking and Currency, "Sale of Participations," 18.

99. See ibid. Also see "'Participations' Approved as Borrowing Device," in *CQ Almanac 1966* (Washington, D.C.: Congressional Quarterly, 1967), https://library.cqpress.com/cqalmanac /document.php?id=cqal66-1300307.

100. U.S. House Committee on Banking and Currency, "Sale of Participations," 18.

101. Ibid., 22.

102. See Lyndon B. Johnson, "Letter to the President of the Senate and to the Speaker of the House Transmitting Bill Encouraging the Substitution of Private for Public Credit," ed. John T. Woolley and Gerhard Peters (Santa Barbara, Calif.: American Presidency Project, 1966). See also "Chronology of Action on the Budget," in *Congressional Quarterly: Congress and the Nation* (Washington, D.C.: Congressional Quarterly, 1966).

103. Brock Adams, letter to Barefoot Saunders, October 27, 1966, in White House Central Files, Box 55, Folder "LE/FI 5," Lyndon Baines Johnson Library, Austin, Texas.

104. Johnson, "President Johnson to Gerald Ford."

105. These six agencies were the Federal Housing Administration, the Farmers Home Loan Administration, the Department of Education, the Department of Housing and Urban Development, the Veterans Administration, and the Small Business Administration.

106. See Lapin, interview by David G. McComb, 1968.

107. Richard F. Janssen, "How Fannie Mae Helps U.S. Budget Makers Trim Spending Figures," *Wall Street Journal*, January 20, 1966.

108. "Memo on Debt Limit from Secretary of Treasury's Office to the White House, 1967," in White House Central Files, Box 55, Folder "FI 10 5/26/66–1/27/67," LBJ Library.

109. "Memo Ca. November 1966," in White House Central Files, Box 55, Folder "FI 10 5/26/66–1/27/67," LBJ Library.

110. "Fannie Mae Undecided on When It Will Sell $3.2 Billion Certificates," *Wall Street Journal*, September 1, 1966; "Treasury Changes Its Policy on Sale of Agency Issues," *Wall Street Journal*, September 12, 1966. See also "Memo on 6 September 1966," in White House Central Files, Box 35, Folder "FI 5 Credit–Loans 4/21/66–9/6/66," LBJ Library.

111. Lyndon B. Johnson and Henry Fowler, "President Johnson and Henry 'Joe' Fowler, 11 January, 5:25 Pm," Tape WH6701.03, Program 8, Citation 11340, in Recordings of Telephone Conversations—White House Series, Recordings and Transcripts of Conversations and Meetings, LBJ Library.

112. Henry Fowler, "Memorandum for the President, January 4th" in RG 51, Box 119, Folder "PCBC—Appointment of Commission Members. Jan–March 1967, Jan 12, 1967," National Archives, College Park, Maryland.

113. U.S. Bureau of the Budget, "Memo to the President's Commission," later published in United States President's Commission on Budgetary Concepts, "Staff Papers," 292.

114. Johnson and Fowler, "President Johnson and Henry 'Joe' Fowler."

115. The debt limit would be raised from the $285 billion level at which it had stayed since 1960 (all interim raises were to the temporary limit) to $365 billion on June 30, the last day of the 1967 fiscal year. Johnson got his deal.

116. U.S. Bureau of the Budget, "Memo to the President's Commission," 105.

117. Ellsworth H. Morse, "Report of the President's Commission on Budget Concepts in Retrospect," *Public Administration Review* 31, no. 4 (1971).

118. Ibid., 294.

119. Ibid., 406.

120. Ibid., 294.

121. "Administrative History of the Bureau of the Budget, Ca. 1968," 29, in Administrative Histories Collection, Box 1, LBJ Library.

122. President's Commission on Budgetary Concepts, "Report," 55.

123. "Administrative History of the Treasury, Ca. 1968," in Administrative Histories Collection, Box 1, LBJ Library; Raymond Lapin, "Raymond Lapin to Robert Weaver," January 3, 1967, in White House Aides, Office Files of James Gaither, Box 7, Folder: "FNMA Spin-Off," LBJ Library; Philip Brownstein, interview by David G. McComb, 1968, http://web2.millercenter.org /lbj/oralhistory/brownstein_philip_1968_1122.pdf.

124. DeVier Pierson, "Memorandum for the President," March 9, 1968, in White House Central Files, Box 37, Folder "EX FI 5 Credit–Loans 4/21/66–9/6/66," LBJ Library.

125. "Memorandum for Devier Pierson, Subject: Secretary Freeman's Proposal on Budget Concepts," March 6, 1968, in White House Central Files, Box 37, Folder "e FI 5 Credit–Loans 4/21/66–9/6/66," LBJ Library.

126. David M. Freund, *Colored Property: State Policy and White Racial Politics in Suburban America* (Chicago: University of Chicago Press, 2007); Jones and Grebler, *Secondary Mortgage Market.*

127. Krippner, *Capitalizing on Crisis*; Monica Prasad, *The Politics of Free Markets: The Rise of Neoliberal Economic Policies in Britain, France, Germany, and the United States* (Chicago: University of Chicago Press, 2006).

128. Sherman Maisel, "Minutes of the Housing Credit Committee Meeting," May 11, 1967; "Subject: Some Notes on Proposed Secondary Market Operations," May 8, 1967; "Memorandum to Mr. J. S. Duesenberry, Council of Economic Advisers, Subject: Primary Review of Two Mortgage Proposals," September 27, 1967, all in Private Papers of Sherman Maisel, Berkeley, California.

129. See Sellon and VanNahmen, "Securitization of Housing Finance"; Charles M. Sivesind, "Mortgage-Backed Securities: The Revolution in Real Estate Finance," *Federal Reserve Bank of New York Quarterly Review* 4, no. 3 (1979).

130. Paul E. Junk and Lonnie Nickles, "Federal Participation Certificates," *Nebraska Journal of Economics and Business* 9, no. 2 (1970).

131. Maisel, "Minutes."

132. Idem, "Subject: Some Notes."

133. U.S. House Committee on Banking and Currency, "Housing and Urban Development Act of 1968, Report of the Committee on Banking and Currency, Together with Minority Views, on H.R. 17989" (Washington, D.C.: Government Printing Office, 1968), 79.

134. "Summary of Meeting on Fannie Mae," January 19, 1968, in White House Aides, Office Files of James Gaither, Box 7, Folder "FNMA Spin-Off," LBJ Library.

135. On the changing debt-to-equity ratio of Fannie Mae, see Lapin, interview by David G. McComb, LBJ Library Oral Histories, 11, 35, https://www.discoverlbj.org/item/oh-lapinr -19681121-1-74-37.

136. "The Fannie Mae Flap," *Wall Street Journal*, December 18, 1969; Richard F Janssen, "The Outlook," *Wall Street Journal*, December 15, 1969.

137. Hyman, *Debtor Nation*, 221–32.

138. See the discussion of the "rat bill" in Robert Weaver, interview by Joe B. Frantz, November 19, 1968, LBJ Library Oral Histories, https://www.discoverlbj.org/item/oh-weaverr -19681119-1-73-26.

139. "Housing Bill Provides Home-Buying, Riot, Other Aid," in *CQ Almanac 1968* (Washington, D.C.: Congressional Quarterly, 1969); Alexander von Hoffman, "Calling upon the Genius of Private Enterprise: The Housing and Urban Development Act of 1968 and the Liberal Turn to Public-Private Partnerships," *Studies in American Political Development* 27, no. 2 (2013): 186.

140. Johnson, "President Johnson to Gerald Ford."

141. Sivesind, "Mortgage-Backed Securities."

142. Richard F. Janssen, "Fuss over Dismissal of Fannie Mae Head Unlikely to Fade Soon," *Wall Street Journal*, December 16, 1969.

143. James Hill, "GNMA Mortgage Backed Securities," 1971, in RG51, E202, Folder: "Housing CVA: HUD 1971–72G(2)," National Archives and Records Administration, Washington, D.C.

144. Congressional Research Service, "The Federal Financing Bank: Its Role and Functions" (Washington, D.C.: Congressional Research Service, Library of Congress, 1975); U.S. Department of Treasury, "Federal Financing Bank Annual Report" (Washington, D.C.: U.S. Department of Treasury, 2014).

145. Congressional Budget Office, "Loan Guarantees," 24–31.

146. Krippner, *Capitalizing on Crisis*.

147. K. H. Lin and D. Tomaskovic-Devey, "Financialization and US Income Inequality, 1970–2008," *American Journal of Sociology* 118, no. 5 (2013); D. Tomaskovic-Devey and K. H. Lin, "Income Dynamics, Economic Rents, and the Financialization of the U.S. Economy," *American Sociological Review* 76, no. 4 (2011).

148. There is a large literature on financialization. On finance and income inequality, see Lin and Tomaskovic-Devey, "Financialization and US Income Inequality"; Tomaskovic-Devey and Lin, "Income Dynamics." For book-length treatments on financialization, see especially Krippner, *Capitalizing on Crisis*; Gérard Duménil and Dominique Lévy, *The Crisis of Neoliberalism* (Cambridge, Mass.: Harvard University Press, 2011); Randy Martin, *Financialization of Daily Life* (Philadelphia: Temple University Press, 2002). For sociologically minded review articles, see Gerald F. Davis and Suntae Kim, "Financialization of the Economy," *Annual Review of Sociology* 41 (2015); Bruce G. Carruthers and Jeong-Chul Kim, "The Sociology of Finance," *Annual Review of Sociology* 37, no. 1 (2011); Natascha van der Zwan, "Making Sense of Financialization," *Socio-Economic Review* 12, no. 1 (2014). For an analysis of housing and financialization, see Manuel Aalbers, *The Financialization of Housing: A Political Economy Approach* (New York: Routledge, Taylor & Francis Group, 2016). I approach the related concept of neoliberalism as an ideological system that is conducive to financialization; for an incisive overview of neoliberalism, see Stephanie Lee Mudge, "What Is Neo-Liberalism?," *Socio-Economic Review* 6, no. 4 (2008).

149. Wolfgang Streeck, *Buying Time: The Delayed Crisis of Democratic Capitalism* (New York: Verso, 2014), 3.

150. For a similar argument that focuses on securitization as part of a larger trend of the rise of derivatives, see Dick Bryan and Michael Rafferty, *Capitalism with Derivatives: A Political Economy of Financial Derivatives, Capital and Class* (New York: Palgrave Macmillan, 2006). On the emergence of securitization as one of various new forms of property rights that emerged with financialization, see Bruce G. Carruthers, "Financialization and the Institutional Foundations of the New Capitalism," *Socio-Economic Review* 13, no. 2 (2015). For insight into how the use of trusts promotes financialization through securitization and derivatives, see Brooke Harrington, "Trusts and Financialization," *Socio-Economic Review* 15, no. 1 (2017).

151. Krippner discusses the process of "deregulation" under financialization as "a continual process of institutional innovation in which functions are transferred to markets, but under the close control of the state." Aalbers uses the phrase "regulated deregulation" to note that deregulation, while a removal of market rules and regulations, does not involve the removal of the state from market spaces so much as a reconfiguration of the government's role in those spaces. Greta Krippner, "The Making of US Monetary Policy: Central Bank Transparency and the Neoliberal Dilemma," *Theory and Society* 36, no. 6 (2007): 477; Aalbers, *Financialization of Housing*, 170–92.

Chapter 10: What We Owe One Another

1. See, for example, Gérard Duménil and Dominique Lévy, *The Crisis of Neoliberalism* (Cambridge, Mass.: Harvard University Press, 2011); Fred Block, "Financial Democratization and the Transition to Socialism" (University of California Davis, 2018), https://ssc.wisc.edu/~wright/929-utopias-2018/wp-content/uploads/2018/01/Block-Democratizing-Finance-April-2017.pdf; Robert C. Hockett, "Finance Without Financiers" (Cornell Law School, 2018), https://ssc.wisc.edu/~wright/929-utopias-2018/wp-content/uploads/2018/01/Hockett-Finance-without-Financiers-17-June-2017.pdf.

2. Jeffrey Haydu, "Making Use of the Past: Time Periods as Cases to Compare and as Sequences of Problem Solving," *American Journal of Sociology* 104, no. 2 (1998): 339–71.

3. Louis Hyman, *Debtor Nation: The History of America in Red Ink* (Princeton, N.J.: Princeton University Press, 2011); Jan L. Logemann, "From Cradle to Bankruptcy?: Credit Access and the American Welfare State," in *The Development of Consumer Credit in Global Perspective: Business, Regulation, and Culture*, ed. Jan L. Logemann (New York: Palgrave Macmillan, 2012).

4. Barry Bosworth, Andrew S. Carron, and Elisabeth Rhyne, *The Economics of Federal Credit Programs* (Washington, D.C.: Brookings Institution, 1987); Raymond J. Saulnier, Harold G. Halcrow, and Neil H. Jacoby, *Federal Lending: Its Growth and Impact* (New York: National Bureau of Economic Research, 1957); Douglas J. Elliott, *Uncle Sam in Pinstripes: Evaluating U.S. Federal Credit Programs* (Washington, D.C.: Brookings Institution, 2011); Clifford M. Hardin and Arthur T. Denzau, "The Unrestrained Growth of Federal Credit Programs" (Center for the Study of American Business, Washington University, 1981).

5. David M. Freund, *Colored Property: State Policy and White Racial Politics in Suburban America* (Chicago: University of Chicago Press, 2007).

6. Isaac William Martin, *The Permanent Tax Revolt: How the Property Tax Transformed American Politics* (Stanford, Calif.: Stanford University Press, 2008), 20.

7. On organizational imprinting, see especially Arthur L. Stinchcombe and James G. March, "Social Structure and Organizations," *Handbook of Organizations* 7 (1965); Victoria Johnson, "What Is Organizational Imprinting?: Cultural Entrepreneurship in the Founding of the Paris Opera," *American Journal of Sociology* 113, no. 1 (2007); Zeki Simsek, Brian Curtis Fox, and Ciaran Heavey, "'What's Past Is Prologue': A Framework, Review, and Future Directions for Organizational Research on Imprinting," *Journal of Management* 41, no. 1 (2014).

8. I note that this insight is at the core of Lipset's work on American exceptionalism, although I ultimately draw different conclusions about the results of this for American markets. Seymour Martin Lipset, *The First New Nation: The United States in Historical and Comparative Perspective* (New Brunswick, N.J.: Transaction Publishers, 2003 [1963]); idem, *American Exceptionalism: A Double-Edged Sword* (New York: W. W. Norton, 1996).

9. Marc Schneiberg, "What's on the Path?: Path Dependence, Organizational Diversity and the Problem of Institutional Change in the US Economy, 1900–1950," *Socio-Economic Review* 5, no. 1 (2007); Gerald Berk, *Alternative Tracks: The Constitution of American Industrial Order, 1865–1917* (Baltimore: Johns Hopkins University Press, 1994); Michael Schwartz, *Radical Protest and Social Structure: The Southern Farmers' Alliance and Cotton Tenancy, 1880–1890* (Chicago: University of Chicago Press, 1988).

10. Lipset, *American Exceptionalism*, 154.

11. Karl Polanyi, *The Great Transformation: The Political and Economic Origins of Our Time* (Boston: Beacon Press, 1957).

12. Benjamin Braun, "The Financial Consequences of Mr. Draghi?: Monetary Policy and Market-Based Banking in the Euro Area" (Max Planck Institute for the Study of Societies, 2016); Ewald Engelen and Anna Glasmacher, "'Simple, Transparent and Standardized': Narratives,

Law and Interest Coalitions in Regulatory Capitalism," (University of Amsterdam, 2016); Marina Hübner, "'Securitization Is Dead—Long Live Securitization!': The European Sovereign Debt Crisis, Market-Based Banking, and the Dream of an Integrated European Financial Space" (Max Planck Institute for the Study of Societies, 2016).

13. Ewald Engelen and Anna Glasmacher, "The Waiting Game: How Securitization Became the Solution for the Growth Problem of the Eurozone," *Competition & Change* 22, no. 2 (2018): 167.

14. Xavier Debrun, Laurent Moulin, Alessandro Turrini, Joaquim Ayuso-i-Casals, Manmohan S. Kumar, Allan Drazen, and Clemens Fuest, "Tied to the Mast?: National Fiscal Rules in the European Union (with Discussion)," *Economic Policy* 23, no. 54 (2008); James M. Poterba and Jürgen von Hagen, *Fiscal Institutions and Fiscal Performance*, National Bureau of Economic Research Conference Report (Chicago: University of Chicago Press, 1999).

15. Gene Park, *Spending Without Taxation: Filp and the Politics of Public Finance in Japan*, Studies of the Walter H Shorenstein Asia-Pacific Research Center (Stanford, Calif.: Stanford University Press, 2011).

16. Y. Wang "The Rise of the 'Shareholding State': Financialization of Economic Management in China," *Socio-Economic Review* 13, no. 3 (2015).

17. On state-level banking, see chapter 2. Josh Pacewicz, "Tax Increment Financing, Economic Development Professionals and the Financialization of Urban Politics," *Socio-Economic Review* 11 (2012).

18. Pierre Bourdieu, *On the State: Lectures at the College de France, 1989–1992* (Malden, Mass: Polity Press, 2014).

19. Benjamin Braun, "Central Banking and the Infrastructural Power of Finance: The Case of ECB Support for Repo and Securitization Markets," *Socio-Economic Review*, February 20 (2018).

20. Special purpose vehicles (SPVs) are also sometimes called special purpose entities (SPEs) or special purpose companies (SPCs). They can be trusts, partnerships, or even corporations.

21. Gerald F. Davis, *Managed by the Markets: How Finance Reshaped America* (New York: Oxford University Press, 2009).

22. For more on important changes in the securitization market in the 1970s and 1980s, the best sources are Hyman, *Debtor Nation*; Natalya Vinokurova, "How Mortgage-Backed Securities Became Bonds: The Emergence, Evolution, and Acceptance of Mortgage-Backed Securities in the United States, 1960–1987," *Enterprise & Society* 19, no. 3 (2018). For accounts of the rise of finance and the crisis of 2007, see Davis, *Managed by the Markets*; Gillian Tett, *Fool's Gold: How the Bold Dream of a Small Tribe at J. P. Morgan Was Corrupted by Wall Street Greed and Unleashed a Catastrophe* (New York: Free Press, 2009); Bethany McLean and Joseph Nocera, *All the Devils Are Here: The Hidden History of the Financial Crisis* (New York: Portfolio/Penguin, 2010); George A. Akerlof and Robert J. Shiller, *Animal Spirits: How Human Psychology Drives the Economy, and Why It Matters for Global Capitalism* (Princeton, N.J.: Princeton University Press, 2009); Atif Mian and Amir Sufi, *House of Debt: How They (and You) Caused the Great Recession, and How We Can Prevent It from Happening Again* (Chicago: University of Chicago Press, 2014); Raghuram Rajan, *Fault Lines: How Hidden Fractures Still Threaten the World Economy* (Princeton, N.J.: Princeton University Press, 2010); Anat R. Admati and Martin F. Hellwig, *The Bankers' New Clothes: What's Wrong with Banking and What to Do About It* (Princeton, N.J.: Princeton University Press, 2013); Daniel Immergluck, *Foreclosed: High-Risk Lending, Deregulation, and the Undermining of America's Mortgage Market* (Ithaca, N.Y.: Cornell University Press, 2009); Herman M. Schwartz and Leonard Seabrooke, *The Politics of Housing Booms and Busts* (New York: Palgrave Macmillan, 2009).

23. Greta Krippner, *Capitalizing on Crisis: The Political Origins of the Rise of Finance* (Cambridge, Mass.: Harvard University Press, 2011); Wolfgang Streeck, "The Crises of Democratic Capitalism," *New Left Review* 71 (2011); Colin Crouch, *The Strange Non-Death of Neo-Liberalism*

(Malden, Mass.: Polity, 2011); Raghuram Rajan, "The True Lessons of the Recession: The West Can't Borrow and Spend Its Way to Recovery," *Foreign Affairs* 91, no. 3 (2012).

24. Daniel Immergluck, "From Risk-Limited to Risk-Loving Mortgage Markets: Origins of the U.S. Subprime Crisis and Prospects for Reform," *Journal of Housing and the Built Environment* 26, no. 3 (2011): 251.

25. Patric H. Hendershott, "The Market for Home Mortgage Credit: Recent Changes and Future Prospects," NBER Working Paper Series (1990), http://www.nber.org/papers/w3548.pdf.

26. Ibid.

27. Jacob S. Hacker, "Privatizing Risk Without Privatizing the Welfare State: The Hidden Politics of Social Policy Retrenchment in the United States," *American Political Science Review* 98, no. 2 (2004); J. Hacker and P. Pierson, "Business Power and Social Policy: Employers and the Formation of the American Welfare State," *Politics & Society* 30, no. 2 (2002); Duménil and Lévy, *Crisis of Neoliberalism*; Anthony Ross, "The Ownership Society: Mortgage Securitization and the Metropolitan Landscape Since the 1960s" (Ph.D. diss., University of Michigan, 2015).

28. Key innovators Lewis Ranieri and Lawrence Fink both discussed how hard they worked to sell these bonds in early years. Fink later recalled: "Investor seminars were conducted, research pieces disseminated, conferences hosted, and sales calls made in record numbers." Lawrence Fink, "The Role of Pension Funds and Other Investors in Securitized Debt Markets," in *A Primer on Securitization*, ed. Leon T. Kendall and Michael J. Fishman (Cambridge, Mass.: MIT Press, 1996), 122.

29. Michael J. Lea, "Innovation and the Cost of Mortgage Credit," *Housing Policy Debate* 7, no. 1 (1996): 166.

30. Bruce G. Carruthers and Arthur L. Stinchcombe, "The Social Structure of Liquidity: Flexibility, Markets, and States," *Theory and Society* 28, no. 3 (1999). See also Lea, "Innovation."

31. See Vinokurova for an excellent analysis of how private firms accomplished this by changing both the structure of the instruments and investors' understanding of what constitutes a bond. Natalya Vinokurova, "How Mortgage-Backed Securities Became Bonds: The Emergence, Evolution, and Acceptance of Mortgage-Backed Securities in the United States, 1960–1987," *Enterprise & Society* 19, no. 3 (2018).

32. This list of "exotic securitization deals" is from Vinod Kothari, *Securitization: The Financial Instrument of the Future*, Wiley Finance (Hoboken, N.J.: John Wiley & Sons, 2006), 65.

33. On securitization and the change in banking, see Davis, *Managed by the Markets*.

34. John J. McConnell and Stephen A. Buser, "The Origins and Evolution of the Market for Mortgage-Backed Securities," *Annual Review of Financial Economics* 3 (2011): 181.

35. Ruth Simon and Michael Hudson, "Whistling Past Housing's Graveyard?: Bad Loans Draw Bad Blood," *Wall Street Journal*, October 9, 2006.

36. Mian and Sufi, *House of Debt*.

37. See ibid.; McConnell and Buser, "Origins and Evolution."

38. Adam J. Levitin and Susan M. Wachter, "Explaining the Housing Bubble," *Georgetown Law Journal* 100, no. 4 (2012).

39. Adam B. Ashcraft and Til Schuermann, "Understanding the Securitization of Subprime Mortgage Credit," *Federal Reserve Bank of New York Staff Reports* 318 (2008), https://www.newyorkfed.org/medialibrary/media/research/staff_reports/sr318.pdf.

40. Gary B. Gorton, "The Subprime Panic," NBER Working Paper Series (2008), http://www.nber.org/papers/w14398.pdf.

41. Benjamin Keys, Tomasz Piskorski, Amit Seru, and Vikrant Vig, "Mortgage Financing in the Housing Boom and Bust," in *Housing and the Financial Crisis*, ed. Edward L. Glaeser and Todd Sinai (Chicago: University of Chicago Press, 2013), 149.

42. Gorton, "Subprime Panic," 3.

43. Keys et al., "Mortgage Financing," 144.

44. McConnell and Buser, "Origins and Evolution," 180. See also Mian and Sufi, *House of Debt*.

45. Donald MacKenzie, "The Credit Crisis as a Problem in the Sociology of Knowledge," *American Journal of Sociology* 116, no. 6 (2011).

46. McConnell and Buser, "Origins and Evolution," 181.

47. CoreLogic, "United States Residential Foreclosure: Ten Years Later" (2007), http://www.corelogic.com/research/foreclosure-report/national-foreclosure-report-10-year.pdf, 4–5.

48. McConnell and Buser, "Origins and Evolution," 181.

49. Christopher Lewis Peterson, "Fannie Mae, Freddie Mac, and the Home Mortgage Foreclosure Crisis," *Loyola University New Orleans Journal of Public Interest Law* 10 (2009): 165.

50. McConnell and Buser, "Origins and Evolution," 179.

51. Peterson, "Fannie Mae, Freddie Mac," 166.

52. Mian and Sufi, *House of Debt*.

53. United States Bureau of Labor Statistics, "The Recession of 2007–2009," *BLS Spotlight on Statistics* (2012), https://www.bls.gov/spotlight/2012/recession/pdf/recession_bls_spotlight.pdf.

54. McConnell and Buser, "Origins and Evolution," 182.

55. For an analysis of exclusion and exploitation as mechanisms of inequality, see C. Tilly, "Relational Origins of Inequality," *Anthropological Theory* 1, no. 3 (2001).

56. On the continuance of racially biased risk management systems, see especially Guy Stuart, *Discriminating Risk: The U.S. Mortgage Lending Industry in the Twentieth Century* (Ithaca, N.Y.: Cornell University Press, 2003).

57. Alyssa Katz, *Our Lot: How Real Estate Came to Own Us* (New York: Bloomsbury, 2009), 43, 48.

58. Debbie Gruenstein Bocian, Wei Li, Carolina Reid, and Roberto G. Quercia, "Lost Ground, 2011: Disparities in Mortgage Lending and Foreclosures" (Center for Responsible Lending, 2011), http://www.responsiblelending.org/mortgage-lending/research-analysis/Lost-Ground-exec-summary.pdf, 4.

59. Gorton, "Subprime Panic," 5.

60. Katz, *Our Lot*; Harvard University Joint Center for Housing Studies, "The State of the Nation's Housing 2009," http://www.jchs.harvard.edu/research/publications/state-nations-housing-2009; Renae Merle, "Minorities Hit Harder by Foreclosure Crisis," *Washington Post*, June 19, 2010.

61. Jacob S. Rugh and Douglas S. Massey, "Racial Segregation and the American Foreclosure Crisis," *American Sociological Review* 75, no. 5 (2010); Matthew Hall, Kyle Crowder, and Amy Spring, "Variations in Housing Foreclosures by Race and Place, 2005–2012," *Annals of the American Academy of Political and Social Science* 660, no. 1 (2015).

62. Katz, *Our Lot*; Harvard University Joint Center for Housing Studies, "State of the Nation's Housing." See also Melvin L. Oliver and Thomas M. Shapiro, *Black Wealth, White Wealth: A New Perspective on Racial Inequality*, 10th anniversary ed. (New York: Routledge, 2006), 211–20, 46–50.

63. Jonathan G. Katz, "Who Benefited from the Bailout?," *Minnesota Law Review* 95, no. 5 (2011): 1586.

64. Ibid., 1587.

65. See especially Elliott, *Uncle Sam in Pinstripes*.

66. Avi Lerner and Elizabeth Cove Delisle, "Report on the Troubled Asset Relief Program—June 2017," http://www.cbo.gov/publication/52840.

67. Katz, "Who Benefited from the Bailout?," 1584–85.

68. For critiques on the bailout as ineffective, see Olga Pierce and Paul Kiel, "By the Numbers: A Revealing Look at the Mortgage Mod Meltdown" (ProPublica, 2011), https://www.propublica.org/article/by-the-numbers-a-revealing-look-at-the-mortgage-mod-meltdown.

69. Katz, "Who Benefited from the Bailout?," 1584.

70. Office of the Special Inspector General for the Troubled Asset Relief Program, "Quarterly Report to Congress," October 26, 2016, https://www.sigtarp.gov/Quarterly%20Reports/October_26_2016_Report_To_Congress.pdf, 99.

71. Mian and Sufi, *House of Debt*.

72. Levitin and Wachter, "Explaining the Housing Bubble."

73. White House, "President Trump's Plan to Rebuild America's Infrastructure," https://www.whitehouse.gov/blog/2017/06/08/president-trumps-plan-rebuild-americas-infrastructure; idem, "Fact Sheet 2018 Budget: Infrastructure Initiative," https://www.whitehouse.gov/sites/whitehouse.gov/files/omb/budget/fy2018/fact_sheets/2018%20Budget%20Fact%20Sheet_Infrastructure%20Initiative1.pdf.

INDEX

Adams, Brock, 189
Adams, John Quincy, 31
Ade, George, 40
Agency for International Development,
    United States (USAID), 4–5, 156, 167
Agricultural and Marketing Act of 1929, 136
Agricultural Wheel, 60
agriculture: American political development
    and, 52; credit needs of settlers, 39–41;
    farm loans secured with a mortgage,
    41–46; the Federal Farm Loan Act of
    1916 (*see* Federal Farm Loan Act of 1916);
    growth of in the late nineteenth and early
    twentieth centuries, 49–50; investigation
    of European models for, 73–74; the New
    Deal and, 136–38; politics of in the late
    nineteenth and early twentieth centuries,
    50–52; postwar farm credit, 158; racial
    inequality, farm loan programs and,
    258n99; sharecropping and tenancy in
    the South, 58–60
Agriculture, United States Department of
    (USDA), 79, 158
Alger, George W., 111, 117–18
alliance exchanges and the joint-note
    program, 48; background to, 57–60;
    cooperative model of credit, develop-
    ment of, 60–63; joint-note plan, origin
    of, 62; populist politics and, 63–64; as
    a republican solution to credit distribu-
    tion, 52; the Texas Alliance Exchange (*see*
    Texas Alliance Exchange)
American Bankers Association, 71, 80, 135, 159

American Bond and Mortgage Company,
    110, 112
American Commission, 73–79
American Construction Council, 115
American Federation of Labor, 102
American Institute of Architects, 102
American political development: credit pro-
    grams and, 11–17, 130–31, 171–73, 200–
    204 (*see also* Reconstruction Finance
    Corporation); farmers' contributions to,
    significance of, 52, 68; the Federal Farm
    Loan Act and, 70, 84; fractured political
    institutions and, 7–11; research methods
    and, 19; state-level policies, potential for
    future research on, 204–5; wars and, 99
American Research Development (ARD),
    153–54
Amerikanischer Darlehen und Bau-Verein, 94
Ansell, Christopher K., 85, 217n49
ARD. *See* American Research Development
associational state, 8–12, 104–5, 126–27,
    130–31

B. F. Goodrich, 151
Balough, Brian, 32
Bank for Cooperatives, 137
Bank of America, 132, 138
banks and banking: commercial banks
    (*see* commercial banks); crises of the
    1930s, 131; Federal Farm loan legislation,
    political action regarding, 79–80; "free
    banking," 43; joint-stock land banks,
    81–83; marketing of new instruments to

banks and banking (*continued*)
attract capital, 184; mutual savings banks, 93–94; national in the nineteenth century (*see* national banks, nineteenth century); in nineteenth-century farm mortgage markets, 42–44; the Reconstruction Finance Corporation, assistance from, 132–33, 135–36; regional distribution of, 1870, 57–58; regulations enacted in the 1930s, 153, 177–78; Second Bank of the United States (*see* Second Bank of the United States); S&Ls (*see* savings and loans); southern property banks (plantation/planters' banks), 38–39, 43; in Southern states, 1880, 58; state (*see* state banks); Texas Alliance Exchange, refusal to work with, 62–63; thrifts (*see* thrifts)

Baptist, Edward, 37–39
Baradaran, Mehrsa, 166
Barnes, Heather, 232n76
Barnes, Maria Catherine, 94
Bathrick, Ellsworth, 79
Baughman, J. Stanley, 189
Bear Stearns, 208–9
Beckert, Sven, 37
Beecher, Catherine, 92
Bell, Daniel, 268n92
Benton, Thomas Hart, 29–30
Berk, Gerald, 202, 231n47
Berle, Adolf, 56, 134–35
Bestor, H. Paul, 132
Better Homes of America, 105
Better Housing Program, Title I loans, 105
Blank, Clark, 78
Block, Fred, 14–15, 268n92
Bodenhorn, Howard, 43, 225n104
Bodfish, Morton, 96
Bogue, Allan, 44, 53
Bond and Guarantee Mortgage Company, 114
Bourdieu, Pierre, 12, 205
Boustan, Leah Platt, 263n31
Brandeis, Louis, 126
Braun, Benjamin, 205
Breitwieser, Hubert, 112
budget and budgeting: battles of the 1960s, 186–92, 195–96; credit programs and, 12; debt limit, 1960s adjustments to, 187; as an economic policy instrument, 130; "emergency" and "general" expenditures, distinction between, 147; Fannie Mae moved off-budget, 194; future research on, potential for, 204–5; New Deal credit programs as off-budget, 147–48; pooled

asset sales as off-budget, 180–81, 187; postwar credit programs and, 167–69; President's Commission on Budgetary Concepts, 191–92, 195
building and loan societies, 94
Bulkley, Robert, 80
Bureau of the Budget, 130
Burlington & Missouri Railroad Co., 33, 35
Burr, Aaron, 45
Byrd, Harry, 128–29

California Fruit Growers' Union, 72
Carruthers, Bruce, 6
Castles, Francis G., 16
CCC. *See* Commodity Credit Corporation
Chandler, Alfred, 56
Chrysler Corporation, 155
Ciepley, David, 55
Citizens Bank (Louisiana), 38
classification: credit and, 11–18; farm credit and theories of, 85–86; of housing programs as market corrections, 17–18, 140, 145–46, 201
Clay, Henry, 31
Clemens, Elisabeth, 11, 52, 66
CoBank (Banks for Cooperatives), 158
Cohen, Lizabeth, 18, 176
Cole, Albert, 260n137
Colean, Miles, 46, 213n2
collateral: crops as, 41–45, 58–60, 62; land as, 41–45, 225n93; slaves as, 23, 37–39, 58
Collins, Robert M., 262n10
Colm, Gerhard, 148
Colored Farmers' Alliance, 60–61
Commerce, United States Department of, 104–6
commercial banks: farm loans by, 71; Glass-Steagall limitations on, 153; interest rates offered by, 183–84; joint-stock banks set up by, 82; mediation of disputes among, 83; in nineteenth-century mortgage markets, 42–44; residential mortgage debt held in the early twentieth century by, 93; residential mortgage debt held in the postwar era by, 160–61
Commodity Credit Corporation (CCC): emergency response to a budget overage by, 181; farmers subsidized through loans from, 4; local warehouses, organized through, 148; non-recourse loans as grants by, 167; price supports by, 137–38, 158; sale of pooled assets in the 1930s, 265n52; straddling of governmental boundaries by, 12

Conference on Home Building and Home Ownership, 140

Consolidated Association of Planters of Louisiana, 38–39

cooperatives: in American history, 203; campaign to create under the Federal Farm Loan Act, 81; concerns about in the U.S. context, 78–79; credit support for, 158; European models for, 71–74, 77–78; failed experiments with, late nineteenth-century, 48–49, 57, 60–64; logic as relates to western mortgage bonds, 55; political and administrative burdens, as solution for, 76–79; on the Western frontier, 41. *See also* savings and loans (S&Ls)

corporations: as collectives, exchange system's view of, 63–64; disputed nature of, 55–56; liberal-republican division regarding, 126; populists' targeting of, 51–52; property rights and, 56; regulation of, the Crash of 1873 and government, 36

Couch, Harvey, 132

Council of Economic Advisers, 130

Country Life movement, 71–72

Cowrie, Jefferson, 176

credit/credit programs: federal, 4–5; financial crisis and (*see* financial crisis); governmental support for development of, 14–15; for housing (*see* housing policy); lightness of, 13–14, 16, 18, 21, 86, 200; mixed-enterprise partnerships and, 84–85; money and, relationship of, 217n46; moral judgments associated with, 49, 67; the New Deal and (*see* New Deal; Reconstruction Finance Corporation); as a policy tool, 1, 18, 130–31, 140, 144–49, 156–57, 200–201; post–Revolutionary War land sales and, 25–30; for railroad development, 33, 36; securitization and, paired histories of, 5–7; as social policy, 16–17; in the South, 37–39; on the Western frontier, 39–45

credit/credit programs, Second World War and beyond, 150; business, programs to support, 153–56; changes in postwar, 152–58; costs and benefits of, 169–71; credit crunch of 1966, 184–86; disaster relief, 152; farm credit, 158; financialization of, 196–98; housing programs, 159–63; loans as foreign and military policy, 156–57; in 1963, 150; political/economic development and, 171–73; politics of, 167–69; racial inequality and, 163–67 (*see also* racial inequality);

Reconstruction Finance Corporation, end of the, 151–52 (*see also* Reconstruction Finance Corporation); reforms called for by homebuilders and lenders in the early 1960s, 267n77; regulations impacting, 177–78, 181; school loans, 157–58, 169; securitization of mortgages (*see* securitization)

credit distribution: as an alternative to wealth distribution or expenditure, 16–19, 77, 181–82, 196–98; European models for, 73–79; failed experiments in, 48–49, 67–68 (*see also* alliance exchanges and the joint-note program; subtreasury plan; western mortgage bond market failure); the Federal Farm Loan Act of 1916 (*see* Federal Farm Loan Act of 1916); government land sales and, 25; land distribution on the frontier and, problem of, 45–47; postwar growth liberalism and, 177–78; rural credit problem, rediscovery of, 70–73

"Crime of 1873," 51

Cromwell, Oliver, 61

Crouch, Colin, 18

D'Arista, Jane, 215n19

Davis, Gerald, 205

Davis, Lance E., 224n80

Dawes, Charles G., 132–33

Dayton plan, 97

debt: land sales and repayment of, 24–27, 30; post–Revolutionary War, 23

debt disease, 28

Defense Advanced Research Projects Agency (DARPA), 14

Defense Homes Corporation, 151

Defense Plant Corporation, 151

Defense Supplies Corporation, 151

derivatives, 207

developmental state, 14–16, 171–73. *See also* credit/credit programs; internal improvements

Dexter, Seymour, 98

Disaster Loan Corporation, 138

disaster relief, 152

discounts, 264n42

distributional politics, postwar, 175; budget battles of the 1960s as, 186; credit and, 18, 203–4; end of growth, the political response to, 182–83; financialization and, 196–98; perpetual growth and economic equality, 175–77; risk redistribution, 202

Dobbin, Frank, 36, 83–84

Douglas, Lewis, 129, 146

Douglas, William O., 120
Dow Chemical, 151
Du Bois, W.E.B., 57, 59, 94
Duesenberry, James, 192

Eccles, Marriner, 129, 144–45
economy, the: bank regulations as automatic
    stabilizers, 177–78; boom and bust, pat-
    tern of, 27–28 (*see also* financial crisis);
    limitations on planning, the *Schechter*
    decision and, 127; planning during World
    War II, Southern Democrats and, 128–29;
    postwar era affluence, end of, 182–86;
    postwar era "Golden Age" of, 174–76; in
    the summer of 1965, 184. *See also* growth
    liberalism
Education Amendments of 1972, 157
Eisenach, Eldon, 104
Eisenhower, Dwight D., 152, 162, 195
Emergency Banking Act of 1933, 135
Emergency Farm Mortgage Act of 1933, 137
Emergency Fleet Corporation, 99, 101–3
Emergency Relief and Construction Act of
    1932, 133, 136, 141
Engelen, Ewald, 204
Equal Opportunity Loan program, 166
Export-Import Bank, 5, 152, 156, 167–70,
    180–81

factors, 37
Fair Housing Act of 1968, 165
Fannie Mae (Federal National Mortgage
    Association): commercial loans, as
    source of, 167; credit crunch of 1966
    and, 185; developmental state, as part of,
    14; financial crisis in 2008 and, 208–9;
    leadership, change of, 189–90; macro-
    economic policy and, 169; origins of,
    142–44; participation certificates, au-
    thorization to sell, 181, 189; pass-through
    certificate as replacement for PCs, 193,
    196; pooled government assets, sale of,
    180–81; privatization/spin-off of, 192–95;
    reorganization of in 1954, 162–63; S&Ls
    and brokers, relationship with, 160; as a
    shadow government agency, 196; Tan-
    dem Plan, 194–95; uninsured mortgages,
    conditions for purchasing, 252n108
Farm Bureau, 137
Farm Credit Administration, 158
Farm Credit System Insurance Corporation,
    158
Farmer Mac (Federal Agricultural Mortgage
    Corporation), 158

Farmers Home Administration, 158, 256n65
Farm Loan Associations (FLAs), 81, 83, 136
Farm Mortgage Bankers Association, 80
Farm Security Administration, 137
Farm Service Agency, 158, 256n65
Farm Tenancy Act of 1937, 137
Federal Credit Reform Act of 1990, 169
Federal Deposit Insurance Corporation
    (FDIC), 135–36, 210
Federal Emergency Management Agency
    (FEMA), 5, 152
Federal Farm Loan Act of 1916 (FFLA): as a
    dual-system compromise, 80–83; legisla-
    tive path to, 79–80; long-term amortiz-
    ing mortgage, promotion of, 5; as a new
    path for credit policy, 86–87; passage of,
    69–70, 80; political economy of, 83–86
Federal Farm Loan Board, 81–82
Federal Farm Loan Bureau, 81
Federal Financing Bank, 196
Federal Home Loan Bank Board (FHLBB),
    160, 177, 263n34
Federal Home Loan Bank (FHLB) system:
    conservative movement of credit, com-
    plaints about, 183; guarantees, concerns
    of fiscal conservatives regarding, 146;
    land bank system as model for, 86; S&Ls,
    created to support, 140–41, 145, 148, 159
Federal Housing Administration (FHA):
    accounting and financial management of,
    167–68; disaster relief and, 152; lenders,
    relationship to the different, 160–62;
    mortgage contracts, shaping of, 170–71;
    mortgage insurance by, 142, 159; origins
    of Fannie Mae and, 142–44; racial in-
    equality reinforced by, 17, 164–65; regula-
    tions of, securitization of mortgages and,
    178–80; unemployment, as inexpensive
    way to reduce, 146–47; as the world's
    largest mortgage insurer, 14
Federal Intermediate Credit Banks, 86, 137,
    158
Federal Reserve: the credit crunch of 1966,
    response to, 184; farm loans and, 71;
    financial crisis of 2007–2008, response
    to, 210; reclassification of Ginnie Mae-
    guaranteed securities, proposal for, 196;
    Regulation Q, 177–78, 184, 267n83
Federal Reserve Act of 1913, 71, 79, 83–84
Federal Savings and Loan Insurance Corpo-
    ration (FSLIC), 140, 159–60
FFLA. *See* Federal Farm Loan Act of 1916
FHA. *See* Federal Housing Administration
FHLBB. *See* Federal Home Loan Bank Board

financial crisis: banking crises of the 1930s, 131; bubbles, 28, 53–55; Crash of 1819, 29–30; Crash of 1837, 39; Crash of 1873, 36; Crash of 1907, 70; early nineteenth-century, 28–30; the Great Depression, 125 (*see also* New Deal); housing boom and bust of the 1920s, 107–8, 113–18; mortgage markets in the 1960s, 183–86; pattern of, 27–28, 201–2; of 2007–2008, 205–10; of 2007–2008, responsibility for, 210–11

financialization, 196–98

Fine, Sydney, 56

Fink, Lawrence, 274n28

First National Bank of New York, 266n73

fiscal conservatives: Keynesian spending, opposition to, 129–30; New Deal accounting changes, opposition to, 147; New Deal credit programs, opposition to, 146 ·

Fisher, Ernest M., 123

Fisher, Irving, 28

Flannery, J. Rogers, 102

Fletcher, Duncan, 79–80, 100

Food for Peace program, 156

Ford, Gerald, 191

foreclosures: between 2007 and 2016, 208; in the late 1920s and early 1930s, 139; life insurance as protection against, 53, 55; during the mortgage bond crash of the 1920s, 116; as the ultimate degradation, 50

foreign policy, 156–57

Fortas, Abe, 120

Fourcade, Marion, 6

Fowler, Henry "Joe," 190–92

France, agricultural credit system in, 77–78

Franklin, Benjamin, 45

Freddie Mac (Federal Home Loan Mortgage Corporation), 195, 208–9

Freund, David: credit, inoffensive language of, 140, 201; federal credit allocation, call for in-depth examination of, 5; myth of free markets, use of credit to maintain the, 145–46; New Deal housing credit programs, designers' understanding of, 13; racism shaped by credit supports, 17–18, 164

Frymer, Paul, 24

Fukuyama, Francis, 8

Fulbright, J. William, 151–52

Funk, Russell, 85

G. L. Miller & Co., 110, 114–15, 118

Gallatin, Albert, 27

Gallman, Robert E., 224n80

Gates, Paul, 25, 30

General Motors, 151

Germany, system of rural credit in *(Land-schaften),* 70–76

Gerstle, Gary, 8

G.I. Bill (Servicemen's Readjustment Act), 157, 159

gift exchange, theory of, 218–19n68

Gilded Age: corporations in, new vision of, 36; laissez-faire in, 52

Ginnie Mae (Government National Mortgage Association), 194, 196

Glasmacher, Anna, 204

Glass, Carter, 134

Glass-Steagall Act of 1932, 153

Goetzmann, William, 11, 107, 115

Goldin, Claudia, 176

Goodrich, Carter, 32

Goodwyn, Lawrence, 63, 65

Graduation Act of 1854, 40

Grain Stabilization Corporation, 136

Great Depression, 125. *See also* New Deal

Grebler, Leo, 143–44, 237n82, 257n83

Greenwood, Robin, 3

Griswold, Wendy, 85

growth liberalism: control of financial markets under, 181–82; homeownership as the cornerstone of consumption for, 175–76; as new means and tools to support market growth, 262n10; as political response to the end of growth, 182–83; the postwar "Golden Age" and, 174–75

Hacker, Jacob, 174

Halsey Stuart Co., 114

Hamilton, Alexander, 23

Hamilton, Charles, 166

Haveman, Heather A., 96–97

Hawley, Ellis Wayne, 104–5, 126–27, 130, 248n7

Haydu, Jeffrey, 19, 200

Herrick, Myron, 71

Higher Education Act of 1965, 157

Hirsch, Arnold, 163

Hirschman, Dan, 85

Hockett, Robert, 14

Hollis, Henry, 80

Home Affordable Modification Program, 210

Home Loan Bank Bill, 103

Home Modernizing Bureau, 105

homeownership: costs for, 92; high levels of, 2; increase in, 92; mortgages, sources of, 93–99 (*see also* thrifts); Own-Your-Own-Home campaign, 100, 105; postwar

homeownership (*continued*)
  growth liberalism, as a central pillar of,
  175; suburbanization and, distinction between, 91; vision associated with, 88–92;
  wartime promotion of, 100
Home Owners Loan Corporation (HOLC),
  140–41, 144, 164, 170
Homestead Acts, 40–41
Hoover, Herbert: associational state, vision
  of, 104–5, 126–27, 130–31; farmers, relief
  for, 136; housing, interest in, 103–5; housing market crash, response to, 140–41;
  Reconstruction Finance Corporation,
  creation of, 131–33
Houghteling, Peabody, 108
Housing and Home Finance Agency, 163
Housing and Urban Development (HUD),
  United States Department of, 183
Housing and Urban Development Act of
  1968, 193–95
Housing Corporation, United States, 101–3
housing policy: challenges of the 1960s,
  183–84; credit crunch of the 1960s,
  failure to respond to, 184–86; crisis of
  2007–2008, role in, 207–9; federal housing programs, initiation of in the New
  Deal, 125–26; financialization of, 196–98;
  as industrial policy, 103–4; institutional
  context for, 106; managing the economy
  through, 144–49; New Deal, 139–44;
  postwar programs, 159–63; post–World
  War I, 104–5; racial inequality in, 17–18,
  163–65; Section 235 program, 195; social
  policy as, 16–17; World War I, 100–104;
  the World War I housing crisis, 99–100.
  See also Fannie Mae
Howard, Christopher, 5, 84
Howe, Daniel Walker, 222n55
Hurley, Edward Nash, 100
Hyman, Louis, 4, 170

inducements and incentives, 9–10. *See also*
  tax expenditures
inflation, 186
infrastructure plan, 211–12
Institutional Securities Corporation, 178
Instlcorp, 178–79
insurance companies: in farm mortgage
  markets, 42; life insurance as a protection
  against foreclosure, 53, 55; mortgages
  and mortgage bonds, insuring of, 110; in
  residential mortgage markets, 93, 160–61
interest rates: adjustable-rate mortgages,
  206; commercial banks compared to

S&Ls, 183–84; development of securitization and, 210–11; for farm mortgages in
  1922, 82; the money supply and, 50–51;
  offered by S&Ls, 267n76; for short-term
  credit in the post–Civil War South, 59
intermediaries, 44–45
internal improvements: land grants and
  credit supporting railroads and, 32–36;
  politics of, 30–32
international credit support, 156–57
International Institute for Agriculture, 72
Interstate Commerce Commission, 84
Investors Central Management Corporation,
  264n46
Ippolito, Dennis, 168

Jackson, Andrew, 31
Jackson, Kenneth T., 213n1, 238n2
Jacksonian Democrats, 30–31
Jefferson, Thomas, 24, 31, 37, 90
Jensen, Laura, 16, 24
Johnson, Ernest A., 244n16
Johnson, Lyndon: credit crunch of 1966,
  response to, 185; distributional choices,
  budget battles and refusal to make,
  186–87; housing improvements, recognition of need for, 183; on SBICs, 154;
  securitization, promotion of, 187–91,
  211; student loans, promotion of, 157; tax
  increase, resistance to, 184–85, 268n94;
  Vietnam War finance and, 267n80; War
  on Poverty, 176
Johnson, Oscar, 138
joint-stock land banks, 81–83
Jones, Jesse H.: background of, 133–34;
  board of the RFC, appointment to, 132;
  credit and government spending, distinction between, 146; exit from the RFC,
  151; leadership of the RFC, 130, 134–35;
  Roosevelt's idea for non-recourse loans
  against farm crops, 138; war production,
  support for, 151
Jones, Oliver, 143–44, 178, 180, 237n82,
  257n83

Karolak, Eric, 103
Kassis, Annette, 234n23
Katz, Jonathan, 210
Katznelson, Ira, 128, 130, 248n3
Keehn, Richard H., 226n126
Kemeny, Jim, 16
Kennedy, David, 191
Kennedy, John F., 165
Kennedy, Joseph, 120

Kerner Commission, 183
Keynesian economics: decentralized government, problem of dealing with, 148–49; fiscal conservatives and, 129–30; mortgage credit and, 144–45; Southern Democrats and, 127–29. *See also* growth liberalism
Kindleberger, Charles, 27
Kissell, Howard, 148
Klaman, Saul, 123, 257n82
kludgocracy, 11
Knapp, Joseph Grant, 232n77
Kohler, Walter, 105
Krippner, Greta: banking regulations as a macro-economic tool, 177; deregulation to avoid political responsibility, 18, 206; deregulation under financialization, 197, 271n151; government involvement in markets, 6; the housing industry as a macro-economic tool, 145; inflationary pressures of the 1960s, 186; scarcity, the political reaction to, 182

laissez-faire: corporations and, 126; the Crash of 1873 and reduction of government regulation, 36; as exclusively a federal issue, 31; the judiciary and, 56; mortgage bonds and, 52, 55–57 (*see also* western mortgage bond market failure); rethinking after the bond market collapse of 1927, 120–21; as a utopian dream, 203
land: fiscal functions of, 23–24; investment/speculation in, 45; lending intermediaries as promoters, 44–45; as military policy, 24; mortgages on, 41–45 (*see also* lenders); as social policy, 16–17; states' ceding of to the public domain, 219–20n4
land banks, 81–83
land distribution: credit markets and, problem of, 45–47; for internal improvements, 30–36; Land Grant Map of Franklin County, Arkansas (1893), 34; laws governing, late-eighteenth and nineteenth century, 25–26, 30; post–Revolutionary War, 24; railroads and, 32–36; as a welfare program, 16
land sales: Advertisement for Land Bought on Credit from Railway, 1872, 35; collections and, 1813–1819, 27; early nineteenth-century financial crisis and, 27–30; post–Revolutionary War, 24–27; revenue from, 30; revenue from in England, 220n6
Landschaften: origins of the Federal Farm Loan system and, 70, 74–75; southern

property banks, as possible inspiration for, 225n59
Lapin, Raymond H., 185, 189–90, 196–97
Larson, John Laritz, 222n54
Lawyers Mortgage Company, 112
Leflore County Massacre, 61
Lehman, Herbert H., 118
Lehman Brothers, 209
lenders: banks (*see* banks and banking; commercial banks); brokers and boosters, 44–45, 141–42, 160, 162; insurance companies (*see* insurance companies); non-institutional, 42, 93, 160–62; post–Second World War, 159–62; thrifts (*see* thrifts)
Lerner, Josh, 155
Levitin, Adam J., 210
Levy, Jonathan, 53, 55, 230n37
life insurance companies. *See* insurance companies
Lippmann, Walter, 176
Lipset, Seymour Martin, 203, 272n8
Lockheed, 155
Lubin, David, 72–73
Lucas, Deborah, 170

MacKenzie, Donald, 208
MacLaury, Bruce K., 167, 260n126
Macune, Charles W., 61–66, 83
Maisel, Sherman, 192
Mappin, W. F., 230n32
Margo, Robert A., 176, 263n31
market forms, 9–10
Marshall Plan, 156
Martin, Bonnie, 23, 37
Martin, Isaac, 201
Martin Act (New York), 118–19, 246n91
Mason, James, 136
Mauss, Marcel, 218–19n68
Mayrl, Damon, 8, 13, 85, 248n3
Mazzucato, Mariana, 4, 14, 171
McCarthy, Wilson, 132
Means, Gardiner, 56, 134
Mellon, Andrew, 132
Mercantile Trust, 54
Merrill Lynch, 209
Metals Reserve Company, 151
Metcalf, Ralph, 78
methodology, 19–20
Mettler, Suzanne, 5, 11, 169
Meyer, Eugene, 132–33
Mian, Atif, 209–10
Mills, Ogden, 132
Mills, Wilbur, 186

Minicucci, Steven, 32

Minsky, Hyman, 27, 185

mixed-enterprise partnerships, 84–85

Moffet, Jimmy, 144

money supply: Alliance cooperatives and, 63; contraction of, farmers and, 51; farm credit and, 50–51; the subtreasury plan and, 65

Mooney, Edward, 134

Morgenthau, Henry, Jr., 129–30, 146, 151

Morrill, Chester, 147–48

mortgage-backed securities: Fannie Mae's pass-throughs, 193–96; political attractions and risks of, 211; securitization, as a form of, 3; the social logic of Fannie Mae's pass-throughs, 196–98. *See also* mortgage bonds; pooling

Mortgage Bankers Association, 95, 159

mortgage bond bust of the 1920s: the crash, 115–17; fleecing investors in the wake of the crash, 117–18; laissez-faire and, 120–21; legacy of, 121–23; marketing of mortgage bonds, 113–15; regulatory responses: federal securities regulation, 119–20; regulatory responses: New York, 118–19; shareholder democracy and, 108, 113–14

mortgage bonds: decline of early market for, 121–23; mortgage-backed securities (*see* mortgage-backed securities); participation certificates, 110–13; post–World War I market for, 108–13; proposal for from the United States Commission, 76; real estate bonds as a portion of nonfarm mortgage debt, 1896–1952, 109; shareholder democracy and, 108; skyscrapers and, 107–8; tranches, division into, 3, 206; the western mortgage bond market failure (*see* western mortgage bond market failure)

mortgage brokers, 44–45, 141–42, 160, 162

Mortgage Corporation of America, 264n46

Mortgage Finance Task Force, 193

mortgages: conventional and government-guaranteed, convergence of terms of, 261n151; for existing homes by maturity and loan-to-value ratio, 171; importance for American history, 2; insuring, 110; leading up to the crisis of 2007–2008, 207–8; New Deal responses to a patchwork market for, 139–40; pooling (*see* pooling; securitization); residential held by S&Ls and mutual in 1940 and 1970, 257n80; shaping of the modern, 170–71; in the South with slaves as collateral,
37–39; in the West with land as collateral, 41–45. *See also* lenders

Moss, Ralph W., 80

Moussier, J. B., 38

Mudge, Stephanie, 175

Mumford, Lewis, 107

Murphy, Paul, 100

mutual savings banks, 93–94

Naopala, Maria K., 95

National Association for the Advancement of Colored People (NAACP), 165

National Association of Home Builders, 159

National Association of Mutual Savings Banks, 95, 159

National Association of Real Estate Boards, 95, 121, 148, 159

National Association of Real Estate Brokers, 102

National Association of Real Estate Builders, 103

National Banking Acts of 1863 and 1864, 224n77

national banks, nineteenth century: in nineteenth-century mortgage markets, 43; railways and, 224n77; Second Bank of the United States, 28–30

National Building and Loan Protective Union, 97

National Conference of City Planners, 240n59

National Credit Corporation, 131

National Defense Education Act of 1958, 157

National Farmers' Alliance and Industrial Union, 60

National Federation of Construction Industries, 95

National Housing Act of 1934 (NHA), 140, 142, 144–45

National Recovery Administration (NRA), 127

National Resources Planning Board, 128–30

Neu, Irene, 225n95

New Deal: credit programs of, 125, 130–31, 149 (*see also* Reconstruction Finance Corporation); housing programs of, 139–44; ideological division and policy deadlock, problem of, 126–27; Keynesian spending, fiscal conservatives and, 129–30; Keynesian spending, Southern Democrats and, 127–29

Newman, Frank, 107, 115

New York, regulatory response to the bond collapse in 1927, 118–20

New York Real Estate Board, Real Estate Securities Exchange, 115–16

New York Stock Exchange, 113
NHA. *See* National Housing Act of 1934
Niagara Permanent Savings & Loan
    Association, 95
Nixon, Richard, 166
non-institutional lenders: in farm mortgage
    markets, 42; in residential mortgage
    markets, 93, 160–62
non-recourse loans, 138, 167
Norris, George, 79
Northern Farmers' Alliance, 60

O'Connor, James, 268n92
Ohio Land Company, 25
Okun, Arthur, 191
Olmsted, Frederick Law, Jr., 101
Olson, James S., 130, 134
Omarova, Saule, 14
Ordinance of 1785, 24
Ott, Julia, 108, 113
Ottinger, Albert, 118, 121
Overseas Private Investment Corporation, 156
Own-Your-Own-Home campaign, 100, 105
Oxford Provident Building Association, 94

Pacewicz, Josh, 205
Pacific Rail Act of 1862, 33
Padgett, John F., 85, 217n49
participation certificates (PCs): the bond
    market crash of the 1920s and, 117–19;
    budgetary status of, 190–92; Fannie Mae
    authorized to sell, 181; interwar, 110–13;
    as Johnson's response to the budget
    impasse of 1966, sale of, 187–90; politics
    and, 195; replacement of as a mechanism
    to fund Fannie Mae, 193
Participation Sales Act of 1966, 187–91, 193,
    196
partnerships, 8–10
pass-through certificates, 193, 196
Patman, Wright, 154
Patterson, James, 175
PCs. *See* participation certificates
Pell Grants, 157
People's Party: Omaha Platform, call for
    subtreasury in (*see* subtreasury plan);
    populism of, 49, 64–65
Petroleum Oil Reserve Company, 151
Pierson, Paul, 19, 89, 174
Plunkett, Horace, 71, 74
Polanyi, Karl, 124–25, 203
policy work-arounds, 8–11
politics/political economy: agriculture
    and, late-nineteenth and early-twentieth
century, 50–52; the Alliance exchanges
    and, 63–64; budget battles of the 1960s,
    186–92; contentious and the turn to
    finance, 18, 201–2; the credit crunch of
    1966, options for responding to, 185–86;
    of the credit programs for housing, 114–
    49; credit's ideological lightness and,
    13; deregulation and the rise of finance,
    197; distributional (*see* distributional
    politics, postwar); of the Fannie Mae
    spin-off, 195–96; of the Federal Farm
    Loan Act, 83–86; of internal improve-
    ments, 30–32; of the New Deal (*see* New
    Deal); policy work-arounds, institu-
    tional complexity and, 8–11; of postwar
    credit programs, 167–69; of Progressive
    approach to rural credit distribution,
    72, 83; the rhetoric of laissez-faire and,
    56; the subtreasury plan and, 65–67; the
    Trump infrastructure plan and, 211–12.
    See also American political develop-
    ment; state, the
pooling: as off-budget financing, 178; of
    postwar government-held assets, 180–81;
    of slave-backed mortgages, 37; of western
    mortgages, 53 (*see also* western mortgage
    bond market failure). *See also* mortgage-
    backed securities; securitization
populist movements: the Alliance exchanges
    as, 63–64; corporations, targeting of,
    51–52; decline of among farmers, 66–67;
    pattern of, 51; the People's Party, 48–49,
    63–66
Postel, Charles, 63, 233n85
Prasad, Monica: consumption in postwar
    European economy, 175–76; farmers'
    contribution to a pro-credit coalition, 16;
    farm prices and production costs, rela-
    tionship of, 229n11; "Mortgage Keynes-
    ianism" of post-war economic policy,
    145; unprecedented growth of the United
    States, 49; volatility of real interest rates
    on mortgages, 50
President's Commission on Budgetary Con-
    cepts, 191–92, 195
Progressive National Housing Association,
    102
Progressives, the: farm credit distribution,
    the legislative answer to problem of, 69–
    70; politics of compromise for, 83; rural
    credit problem, rediscovery of, 70–73
property/plantation banks, 38–39, 43
protective committees, 117–18, 120
Public Works Administration, 138

racial inequality: in business programs, 165–67; credit and, 17–18; in farm loan programs, 258n99; the financial crisis of 2007–2008 and, 209; in housing programs, 163–65; postwar economic growth, in the midst of, 177

Radford, Gail, 84, 103

Rae, Ann E., 95

railroads: land grants and credit supporting, 32–36; participation certificates to finance, 111

Rajan, Raghuram, 18

Ranieri, Lewis, 274n28

Rao, Hayagreeva, 96–97

Realty Collateral Corporation of New York, 264n46

Reconstruction Finance Corporation (RFC): banks, rescue of, 135–36; budgetary advantages of, 147–48; China, loan to, 156; congressional expansion of, 133; development of credit policy, institutional center for, 125–26; Fannie Mae and, 143–44; farmers, increased credit for, 136–37; farm price supports, credit as, 137–38; origins of and initial limits to, 131–33; political "middle way" offered by, 130; postwar scandal and liquidation of, 151–52; profit from amortizing business loans by, 170; range of efforts beyond banks and farms, 138–39; relationship of Jones and Berle to, 133–35; relief funds for land and joint-stock banks in 1932 from, 83; securitization to help unwind, 181; War Finance Corporation as justification for, 99

Redlich, Fritz, 38, 225n95

Regional Agricultural Credit Corporations ("Regionals"), 136–37

republican ideals: corporations and, 126; independent yeoman farmers, Jefferson's vision of, 24; internal improvements and, 31; joint-note program and subtreasury plan as reflecting, 52; property ownership and, 90

Resettlement Administration, 137, 158, 256n65

RFC. See Reconstruction Finance Corporation

RFC Mortgage Company, 143–44

Rich, Comly, 94

Riis, Mary, 245n47

Rodgers, Daniel, 73

Roosevelt, Franklin Delano: balanced budget, initial commitment to, 129; banking crisis, response to, 135; construction industry, focus on, 115, 175; credit, use of in the New Deal, 125; emergency spending in federal budgeting, defense of, 147; farming crisis, response to, 137–38; Hoover's precedents, building on, 105; housing, early interest in, 103; Jones, support for, 134; Keynesian spending, embrace of, 129–30; National Recovery Administration (NRA) and, 127

Roosevelt, Theodore, 71, 126

Rouse, James, 264n42

Roy, Ananya, 90

Roy, William, 55, 231n47

Rubber Reserve Company, 151

Rural Electrification Administration, 138, 152

S. W. Strauss & Co., 110, 113–14

Sabath, Adolf, 120

Sabath Committee, 120

Sallie Mae (Student Loan Marketing Association), 157

Sandel, Michael, 8

Sanders, Elizabeth, 52, 68

Saperstein, David, 121–22

savings and loans (S&Ls): the credit crunch of 1966 and, 184; deposit insurance for, issue of, 251n88; federal supports for, 140–41; interest rates compared to commercial banks, 183–84; interest rates offered by, 267n76; postwar housing and, 159–62; thrifts, as one of the, 94 (see also thrifts)

SBA. See Small Business Administration

SBICs. See Small Business Investment Corporations

Scharfenstein, David, 3

Schlesinger, Arthur, 133–34, 136

Schlesinger, Arthur, Jr., 148

school loans, 157–58, 169

Schultze, Charles, 192

Schuykill Company, 111

Schwartz, Herman, 16

Schwartz, Michael, 60–61, 202, 232n76

Second Bank of the United States, 28–30

Securities Act of 1933, 119–20

Securities and Exchange Commission (SEC), 120

Securities Exchange Act of 1934, 120, 247n97

securitization, 2–4; crisis of 2007–2008, role in, 3, 205–8, 210–11; federal credit programs and, paired histories of, 5–7; future research on, potential for, 204; mortgage-backed securities, the Fannie

Mae spin-off and, 193–96; mortgage
bonds (*see* mortgage bonds); as off-
budget financing for credit programs,
180–81; the Participation Sales Act of
1966, 187–91; pass throughs, 193, 196;
private efforts in the postwar era, failure
of, 178–80; separation of profits from risk
by, 56; social logic of modern, 196–98
self-correcting markets as utopian fantasy,
124–25
serial plans, 96
settlers, credit needs of, 39–41
shareholder democracy, 108, 121. *See also*
mortgage bond bust of the 1920s
Shaw, Christopher, 72
Sheinberg, Marc, 202
Shickler, Eric, 8
Skocpol, Theda, 19
Skowronek, Steven, 67
slaves/slavery: as human collateral, 23,
37–39, 58; moral economy of, 39;
sectionalism before the Civil War and,
31–32; tenancy and sharecropping as
relates to, 60
Small Business Administration (SBA): creation of, 153; disaster relief, 5, 152; racial
inequality and, 165–67; revolving fund for
loans, size of, 254n15; sales of assets after
the Fannie Mae spin-off, 196; Small Busi-
ness Investment Corporations (SBICs),
154–55, 167
Small Business Investment Act of 1958, 154
Small Business Investment Corporations
(SBICs), 154–55, 254n23
Smaller War Plants Corporation, 151
Small House Service Bureau, 104
Smiley, Gene, 226n126
Smith, Charles W., 82
Smith, Harold, 130
Snowden, Kenneth, 54, 95, 141
South, the: alliance exchanges and the joint-
note program (*see* alliance exchanges and
the joint-note program); early form of
credit in, 37–39; Louisiana corn prices
with implied interest rates, 59; post–Civil
War poverty and decimated banking
system in, 57–58; sharecropping and
tenancy in, 58–60; the subtreasury plan
(*see* subtreasury plan)
Southern Building and Loan Association, 98
Southern Commercial Congress (SCC), 73
Southern Democrats: economic planning
during World War II and, 128–29; the
New Deal and, 127–28

Southern Farmers' Alliance, 48, 60–61
special purpose vehicle (SPV), 205–7, 273n20
speculators: land companies formed by, 25;
land sales on government credit and, 27
Sputnik, 154, 157
state, the: administrative capacity, lending
through farmers' cooperatives and,
76–79, 78–79; associational state,
Hoover's ideal of, 104–5, 126–27, 130–31;
classifications by, significance of, 217n47;
development of (*see* American political
development); development of credit
markets and, 14–15; finances of, potential
for future research on, 205; financial bailout of 2009, 209–10; fragmentation of,
7–8, 11, 200–201; internal improvements
and development of, 32; laissez-faire
and (*see* laissez-faire); late nineteenth-
century, 67–68; management of, involvement in financial markets and, 181–82;
markets and, western markets as a test
case for understanding, 227–28n145; regulations as economic stabilizers, 177–78;
securities regulation, the issue of, 120–21.
See also politics/political economy
state banks: in nineteenth-century mortgage
markets, 43–44; property/plantation
banks, 38–39, 43
Stein, Clarence S., 101
Strauss, S. W., 121
Streeck, Wolfgang, 18, 197–98
student loans, 157–58
subtreasury plan, 48; political economy of,
65–67; as a republican solution to credit
distribution, 52; rise and fall of, 64–66
suburbanization, 88, 91–92
Sufi, Amir, 209–10
Sunstein, Cass, 10
Supreme Court, United States: *Schechter* decision ruling the NRA unconstitutional,
127; tax exemption for FFLA bonds,
legality of, 82
Sutch, Richard, 92, 239n29
Sylla, Richard, 43

Taft, William Howard, 70–71
Taft-Hartley Act of 1947, 128
Tandem Plan, 194–95
TARP. *See* Troubled Asset Relief Program
tax expenditures: early land sales and, 26;
government credit support and, 4; political
advantage of, 10, 84–85; for Small Business
Investment Corporations (SBICs), 154
Taylor, A. Merritt, 101

Teles, Steven, 11
Texas Alliance Exchange: political economy of, 63–64; rise and fall of, 61–63
Thaler, Richard, 10
thrifts: cooperative lenders, development as, 93–95; limitations and evolution of, 96–97; moral identity of, 95–97; the nationals, 97–98; postwar mortgages held by, 160; S&Ls (*see* savings and loans); vision of, 88–89; women's participation in, 94–95
Thurston, Chloe, 17, 165
Title and Guaranteed Company, 110
transaction costs, pooling mortgages to reduce, 53
Troubled Asset Relief Program (TARP), 15, 209–10
Trumbull, Gunnar, 16
Tugwell, Rexford, 137
Ture, Kwame (Stokely Carmichael), 166

Union Bank (Louisiana), 38
Union Carbide, 151
Union Pacific, 36
United States Building and Loan League (USBLL), 89, 95–96, 98, 140–41, 251n88
United States Commission, 73–79
United States Savings and Loan League, 159
Untermyer, Samuel, 247n103
urbanization, 89
Urban League, 165
urban mortgage credit: federal support for, beginnings of, 89; rural credit, differences from, 88
U.S. Army, Ordnance Department, 101
U.S. government bonds, 53
U.S. Steel, 151
USAID (United States Agency for International Development), 4–5, 156, 167
USBLL. *See* United States Building and Loan League
USDA. *See* Agriculture, United States Department of

Veiller, Lawrence, 91, 101, 240n59
venture capital, 153–56
Venture Economics, 155
Veterans Administration (VA), 159–60, 162, 171

vetocracy, 8
Voluntary Home Mortgage Credit Program, 165
von Hoffman, Alexander, 195

Wachter, Susan M., 210
Wagner Act of 1935, 128
Walgreen, Charles, 116
Wallace, Henry, 138
War Damage Corporation, 151
War Finance Corporation, 99, 132
Warner, Sam Bass, 238n2
War on Poverty, 176
Washington, George, 45
Watkins, J. B., 53–54
Weaver, Robert, 183, 195
Webster, Pelatiah, 24
Weinstock, Harris, 72
West, the: credit on the frontier, 39–45; postwar need for mortgage credit in, 179; western mortgage bond market failure (*see* western mortgage bond market failure)
western mortgage bond market failure: the bubble, 53–55; as a laissez-faire solution to credit distribution, 52, 55; political economy of, 55–57
Westropp, Clara, 95
Westropp, Lillian, 95
White, Richard, 33, 223–24n76
Whitman, Walt, 92
Williamson, Charles, 45
Wilson, Woodrow, 71, 80, 126
Wolff, Henry, 78
Wolner, Edward W., 243n6
women: marketing of mortgage bonds to, 113–14; thrift movement, activity in, 94–95
Women's Savings & Loan Company, 95
Wood, Edith Elmer, 91–92, 102–3
Woodman, Harold D., 59, 231–32n58
Works Progress Administration, 138
World War I: housing crisis during, 99–100; housing policy during, 100–104
Wray, Randall, 4

Zelizer, Julian, 129
Zelizer, Viviana, 6
Zysman, John, 15

Princeton Studies in American Politics
Historical, International, and Comparative Perspectives
Series Editors
Ira Katznelson, Eric Schickler, Martin Shefter, and Theda Skocpol

American Bonds: How Credit Markets Shaped a Nation by Sarah L. Quinn

The Unsolid South: Mass Politics and National Representation in a One-Party Enclave by Devin Caughey

Southern Nation: Congress and White Supremacy After Reconstruction by David A. Bateman, Ira Katznelson, & John S. Lapinski

California Greenin': How the Golden State Became an Environmental Leader by David Vogel

Building an American Empire: The Era of Territorial and Political Expansion by Paul Frymer

Racial Realignment: The Transformation of American Liberalism, 1932–1965 by Eric Schickler

When Movements Anchor Parties: Electoral Alignments in American History by Daniel Schlozman

Paths Out of Dixie: The Democratization of Authoritarian Enclaves in America's Deep South, 1944–1972 by Robert Mickey

Electing the Senate: Indirect Democracy Before the Seventeenth Amendment by Wendy J. Schiller & Charles Stewart III

The Substance of Representation: Congress, American Political Development, and Lawmaking by John S. Lapinski

Looking for Rights in All the Wrong Places: Why State Constitutions Contain America's Positive Rights by Emily Zackin

Fighting for the Speakership: The House and the Rise of Party Government by Jeffery A. Jenkins & Charles Stewart III

Three Worlds of Relief: Race, Immigration, and the American Welfare State from the Progressive Era to the New Deal by Cybelle Fox

Building the Judiciary: Law, Courts, and the Politics of Institutional Development by Justin Crowe

Still a House Divided: Race and Politics in Obama's America by Desmond S. King & Rogers M. Smith

The Litigation State: Public Regulation and Private Lawsuits in the U.S. by Sean Farhang

Reputation and Power: Organizational Image and Pharmaceutical Regulation at the FDA by Daniel Carpenter

Presidential Party Building: Dwight D. Eisenhower to George W. Bush
 by Daniel J. Galvin

*Fighting for Democracy: Black Veterans and the Struggle Against White Supremacy in
 the Postwar South* by Christopher S. Parker

The Fifth Freedom: Jobs, Politics, and Civil Rights in the United States, 1941–1972
 by Anthony S. Chen

Reforms at Risk: What Happens After Major Policy Changes Are Enacted
 by Eric M. Patashnik

The Rise of the Conservative Legal Movement: The Battle for Control of the Law
 by Steven M. Teles

Why Is There No Labor Party in the United States? by Robin Archer

*Black and Blue: African Americans, the Labor Movement, and the Decline of the
 Democratic Party* by Paul Frymer

*The Transformation of American Politics: Activist Government and the Rise of
 Conservatism* edited by Paul Pierson & Theda Skocpol

*Political Foundations of Judicial Supremacy: The Presidency, the Supreme Court, and
 Constitutional Leadership in U.S. History* by Keith E. Whittington

Governing the American State: Congress and the New Federalism, 1877–1929
 by Kimberley S. Johnson

*What a Mighty Power We Can Be: African American Fraternal Groups and the
 Struggle for Racial Equality* by Theda Skocpol, Ariane Liazos, & Marshall Ganz

When Movements Matter: The Townsend Plan and the Rise of Social Security
 by Edwin Amenta

Disarmed: The Missing Movement for Gun Control in America by Kristin A. Goss

Why We Vote: How Schools and Communities Shape Our Civic Life
 by David E. Campbell

Filibuster: Obstruction and Lawmaking in the U.S. Senate by Gregory J. Wawro &
 Eric Schickler

Shaping Race Policy: The United States in Comparative Perspective
 by Robert C. Lieberman

How Policies Make Citizens: Senior Political Activism and the American Welfare State
 by Andrea Louise Campbell

*Managing the President's Program: Presidential Leadership and Legislative Policy
 Formulation* by Andrew Rudalevige

Dividing Lines: The Politics of Immigration Control in America by Daniel J. Tichenor

Shaped by War and Trade: International Influences on American Political Development
 edited by Ira Katznelson & Martin Shefter

The Forging of Bureaucratic Autonomy: Reputations, Networks, and Policy Innovation in Executive Agencies, 1862–1928 by Daniel P. Carpenter

Dry Bones Rattling: Community Building to Revitalize American Democracy by Mark R. Warren

Disjointed Pluralism: Institutional Innovation and the Development of the U.S. Congress by Eric Schickler

The Rise of the Agricultural Welfare State: Institutions and Interest Group Power in the United States, France, and Japan by Adam D. Sheingate

In the Shadow of the Garrison State: America's Anti-Statism and Its Cold War Grand Strategy by Aaron L. Friedberg

Stuck in Neutral: Business and the Politics of Human Capital Investment Policy by Cathie Jo Martin

Uneasy Alliances: Race and Party Competition in America by Paul Frymer

Faithful and Fearless: Moving Feminist Protest Inside the Church and Military by Mary Fainsod Katzenstein

Forged Consensus: Science, Technology, and Economic Policy in the United States, 1921–1953 by David M. Hart

Parting at the Crossroads: The Emergence of Health Insurance in the United States and Canada by Antonia Maioni

Bold Relief: Institutional Politics and the Origins of Modern American Social Policy by Edwin Amenta

The Hidden Welfare State: Tax Expenditures and Social Policy in the United States by Christopher Howard

Morning Glories: Municipal Reform in the Southwest by Amy Bridges

Imperiled Innocents: Anthony Comstock and Family Reproduction in Victorian America by Nicola Beisel

The Origins of the Urban Crisis: Race and Inequality in Postwar Detroit by Thomas J. Sugrue

The Road to Nowhere: The Genesis of President Clinton's Plan for Health Security by Jacob S. Hacker

Party Decline in America: Policy, Politics, and the Fiscal State by John J. Coleman

The Power of Separation: American Constitutionalism and the Myth of the Legislative Veto by Jessica Korn

Why Movements Succeed or Fail: Opportunity, Culture, and the Struggle for Woman Suffrage by Lee Ann Banaszak

Kindred Strangers: The Uneasy Relationship Between Politics and Business in America by David Vogel

From the Outside In: World War II and the American State
    by Bartholomew H. Sparrow

Classifying by Race edited by Paul E. Peterson

Facing Up to the American Dream: Race, Class, and the Soul of the Nation
    by Jennifer L. Hochschild

Political Organizations: Updated Edition by James Q. Wilson

*Experts and Politicians: Reform Challenges to Machine Politics in New York, Cleveland,
    and Chicago* by Kenneth Finegold

Social Policy in the United States: Future Possibilities in Historical Perspective
    by Theda Skocpol

Bound by Our Constitution: Women, Workers, and the Minimum Wage by Vivien Hart

Prisoners of Myth: The Leadership of the Tennessee Valley Authority, 1933–1990
    by Erwin C. Hargrove

Politics and Industrialization: Early Railroads in the United States and Prussia
    by Colleen A. Dunlavy

Political Parties and the State: The American Historical Experience by Martin Shefter

The Lincoln Persuasion: Remaking American Liberalism by J. David Greenstone

Labor Visions and State Power: The Origins of Business Unionism in the United States
    by Victoria C. Hattam

A NOTE ON THE TYPE

This book has been composed in Adobe Text and Gotham.
Adobe Text, designed by Robert Slimbach for Adobe,
bridges the gap between fifteenth- and sixteenth-century
calligraphic and eighteenth-century Modern styles.
Gotham, inspired by New York street signs, was designed
by Tobias Frere-Jones for Hoefler & Co.